Legends Of The War Of Independence
And Of The Earlier Settlements In The West

T. Marshall Smith

Alpha Editions

This Edition Published in 2021

ISBN: 9789354503245

Design and Setting By
Alpha Editions
www.alphaedis.com
Email - info@alphaedis.com

As per information held with us this book is in Public Domain.
This book is a reproduction of an important historical work. Alpha Editions uses the best
technology to reproduce historical work in the same manner it was first published to preserve its
original nature. Any marks or number seen are left intentionally to preserve its true form.

LEGENDS

OF THE

War of Independence,

AND OF

THE EARLIER SETTLEMENTS

IN THE

WEST.

BY T. MARSHALL SMITH.

Louisville, Ky.
J. F. BRENNAN, PUBLISHER.
1855.

To the

CHERISHED MEMORY

OF THE

COMPANION OF MY EARLIEST YOUTH,

AND MY FRIEND THROUGHOUT A SOMEWHAT EXTENDED LIFE, THE

HON. JAMES T. MOREHEAD,

NOW NO MORE AN INHABITANT OF EARTH,

THIS BOOK

IS DEDICATED,

AS A TESTIMONIAL OF THE ADMIRATION,

AND JUST APPRECIATION OF HIS LIFE

OF ENLIGHTENED AND VIRTUOUS DEVOTION

TO THE

SERVICE OF HIS COUNTRY.

PREFACE.

THE author of the book here presented to the public, has often heard persons regret that histories, which profess to treat of our revolutionary struggle, or of the no less arduous and dangerous conflicts attending the settlement of the vast wilderness of the West, contains so little of the personal history of many of the actors.

Historians, for the most part, confine themselves to the notice of what the world calls important events—the movements of armies, the result of battles, the conclusion of treaties, and the general legislation of the State. If they notice individuals at all, it is, generally, only those the most distinguished, the most highly and extraordinarily endowed by nature, the most fortunate in position, or who, attended by fortuitous circumstances, have been enabled to perform some astounding feat or semi-miracle; while their superiority consists in nothing, in point of real worth or merit, above that of the thousands of faithful and honest cotemporaries around them.

Historians, necessarily, even those most highly esteemed, are but the mere chroniclers of periods, men, and events of nations, generalized. And it is admitted, if all the incidents of all who have acted and preceded us were recorded in histories, then, indeed, could no man, however long his life might be protracted, read more than one half. But we are persuaded histories would furnish clearer conceptions of past events and prove more instructive and at

PREFACE.

the same time more interesting, if they indulged more in personal sketches.

Biography to the writer has always possessed peculiar charms, and it, indeed, may often be regarded as the most instructive branch of history. From his boyhood and his earliest recollection, to stand or seat himself at the foot of a venerated revolutionary father and listen to his unvarnished tales of the War of Independence, the battles in which he participated, and the thrilling scenes he witnessed, or sit by the side of an old soldier or pioneer of the West, detailing his own and his neighbors adventures, wants, privations, sufferings, and hair-breadth escapes from the furious monsters of the forest, and the no less wily and ferocious savages that everywhere pervaded the vast wilderness around them, he has been entranced, and felt, even then, a young heart expand, and new impulses for manly action result in making him a better and a happier boy, and in riper years a better and happier man. Such, we believe, are among the natural and legitimate effects of history—telling upon the hearts and lives of the young, the middle-aged, and the old in all ranks of society. To accomplish such end has been to a great extent our aim in this little book,—the chief fruition hoped for during our labors.

It is not proposed to make this work a chronological or regular statistical history of the revolution, or of the earliest emigrations to the West. Very creditable productions for this purpose have already appeared. Here are given only sketches of the acts and lives of those as they have stood connected with the facts narrated of, and by the individuals whose biographies are introduced. The *facts* are vouched for as given by old soldiers, their wives,

PREFACE.

pioneers and their cotemporaries; confided in and of whose narrations memoranda have been made by the author at various times within the last forty years, but who now are believed to be all in their graves. Such memoranda were originally made for his own entertainment; but now, as they are believed justly to belong to the history of his beloved country, and would otherwise sleep with the dead in the grave forever, they are freely here recorded.

T. M. S.

Louisville, January, 1855.

CONTENTS.

CHAPTER I.

Col. Davidson sets forth to Charlotte to attend the Convention of the Whigs of Mecklenburg and of other portions of the Colony of North Carolina—Meets with two Scotch Tories, John and William Harpe—Their Conversation and Doctrines—Col. Davidson and Family—The Harpes and Family.   -   -   - 17

CHAPTER II.

Col. Davidson meets with and renews his acquaintance with Capt. J. Wood—Spends the night at his house.   -   - 26

CHAPTER III.

Col. Davidson resumes his journey to Charlotte, accompanied by Capt. Wood—Meet with Dr. D. Caldwell, Dr. E. Bavard and other Patriots, destined for the same place and the Mecklenburg Convention—Discussion upon the causes of the Revolution—Brief biographical sketches of Drs Caldwell, Bavard and others.   -   -   -   -   -   -   -   -   - 32

CHAPTER IV.

Mecklenburg Convention—How organized—Speeches by Rev. H. J. Balch, Mr. Kennon and E. Bavard.   -   -   - 45

CHAPTER V.

Declaration of Independence and other resolutions passed by the Convention—Character and patriotism of the women of the Revolution.   -   -   -   -   -   -   -   - 54

CHAPTER VI.

Original letters of Presidents, John Adams and Thomas Jefferson, on the subject of the Mecklenburg Declaration of Independence in 1775, and as identical in substance with that of 1776.   -   -   -   -   -   -   -   -   - 61

CONTENTS.

CHAPTER VII.

Proceedings of the Whigs in the colony of North Carolina—
Questions asked and answered as to the causes of the tyranny
that overrides the nations of the earth, and how the freedom
of a nation can be effected. - - - - - - - 68

CHAPTER VIII.

A somewhat minute examination of the principles and spirit of
the Whig and Tory population in the country, generally, and
particularly in North Carolina—The Scenery of North Carolina, &c. - - - - - - - - - - - 81

CHAPTER IX.

The Whig women of North Carolina—A few touching biographical sketches of them during the war—Uncle Dan and his
colored company, with his old "ooman" at her cabin—Maj.
Kidd and his corps on a trip to Maj. John Adair—A hard
fought battle between two African slaves, Cæsar and John,
servants of Lawrence Smith, against five Tories and one Indian—They effectually defend their mistress and daughters,
killing two of the enemy and desperately wounding a third. - 91

CHAPTER X.

Rev. James Frazier makes appointment to preach—On his way
to church rescues Miss Happy Thompson from being precipi-
tated over the Pomonkee bridge—Her acknowledgments of the
service—Mr. Frazier's peculiar courting sermon—The return party's comments thereon. - - - - - - 107

CHAPTER XI.

Thoughts on the designs of Providence in opening up the way
from the old world to the new—The almost miraculous preservation and prosperity given to the earlier emigrants from
Europe, &c.—Some touches of the history of the revolution in
the middle colonies, particularly in North Carolina—The conflicts with the Tories—Their abduction of three young and
beautiful Whig ladies—The pursuit and execution of a number by Capt. John Wood and others. - - - - - 116

CHAPTER XII.

The attack upon and murder of Capt. John Wood, by twelve
Tories, sent forth by Col. Ferguson, of the British army to
destroy him—His burial by his son. - - - - 135

CHAPTER XIII.

Parson Frazier again—His return to the neighborhood of Elder Brame—His courtship and marriage with the rich, young, and accomplished Virginia lady, Miss Happy Thompson, and their settlement upon a portion of her fine estate at Hillsboro,' North Carolina, together with other interesting touches of Virginia gallantry and courtship in the Old Dominion. - 145

CHAPTER XIV.

Frank Wood, after the burial of his murdered father, endeavors to find his mother and sisters—Uncle Dan and his brave African troops are introduced at his cabin—Frank returns home, and immediately afterwards enters upon his first campaign in the army of the revolution—He joins the command of Gen. Morgan, at Waxaw Bottoms—Is with the Whigs in the battle of Kings Mountain—Kills several of the Tories that assassinated his father, and in that battle, shoots from his horse, the British commander, Col. Ferguson, while the latter is rallying his retreating troops—Other details of Frank Woods' adventures in the service of the country, and in fulfillment of his vow of vengeance. - - - - - - - - 160

CHAPTER XV.

Measures taken by Cornwallis—Battle of Kings Mountain—Death of Col. Ferguson, by the hand of Frank Wood—His narrative of the battle and subsequent action. - - - 174

CHAPTER XVI.

Lord Cornwallis encamped at Hillsboro'—Marauding parties of British and Tories sent out to ravage and plunder the inhabitants—Anecdote of Maj. Hinton, in his attempt to rob Mrs. Slocum—Falls into a dry well in her cellar—A love adventure of his lordship with Maria Davidson—His utter overthrow—The Toryism and base treachery of the Rev. Mr. James Frazier toward his wife, and flight to and with the British army, after embezzling his wife's fine estate—The hypocrite's picture. - - - - - - - - - - - 185

CHAPTER XVIII.

Frank Wood again at home—Learns the dreadful intelligence of the abduction of his sister Susan and Maria Davidson by the Tories and Indians—Visits with his mother the monu-

XII   CONTENTS.

ment she had erected over the grave of his father—Visits with
his sister Rosa, the family of the Simpsons, and something is
told strongly signifying a love match between two young
lovers. - - - - - - - - - - - - 201

CHAPTER XIX.

Frank Wood sets out from his home in North Carolina to join
his regiment under Gen. Green, according to his furlough—
He is transferred and attached to the division of the army
then under Gen. Lafayette in Virginia—In course of time,
with that division, he was marched to the vicinity of Yorktown, and when joined to the other force of Gen. Washington,
marched to entrap and besiege Cornwallis at Yorktown—
When Cornwallis capitulated and provisions were made and
completed by Gen. Washington, safely and securely, to dispose of the many thousands captured at Yorktown and dispose
of the large amount of munitions of war there given up in the
capitulation, he obtains leave from Marquis Lafayette to return
to his home and his friends in North Carolina—On his way
Frank Wood has many thoughts of his country, seeks to look
into her future, and prays for her prosperity—Finds and consummates his previous engagement in marriage with Mary
Simpson. - - - - - - - - - - - 216

CHAPTER XX.

Thoughts on the effects of times, surrounding localities, circumstances, physical and metaphysical, climate, topography of
country, education, manner of life and action to make the
man a giant or a pigmy, a philosopher or an ape, a hero or a
poltroon—Capt. Jack Ashby—His feats of activity and bravery—Trip to Kentucky—Escape from the Indians at the falls
of the Ohio. - - - - - - - - - - 226

CHAPTER XXI.

Capt. Jack and his companions shoot at the Indian party—
They kill the principle one, and wound another and the white
man—The third Indian dives into the river and escapes—
Salona Maron, the young French girl's story—She informs
the Captain that the white man, Ben. James is from Virginia
—Ashby questions him and discovers his knowledge of his
family—He gives an account of himself—Porter is taken sick
with fever—They start down the Mississippi, taking Ben.

James with them, after sinking the two dead Indians in their canoe—Porter dies and is sunk in the remaining Indian canoe, opposite Chickasaw Bluffs—Ben. James is allowed to depart for his Indian home—Capt. Ashby, Wells and Salona Maron, proceed down the Mississippi—They arrive at New Orleans safely—Are treated well by Miss Maron's aunt and family—Capt. Jack and Wells arrive at San Augustine, where Wells is taken sick and dies—Capt. Jack finally gets home after an absence of two years. - - - - - - 241

CHAPTER XXII.

Thos. McClanahan, another native Virginian—Incidents of his boyhood—His skill and perseverance as a huntsman—Chases a buck on foot six miles—Runs him into a farmer's cellar, where he is found next morning, killed and taken home in triumph—Tom, at the age of eighteen leaves his home, and joins the continental army—Travels one hundred miles on foot to whip a man who insulted his father, and having done so, immediately returns—Is engaged in the battles of Brandywine, Morristown, Monmouth and Trenton—Returns home after the surrender of Cornwallis—Renews his acquaintance with Miss Ann Green—Courts her—Asks the consent of her brother, Col. Robert Green—Is refused. - - - - 259

CHAPTER XXIII.

Young McClanahan informs his mother of his determination and requests her assistance—She breaks the subject to her husband, and they agree to provide their son with funds to consummate his object—Miss Nancy and her lover fix upon the course they intend to adopt. - - - - - - 266

CHAPTER XXIV.

The lovers consummate their marriage—A description of the bride's person—Col. Green's chagrin and disappointment—His wife's sensible advice, and the colonel's final reconcilement to what he could not help. - - - - - - 277

CHAPTER XXV.

McClanahan removes to New River—Is famed for his pugilistic encounters and victories—A conspiracy to whip him—Seven men undertake to do so, but after five of them being by him nearly killed, the other two run and leave him victor—He, with his family, emigrate to Kentucky—Reach and reside at Boone's Station—McClanahan's intimacy with Daniel Boone—Has several severe combats with Indians—Delights in the occupation—Boone makes him commander of a company of rangers, and sends him to the settlements on the Ohio to watch the Indians—His success. - - - - - 283

CHAPTER XXVI.

The party overtakes the Indians—After destroying forty of them, they release Miss Lucy Smith and Harriet Lane, and conduct them in triumph to Fort Washington, now Cincinnati—Lucy Smith is married to one of the Rangers—The first wedding ever celebrated at Cincinnati. - - - - - - 295

CHAPTER XXVII.

McClanahan's account of Harmar's defeat—His own miraculous escape from death—Makes his way back to camp, much to the surprise of his comrades, who had given him up for lost. - 303

CHAPTER XXVIII.

Lord Rawdon's inhuman execution of Col. Isaac Hayne—Death of Hayne's wife and child—Some thoughts on these sad occurrences. - - - - - - - - - 309

CHAPTER XXIX.

Particulars of the abduction of Susan Wood and Maria Davidson by big Bill and Josh. Harpe—Their treatment of the girls on their journey to the hunter's cave, and from thence to Nickajack on the Tennessee River, a town of the Cherokee's—Destruction of that town by Gen. Jackson, and flight of the Harpes with their victims to the Cumberland mountains. - 317

CHAPTER XXX.

Rev. William Lambeth's adventure with Big Harpe—The Harpes leave their camp at the Cumberland Mountain, and start for the Ohio—Meet with, murder and rob two Marylanders—Maria Davidson's account of that horrible crime—They waylay, murder and rob a young Virginian—They are chased and secured in Danville jail—They escape and make their way to Springfield—The two ruined girls their victims, being free, discuss the propriety of seeking the sympathy and protection of the settlers—They decline doing so—The Harpes return to the

women and start for the neighborhood of Snelling's Station
—Again they steal horses and journey towards what is now
Columbia, Adair Co., Ky., where they are believed to have
murdered Col. Trabue's little son—Continue their journey
and operations of murder and robbery into Tennessee, are
chased back to the Mammoth Cave, but not captured—Big
Harpe murders his own child.   -   -   -   -   -   - 325

CHAPTER XXXI.

The Harpes and Cherokees continue their blood-thirsty journey
—At the point of the Clay Lick woods they murder, strip,
and mutilate the families and servants of two brothers—They
are chased by a party from Russellville and Drumgool's stations—The Harpes, in the meantime, murder Stegall's family
near the Double Licks, rob and burn up his home—They
are overtaken at the "Lonesome Oak" by the pursuing party—Big Harpe and one Indian is killed, and the head of the
former hung on a tree—Stegall attempts to murder Susan
Woods—Is restrained and wholly checked by Wm. Stewart,
of Russellville—Maria Davidson and Susan Woods are taken
with the return party to Russellville—Excitement of the populace against them—They are privately conveyed out of town
to a place of safety—Maria is subsequently married.   -   - 334

CHAPTER XXXII.

Further narrative of the adventures of Josh Harpe—His escape
—His appearance at Natchez with Peter Alston—They conspire to murder and decapitate Mayerson for the government
reward—They do so and while waiting for the reward are
recognized and seized, tried, condemned and executed.   -   - 341

CHAPTER XXXIII.

Major Bland Ballard—His parentage—His father locates at
Boonsboro—Removes to Tick Creek—Family locates at Tyler's Station—Maj. Bland marries—The Station becoming
crowded, the Ballards remove outside the stockades—Danger
from the Indians anticipated—The family of old Mr. Ballard
is attacked and nearly all murdered by the Indians—Maj.
Bland, hearing the attack, rushes to the door of his cabin to
receive the last groan of his murdered mother—Decides to
take the open ground and defend himself and wife—Is heroically assisted by his wife—After shooting seven Indians, he

finds his bullet-pouch exhausted—Is supplied by his wife who melts her spoons for the purpose, and exposes her life to hand the bullets to her husband—He finally triumphs. - - - 345

CHAPTER XXXIV.

" William Stout "—Thoughts on the adage " Murder will out" —Why Stout came to Kentucky—His dark deeds of blood— His care of his family—Tracks and destroys the murderer of his son—Redresses the widow's wrong—Prevents Jerry Moore's trip to Missouri—Dies. - - - - - 350

CHAPTER XXXV.

A picture of the earlier settlements in the West—State of Society —Who gave it tone and polish. - - - - - - 362

CHAPTER XXXVI.

Religious revival in the West—Rev's John and William M'Ghee —Their appointments to preach—Preaching at Red River Meeting House—Its results—Preaching at Beech Meeting House—Results, especially on those who came to mock, but remained to pray—Meeting at Muddy River Church—The Meeting House too small to accommodate—They go out into the open air—A pulpit is erected—First Camp Meeting— Great results. - - - - - - - - - 370

CHAPTER XXXVII.

State of Western Society—Dr. Gist's story of the honey—Its disastrous results—Is confirmed by Dr. Wilmot—His additional remarks. - - - - - - - - - 374

CHAPTER XXXVIII.

Religion in the West—The revival of 1799—Its effects—Dissenting of the Presbyterians and denial of God's hand in the work—Results of such denial—Cause of the organization of the Cumberland Presbyterian Church—Conclusion. - - 389

LEGENDS

OF THE

WAR OF INDEPENDENCE

AND OF THE

EARLIER SETTLEMENTS IN THE WEST.

CHAPTER I.

Col. Davidson sets forth to Charlotte to attend the Convention of the Whigs of Mecklenburg and of other portions of the Colony of North Carolina—Meets with two Scotch Tories, John and William Harpe—Their Conversation and Doctrines—Col. Davidson and Family—The Harpes and Family.

> "Well, honor is the subject of my story.
> I cannot tell, what you and other men
> Think of this life; but, for my single self,
> I had as lief not be, as live to be
> In awe of such a thing as I, myself.
> I was born as *free* as Cæsar; so *were* you;
> We both have fed as well—and even can both
> Endure the winter's cold as well as he."—*Shakspeare.*

In the year 1775, and on one of those beautiful evenings in May, after hours of heavy rain from dark clouds, with repeated claps of thunder; and when the effulgent source of day had brushed the mists that intervened between him and field, and flower, three neighbors—John and William Harpe, brothers, and Capt. John Davidson,

2

18   LEGENDS OF THE

afterwards Col. Davidson, in the army commanded by
Gen. Nathaniel Green—met at a small country Inn, on
the road leading, at that time, from Hillsboro' to Charlotte, the county seat of Mecklenburg county, colony of
North Carolina.   Their meeting was more than usually
cordial ; and, after the ordinary salutations between them,
Capt. Davidson, who, though a Virginian by birth, had
been reared, from an early age, in Mecklenburg; and
having married when but little passed minority, settled
and cultivated a very productive farm near one of the
tributary streams of the Yadkin.   He said to the two brothers :

"I am glad, neighbors, to meet you here, for many
reasons : First, because we shall be company to Charlotte, which is yet a good long ride; and secondly, because I am glad to find you, at last, coming into our
views of the necessity of resisting, some way, the doings
of old George, and his vile officers of the Crown—extort-
ing, on all occasions, their high taxes without our consent, in any way—and levying and exacting the most ex-
travagant fees for the least official service—sacrificing,
without restraint of even the proclamations of the Governor, the citizen's property, to satisfy them.   For I suppose you are going to the meeting, to-morrow, called by
our chief-committee-man, Col. Polk ? "

" You need nae think that, Jonny Davison," said John
Harpe, the elder; " 'Tis a' thrue, we seed the writin' of
Col. Polk—and read it, too—callin' the meetin', but din
nae heed it.   The regulations is nae the work for mea.
And ye, Jonny Davison, afthur you're fitin' givinor
Thryon and his guid boys at the Allemance, three years
agone, and runnin' awa' half kilt, yoursel', and more nor
half the regulation kilt and bleedin' on the ground at the
Allemance, ye, yoursel', wad nae more be creepin' afthur
the regulation, nae anny biddy else.   Mouthin' and scald-
in' the king, and the givinor, and the Clarks and the
Sherricks.   Din nae hear, twad be far bether to tarry at

WAR OF INDEPENDENCE. 19

hame, luvin' and cheerin' yere bonny wife, and the bonny dather, jist bloomin' like the pretty fluer, nor ridin' to town to flout and fiaro! Nae, Jonny Davison, the aith the givinor mad' mea and mea brither tak' and aboon that, the la' o' the kirk forbids the regulation with us."

"Aye, Jonny, we ken you a gude sojer," said the younger brother, William Harpe; "Nae man iver made a bonny rifle crack bether nor you, whene the cluty injin stude annent ye, or the glowerin' panther, or creepin' bear across yere thread, dore stand, and ye tak' a hunt to the Blue Mountains. But Jonny Harpe tells ye thrue, the givinor's aith and the la' o' the kirk tither the hauns of the gude man, and no meeting the regulations for me, either. Ye're fitin' the injins, and the bears nae ilka the givinor's thrupes. The beasts ye ma' kill; but God and the big buke forbids ye kill the king's men—and that ye'll ha' to do."

"Well, well; I have no time to talk these matters over with you, now. I shall have a hard ride to get to Charlotte in time to attend the meeting. I confess I do not understand what you mean by the law of the Church, forbidding your resisting the oppressions of the king and his officers, in their unjust taxes and unlawful fees. In this way the people here or any where could have no rights, and must become slaves. Indeed, so it is, all nations in Europe are now subjects of tyranny, and must forever remain so. I don't believe a word of it. I was born free and I mean to die so."

"Why, Jonny Davison," said John Harpe, "ye din nae untherstand how the la' o' the kirk, and the big buke forbids ye're fitin' the king? An' din nae ken the scripther saith, 'ye'll abide the powers that be, an' that ev'ry gude covenanter sweareth like he will stand by the king, and his auldest boy or dather, as next the king.' But we know ye'll gang, Jonny, to the meetin'—take gude care, howndeavor, ye ha' nae rebels among ye. The big presbyther, Docthur Killwell fra' the Gilfords we knoo'll be thare, an' the mickle-larned man, Bavard, talk-in' like a buke, an' a' the rist o' the regulation who's nae luve for the gude King George, 'ill be thare."

"I have no love, I confess, said Capt. Davidson, for kings, and little respect for them that do love them. With the people of the Colonies it has now come to this: 'They must decide whether they will quietly submit to the king's arbitrary assumptions of power and parlia-ments; or resist by revolution or otherwise. Submit now, and we are slaves; resist, and with the blessing of God, we will be free. Farewell."

Capt. Davidson was tall in stature; somewhat slender in person, with light hair, fair skin, deep blue eyes; nose prominent, but finely turned, and a mouth little more than ordinarily broad; lips generally compressed; expres-sive of moral courage and personal prowess—in respect to which, he had been distinguished in several panther and bear hunts, in the adjacent mountains, and in seve-ral perilous conflicts with marauding invaders from the several Indian tribes, bordering on the Northern and North-western boundaries of the Colony, and still more by his courage and efficient deportment in the battle fought by the Regulators, as they were then called, at the Allamance, against Gov. Tryon, and his myrmidons, in the year 1771. And in which—though the royalists tri-umphed and slew many of Capt. D.'s bravest and best fellow-citizens, (left dead on the field,) wounding and most brutally and cruelly maltreating many more, him-self among the rest, but in which, or the results of which, although the bloody Tryon framed a new oath of allegi-ance and extorted from each of the survivors and all the inhabitants of the Colony, to swear the most humiliating and unlimited submission to the king and the British Parliament—there was kindled in the breasts of the peo-ple, (certain Scotch and Irish religionists always except-ed,) a flame of resentment and indignity toward the king, that never ceased to blaze and burn intensely, till

WAR OF INDEPENDENCE.   21

full independence and freedom was nobly fought for, and gloriously obtained for the whole country, as will be abundantly shown in the further progress of this narrative.

At home Capt. D. was very happily situated. His companion was what might be called a handsome lady, the daughter of —— Graham, a farmer of great respectability, in the vicinity of Hillsboro. She was pretty well educated in most of the English branches, and thoroughly instructed in, and accustomed to all the most useful and approved departments of housewifery; full of love and reverence for her worthy husband; and of earnest affection and maternal solicitude for the proper instruction and rearing of an only daughter, now arrived at the age of fifteen years, and under the tuition and care of a Presbyterian Minister, the Rev. James Frazier, who, in conjunction with his very accomplished and highly educated lady, Mrs. Happy Frazier, had charge of one of the finest female Colleges, ever, for many years, opened in North Carolina.

In respect to estate, Capt. D. owned an ample farm—fertile, and made by his own industry, economy, and management, and the aid of several sturdy and well-trained farm-servants—exceedingly productive; yielding not only an abundant supply of everything common to the country, and for all domestic and culinary purposes, but sent to the markets abroad a profitable surplus. He was born in Bedford county, Virginia, of Irish parents, who early removed to Mecklenburgh, North Carolina, where he was principally reared and educated. The country being then well filled with game, such as elk, deer, and turkies and other wild fowls, and sometimes with bear and panther; he became, early, an adept in the use of the rifle, and a most successful huntsman; and when the savages would sometimes make down from the mountains and cross into the valleys below the Blue-Ridge, in companies of fifty and sometimes a hundred in number

22   LEGENDS OF THE

for the purpose of murder, rapine and robbery—young
Davidson was often foremost in pursuing them, and the
most successful in overtaking and inflicting the severest
punishment and most summary justice upon them.

Of the two Scotchmen with whom Capt. D. held the
above detailed narrative, little need be said. Both had
emigrated with their wives to the new world together,
some fifteen or sixteen years before the period of which
we are writing and settling in the county of Orange, near
Hillsboro—purchased each a small farm and chiefly employed themselves in its cultivation and hunting in the
contiguous and extensive forests, reaching to, and beyond
the blue mountains. These Scotchmen, as is perceived
from their conversation with Capt. Davidson, had been
thoroughly educated and brought up under the superstitious notions that sprung from the feudal teachings of
many centuries since, spread and obtained all over Europe;
the doctrine of "The Divine Rights of Kings!" a scheme
cunningly devised and propagated by priests and the flatterers and fawners of power in church and State, in order
to employ the superstition of men, as a chief instrument
in subjecting them to the arbitrary control and iron heel
of monarchical authority; to build up and perpetuate
over the nations, a theology teaching a dread of opposing
tyranny in any form; under color of which, kings and
other potentates have made their persons sacred, whatever their crimes, and sanctify to all patient endurance and
submission, whatsoever iniquities they perpetrated—whatsoever cruelties they inflicted! A doctrine doubtless con-
cocted in the deep pits of infernal darkness, seized and assiduously and insiduously wielded by the pride of rulers
and the lovers of oppression! Under the sanction of
which kings and rulers have practiced such tricks, in
the sight of heaven as should make even fallen angels
blush! But in respect to this stratagem of darkness,
these illiterate Scotch brothers had been—like many thousands of others who lived in the Colonies, that wrought,

with might and main, to thwart the progress and success of the struggle for liberty, and to perpetuate the tyranny and oppression of king and parliament,—the pupils of their peculiar church, the Scotch kirk or covenanters, known to have a fundamental principle in their *confession of faith* and discipline, as the Harpes declared, from which circumstance the name of the covenanters actually takes its rise. All who are in its communion or are subjected to its laws and control are understood expressly, or tacitly, to be forever bound by a covenant and a most sacred, solemn and religious promise or pledge, never to yield or submit to, or permit the exercise of the sovereign reign, of any prince, potentate, or other power, save, and except, the kings and queens of the throne of England and the heir apparent to the throne. This is the bonus given by conquered Scotland, for a few extra and minor privileges granted to the people, and for the protection of the Scotish kirk as a separate establishment, wholly independent of the discipline and organization of the Protestant Episcopal Hierarchy. No wonder, then, that these, and all others of like religious opinions taught to feel and be ruled by these obligations to the royal family as no less than the essence of religion and faith, even the most unexceptionably among them in other respects, should feel disposed to favor the parent government, and take sides against the patriots. John and William Harpe so thought and so acted. With them it was not only in accordance with their opinions to approve the course of that government in its conduct toward the colonies, provoking resistance, but also a principle of religious faith. Each had one son. William, the son of John, was very stout, surpassingly strong and active; now about twenty years of age—commonly called, " Big Harpe."

Joshua, the son of William, was not so strong as John, but able to perform more feats of activity and great endurance. No one, who was at all conversant with physiognomy, and accustomed to form opinions of the moral traits of

24   LEGENDS OF THE

character, from the lineaments of the face, the formation
of the head, and the expression of the eye, could look upon either of these young Harpes, without being disagree-
ably and disgustingly impressed with the bull-dog head
and face of the former, and the sly lynx or hyena appearance of the head and face of the latter, now about eighteen
years old.

Neither had received even the least literary cultivation,
or had been taught anything but the mere questions and
answers of the Calvinist confessions and catechisms of
the day. From their fathers they received no examples
of practical piety, no words of kindness calculated in the
slightest to awaken final respect, and cherish the sympathies and obligations of their humanity for their fellow
men ; never having enjoyed a father's look, but enveloped
with frowns, and seldom heard a father's voice but in
abuse of some one, and most frequently, themselves. All
their moral instruction and training, consisted in being
imbued thoroughly with the doctrine of their father—
that God's immutable decrees fixed everything, and determined the fate, for Heaven or hell, of every one born
into the world, without regard to moral character or faith
or practice, good or base ! These were the sentiments, at
least, that they entertained, whether the legitimate de-
ductions of the teachings they had received or not, the
ferocity of their lives and the desperation of their characters too well attest the fact. While young, they had few
associates; living in a neighborhood sparsely populated,
and never at school, they formed few acquaintances.
When not immediately at labor on the farms of the two
families to which they respectively belonged, they spent
almost all their time upon hunting excursions to the Blue
Ridge, or upon fishing tramps along the adjacent rivers.
Each had a sister, a few years younger than themselves,
and each as uncouth in manners and mind as themselves.
On a few occasions, these Misses Harpe, had met Maria
Davidson, till they had reached womanhood; and when

WAR OF INDEPENDENCE. 25

she would occasionally spend the vacations of the school at Hillsboro, at her father's, in company with her excellent mother, she visited at the house of old John Harpe, on cotton picking, quilting, or log-rolling occasions—common in those early days of the country, and, indeed, almost the only high days and holidays enjoyed by the young in those semi-savage times, in that portion of North Carolina. On such occasions, also, William and Joshua Harpe saw and became known to Maria, and sometimes danced with her, or played thimble, &c., at the frolics, with which these gatherings generally ended; and when their mothers and fathers would also enjoy themselves in minuets, reels and jigs, to the great delight and entertainment of the sons and daughters, and all other spectators.

CHAPTER II.

Col. Davidson meets with and renews his acquaintance with Capt.
J. Woods—Spends the night at his house.

> "Vouchsafe to those that have
> Not read the story,
> That I may prompt them; and of such as have
> I humbly pray thee to admit the excuse
> Of time, of numbers, and due course of things,
> Which in their huge and proper life
> Be here present."—*Shakspeare.*

WE parted with Capt. Davidson, where he left the two elder Harpes, at the little inn on his way to Charlotte. On he pushed until about eight o'clock at night, when, as he had yet fifteen miles to reach that place, the roads deep and the weather somewhat mirky, he turned to a farm house for an evening's repose, which he was well pleased to find belonged to and was occupied by Capt. J. Woods, whom he had seen several years before on one of the excursions of the citizens of that part of the country, against the Cherokee Indians, who had stealthily crept into the white settlements, murdered some of the inhabitants and carried off a great many horses, cattle, &c. He had been with him also on a bear and buffalo hunt, when they for the first time crossed the Blue Ridge, and penetrated the dense and unbroken forests west of the mountain. Our traveler alighted from his horse, which he left near the gate, entered the yard, approached and knocked at the door, and was speedily responded to by a clear and sonorous voice from within, enquiring his object, and requesting him to wait till a light should be procured. In a brief space, a light was brought out, made by a pine knot, borne in the hand of Capt. John Wood, who was immediately recognized though he had not seen him for ten years. He requested entertainment for the night, explaining that he was on his way to Charlotte, which he presumed was yet fifteen or twenty miles off, and as it was now quite dark, and as he could reach the place by an early morning ride, and in time for his business, he would be glad to be permitted to stay till then, and would be pleased to give any reasonable compensation for it

"You can't pay anything here, friend, for so small a favor," responded Wood. "We live near the road, it is true, leading across the upper part of the colony pretty much, and on into South Carolina We don't keep tavern, yet we are not apt to turn folks off when they call for quarters. We don't charge them for it neither. Where's your horse, stranger? Is he at the gate. Here, Frank," called to his eldest son, "the gentleman's horse is hitched at the yard gate. See that he is cared for—tell Pete to feed him well. Now come in sir, and rest, for travelers are generally pretty glad, after a hard day's ride, to get a comfortable seat by a warm fire; but we have no fire in the room, the weather has been so warm we have not thought it necessary. My daughter, call old Cæsar out of the kitchen to make a fire at once, and then we can see better to talk, for after we get our travelers a little warm and rested, and something comfortable to eat, we expect them to tell something good and interesting of the parts they are from, and that's our charge. Wife, here's a gentleman who wants to stay with us till morning, when he is going to Charlotte, and would like to get a rasher or two of that good venison stew you have handy, and some bread, milk and butter. I don't know your name, sir, but since I can see better, and you've come in, it seems to me I had ought to—for I think I've seen you before—but it don't now matter. This is my wife, sir, and there's my two girls. I have two boys. Harry's our pet, and Frank, who I sent to look after your horse, is our biggest boy, and a rousin' boy he is too, being only fourteen last April. My boys, sir, young as they are, do a great deal for me, and when not away at school, work as hard as any of my negroes, and I have two fine darkies to work, I assure you."

Capt. Davidson, as soon as his host ceased these remarks about his family, informed him what his name was, that he was from the neighborhood of Hillsboro, and that he very well remembered to have seen him on the chase after the Indians in June, 1762.

"Aye, yes," said Capt. Wood, "I was on that hunt, and now remember you. And you are the man that all believe killed big Washita, at the mouth of the Great Cave, where the Injins hid themselves when we were hot upon them. Big Washita had four scalps tied with a deer sinew string, fastened around his waist. I saw you cut them loose and run behind that big tree, that stood near, a little to one side of the mouth of the cave—the infernal Injin den, and that was right enough. For the villains sent many a ball whistling after you, just as you got behind the tree. You hung on to the string and the skalps, though."

"No more of the Injins came out; and we could not get them out of the cave. I thought since, we ought to have built a great log fire across the mouth, and smoked them all out, like rabbits; and proposed to do so, but Major Goodin said he reckoned we could not do anything that way, and said there was, probably, on the other side of the mountain, another mouth of the cave, through or under which the plaggy hollow seemed to run, and the smoke and even the Injins would get out at it, and it would'nt do no good, and so we all came home, you know, being a little skittish about going any further out into the big wilderness. Them Injins have been a little more scarce since that time; they hain't took many horses since—well enough they don't, for there's many a horse stole now, and carried off to Georgia, through Virginia to Pennsylvania, or some of them forin parts, by some devilish Injins, what, I guess lives here, right amongst us; they will be caught and hung some of these days, and I wish they was. Well, now, there's a bite of supper for you on the table, and I'll not keep you from it any longer. When you have got done with the eating, I guess we can talk a bit more before you must go to bed." So the traveler took his seat at the table, and had but little more than began his repast before his friend began to talk to him again.

"Ah! now I think of it," he said, "It is very likely you are going to Charlotte, to meet the regulating friends. I guess you seen the letter of Col. Polk and are going to the meeting to-morrow. I hope so, at least; for my heart and soul is in that business. I forgot to tell you, I was going myself to Charlotte, pretty early in the morning, to see what they'll do about it. So if that's your business we'll go together." "That is my business there, Capt. Wood, and I am glad, not only to have your company, but that we are very likely to agree in respect to the object and necessity of such a meeting. We want men there that have the heart and mind to think and act for themselves, and for their country, independently!— men of firm minds and strong arms; for if we do not now, I am sure we will need all we can get of that stamp, very soon. As I do not see that the king and parliament and colonial officers are likely to get any better soon, but worse and worse; and I, for one, let me tell you, cannot see how the people of the colonies are to stand it peaceably much longer."

"Well, now indeed, friend Davidson, we do seem to agree very well; and if you say so, we'll not only go together to Charlotte, but throughout this whole business, come what will," said the bold and generous Capt. Wood.

By this time the traveler had finished his sumptuous supper, so promptly and abundantly supplied by the hos-

30   LEGENDS OF THE

pitable matron, and taking his seat near the comfortable fire, briskly and cheerily blazing away on the hearth, he said:

"How very different men are in their opinions and views upon every subject. I confess I was a little disappointed, if not actually grieved, when John and William Harpe, my neighbors, (two Scotchmen who settled among us twelve or fourteen years back,) talked with me as they did this evening. They were at a little tavern on the road. I found them there, and was in hopes they were also on their way to Charlotte, to attend the meeting, and so told them; and really, they almost quareled with me, for supposing such was their purpose. They had a great deal to say in favor of the king—said that God and religion forbid saying and doing anything against the king, or any of his men in authority; and said a good deal about the regulators, seeming to rejoice that old Tryon had whipped them all, at the Allemance, and talked much about the treason of our meeting to-morrow. So I came to the conclusion that if we got into a scuffle with old George, we might not rely much upon those sort of foreigners, as indeed, there was much greater room to fear they would most of them, fight against us."

"They are not going to fight us much in the way of a regular field fight," said Capt. Wood, "but will be likely to do worse. They will, most probably, if we get in a war, turn their attention to robbery and plunder, and sly attacks upon our defenceless families, when we are out campaigning for the country. O, I say, wife, was it not a young man by the name of Bill Harpe, who it was said, had stolen Squire Dennis' fine riding horse, the week before last, and was followed into the neighborhood of Abington, but there dodged Crane and Collins, that folfowed him? I say, wife?"

Mrs. Wood answered, she thought that was the name.

"Aye, well, I wonder if he is any 'kin to those two Scotchmen. Yes, the name was Bill Harpe, for certain, and I should like to know whether he is a son or cousin of them."

"Indeed," said Capt. Davidson, "you surprise me. John Harpe has a son by the name of Bill, or William, now about twenty or twenty-one years of age, and a very stout active man at that."

"Ah, there it is," said Capt. Wood, "I should calculate it was the same; and that such men as you say they are, are likely to raise such scamps of sons—cowards or thieves, you may be sure."

"Truly," said Capt. Davidson, " if it be big Bill Harpe, as he is called in the neighborhood, it is only fulfilling the fears many of us have had about him, for some years; but I never heard of his stealing anything before, if indeed, it was he. I don't remember to have seen him in our parts for some month or so, and now I remember it, his uncle, William Harpe, at the mills, the other day, said that big Bill, and his own son, Joshua had gone over into Virginia, for a spell, to get some employment as overseers of negroes. Well, indeed, it may be the same that took the horse, and I'll vouch more than one horse is gone ; for they are known to be very intimate, always together, if any mischief is to be done. I do not know that any of us have suspected them for stealing, but they are universally hated and shunned in the neighborhood, as bad young men."

" Capt. Davidson," said Capt. Wood, " I guess you're tired enough to lie down a while. Here, Rosa, my daughter, take that lamp and show Capt. Davidson his room. I hope you'll sleep pretty fast, so as to be up to a bite of breakfast, we must have before we go, as we ought to get to Charlotte early, and ready to attend the meeting, as soon as any of our friends. Go, now Rosa, sweet girl, and direct the gentleman to his bed."

Capt. D., followed the pretty Rosa, and was speedily wrapt in a sound and refreshing slumber.

CHAPTER III.

Col. Davidson resumes his journey to Charlotte, accompanied by Capt. Wood—Meet with Dr. D. Caldwell, Dr. E. Bavard and other Patriots, destined for the same place and the Mecklenburg Convention—Discussion upon the causes of the Revolution—Brief biographical sketches of Drs. Caldwell, Bavard and others.

> " Those are they
> That most are willing; if any such be here
> (As it were sin to doubt,) that love this painting
> Wherein you see me smear'd; if any fear
> Less his person than an ill report;
> If any think brave death outweighs bad life
> And that his country's dearer than himself,
> Let him, alone, or so many, so minded,
> Wave thus (waiving his hand) to express his disposition
> And follow Marcius."—*Shakspeare.*

At five o'clock the entire family of Capt. Wood was aroused, and white and black were engaged in preparing an early breakfast for the two patriots, Davidson and Wood, before they proceeded to the gathering of their countrymen at Charlotte. Quickly it was upon the table, and in haste the gentlemen partook of the sumptuous fare, so that by morning's dawn they were hastening to the place of destination. They had not traveled far before they fell in with a goodly company of the hardy sons of North Carolina, ready in heart and mind to do, or die in the attempt, whatsoever the meeting should decide to be proper and honorable in resistance to oppression. Their destination was soon known to Capt. Wood and Davidson, a very ready acquaintance was formed with each other, and a cordial interchange of sentiment began as they chatted on the way.

WAR OF INDEPENDENCE. 33

To our two friends, Wood and Davidson, the names and characters of several of the company, by whom they were thus joined, were well known. Amongst them was Dr. Caldwell, a Presbyterian minister at Guildford Court-House, having charge of a congregation at that place, also one at Allemance, a short distance off—a man of great learning and in charge of an institution of education unsurpassed by any, even up to that time, established in the colony, and whose public and private characters were well known throughout the entire country; also Dr. Ephraim Bavard, an elder at Allemance—a man of very superior mind and profound erudition—with others who afterwards made themselves greatly useful to the country and were distinguished for indomitable courage and unvarying love of country. All, all, soon made themselves known as deeply interested in the objects of the meeting before them, and resolved and prepared in mind to act on the occasion.

Dr. Bavard told them he had, that morning, received by letter, intelligence of the conduct of the Governor and British military officers at Boston; the resistance of the friends of the country to their cruel, arbitrary and wicked attacks upon the people at Lexington and Cambridge, as well as the fight at Breed's and Bunker's Hill, and the glory won by the Americans on those occasions. The letter received he promised to read so soon as the meeting was organized. This startling intelligence aroused, as may well be supposed, the most intense feeling and profound consideration in the minds of all who heard it. For some minutes perfect silence prevailed, and it was first broken by the voice of Capt. Wood, who, evidently under the influence of the most powerful excitement, said—

"I am an American by birth; born free as George III. in the good colony of Massachusetts. My grand-father sacrificed his all of lands and money in England to look for and find a home freed from the iron tread of British

3

tyranny. In this country he found it. Hard by old Plymouth Rock my ancestors lived and died; there I was born, and there I tasted the sweets of Liberty, I shall say 'Heaven's best earthly gift to man;' and here, in North Carolina, I am prepared to follow the example of my old comrades and fellow-citizens in that good old colony in resisting unto blood and death, if need be, the Stamp Act, Tea Tax, and every other act or thing on the part of the king and parliament calculated to enslave or even to abridge, to any material extent, the chartered rights of free Americans! I am no orator, Capt. Davidson and gentlemen; I am no preacher, nor am I learned enough, like our good Dr. Caldwell and Dr. Bavard, to do much in speech-making, but I have a good strong arm and as keen a sight along the straight edge of my bright and well-tried rifle, as any man. You saw me a little tried at the Allemance against Tyron and his men, fighting the friends of the country, and all who felt the oppressions of the officers in their fee-exactions and the tax-collectors. Yes; you will guess, too, I made some of them feel the loving touches of that rifle. Now I don't know what you may all think best to be done and shall resolve to do, at this meeting, but I say resolve upon what you please to oppose this tyranny, and if you do not find old John Wood on your side, you may know he has forgot his wife and children and has ceased to tell his sons, ' Die sooner than live slaves.' "

Every one within hearing of these thrilling remarks of this firm and most intrepid man—several, while he was addressing them, seemed to have unconsciously pressed their horses near to his side—involuntarily surrounded him, their countenances expressing an almost unspeakable interest and admiration for the speaker, from whose flashing eyes and pallid features there seemed to irradiate new lights of thought and patriotic inspiration, which, for more than a minute, enchained them in silence, until the venerable Caldwell, who, with others, had gathered near him, addressed him in tones at once soothing and instructive, by saying:

"Please be careful, my friend, and temperate as possible in your expressions. We know you love your country, love liberty, and are as ready to act as bravely as any man. But should we not, while our enemies may, under cover of law, question our rights and persecute us for what we say, or do, be very cautious lest we give grounds for persecution. I know your determination on resistance of tyranny in every political shape. But it is always wise to do nothing in rashness, or which is not calculated to accomplish a certain good. It is certain there is a great crisis at hand; the intelligence we have heard from Boston of the conduct of the Governor and other British officers, prove the fact beyond question that war there, and here, and throughout the land, is most likely to ensue; and it will then be to be determined by us whether we will be free or more and more continually the slaves of British dictation and power."

"That question with me, reverend sir," said Capt. Wood, "is already settled. The roaming bear, the sculking panther, the bounding deer and elk of the boundless forests or prairies of the far west, are no less fettered by the chains of arbitrary power than John Wood intends to live and die."

"These, your reverence, after all, seem to be the nat'ral sentiments of a true American. They are mine, at all events," said Lawrence Smith, who had been listening with fixed and the most absorbing interest to all that passed between the parson and the brave border patriot, adding, "and it is certain, if the people give up now, it will not be long before we will have to be ordered and submit to it without grumbling, as the slaves have to do in old Virginia when the overseers say, 'cross your hands.' We shall have to cross our hands to old George and to the very meanest of his officers and take the whipping. I reckon we'll fight awhile first."

"Well, my countrymen," said Doctor Bavard, "it is with great joy I hear, even on our way to the meeting, the expression of such natural and firm opinions and views, on these momentous subjects, as I have this day heard expressed by my countrymen, whose habits and walks in life promise more of action than mere words and opinions. I fully concur with you, the colonies must now stand for their rights or they are gone forever. It is of no use to further petition and pray his majesty and parliament for a redress of grievances. They believe, or pretend to believe, they have the right to tax us, while we have no representative, no voice in the act to any necessary extent, to replenish their empty coffers and treasury, by wringing from the people of America their hard earnings to fatten and pamper the ministers and fawning sycophants of arbitrary power, and to coerce our submission, if we resist. I trust in God, and confidently expect we shall meet many at Charlotte to-day, like yourselves, ready to do or to die."

Many others during the ride that morning, besides those named, fell into the road with Davidson and Wood, and more or less interchanged sentiments.

Of the four, however, already introduced to our readers, Capt. Wood, Dr. Caldwell, E. Bavard and L. Smith, as they and their families are to figure considerably in many of the scenes and events of the greatest interest the narratives yet to be given, it may be proper to indulge our kind readers in a more particular analysis of their characters, &c.

Relative to Capt. Wood, little in addition to what the reader has already seen of him need here be said. Few who have had the opportunities to form an acquaintance with the characters and lives of that portion of our colonial inhabitants occupying the frontier borders of the

Southern States, during the commencement and the progress of the war of Independence, will be likely to fail to understand the solid integrity of his mind and heart, the stern indomitableness of his will, and his unconquerable moral courage. He was a man of six feet four inches heighth, of limbs finely developed, fitted for great activity and endurance; reared in his native colony to the active life of the farmer, it was natural that in emigrating to the fertile region of North Carolina, promising the richest and most abundant rewards of the tiller's toil, he should settle and engage in the culture of a farm. But notwithstanding his steady habits, acquired and industriously pursued as a farmer, he was passionately fond of adventure. He had married at the early age of twenty-three to a lady, like himself descended from a respectable Puritan stock, three years younger than himself, of handsome and healthful person, and tolerably educated in the most useful branches of an English education. Nor was her rearing deficient in regard to the more useful qualifications of a good house-wife, for it was most unquestionably asserted by Capt. Wood, and all who knew her at that early period, that not a lass or matron in all the old Bay State could with more than equal dexterity perform those distinguishing feats of all good cookery in her day—toss a pan-cake as high as the kitchen chimney, and make the butter come from the churn. She was industrious and ingenious, spinning and weaving all the clothing for her husband and herself, children and servants, and in all other respects filling creditably the important relations of wife, mother, and mistress of her household. Four children in due time blessed their union—the two oldest girls, the others boys. Capt. Wood, as a farmer, was very successful. His farm was situated in the neighborhood of the shallow ford of the Yadkin river and in the midst of a rich champaign country. Often, however, in the less busy seasons of the year, in the gratification of his natural fondness for a more heroic and adventurous life, he would leave the management of his farm in the hands of a portion of his skillful and faithful Yankee help, brought from Massachusetts at his removal, and with another portion of them, who were always delighted with the huntsman's sports and whom he had taught to wield with efficiency the deadly rifle, he made excursions for weeks far into the regions covered by the Blue Ridge, or Blue Mountains as they were often called; penetrating sometimes even into the wilderness approaching the vast Alleghanies, in pursuit of deer, elk, buffalo, and bear; and having been always more or less successful, returned with many packs, richly filled with the spoils of victory, prepared in the forests, by means of salt taken out and the process of jerking as it was called, for the winter's consumption of his family. He had also frequently been upon expeditions in pursuit of marauding Cherokee, Choctaw, Creek, and other hostile Indians, inhabiting the country west of the Blue Ridge, but chiefly the Alleghanies, who suddenly permeating the sparcely populated portions of Georgia, North Carolina, and Virginia, lying south of those mountains, murdered many without discrimination of age, or sex, or color—stealing horses and cattle, sometimes burning houses and consuming the inhabitants, amounting in some instances to entire families. On these expeditions, he was often placed in command, and learned much of the science of war, especially that with the aborigines of the country. Endowed with a mind naturally good, a will indomitable, a courage seldom if ever surpassed, with a giant strength of body and power of action, it was to be expected, as it really was the case, his countrymen living in his neighborhood and about to join the scouts after the Indians, invariably selected him to command the company, and even when in batallions of volunteers that would be formed and a colonel or major was placed in command—for he always declined taking any position higher than captain—his opinions and plans of attack were more relied on than even their own, and his influence was paramount. These campaigns always brought him into acquaintance with the most distinguished and public spirited men of the colonies, such as Davidson, Bavard, Graham, Alexander, Sumpter, Ashe, Marion, and a host of others, of great deeds in the revolutionary struggle. One inducement, subordinate to be sure, to his great solicitude to witness the result of the meeting at Charlotte, was the hope of seeing there many of those old valued friends, and with them consider and resolve upon the best measures to be pursued in the crisis then upon the country. We have said he had four children—two daughters and two sons.

Rosa, the eldest daughter, was now about nineteen years of age; fair, blue eyes, flaxen hair, a finely developed person, and mind much more than ordinarily cultivated for those frontier regions and times, through the timely industry and care of her affectionate mother.

Susan, about the age of seventeen, was a little less perfected in womanhood, well-looking, with her slightly brunette skin, black hair and eyes, fully as intellectual, though not so affable and amiable in disposition; a little more inclined to flashiness, and much less under the control of her prudent and most affectionate mother. Great was the affection of Rosa for her sister, and Susan usually felt and acted toward her with a kindness manifesting a reasonable regard. But when it was thought necessary, and her duty, by the elder sister, to advise and gently admonish Susan of errors and dangers, she often seemed a little provoked, and too often retorted with some bitterness and ascerbity, saying as much as, "it was none of her business, she was her own mistress as far as she was concerned." Their intercourse was usually harmonious and pleasant, notwithstanding these little bickerings to the contrary. They were not exactly, what in modern phrase, would be called the belles of the neighborhood. True, they had not been taught many of those branches of education without which our young ladies, of the modern days of the republic, would esteem themselves greatly destitute. But although they neither had, from a French or German master, received lessons on the piano-forte or dulcet harp, it was a fact well known to all their acquaintances that they could occasionally sing sweetly the pieces then most fashionable, such as " Crazy Jane," "Barbary Allen," "My Mamma did so before me," and numerous others, in voices sweet and subduing—and thus bewitching many languishing swains and lovers, who made them their "thoughts by day and dreams by night." Yet in no music of their day of girlhood, did they so excel or display so finely to advantage the symmetry and luxury of their elegant persons, as when they with much grace of action and poetry of motion, danced back and forth to the useful and most charming music of their mother's spinning wheel. Whether or no it was the skill and rapturous grace of these blooming and truly lovely damsels that first filled, captivated and inspired the lofty poetic rhapsody of Homer, in his Iliad, on looms and shuttles, is not known.

Their brothers were still younger. Frank, though only fifteen, at the time of which we now write, was remarkably grown for a boy of such tender years; tall and quite athletic in appearance, promising at manhood to rival his gigantic father in every quality. Considerable care had already been bestowed on his education, having been more than two years under the tuition of a fine teacher at Newberne, and during that time having made very creditable progress in the attainment of a good English education.

Henry, or Harry as he was always designated in the family, was only twelve years of age; still he was the pet, and then might well be so considered, being the youngest of the family—as it is to this day in this land, with all ranks of society, the youngest son is indulged beyond the common walks of boys, and preëminently entitled to imitate the celebrated Alexander Selkirk, and exclaim:

> "I am monarch of all I survey,
> My right there is none to dispute."

These young Woods, however, to use a homely phrase of those earlier days, were still in the rough, roll, and tumble of boyhood, and too young to have given any decided *indicia* of future character.

Frank, however, was never more delighted or observed to be so absorbed in interest, as when listening to his father, or some other, narrating hunting adventures, hair-breadth escapes from the crushing embrace of the bear, or the terrific fangs of the panther, or more desperate fights with Indians, combats with bandits and highway robbers. And when entertained by graphic and spirited descriptions, in story or history, of the destruction of human life in the conflicts of infuriated armies, his physical as well as mental nature would seem to put on a new aspect, as it were. His countenance showed visibly the deep workings of his own heart and mind; and unmistakably, though dimly, while quite young, shadowed forth some deeply embedded principles in his soul of bitterness and vengeance—some reveries and presentiments of bloody strife and future horror.

Dr. Cadwell's reputation for learning, benevolence, and widely extended usefulness, needs here no panegyric; for they were long known, written and spoken of by all who knew him. He may be said ever to have preached as a minister of the gospel of Christ what he practiced; and as forcibly taught, or more so, most likely, by his religious life and practice than by his fervid and powerful discourses from the pulpit. Aside from his general acquiescence in, and submission to the Calvinistic system of election and reprobation, as engrafted into the Westminster confession of faith, though in the discussion of which he never entered in his pulpit, his whole life was truly a most convincing commentary on and illustration of the truth and saving efficacy of the gospel of a most merciful and beneficent Creator. The nation has long and extensively reaped the rich harvests of those patriotic and enlightened, civil, naval, and military gentlemen, whose minds and morals have received at the institution of learning and science, established by Dr. Caldwell's benevolence, and fostered long by his untiring solicitude and vigilance at Guilford Court-house, the happiest culture and qualifications for the usefulness justly ascribed to them in the nation's records. No historian worthy of the name,—poor as invariably their narratives of North Carolina appear,—has ever failed to enlarge and enrich his pages by respectful mention of the life and character of this most estimable man. His warm and unwavering *amor patria*, ever through his long life, and in the times of her greatest trial and despondency, so far as a just appreciation of his sacerdotal mission would justify, in feeling and action, kept on his country's side. Never did he, like some of his brother ministers, and many of the laity of his own community and unhappily of others, plead his sacerdotal office or religious obligations in excuse, as many unfortunately and under the blind influence of a love of power or pusillanimity for their disgusting tirades, preach from the pulpits of the country against the revolution and the impiety and folly of its advocates. He did not as an officer or soldier enter the army of the republic to do battle. And yet, was there a battle fought within the reach of a reasonable travel; were there wounded and dying, of any grade on either side, needing the consolation of his well instructed, quiet, sympathizing heart and voice to cheer and console them amidst suffering and extreme pain, or by well-timed words, to lift the desponding faith and hope of the dying to the cross of the Redeemer and a home in Heaven, there was he to be found. He lived to the age of ninety years— marked the entire progress of that Heaven-directed struggle for the liberty of the country—suffered much in person, property, and in his most tender social relations on account of his cordial approbation, throughout that con-

WAR OF INDEPENDENCE. 43

flict, of the principles prompting the efforts of his countrymen—hailed in grateful adoration the providence of his God, whose inspirations had directed and nerved their arms for the fray, and finally led them to victory and independence.

Yet it must be recorded here and ought everywhere to be recorded to the everlasting dishonor of that boasted Christian nation, Great Britain, that often even her own troops, but especially her allies, the Tories, received and cherished in her service, more than once sought this venerable man's life; and on one occasion, when a British corporal and his guard, together with a half dozen or more Tories, who had wandered a short distance from the main British encampment, sought him at his home to destroy and sacrifice him to their brutal rage, and who, finding he was away, induced one of those Tories to shoot his wife through the window of her chamber, where she was walking the floor with her infant in her arms. She fell, and instantly expired in the midst of the screams of three or four young and helpless children, to satisfy and appease the disappointment of these wretches.

Oh, if there was anything yet needed to add to the dark catalogue of Christian England's vile atrocities, countenanced and sanctioned by her armed, plumed and commissioned officers, occurring in the acts of her tory and savage subsidiaries in both her wars with the United States, this, it truly may be said, claims the most marked preëminence. But the finishing touch of this most tragic item in the history of the revolutionary conflict, in regard to the sufferings of this most estimable man, is given in the wanton act of burning, within a few days after the above-mentioned incident, his dwelling house, containing a library of the most valuable character, collected at great pains and cost, and the best that at that time existed in the land.

Here, however, for the present, at least, we dismiss this melancholy picture and turn with pleasure to the contemplation of one more pleasant. It is, as we ere this promised, to give the reader a better acquaintance with the very erudite and most estimable man, Dr. Ephraim Bavard.

He was a man of great modesty, yet imbued with a spirit of indomitable moral courage, fervid and glowing with the love of country; with a mind fully and richly instructed in the science of practical christianity, exemplified throughout his too short life in deeds of kindness to his suffering neighbors. And we feel assured the intelligent reader, when we have introduced to his admiring view the great State paper, the production of his pen at Charlotte, as we shall now speedily do, will conclude with us, had Providence spared him yet a little longer, his name and fame would have stood out prominently in the history of our beloved nation, and as one of her greatest men. But he was cut off in the meridian of his useful life!

CHAPTER IV.

Mecklenburg Convention.—How organized.—Speeches by Rev. H. J. Balch, Mr. Kennon, and E. Bavard.

> "By the hope within us springing,
>   Herald of to-morrow's strife;
> By that sun, whose light is bringing,
>   Chains of freedom, death or life!
> Oh, remember life can be
> No charm for him, who lives not free!
> Like the day-star in the wave,
> Midst the dew-fall of a nation's tears!
> Happy is he o'er whose decline
> The smiles of home may soothing shine
> And light him down the steep of years;
> But O, how grand they sink to rest,
> Who close their eyes on victory's breast!"—*Moore.*

At about 10 o'clock on the morning of the 19th day of May, 1775, our two friends, Davidson and Wood, together with those we have already mentioned, and others, met on the route, arrived at the little village of Charlotte; and from the many coteries, or clusters of plain and neatly attired citizens they at once saw, standing in numbers varying from four to ten and a dozen, in every direction, on the public square, and along the streets, they conceived the most favorable hopes for the success of the convention, so far as numbers were concerned, and felt a fresh inspiration for the success of the results to flow to the country from the doings of that day. Oh, it was a lovely day; the sun had risen, beaming on the world his brightest effulgence; and calm and cloudless the day looked forth, with blissful promises of life and joy to all nature.

As our friends strolled along one of the streets, having

disposed of their horses, they drew near to the small parties or clusters of talkers standing in the way and listened
to the conversation; all seemed serious and exhibited an
interest the most intense. They had not gone far before
they approached some, who appeared to be villagers, engaged in conversation, and they listened to the words that
passed between them.

"Who," said one of them to the others, "are these that
are crowding to our town, so early this morning? Is
there a court of any kind to sit here, to-day, or what is
the cause of our seeing farmers, mechanics, lawyers, doc-
tors, and even preachers coming in from all parts of the
country, and, indeed, from all parts of the colony?"

To these enquiries, one and another answered, "they
knew not."

One said: "Indeed, neighbors, I should like to know,
myself. It must be something of great importance, bringing, as it were, the whole country together at this place.
I am getting anxious to know, myself, what it is?"

Within hearing of these remarks, but appearing not of
their acquaintance, there stood an elderly-looking gentleman, about sixty years of age, perhaps, whom they afterwards learned was George Wolden, of Allemance. He,
in a calm and unobtrusive manner, addressed himself to
the villagers, and said:—

"Know ye not, my countrymen, that this is the day
appointed for the meeting of the Committee of Safety of
our country, and of the friends of liberty in all parts of
the colony, at this place, as notified and invited by our
Chief Secretary, Mr. Thomas Polk; and that the business
is to deliberate and determine upon what should be done,
in the present crisis, to save our political and religious
rights from being trodden down by the king and parliament?"

"Ah, is that it, sir?" replied one of the neighbors.
"God give them wise heads and right hearts, for I have
been thinking, myself, something more ought to be done

WAR OF INDEPENDENCE. 47

to check up the big folks at home; the parliament and the old king always making tax laws, and such like, and never knowing or enquiring of us whether they suit us or not! And then they do, with the money they get out of us, what they please—and they don't ask us about that neither! Some tell us it goes to pay our own officers and for the good of our own country, but I hav'nt seen none of it yet. I think its all tyranny any how. I don't love tyrants, nor taxes, no way you can fix it."

"For my part," said another villager; "I don't know nothing about it. All I want's for everybody to let everything alone and mind his own business. I hope thar'll be no more fighting, like there was t'other year at the Allemance—killin' and criplin' one another!"

"Well," said the other speaker; "I don't pretend to know much about these things, neighbor. I love, and want peace, but if they make it necessary to keep our liberties and not live like slaves, to fight, I reckon I can do a little as well as the next man."

Leaving the villagers still conversing, and seeing the gathering of the people into the Court-house and around the door, the venerable stranger and ourselves, supposing the time had arrived for the sitting of the convention, proceeded thitherward.

Abraham Alexander was called upon to preside, and J. McKnight Alexander, and Dr. Ephraim Bavard were appointed Secretaries.

It was then proposed that the meeting should open with prayer, and the chairman called upon the venerable Dr. Caldwell to lead.

The Chairman then proceeded to read to the convention the intelligence brought on that day, by express, giving a short but reliable detail of the attack made by the British troops from Boston on the citizens of Massachusetts, at Lexington, on the 19th, and at Cambridge on the 20th of April; and as the same was being read by the Secretary it would be difficult to describe the deep feeling and excitement every face exhibited in that large assemblage, though without noise or any sort of indecorum on the part of any. Several gentleman then arose in succession and addressed the assemblage.

Rev. H. J. Balch first spoke, and in a calm and manly diction, recurred to a history of the course pursued, for ten or twelve years, by the king, ministry, and parliament toward the colonies; reciting each separate act, explaining their respective effects and purposes; charged the government with the unconstitutional design, and with practically carrying out the purpose, to tax them to any amount deemed necessary, without their consent, or any manner of voice in the parliament, but upon the vague and uncertain principles as they pretended, that their charters were the grants of the Sovereigns of England, and therefore, the king retained the right to tax. Then reasoning and arguing in a most convincing and simple view of this delusive and sophistical doctrine, exposing its fallacies and tyrannical tendencies, he took his seat.

Mr. Kennon next arose, and with great justice touched and vanquished these false pretences in favor of British arbitrary power under their own constitution. He took a rapid glance at the rights guaranteed to the colonies by their several characters, securing self-government, the sole power to make all taxes, or for any other purpose not incompatible with charters, and subject to the king's negation; and concluded, urging from arguments drawn from Holy Writ, that there were times when it was the religious and political duty of every man to resist power with war and bloodshed. In rapid and vivid coloring he pointed out the present condition of America, the trial now upon the people, and, with great promptness, showed that the present condition of the country was not unlike that of a certain ancient nation, unto whom God, by the mouth of his prophet, said to them, "cursed is every man that keepeth back his sword from blood!"

WAR OF INDEPENDENCE. 49

Still the profoundest silence pervaded the audience. It evidently seemed that sentiments and feeling too big for utterance, too serious to permit boisterous expressions of applause, filled every thinking mind and thrilled every beating heart.

Slowly, then, the distinguished, learned and universally beloved Bavard rose from his seat, and standing six feet and four inches in person, with a face pale with intense thought, yet his eyes flashing promethean fire, in a deep-toned melody of voice, said:—

"My Countrymen—Americans—We have listened to the just and most impressive remarks made by the gifted and patriotic gentlemen who have preceded me in this discussion upon the present crisis of our whole country. As to its nature and the mighty consequences involved, there can be in my humble judgment but little difference of opinion among men who love right and are capable of appreciating civil liberty. I am myself now, as I have been for some time, prepared boldly to assert, now is the time for decisive action. What that action should be, we are now here to determine. On the part of the king, who is the head and constitutional representative of the parent government, we are, as the proclamation just read and commented upon by Mr. Balch, declared to be rebels and traitors!—no longer under the protection of the laws of the realm, nor worthy of such protection. The rights of the government and governed must, according to all just principle and sensible construction, be forever reciprocal, coincident, and corelative with, and dependant upon faithfulness in the governor. This is the foundation of all claim in the government to obedience and allegiance from the governed. And when protection and a just administration of the laws cease, then cease also obedience and allegiance. For more than ten years, nay twelve, the people of these colonies have been made, under the unwarranted and misguided policy of the ministry, the king, and the parliamentary enactments, to groan and endure

4

50   LEGENDS OF THE

till submission has ceased to be a virtue. Petitions, me-
morials and remonstrances, couched in language no less
respectful than pathetic, and urgent, addressed to the
king, parliament, and the ministry, for a redress of grievances in the taxes imposed, and the cruel exactions upon
them in the way of fees, and in every variety of way by
the civil and ecclesiastical officers appointed and commissioned by the English government, have flown like
carrier-pigeons or doves of peace across the Atlantic and
been laid at the foot of the throne. Yet none have been
regarded further than to elicit still greater burthens and
such violent and cruel denunciations as you have just
listened to. Yea, truly, "we have asked for bread and
they have given us a stone." They have sent to us hungry cormorants to feed and fatten on fees and exactions
wrung from our labor, care and toil, in amounts the most
unreasonable, and in forms the most unusual; and sold,
or otherwise furnished to neighboring, ferocious savages,
arms the most deadly, who have come down upon us to
rob, murder, and devastate the country! Are these, my
countrymen, the foundations on which rest his most royal
and gracious majesty's claims to our fealty—to our allegiance? Nay, let me tell you, there is no alternative but
to make our necks ready for the riveting of the tyrant's
yoke, or, to resolve like men, born free, to declare ourselves independent; to resist to the uttermost, yea, unto
death, the aggressions of power, so long and so inevitably designed and practiced to make us crouching slaves.
For my part, my countrymen, I choose the latter alternative, and I here propose that the convention immediately
proceed to appoint a committee of three to draft and report to us, as speedily as convenient, a declaration and
resolutions to that effect, for our consideration and adoption. I know, gentlemen, that we, here now assembled,
constitute but a small integral part of the colony of North
Carolina, and but few, very few, of the people of the colonies. I am fully warned that that which I now propose

WAR OF INDEPENDENCE. 51

to be done by us, through this committee, can not be any more than obligatory upon ourselves, further than that of an example persuasive in its nature, and may influence, not only this whole colony, but also, in some degree, the Continental Congress, now at Philadelphia, to pass, for the whole nation, a like declaration of independence, for ourselves, our children, and all coming posterity, freed by the will and blessing of Almighty God, forever from all British domination and tyranny!

On the question being put by the chairman and decided in the affirmative, the three gentlemen whose addresses we have been here so imperfectly reporting, Messrs. Bavard, Balch, and Kennon, were appointed upon that committee, and soon after retired to an adjacent apartment to perform the services proposed. During Mr. Bavard's speech, however, we may here remark, great silence was maintained, and attention deep and solemn given, with a very singular exception. Toward the close of his address, and, at that point in which he spoke of the declaration of independence, a cry from the back part of the audience, several Irish and Scottish voices, as seemed from the sound of words, were heard to utter:

"Ain't that trason—trason; who iver dar'd the likes o' that?"

The speaker paused for a moment, and then almost the entire assembly cried out as with the voice of one man:

"Let us be independent—let us declare our independence." And some added—"And defend it with our lives and fortunes."

In response, after silence was secured, Dr. Bavard said:—

"Mr. President—It seems, even here, the coward croakings of the slaves of the king are thrust upon us. And here, suffer me to add, by way of conclusion, my first and earliest hatred was, and still is, to all tyranny! My first distinct impressions of history, remembered, are those drawn from its living paintings of the hated tyrant's tread, and history's records of his atrocities! My first, most ardent, and most lasting love, was, and still is, the love of liberty—liberty of conscience—liberty of speech—liberty of action! And if Heaven favor me, though it be at the hazard of the loss of friends or fortune, though every species of malice and detraction pursue me, though death itself, in all its horrors, frowns and threatens before me, while I am permitted to tread this green and beautiful world, I shall walk in it in the erect soul of a freeman, living as I was born, and dying as I shall have lived, unfettered by any chains which arbitrary power can forge, owning no master but God my maker!"

The committee then withdrew. Several speeches were made by gentlemen, and considerable interest was excited in the room of the assembly by a debate, which arose from a question put by one of the delegates, quite prepossessing in his person and general appearance, but who had been observed hitherto, in rather a moody tone of mind, to occupy his seat, and who arose and addressed himself to the speaker or chairman in words to this effect:

"Mr. President—If you resolve upon declaring independence, which is almost certain to be the purport of the report which the committee you have appointed will make, how shall we all be absolved from the obligations of the oath we took, under Governor Tyron, to be true to King George III. about four years ago, after the regulation fight? Then we were all sworn, whole militia companies, sometimes, together. I should like to know how gentlemen can clear their conscience after taking that oath?"

The excitement thereby produced was instantly and manifestly great throughout the entire assembly. It was certain the gentleman had touched a chord which vibrated quickly upon every reflective mind—all who attached weight to the nature and solemnity of that oath. At once the necessity was seen of a direct, explicit and satisfactory answer to the question. Some, however, in unjustifiable precipitancy, cried out:

"Such questions and difficulties are all nonsense."

Others, with great calmness and respectful consideration, took up, and, with considerable force, presented the argument of Dr. Bavard on the subject of allegiance, or any oath, expressly or impliedly, taken to the government or the king. That the obligations upon the subjects or the governed, to observe and faithfully maintain allegiance to the government or king, was perfectly reciprocal and coincident with the obligations of the government or king to protect and advance the interests and prosperity of the people. That these the king and his government had most grievously failed to do, and that, therefore, those obligations were cancelled—that as the case now was, such being the effect of the acts of the king and his government, to declare independence was but an open public declaration of such cancelment and a determination to set up a government for ourselves that would secure our rights.

One gentleman then arose, the venerable Mr. George Walden, and in a few remarks, introducing a plain and highly illustrative similitude, said :—

"If I am sworn to do a thing as long as that tree," pointing to a large oak that stood in the court-house yard just putting forth its perennial leaves, "continues to retain those leaves and furnish me with shade and comfort, I am bound by that oath. But when the leaves fall, and all shade and comfort is ceased, I am released from that obligation."

It was then decided, that when protection ceased, allegiance ceased also.

The Convention then adjourned to meet again in the morning at 10 o'clock.

54   LEGENDS OF THE

CHAPTER V.

Declaration of Independence and other resolutions passed by the
Convention—Character and patriotism of the women of the Revolution.

"We are accounted poor citizens; the patricians, good; what
authority surfeits on, would relieve us; if they would yield us but
the superfluity while it were wholesome, we might guess they relieved us humanly; but they think we are too dear; the leanness
that afflicts us, the object of our misery, is an inventory to particu-
larize their abundance; our suffrage is a gain to them. Let us revenge this with our pikes, ere we become rakes; for the Gods
know I speak this in hunger for bread, not in thirst for revenge."—
Shakspeare.

THE hour of ten in the morning having arrived, the
chairman, Abraham Alexander, took his seat and called
the Convention to order. The secretaries also took their
position as on the day previous. Prayer was also had
by the Rev. H. I. Balch.

The speaker announced that the first thing in order
was the report of the Committee on Independence if it
was prepared.

Dr. Bavard then presented and handed to the secretary the report, which read as follows, to wit:

THE MECKLENBURG DECLARATION.

"*Resolved*, 1st. That whomsoever directly or indi-
rectly, abetted, or in any way, form or manner, countenanced the unchartered and dangerous invasion of our
rights, as claimed by Great Britain, is an enemy to this
country, to America, and to the inherent and inalienable
rights of man.

"*Resolved*, 2d. That we, the citizens of Mecklenburg

county, do hereby dissolve the political bands which have connected us with the mother country, and hereby absolve ourselves from all allegiance to the British Crown, and abjure all connection, contact, or association with that nation, who have wantonly trampled on our rights and liberties and inhumanly shed the blood of our American patriots at Lexington.

"*Resolved*, 3*d*. That we do hereby declare ourselves a free and independent people; are, and of right ought to be, a sovereign and self-governing association, under the control of no power, other than God and the general government of the Congress; to the maintenance of which independence, we solemnly pledge to each other, our mutual coöperation, our lives, our fortunes, and our most sacred honor.

"*Resolved*, 4*th*. That as we acknowledge the existence and control of no law, nor legal officers, civil or military, within this country, we do hereby ordain and adopt, as a rule of life, all and each of our former laws; wherein, nevertheless, the crown of Great Britain never can be considered as holding rights, privileges, immunities, or authority therein.

"*Resolved*, 5*th*. That it is further decreed that all, each, and every military officer in this county is hereby retained in his former command and authority, he acting conformably to these regulations. And that every member present of this delegation shall henceforth be a civil officer, viz: a justice of the peace, in the charter of committee men, to issue process, hear and determine all matters of controversy according to said adopted laws; and to preserve peace, union and harmony in said county, and to use every exertion to spread the love of country and fire of freedom throughout America, until a general organized government be established in this province."

As the secretary ceased to read, during which time he was listened to with the most profound silence, and when the chair was about to put the question for adoption or other disposition of it, a burly young man by the name of Benjamin Rust, cried out in a most stentorian voice:

"Three cheers, 'cause them's my sentiments."

Instantly the entire assembly, as if startled by an electric shock from a sort of revery into which their deep reflection had carried them, rose up and shouted three times. Nay, a number of ladies, the wives and daughters of the friends of liberty, and especially the whigs, having heard, even to the extremes of the county—nay, nay, indeed, of the adjacent counties—of the Convention and the spirited proceedings of the first day, in great numbers crowded to the village; staid, exemplary matrons, and young, rosy-cheeked and smiling damsels; and, having listened with unspeakable interest and solicitude to the report of the committee, read in words distinct and sonorous by the secretary, joined most heartily in the cheering proposed by Ben. Rust, and mingled with great apparent delight in the general shout that went up that day for liberty and independence. Some of the mothers and daughters, it is said, with tears of joy trickling down their cheeks, in token of their hearty approbation of the resolutions, cast up high in the air their tasty bonnets and fashionable high crowned caps, little thinking of the consequences of the war that must ensue, which had already commenced in Massachusetts, and of the hardships, trials, dangers and devastations of home and country, the sacrifice of the lives of husbands, lovers, brothers and friends that should fall victims to its cruelties and desolating rage.

But like their husbands, brothers and lovers, there that day assembled, and like the heroines of ancient Greece and Rome, they nobly resolved to dare war, and sacrifice everything upon the altar of their country's liberty and glory. Ah, reader, what a powerful stimulant, what an incentive to heroic deeds and chivalric daring was here given by those loved ones to those husbands, brothers and lovers!

WAR OF INDEPENDENCE.

Know ye not that there were no Tories, no fanatical drivelers, no cowardly cringers and crown worshippers among the women of the colonies during the sanguinary struggle of the American Revolution? Ah! but that the men of war, soldiers and officers and all, had here, in this beautiful new world of the West, homes they loved, and continually encouraged by "the smiles from partial beauty won," long ere the eight years' terrible fight with that most powerful nation in the world had ended or transpired, they would have sunk beneath the crush of that mighty power the slaves of usurpation and oppression.

Oh, list to their oft repeated declaration of such inspirations, nerving their arm and cheering their hearts amidst the cannon's loud thunders and the hottest of the fight! Hear him who proved himself an almost unmatched hero while at the front of his forlorn and little band, leading them to storm a redoubt before them, saying to his brave followers:

"That fort must this day be taken, or Molly Stark (his wife) will this day be a widow!"

Nay, listen and mark the exclamation of that courageous soldier, who, being the first to leap, on another occasion, over the walls of an almost impregnable fort, filled with the most experienced and invincible officers and soldiers of the British king, just as he stands erect upon that wall, cries:

"The day is our own! O, my Sallie, 'tis you that makes me brave!"

O, glorious women of the Revolution—ah, how shall we, your children, and your children's children, sufficiently prize, revere and emulate your virtues; and in the gushing fulness of adoring hearts, thank the Almighty God for such mothers—such "unspeakable gifts!"

But to pursue further the narrative of the additional resolutions reported and adopted by this determined and most patriotic body of citizens, in the various meetings held by adjournment from day to day, to regulate and govern themselves and the people whom they represented until a congress of the colony should be called and elected by the whole people, would accomplish but little more for the entertainment and instruction of our respected readers, than to exhibit the sound discretion and resolute conservative action of men determined to be free and preserve and enjoy the rich fruits of a free government instituted by their own hands.

The records of these additional labors are now before us, well authenticated as genuine, but we forbear to transcribe them in this work, as the reader might be wearied too much in the perusal; but he may be assured they unmistakably bear the impress of the heads and hearts that gave forth to the astonished and wondering world the Resolutions and Declaration of Independence above inserted.

Certain it is that no state paper ever given, anterior to its date, of which ancient or modern history gives any record, is its equal for felicity of conception, fitness of diction and perfect aptness of adaptation to the emergencies by which it was brought forth; and no one since its date, except the justly famed Declaration of Independence, made by the Continental Congress, at Philadelphia, on the 4th of July, 1776.

The reader will observe that this last mentioned Declaration of Independence bears date nearly fourteen months after that of the former, and yet it is difficult for one to read and compare them with care, without concluding that both are essentially the production of one head, heart and hand. But this we know from the most indubitable proofs cannot be. Thomas Jefferson, late the President of the United States, more distinguished than almost any man that ever lived in America as a statesman and philosopher, most unquestionably wrote and reported it to the Congress that nobly adopted it. And it is equally certain, that upon its production and his manly support of it before that body, his great fame as a patriot and statesman rested more than upon any one or all of his thousand other distinguished acts in his long and most useful life of public service.

How is it, then, the intelligent reader will very naturally inquire—you have said Mr. Jefferson most certainly drafted and reported this, more admirable and important than any other State paper, and has received, therefor, the highest honors ever awarded to him by his country, for any other act of his long life?—yet you tell me, that the paper above copied from the proceedings of the Convention at Mecklenburg, on the 19th and 20th of May, 1775, was certainly the production of the learned and patriotic Bavard of that Convention. I perceive, upon a careful reading of the two productions, that in every material point, establishing the one or the other to be a declaration of independence, and a clear and final renunciation and abjuration of all future dependence upon, or connection with the British Government, they are, in language, thought, and effect, precisely the same; differing only in those particulars which adapt them to the time and place, as well as the circumstances of their production.

Well, gentle reader, I fully admit the justice of your statement of what I have said, and of your commentary. I do contend, and wish to be distinctly understood to assert only, that although Mr. Jefferson himself drafted and presented this glorious declaration of the Americans, passed by the Congress in 1776, and that in the composition thereof—in regard to the fitness and style to be employed in that sort of production, as well as the emphatic words and burning thoughts to be used—only did, in justice to himself and the immeasurable importance of the objects it was intended to accomplish, what every man, with a tithe of his great intellect, would have done. When the Convention of Mecklenburg selected Capt. James Jack, a resident of Charlotte, to take their declaration to Philadelphia, or rather a copy of it, he placed it in the hands of that distinguished member from Virginia. He, doubtless, perused it with equal wonder and approbation, and with all sound and discriminating discretion, marked its style, force and effect as adapted to an occasion upon which he had thought much already—but postponed as inexpedient at that time, judging it were better still to petition, beseech, and implore "his most gracious majesty" for mercy to his "most loyal subjects in America,"—and taking notes, not of Virginia, but of the Mecklenburg proceeding—as no man who ever lived or ever will live could do better—laid the document aside amongst his private papers, not showing it to his fellow-congressmen, lest they might explode too precipitately before the king could be again heard from, and never afterwards acknowledged that he had seen it, as will be seen by his letter to the elder John Adams, dated July 9th, 1819, and that he believed the document to be spurious.

Well, I just think as the reader will with me, that that glorious old President ought to have had a better memory. But is the courteous reader still disposed to ask, and what of all that?

Why, I say, not much only as the Scriptures say, "one man soweth and another reapeth;" that Dr. Ephraim Bavard sowed the good seed of the American Declaration of Independence, and that President Jefferson cultivated them, and a little more than a year afterward, reaped the rich harvest that gave his name and fame as a proud inheritance to all the future generations of our great republic as the originator, writer and reporter of that stupendous state paper.

Bavard has, doubtless, ere now, reaped his reward in Heaven. Thomas Jefferson has also died, and must stand in judgment before the same righteous God.

In our next chapter we will indulge our readers with a sight of the real correspondence, on the subject of the Mecklenburg Declaration, to which we have alluded, and then leave them to their own just conclusions.

CHAPTER VI.

Original letters of Presidents John Adams and Thomas Jefferson, on the subject of the Mecklenburg Declaration of Independence in 1775, and as identical in substance with that of 1776.

"Fiat justicia, ruat cœlum."—*Cicero.*
"Let justice be done, though the heavens fall."
Sir Matthew Hale.

TRUE virtue, wherever and whatsoever time or occasion exhibited, is always an active, living and fructifying principle; working and diffusing benevolence and good, like God in creation, and in his abiding, overruling Providence, like the Redeemer of the world, its great exemplar, ever going about and doing good! A principle in man and in the economy of human life, God-like in its nature, and no less distinguished for its power under God to create good, than in diffusing and distributing it to each and every one in fairness and justice, "in rendering unto every one his just due—giving glory to him to whom glory is due, honor to whom honor belongs."

In the selection of the maxim placed at the head of this chapter, we have given one, which in our humble judgment must receive the sanction and challenge the admiration of all who love and practice virtue. But virtue, like its legitimate offspring, justice, is always discriminating, always discreet. And in making this selection, we have a motive beyond that of recording and reiterating a sublime and most fascinating axiom; but more materially, for the purpose of furnishing a justification for yet farther continuing these fugitive Legends of the Revolution, and other remarks as to the real authorship of that sublime and Heaven-crowned declaration to which this nation is indebted, no less than to the most signal victory won upon the embattled field. The memory, the reputation, the useful services, the dauntless acheivements of that mighty agony for liberty, are the priceless jewels of the nation's wealth, and must, as long as our republic is prized and preserved, be safely kept and cherished in the great heart-casket of its gratitude.

To perpetuate, however, these in their purity and excellency in the public esteem, and commend them to the popular mind as worthy of all imitation, the history that gathers and records them must maintain and forever observe the virtues of justice and impartiality, must feel and even write in truth, and in conformity to our great maxim—"*Fiat justicia, ruat cælum!*"

Upon these principles alone, would we wish to be understood to act in giving now the correspondence between the two great patriots and Presidents before named, whose consantaneous birth to political and statesmanship's distinction took place in the revolution; and who almost miraculously, in regard to coincidence, died on the same day (4th of July, 1826,) about the same hour that they, with the other members of the august and Heaven-inspired body passed and individually subscribed to the first great continental exponent of American liberty, amidst the loud hosanahs of praise and laudation to them, more so than to any others, for their distinguished eloquence and influence in urging its propriety and necessity.

Aye, on that day, the anniversary of the fourth of July, 1776, the first and greatest jubilee of the nation's triumphant joys, within sight and the hearing of their cannon's roar and hallelujahs of praise to God for the unspeakable gift of civil and religious liberty, these two patriots, full of years and crowned with the highest testimonials of a free and preëminently happy country, lay down to sleep in death, embalmed by that country's tears, and pillowed on its bosom of gratitude.

"But O, how calm they sink to rest,
Who close their eyes on victory's breast!"

In yet father pursuing this subject, we now proceed to give, as above promised, a copy of two letters of the correspondence between these two distinguished statesmen —the authenticity of the originals of which is well attested—on the subject of the Mecklenburg Declaration of Independence:

Copy of a letter from Mr. Adams to Mr. Jefferson.

"QUINCY, June 22, 1819.

"*Dear Sir:*—May I enclose you one of the greatest curiosities and one of the deepest mysteries that ever occurred to me; it is the Essex Register of June 5th, 1819. It is entitled, 'from the Raleigh Register,' 'Declaration of Independence.' How is it possible that this paper should have been concealed from me to this day. Had it been communicated to me in the time of it, I know, if you do not know, that it would have been printed in every Whig newspaper upon the continent. You know that if I had possessed it, I would have made the Hall of Congress echo and reëcho with it, fifteen months before your Declaration of Independence. What a poor, ignorant, malicious, short-sighted, crapulous mass, is Tom Paine's common sense in comparison with this paper. Had I known of it, I would have commented upon it from the day you entered Congress till the 4th of July, 1776.

"The genuine sense of America at that moment was never so well expressed before or since. Richard Caswell, William Hooper, and Joseph Hewes, the three representatives of North Carolina in Congress you know as well as I, and you know that the unanimity of the States finally depended on the vote of Joseph Hewes, and was finally determined by him; and yet history is to ascribe the American Revolution to Thomas Paine, *sat verbum sapienti.*

"I am, dear sir, your invariable friend,
"JOHN ADAMS."

64   LEGENDS OF THE

President Jefferson to John Adams.
           "MONTICELLO, July 9th, 1819.

"*Dear Sir:*—I am in debt to you for your letters of
May 21st, 27th, and June the 22d. The first, delivered
me by Mr. Greenwood, gave me the gratification of his
acquaintance; and a gratification it always is to be made
acquainted with gentlemen of candor, worth, and information, as I found Mr. Greenwood to be. That on the
subject of Mr. Samuel Adam Wells shall not be forgotten
in times and place, when it can be used to his advantage.

"But what has attracted my peculiar notice is the paper from Mecklenburg county, of North Carolina, published in the Essex Register, which you were so kind to
enclose in your last, of June 22d. And you seem to
think it genuine; I believe it spurious. I deem it to be
a very unjustifiable quiz, like that of the volcano so mi-
nutely related to us, as having broken out in North Carolina, some half dozen years ago, in that part of the
county, and perhaps in that very county of Mecklenburg,
for I do not remember its precise locality. If this paper
be really taken from the Raleigh Register, or quoted, I
wonder it should have escaped Ritchie, who culls what is
good from every paper, as the bee from every flower; and
the National Intelligencer, too, which is edited by a
North Carolinian, and that the fire should blaze out all at
once in Essex, one thousand miles from where the spark
is said to have fallen. But if really taken from the
Raleigh Register, who is the narrator, and is the name
subscribed real, or is it as fictitious as the paper itself?
It appeals, too, to an original book which is burnt, to Mr.
Alexander who is dead, to a joint letter to Caswell, Hewes,
and Hooper, all dead, to a copy sent to the dead Caswell,
and another sent to Dr. Williamson, now probably dead,
whose memory did not recollect, in the history he has
written of North Carolina, this gigantic step of its county
of Mecklenburg.

"Horry, too, is silent in his history of Marion, whose scene of action was the county bordering on Mecklenburg. Ramsay, Marshall, Jones, Gerardin, Wirt, historians of the adjacent States, all silent. When Mr. Henry's resolutions—far short of independence—flew like lightning through every paper, and kindled both sides of the Atlantic, this flaming declaration of the same date of the indepencence of Mecklenburg county of North Carolina, absolving it from the British allegiance, and abjuring all political connection, although sent to Congress, too, is never heard of. It is not known, even a twelve months after, when a similar proposition is first made in that body, to have arrived. With this bold example, would not you have addressed our timid brethren in peals of thunder on their tardy fears? Would not every advocate of independence have rung the glories of Mecklenburg county, in North Carolina, in the ears of the doubting Dickinson and others, who hung so heavily on us? Yet the example of independent Mecklenburg county, in North Carolina, was never once quoted. The paper speaks, too, of the continued exertions of these delegates, (Caswell, Hooper and Hewes,) in the cause of liberty and independence.

"Now, you remember as well as I do, that we had not a greater Tory in Congress than Hooper; that Hewes was very wavering, sometimes firm, sometimes feeble, according as the day was clear or cloudy; that Caswell, indeed, was a good Whig, and kept these gentlemen to the notch, while he was present; but that he left us soon, and their line of conduct became then uncertain, till Penn came, who fixed Hewes and the vote of the State.

"I must not be understood as suggesting any doubtfulness in the State of North Carolina. No State was more fixed or forward. Nor do I affirm positively, that this paper is a fabrication: because the proof of a negative can only be presumptive. But I shall believe it such until positive and solemn proof of its authenticity shall be

66   LEGENDS OF THE

produced. And if the name of McKnitt be real, and not a part of the fabrication, it needs a vindication by the production of such proof. For the present, I must be an unbeliever in the Apocryphal gospel. I am glad to learn that Mr. Ticknor has safely returned to his friends; but should have been much more pleased had he accepted the professorship of our University, which we would have offered him in form.

"Mr. Bowditch, too, refuses us; so fascinating *vinculum* of the *dulce natale solum*. Our wish is to procure natives, when they can be found, like these gentlemen, of the first order of acquirement in their respective lines; but preferring foreigners of the first order to natives of the second, we shall certainly have to go for several of our professors, to countries more advanced in science than we are. I set out in three or four days for my other home, the distance of which and cross mails, are great impediments to epistolary communications. I shall remain there two months; and there, here, and everywhere.

"I am, and shall always be,

affectionately and respectfully yours,

"THOMAS JEFFERSON."

Here we should drop the subject of the authorship of the Declaration of Independence, adding simply that the writer of these Legends well remembers to have seen and known the Rev. Hezekiah James Balch, who was one of the committee of three who reported to the Mecklenburg Convention the declaration of that body, 20th April, 1775, more than forty-seven years ago, and after he had removed to the State of Kentucky and engaged in the charge of a school. He died in what is now called Todd county, at more than seventy-five years of age, beloved and esteemed.

One word farther. Rev. Dr. William Henry Foote, in his sketch of North Carolina, published in 1846, by Robert Carter, 58 Canal Street, New York, attests in his work—from personal examinations of old records and conversations with a few aged gentlemen and ladies still lingering on the shores of time and eye-witnesses to the events—not only the truth of the existence of the Mecklenburg Convention, but also of its Declaration of Independence. The genuineness of the letter of Mr. Adams to Mr. Jefferson, and his answer in return, is put beyond question, by the work of Jo. Seawell Jones, entitled, "A defence of the State of North Carolina from the aspersions of Mr. Jefferson."

CHAPTER VII.

Proceedings of the Whigs in the colony of North Carolina—Questions asked and answered as to the causes of the tyranny that overrides the nations of the earth, and how the freedom of a nation can be effected.

> " These things, indeed, you have articulated,
>   Proclaim'd at market-crosses, read in churches;
>   To face the garment of rebellion
>   With some fine color that may please the eye
>   Of fickle changelings, and poor discontents,
>   Which gape and rub the elbow, at the news
>   Of hurlyburly innovation"—*1. Henry IV., Act V., Scene I.*

> " Defiance, traitors, hurl we in your teeth."
>   —*Julius Cœsar, Act V., Scene I.*

In very many towns and villages in the province of North Carolina, after the general intelligence of the proceedings at Charlotte had spread, meetings of the people were called and like resolutions passed by them; declaring the grievances upon them by the crown and parliament of England, and upon the entire country—most particularly upon their brethren, the inhabitants of Boston and the colony of Massachusetts—avowing their determination to resist all innovations upon their chartered rights, by the British ministry, in claiming the right of taxation without representation; asserting that the course pursued by the parent country, the cruelties inflicted upon the people of Boston and the inhabitants of Massachusetts, in the vicinity; that the wanton murders perpetrated by the armed soldiery had forfeited all right of sovereignty and allegiance, and their firm resolve was to resist arbitrary power at home and abroad.

WAR OF INDEPENDENCE. 69

Solemn written covenants were entered into by vast numbers, and individually subscribed with their respective names. As a specimen of this, we subjoin the following, as sufficiently illustrative of the many associations of this character in nearly all the counties of the province, and as expressive of the spirit and firmness of the whole country, excepting the Tories:

"AN ASSOCIATION.—The unprecedented, barbarous and bloody actions, committed by the British troops on our American brethren, near Boston, on the 19th of April, and 20th of May last, together with hostile operations and treacherous designs, now carried on by the tools of ministerial vengeance and despotism for the subjugation of all British America, suggest to us the painful necessity of having recourse to arms for the preservation of those rights and liberties which the principles of our constitution, and the laws of God, nature, and nations have made it our duty to defend. We, therefore, the subscribers, freeholders, and inhabitants of Tryon county, do hereby faithfully unite ourselves under the most sacred ties of religion, honor, and love of our country, firmly to resist force by force, in defence of our national freedom and constitutional rights against all invasions; and at the same time, do solemnly engage to take up arms, and risk our lives and fortunes in maintaining the freedom of our country, whenever the wisdom and counsel of the Continental Congress, or our Provincial Convention shall declare it necessary; and this engagement we will continue in and hold sacred, till a reconciliation shall take place between Great Britain and America, on constitutional principles, which we most ardently desire; and we do firmly agree to hold all such persons inimical to the liberties of America, who shall refuse to subscribe to this association. (Signed by)

"John Walker, Charles McLean, Andrew Neal, Thos. Beatty, Jas. Coburn, Frederick Hambright, Andrew Hampton, Benjamin Hardin, George Peavis, William

Graham, Robert Keandy, David Jenkins, Thomas Espy, Perigrine McNess, James McAfee, William Thomason, Jacob Forny, Davis Whiteside, John Beeman, John Morris, Joseph Hardin, John Robinson, Valentine Maury, George Blake, James Logan, James Baird, Christian Carpenter, Abel Beatty, Joab Turner, Jonathan Price, James Miller, Peter Sedes, William Whiteside, John Dellinger, George Dellinger, Samuel Karbender, Jacob Moony, Jr., John Wells, Jacob Castner, Robert Halclip, James Buckhanan, Moses Moore, Joseph Kuykendall, Adam Sims, Richard Waffer, Samuel Smith, Joseph Neel, Samuel Lofton."

These covenants and associations, thus diffused and circulated industriously among all classes of the inhabitants, settling the principles of resistance and making the subscription thereto the test of enmity or friendship to the country, brought them to the decision and choice of sides they should take in the sanguinary contest to ensue; and thus arose the distinctive names of Whig and Tory. The former, those resolved like true patriots and men, determined to resist and be free, to do or die!—men who, like the Whigs of England, distinguished for opposition to all arbitrary power, and to the new fangled assumptions of prerogative, introduced first and practiced by the Stuarts and their successors to the British throne, and who unwaveringly and manfully stood upon the political platform of the magna charta of England as the palladium of civil liberty, against all mornachial, ministerial, or paliamentary enchroachments or devices infracting the integrity of the British Constitution. The latter, ever the adulators of kings and arbitrary power against popular right and all popular control; advocates forever of monarchial prerogative by construction rather than a just and reasonable regard to the wishes and wants of the masses.

In the revolution, there was an attempt on the part of the sovereign and his ministers to tax, *ad libitum*, the

WAR OF INDEPENDENCE. 71

people of the colonies, resting their right to do so upon the constructive argument of the prerogative of the king; and it was altogether consistent and natural that those Americans here, who subscribed to that doctrine, should go with the king and ministry, and hence all such were called Tories as they are to this day called in England; while on the other hand, the Whigs, always lovers of the largest rational liberty to the people, of the right of self-government, and opposed to all assumptions of power by prerogative, it was utterly incompatible with all their views of right and principle to sanction them in this case; and hence they naturally, and of right, took and maintained at all hazards, the name and principles of Whigs. We pause not here to mention more at large the distinctive claims to approbation or applause belonging to these two parties of the revolution most unhappily existing; retarding very greatly its progress and happy termination, as well as being the fruitful cause of incalculable human suffering, devastation and death. This is no treatise on politics or religion, only as they or either of them enter into, and stand in connection with a plain narrative of facts or just description and appreciation of character—adding only, that in verification of what has almost grown into an adage, "names are nothing; principles everything."

But to return. After the display of the spirit of the people throughout North Carolina, as shown by the paper copied above as a sample of the hundreds that circulated and were subscribed to in all the counties of the province, the reader will anticipate that some general assemblage of the people would speedily take place; and as such an expression of the general mind and feeling of the people may portray, in a more unmistakable light, the general spirit and firm determination of action in the inhabitants generally, of this noble old State, at the very threshold of war, we will now proceed to present to the

reader some of the resolutions passed by the Congress of
the colony, in session at Hillsboro', in the year 1775:

"*Resolved*, That we approve of the proposal of a general
congress, to be held in the city of Philadelphia, on
the 20th of September next, then and there to deliberate
upon the present state of British America, and to take
such measures as they may deem prudent, to effect the
purpose of describing, with certainty, the rights of
America; repairing the breaches made in those rights,
and for guarding them for the future from any such violations
done under the sanction of public authority.

"*Resolved*, That we view the attempts made by the
ministers upon the town of Boston, as a prelude to a general
attack upon the rights of the other colonies; and
that, upon the success of this depends, in a general measure,
the happiness of America in its present race, and in
posterity; and that, therefore, it becomes our duty to
contribute, in proportion to our abilities, to ease the burthen
imposed upon the town, for their virtuous opposition
to the Revenue Acts, that they may be enabled to
persist in a prudent and manly opposition to the schemes
of parliament, and render its dangerous designs abortive.

"*Resolved*, That liberty is the spirit of the British
Constitution, that it is the duty, and will be the endeavor
of us all, to transmit this happy Constitution to our posterity
in a state, if possible, better than we found it; and
that to suffer it to undergo a change which may impair
that invaluable blessing, would be to disgrace those ancestors,
who, at the expense of their blood, purchased
those privileges, which their dengenerate posterity are
too weak or too wicked to maintain inviolate."

And here let me ask the intelligent reader to say,
whether or not, the mind that discerned and dictated
these calm and dignified exhibitions of popular sentiment
and of the duties owed themselves and true Americans,
in this trial of faith, relying upon the justice of their

cause, is not worthy of praise and imitation ? and whether the spirit and manly courage with which these patriots entered into and carried out their great resolves, did not deserve to be crowned with success, and were not most certain to be so by the blessing of a just and overruling Providence ?

Where, in the annals of history, ancient or modern, is there any instance recorded of a people, united in sentiment, spirit and action, moved by a manly emulation to be free and unshackled by the manacles of unreasonable and unnatural authority, looking up, in humble trust and confidence to God, the source and donor of all that is good and merciful, that were not successful ? None ; no, there is none.

Why, then, it may be asked, are not the nations of Europe delivered from the bonds of misrule and oppression under which they have groaned for centuries, nay, thousands of years past? In them, there have been exhibited, from time to time, yea, in most of them, repeated uprisings and signal efforts to throw off their chains and drive oppression from them ! Yet, alas, how futile, or rather terrific, have been the results ! How generally, nay, how uniformly, have all these attempts at revolution turned at last, as if only to mock their most zealous advocates—proved only hot-beds to germinate and rear the hydra monster of riot and anarchy, giving birth and nursing to some ambitious Cæsar or Buonaparte, bold to bestride and with iron will to guide, the destroying Infernal !—gathering from the universal debris of all order, virtue and good, in social life or political structure, intoxicating and blinding the common mind with the delusive glare of ambition, and being far more the children of Belial than of God; having no affinity to anything heavenly and divine, seeking sanctuary in an unholy, perfidious and unhallowed union of church and state, upheld by a corrupted, mercenary, and ambi-

74   LEGENDS OF THE

tious priesthood to tread and crush beneath tyrant heels the fair spirit of liberty! But yet, you say, the question is not solved. It still demands, with doubled interest, to be answered.

Well, and still I insist, no people firmly united in a virtuous purpose, to be politically, morally, and religiously free—free individually, as well as socially, from all external human force or constraint, so far as moral agency and the exercise of choice and untrammeled volition are concerned—can be, with the sanction and approbation of Heaven, enthralled. Because God, in his holy Revelation, has declared that men, yea, nations are to be judged and rewarded or punished in righteousness, according as their deeds shall be! "Because he hath appointed a day in which he will judge the world, in righteousness, by that man whom he hath ordained; whereof he hath given assurance unto all men in that he hath raised him from the dead." Mark you, the judgment of God is to be a righteous judgment—based upon the eternal principle of man's accountability! Upon the principle that he, a rational, accountable subject of his moral government, free to choose that which is right and avoid that which is wrong, and has qualified and required of him, in the full exercise of a virtuous mind, to love, honor, and adore him with a willing and undivided heart. "No man can serve two masters."

Liberty of action, liberty of choice, liberty of conscience, is Heaven's order, then; and whatsoever or whosoever enchains and leaves not "free the human will," treads with unhallowed feet upon Heaven's high behests and cannot have Heaven's smiles and approbation. I assert, therefore, that war unto blood, when entered into by a people oppressed, to obtain and secure to themselves and posterity, natural and moral liberty under God, and a due submission to His law and government as revealed in his Holy Bible, and the right of self-government, I say

WAR OF INDEPENDENCE. 75

a war for these purposes is perfectly right and virtuous. Such, we contend, was precisely the object and aim of the American people in the days of the revolution, and Heaven approved and crowned them with victory.

But when the revolution of a people is but a war between castes for individual aggrandizement, for purpose of revenge, for the exaltation of one set of men by the overthrow of others—however vile and unworthy these others may be, and deserving their fate—for the purpose of deifying and setting up men and worshiping them, to the overthrow of the authority of God, or placing them in the room or 'stead of the Almighty, or as His vicegerent on earth, these may triumph for a season. But God, unto whom "one day is as a thousand years and a thousand years as one day, without change or the shadow of change," who hath declared "vengeance is mine, and I, the Lord God of Hosts, will repay,"—will, ere it is long, for these things bring them into judgment! Look at the old world, look at the present world, look at France! In very little more than half a century there have occurred in her history three thorough and entire revolutions, for the professed and ostensible purpose of acheiving civil and religious liberty. Behold her now, bowed beneath the iron-yoke of a despot! It is true, that in each mighty convulsion there was great apparent union of the people. But analyze and find in what respect did that union consist? May it not be with certainty declared to have consisted in a blasphemy of the power and name of God himself, and a war of extermination of the Bible and the remembrance of it from the face of the whole earth? Did not its infuriated mobs in Paris and other cities make bonfires in the public streets of all that could be found— hunt down and extirpate all God's ministers, and even impotently and impiously burn in effigy what they called Jesus. Nay, who being given over to infuriated rout and riot—maddened maniacs to do the work and bidding

of demons loosed for a season—made oceans of human
gore current along the streets, redden with innocent
blood the green gardens and fields of beautiful France,
and swell the tide of her rivers with sanguinary streams.
"Oh, infidelity where is thy shame, where is thy blush?"

Nor will we stop here in this picture of the mono-
mania of men under the specious guise of liberty; nevertheless, prompted and goaded by principles and motives,
denounced and condemned of all virtuous and enlightened
men, and of God, utterly failing, by reason of those principles and purposes lying deep and smouldering beneath
the general huzza for free, civil, and religious rights!
Turn your eye upon Ireland—Ireland the beautiful Em-
erald Isle of the sea—filled with the most ardent and
generous impulses, when properly directed, above almost
all the nations of the earth—now, as for hundreds of
years past, oppressed and trodden to the dust, to famine
and death. By her cruel destiny, as some are pleased to
call it, Ireland has sometimes seemed united in her uprisings for liberty. But remember the union of Ireland
has always only been in semblance, only plausible, deceitful, hypocritical. Union is strength. But her strength
has been made weakness by her superstition and fanaticism, making liberty and free government licentiousness;
wooing the virgin and chaste goddess, to use a pagan
figure, and sacrificing at her altar with passion and infuriated prejudice in the room of inspirations and ardent
longings and sighs for moral and rational, civil and religious freedom. Ireland, with a population of eight millions, filled with wit and genius of the most dignified
character, what is the matter? Educated in passion, in
the spirit of superstition and revenge, loosed from the
yoke and servitude of England, would, in a day, wildly
rant and riot in blood, and having glutted her rapacious
thirst for blood, drawn from heretic England's boasted
pomp and pride, would most certainly turn the sword of

Ireland against Ireland, as if but to perpetuate her skill in human butchery! What is the matter? Her people, the masses, are untaught of God.

They have listened to the professed expounders of the messages of the meek and lowly Jesus, and been taught for the Gospels of peace the lessons of vengeance and of infernal spirits, and of the creed that all are heretics who dare to think and act, but as licensed and sanctioned by the dictums and decretals of their priestly consociations! Who teach, even to this day, that the crusades carrying fire and sword, death and destruction to the heathens of Palestine, instead of the Bible and the altars of christian worship, were not fanaticisms but in accordance with the christian's faith and charity; nay, prompted and sanctified by the spirit of all holiness and grace! That the *auto da fé* which denounces the anathema of the Church of Rome against a doomed heretic and delivers him or her over to the tortures, the fire and fagot of the holy inquisition, breathes only God's unchanging love and tender mercies which He declares in his revealed word is over and unto all His works! And that the vicegerent of that God, dwelleth at the Vatican, in the eternal city, and sits in solemn state in the once erring Peter's chair, dispensing God's blessings or curse to a fallen world!

Suppose ye, a nation, aye, a people numbering millions, and though ground down with burthens, political and ecclesiastical, not of their choice or consent, yet imbued with these teachings, and blinding, deadening superstitions, can they properly conceive and justly appreciate civil and religious liberty? Can such calmly and correctly consider of the true and judicious construction of a republican government, guaranteeing to all, and to each, equal rights, equal privileges, civil and religious liberty of speech, liberty of conscience, liberty of action? Ah! I would to God it were otherwise than as it is. For that people, your humble writer has long, with all the power of which he is capable, prayed to Almightly God that they might be made wise, not only perfectly to conceive of, but powerful to acheive civil and religious freedom. I know that Ireland has a great number of the most enlightened, the most talented, virtuous and pure patriot citizens, equal to any that are to be found among the nations; but in my poor judgment, if in the days that are past, and now, and onward, the watch-word of her patriot leaders had been as it now should be, educate, educate, instead of agitate, agitate, she would now or soon would be free. I allude to political and religious education. Her patriot sons, many, very many of them, now and in the past, have fully felt, and acting upon the magnanimous sentiment, "a day, an hour, of virtuous liberty, is worth a whole eternity of bondage," lifted high the flag of liberty, too soon, by the treachery of Irishmen, to be dragged down and trailed in the dust and themselves handed over to the merciless English gibbet. But I forbear pressing this subject farther than to say, it is confidently believed that throughout all the nations of the world and in every land where tyranny and despotism prevail, in any or all, however diversified in their degrees, the causes are to be found and assigned therefor as existing in the people—the masses! These are taught the enfeebling, not to say the corrupting, doctrines of men they call spiritual fathers—popes, cardinals, bishops and priests—that they have no right to think for themselves; and in an aggregate point of view, it is astonishing to conceive how large a proportion of them never learn to think to any purpose! Usurpers and tyrants of every grade manage to corrupt, purchase, overawe, or make dupes of those spiritual fathers, and they in turn dupe the people by means of their ghostly authority, chicanery and wizzardism, and pretended mission from Heaven! The priesthood cunningly devise and work upon the wicked and corrupted popular mind for the benefit of the arbitrary power of the state, the king, emperor, or other despotic ruler, relying upon such for the perpetuation of their own power, dominion, and aggrandizement. Aye, friendly reader, in every land, in every country where the unhallowed union of church and state prevails, there is a moral and political putrescence eviscrated—a deadly miasma, as destructive to civil and religious liberty as the fabled breezes passing from or over the Upas tree are destructive to all animal life; or, as the boa constrictor's horrid embrace, in a thousand convolutions, wound around the body of its victim, must bring death. Can a people thus circumstanced, thus taught, made to believe "ignorance is bliss," understand and appreciate the just structure of a free government and with an apprentice skill build it up? Alas! never—never. So true are these statements, the utter incapacity and indisposition of those who, unfortunately, have been reared and schooled in the monarchies of even the most enlightened portions of Europe, that when come to this enlightened land and privileged to enjoy all the guarantees of life, liberty and property of our free constitutions and benign system of laws upon the single condition of conformity thereto, afford ample and sure evidence. The transition is so great it is hard to discipline them to the rational and virtuous proprieties of the country. Often, too often, with them liberty is licentiousness. Look at South America! Look at Mexico! For more than forty years in these, one revolution for liberty has followed in swift and most destructive succession after another; all professedly and, we believe sincerely, for civil and religious freedom, and still what is the liberty acquired? Fearful anarchy, it is true, the worst of governments, has sometimes been brought about; but yet, in every instance of the erection of government, its nature and essence are tyranny and oppression! No, no. You can make no people free, brought up and reared in ignorance, folly and vice. You must first properly educate and prepare them for it. Educate them, and let the pure principles of the gospel, unsophisticated and uncontaminated by a priesthood of any name, be the chief subjects of instruction! Let these furnish the seed and their disciplining influences prepare the "good ground," then republicanism will rise and flourish in every land as if by spontaneous vegetation! Pure religion is the resurrection of the soul of man on earth, to every thing hopeful and good; and when cherished in the heart and practiced in the life, prepares individuals and communities for every good word and work.

CHAPTER VIII.

A somewhat minute examination of the principles and spirit of the Whig and Tory population in the country, generally, and particularly in North Carolina—The Scenery of North Carolina, &c.

"Good, my lord, will you see the players well bestowed? Do you hear? let them be well used; for they are the abstract, and brief chronicles of the time."—*Hamlet, Act II., Scene 2.*

In the preceding pages we have said but little upon the subject of the chief difficulties encountered by the friends of revolution and resistance of the British authorities in the colonies, arising from within their own limits. These, truly, were in many respects very embarrassing. Although it was happily the case, that nineteen-twentieths, at least, of the native Americans, at once cordially and actively engaged in the advocacy of the war, and thereby secured to the Whigs a most flattering prospect of union and ultimate success, still the perfect union of a people necessary to guarantee a speedy and happy consummation of the desires of the patriots, a total independence of all foreign countries, was greatly retarded by Tories or royalists, as they called themselves, apparently actuated by the same general views and motives in their opposition to the war, but in fact, widely differing in many material points. These were four-fifths, or three-fourths, at least, of foreign birth and European education; knowing nothing, practically, of free government, very little theoretically, and as little caring on the subject.

Many stood connected, by marriage and business, with native Whig families, and many by lives of correct deportment, hitherto, had sustained and deserved to sustain unexceptionable characters in the circles of their acquaintance, and for a time wielded much influence.

Fortunately, however, these were generally of the class least corrupted by vicious lives, malignant minds and habits, but chiefly influenced to their opposition from false or mistaken views of religious obligation to God, such as non-resistance to kings, &c.; while as many more, from an honest belief of the inevitable failure of the revolution and the dire consequences to themselves and the whole American country resulting from that failure, using all their influence, by persuasion and power, to frighten others, greatly impeded for a time the progress of the cause. But unfortunately for the country this class of the Tories, were not, by large odds, so numerous as a class of them of whom we must now speak, and who certainly were far less to be tolerated and excused.

There was another class of Tories, or royalists, unfortunately more numerous, and still far more malignant and vicious in their tempers and practices than either the former. All the colonies suffered more or less during the war from these, but especially those of Pennsylvania, Delaware, Maryland, New Jersey, Virginia, North Carolina, South Carolina and Georgia. They were all, or nearly so, the more recent emigrants from Europe, or their immediate descendants.

They were essentially different from the first class described, wholly given up to murder, robbery, theft and pillage; indeed to every species of crime blackening the dark catalogue of human cruelty and iniquity; most of them pleading conscience—truly, as quickened and instructed by their spiritual teachers, popes, cardinals, bishops and priests, Catholics and Protestants, in the old as well as the new country—that it was unlawful to resist magistrates, &c., whether in the right or wrong; but giving in every instance the most unquestionable proofs that conscience was not in the least degree involved, but an insatiable love of crime, cruelty and blood—distrusting. it is probable, like the other class of Tories, the final success of the revolutionists and seeming to espouse from principle the royal cause, nevertheless, only as a cover to the horrible iniquities for which they thirsted, which they deemed the disordered state of the country happily fitted to gratify.

Of the former class, John and William Harpe, the two Scotch brothers heretofore spoken of and described, may be set down with many others—Covenanters, Presbyterians, Methodists and Lutherians.

Of the latter class, the two sons of the Harpes, William, or big Bill Harpe, and Joshua Harpe, with hosts of McDermots, Gleasons, Glutsons, Ernests, Turners, McDonnoughs, Midriffs, Campbells, and many others whose names need not be mentioned—all thieves, murderers and robbers, who seized upon every possible occasion for the gratification of their vile propensities, regardless of time, place, age, sex, or color.

So terrific were their deeds of cruelty and blood, so sly and clandestine were their descents upon the defenceless wives and children of the Whigs, called away in the service of the country and absent from their homes, that all the terror and alarm produced by the invasions of the most merciless and ferocious savages upon the frontiers, in the earliest settlements of the West, never surpassed. Husbands, sons and brothers, whose wives, sisters and daughters were, in their absence from home, made the victims of these worse than savages, were often driven to the greatest excesses of retaliation, and sometimes made themselves the judges and executioners of the most summary justice, in the most unprecedented cruelties, long after peace was declared.

But as it is by no means expected, in these rapid glances at men and things in the great drama of the revolution, to teach ethics or politics, we ask forgiveness of the reader for this seeming digression, and return to a more strict adherence to the purposes of our narratives. Much,

84   LEGENDS OF THE

it is true, biographers and historians have already written in general views of North America and its inhabitants at the time of this great war. Of North Carolina,
however, in the general rivalry that seems to have existed
among them to laud and magnify some other favored
portions of the colonies, and certain favorite heroes of
that struggle for the liberties of freemen from other quarters, they found but little space and few facts to speak or
to more than mention, in meagre praise, indeed, her patriots, and sages; while many of her sons, for civic virtues, deeds of prowess and noble daring, have been passed
by, although entitled to the highest applause. The consequence has been that upon the minds of a large portion
even of our own countrymen, the opinion has been impressed, that, to judge from what is recorded by historians, the people of that State did little of what was
really accomplished by them during the long eight years
of the revolution—that, so far as history credits them,
they are rather facetiously represented in the person of a
feeble old man, who, like old Rip Vanwinkle, greatly
alarmed, and trembling at the first onslaught of battles
and death, closed his eyes that he might not see their
havoc, and falling asleep like an affrighted child, never
awoke till independence was fully established! and whose
first wild waking exclamations were still, as they had
long been before his frightful snooze, in piteous howls,
supplications, and prayers for mercy to "His most gracious Majesty."

" Myne loats, te ging, vat for, you makes de daxes, py
tam ?"

But we are thankful to record, she also had her host of
great and virtuous heroes and statesmen, of sleepless vigilance and dauntless courage, who poured copiously their
richest libations of blood upon the altar of their country's
liberty; whose virtues, patriotism and zeal, worthy of the
cause and all future imitation, shall stand as beacon lights
to earth's teeming generations. Again, on the other

hand, there were, it is lamentably true, in the bosom of this good Whig colony, multiplied hundreds of the inhabitants, who proved themselves to be Tories, capable of the blackest crimes, steeped in the blackest shades of human degradation, followed at last by the swiftest judgments of God, and afflicted even in this world, with the most terrible punishments, the narration of which might be profitable, by way of example, to teach most forcibly, the word of the Almighty, that "the way of the transgressor is hard."

We have already pretty plainly intimated, that to distinguish to some proper extent these different classes of the people of North Carolina, at the time of the " trial of men's souls," under consideration, we will proceed so to do.

First, however, as we must in a good degree speak of various occurrences as well as men acting in a variety of scenes within her limits, then principally the haunts of bears and panthers, and savage tribes no less ferocious, it will be courteous, at least, to introduce our readers and initiate them to a general view of the face of the country. On one side we behold towering mountains, rising in perpendicular grandeur, toward the highest soaring clouds; the summits tipped with the sun's rich and mellow rays; from whence to behold the vast plains beneath, "dressed in Eden's brightest bloom," irrigated by a thousand rivulets, cascading and chiming in joyous praise to Him the maker and builder of these magnificent structures. Again, to be permitted, as in truth the lover of nature may—having ascended those grandly towering mountains, forming portions of the famed Alleghanies—in one sweep of vision count and trace the winding ways of nearly a dozen foaming rivers, taking their rise as it were at his feet, roaring and rolling, some east, south-east, and some south to the Atlantic shores of Maryland, Virginia, the Carolinas, and Georgia; and others, in majesty and power, hastening west and north-west to pour their tributary floods into Mississippi's rushing tide!

In vain may we search the pages of history, poetry, or even geography to find adequate descriptions of the lovely plains, rich and generous soils, always repaying "the tiller's toil," which lie in Virginia, North Carolina and Georgia, east of the Blue Ridge, averaging a width of from fifty to seventy-five miles and stretching along its base more than three hundred. This region of country, within the limits of North Carolina, in the times of the revolution, was comparatively sparsely populated, and agriculture had made but small progress. It may be said the country was yet new, and the inhabitants rough and uncultivated. Relying much upon game for the supply of their families, they engaged in hunting excursions two or three times a year, in which they prepared and preserved for domestic consumption the choice parts of deer, buffalo, elk and bear, found in considerable numbers, bordering upon the Blue Ridge, and in the country beyond. Accustomed to these periodical excursions for game, and occasionally to repel and disperse the marauding Indians, who often stealthily crept within their neighborhood to steal horses and drive off cattle, and sometimes to kill and scalp defenceless families found in their course, the inhabitants of the colonies acquired great expertness in the use of the rifle, and much of the qualities and experience best calculated to make them the most reliable soldiers and dangerous enemies.

But we set out in this part of our book to give the reader a somewhat graphic view of the country at the time of the commencement of the revolutionary war, so far as relates to its sublime and picturesque beauty and general scenery. We will now proceed. But as in a recent publication, the remarks of a very pleasant writer, giving, it is believed, a truthful though glowing description of this very interesting portion of our American

WAR OF INDEPENDENCE. 87

Union, is now before us, we beg leave here to adopt it and quote it in part as equal to any thing that can be written or said on the subject. He says:

"The great artist, in his lavish adornment of our happy land, has not been unmindful of any part, least of all, of that of which we now write. None of the fair sisterhood of States may boast more winning charms than those of the sunny-land; or if, perchance, they be wanting in certain features, they possess compensating beauties peculiar to themselves alone. Proud mountain heights lift th'r voice of praise to Heaven; the thunders of Niagara are echoed by Tallulah; as the gentler prattle of Koaterskill and Trenton is answered by Ammicolah and Toccoa. For the verdant meadows of the North, dotted cottages and grazing herds, the South has her broad savannas, calm in the palmetto and the magnolia; for the magnificence of the Hudson, the Delaware and the Susquehanna, are her mystic lagunes, in whose stately arcades of cypress, fancy floats at will through all the wilds of past and future. In exchange for the fairy lakes of the North, she has the loveliest of valleys, composed and framed like the dream of the painter—turf-covered Horicans and Winnepisseogees. Above her are skies soft and glowing in the genial warmth of summer suns, and beneath lie mysterious caverns whose secrets are still unread. We will briefly speak of the various types of landscape beauty in the South, instancing the most memorable examples of each. The distinguishing mark of the mountain scenery of the Southern States, as contrasted with that of the North, is its greater picturesqueness and variety of form and quantity. The grand ranges of the Catskills and the Adirondes, and the peaks of the Green, and the White mountains, are but outer links of that mighty Alleghanian chain, which, centering in Virginia, rears its most famed summits in Georgia and the Carolinas. The Alleghanies in the Northern States move on in stately and unbroken line, like saddened exiles, whose stern mood is ever the same, and whose cold features are never varied with a smile; while in their home in the South, every step is free and joyous! Here they are grouped in the happiest and the most capricious humor; now sweeping along in graceful outline, daintily crossing each other's path, or meeting in cordial embrace; here gathered in generous rivalry and there, breaking away sullenly in abrupt and frowning precipices. All is Alpine variety, intricacy and surprise. Seen from the general level, the mountains are ever sufficiently irregular in form to offer grateful contrasts, here and there in their unstudied meetings, leaving vistas of the world of hill and dale beyond; while the panorama views command vast assemblages of ridge and precipice varied in every characteristic!—the large in opposition to the small, the barren in contrast with the wooded, the formal and the eccentric, the horizontal and the perpendicular, while a fairy valley in which the Abyssinian prince might have rambled, a winding river, a glimpse of road-side, or a distant hamlet, lend repose without monotony to the landscape."

Thus glowing in the most poetic raptures and imagery, our author proceeds to designate and describe particular instances of the most rare productions of nature in this truly fascinating country, seen and admired by the observant traveler, leisurely passing through the plains lying along and extended for many miles east of the Blue Ridge; or, perhaps, more properly speaking, the Alleghany mountains—mountains of extraordinary height, of every diversity of shape, form and appearance! Cataracts and cascades of greater or lesser note! Vast caverns, yet not fully explored—widening and enlarging from their comparatively narrow debouch, onward and backward to an undefined extent—exhibiting, when powerfully illuminated, a vast cosmogonism beneath terra firma, canopied by a broad expanse, resembling the blue etherial, bedecked with myriads of corriscative lights, emitted by the millions of water drips congealed, giving to the beholder the

WAR OF INDEPENDENCE. 89

complete imagery of an unclouded, moonless night, amid the genial beamings of the stars of Heaven!

In many of these caves, Indians making incursions into the early settlements of Georgia and the Carolinas, to murder, steal, &c., when boldly pursued by the inhabitants, were wont to hide themselves; and, as in the instance referred to in the conversation of Capt. Davidson and Wood, set forth in the first chapter of these narratives, secure themselves perfectly from molestation; but at the mouths of some of which there were sometimes, proportioned to the numbers engaged, the most sanguinary battles fought ever witnessed in the wilds of the South.

We may not, however, in justice to ourselves and consistently with our great desire to impart entertainment to our kind readers, as well as a more perfect view of the country in which many of the most thrilling scenes of the revolution occurred, before turning their attention to other topics more directly indicated by the title of these tales, fail to present a brief description of the stupendous and beautiful Arrarat mountain of North America—standing out proudly, "solitary and alone," in the bosom of the plains we have been considering and within the limits of North Carolina. Many beautiful landscapes are on every hand seen as we approach from the Atlantic shore and arrive in the neighborhood of the Blue Ridge. For many miles the traveler beholds in the distance west, this gorgeous *"lusus naturæ,"* touching, as it were, the blue curtains of the Heavens and the tesselated summits of that ridge! Rising in a pyramidal form, more than two-thirds of a mile, thence culminating to the height of three hundred and fifty feet perpendicularly, a perfect cylinder of solid rock, till it reaches its apex, forming an area of an acre of level surface, and commanding a most imposing and captivating view of the surrounding country for many miles. And as he stands fearfully, yet wishfully, viewing its majestic height, desiring to be borne to its summit and

90   LEGENDS OF THE

catch a Pisgah's sight of some fancied Canaan beyond,
gazing upward, yet despairing of its accomplishment, in
a nearer approach to its base at the northeast side he
finds, in delightful disappointment, a "winding way;"
whether formed by nature in completion of her playful
fancy, or by the art and skill of a race of aborigines
that there once lived—now gone to the dark abyss of
eternal forgetfulness—must forever be unknown! Yet
he finds it perfectly accessible and practicable, by means
of gentle steps, carved semi-horizontally round and round
the vast rock cylinder, to arrive at it.

Arrived, it is true, he sees no Canaan or promised
land, but lovely visions rise and rapturous thoughts gush
in harmonious wonder and praise of the mighty archi-
tect of the universe. Casting his eyes north and north-
east, or west, the Blue Mountain, at the distance of
thirty miles, its nearest point, grandly rises like a broad,
gaudily painted belt, bordered or crimpled with pearl,
kissing the highest rolling clouds! While again, turning
toward the south, he traces with surprising exactness the
transparent current of the beautiful Yadkin, laving the
Arrarat's base with its glittering, gently rolling waters
—like a bright silver cord marking its wandering way
thirty or forty miles in the direction of the broad Pedee.
Captivated by the view of the multitude of objects in nature and art, spread out afar off, his eyes experience no
painful sensation, however taxed, but seem aided all the
time, by a sort of prism formed in the atmosphere, or
thin clouds below, the convexity of the rays of light
bringing these distant objects to a plain and horizontal
line,—an optical illusion, which, though perfectly the
result of natural causes, is nevertheless exceedingly rare,
and not demonstrated at any other place known to the
writer.

CHAPTER IX.

The Whig women of North Carolina—A few touching biographical sketches of them during the war—Uncle Dan and his colored company, with his old "ooman" at her cabin—Major Kidd and his corps on a trip to Major John Adair—A hard fought battle between two African slaves, Cæsar and John, servants of Lawrence Smith, against five Tories and one Indian—They effectually defend their mistress and her daughters, killing two, and desperately wounding a third.

"Here woman reigns; the mother, daughter, wife,
Strews with fresh flowers the narrow way of life;
In the clear heaven of her delightful eye,
An angel—guard of loves and graces lie,
Around her knees domestic duties meet,
And fireside pleasures gambol at her feet.
Where's that land, that spot of earth to be found?
Art thou a man?—a patriot?—look around,
Oh, thou shalt find, howe'er thy footsteps roam,
That land thy country, and that spot thy home."—*Montgomery*

What's hallowed ground?—when mourned and missed
The lips our love has kissed;
But where's their memory's mansion?   Is't
   Yon church-yard's bowers?
No, their souls exist
   A part of ours.—*Campbell.*

HITHERTO these Legends have been dedicated to an exhibition of the causes which led to the war of the American revolution and the inspirations of love of country and liberty which nerved the arms and prepared our patriot fathers for the mortal fray, resulting in the achievement of the independence of the States.   Historians, it is true, in a very few instances, have dropped a thought or two in very brief commendation of a small

number of self-sacrificing and noble citizens of North
Carolina! But in these sparce instances there was a
wide space which might justly have been occupied by
them, left altogether untouched. And it is confessed to
be in some measure the motive, prompting the publication of these reminiscences of the time of the revolution,
to do justice, in some degree, to the memory of her sons
who have gone down to the tomb and whose awards of
gratitude have never yet been made. North Carolina
had, in that distinguished struggle, many men, alike
public-spirited and talented, far less ostentatious and
boastful, it is certain, than many of those of her sister's on
her northeastern border, whose ample praise has long since
been chaunted and sung, and largely rewarded with the
highest offices and honors ever yet conferred, while the
no less distinguished abilities, public and private virtues,
of her Harneys, Harveys, Ashes, Nashes, Cogsdells,
Alexanders, Grahams, Johnsons, and a host of others, are
gone to the tomb unwept; and whose names have been—
if not ungratefully suppressed by the happy and teeming
generations of the nation, who have, and now are reap-
ing and enjoying the rich fruition of their toil and labor,
both in the cabinet and the field—suffered to sleep with
them in their silent graves and not a monument or stone
to tell their worth! Some justice must yet be done in a
nation's gratitude to perpetuate and consecrate their hallowed memories. Nor do the suffering, untiring, and
most self-sacrificing women of any people, claim higher
eulogium than the matrons, wives and daughters of
patriots of that good old State.

We have in the preceding chapter said there were no
Tories among the women of the days of '76 and during
the extended agony which followed—we are sustained in
the assertion by a thousand striking instances illustrative
of the fact. Before, however, entering into a detail of
such proofs, we must bring to the consideration of the
reader, the circumstances which surrounded these fe-

males, during most, if not throughout the revolutionary contest.

They were exposed to four descriptions of enemies and on the frontiers, especially the colonies of Virginia, North Carolina, South Carolina and Georgia, touching the Blue Ridge and Alleghanies, and lying east and south of those mountains, were daily subject to the ravages of the fierce invading savages. These were the King's invading troops, the Tories, the slaves induced by the British and Tories to engage against their masters and mistresses, and lastly the Indians.

Compelled while their husbands, brothers and sons were campaigning and in the fields of battle, often far distant from them, to remain at home, constantly subject to the most insidious and brutal attacks from one or all of them, and made the victims of the most hellish lusts or blood-thirsty massacres, yet these true heroines of the revolution murmured not—endured it all! Nay, when the call came for their husbands, brothers, &c., to muster to the tented-field, instead of a sigh or a groan, or a plea of any kind to stay or impede their march, often and not a few of them were heard to say, in all the gushing feelings of a heroic woman's heart:

"Go, my husband—my son—or my lover, (as the case may be), God is my shield!—Heaven my guard!—and remember LIBERTY is the prize at the end, for you and those you leave at home!"

Aye, there lives even now, within the limits of happy Kentucky, the widowed relict of one of her most highly honored citizens; who, then a girl, witnessed and yet in thrilling tones narrates such scenes. We mean the venerable Mrs. C. P. A., who repeats the very words above quoted as those spoken in her presence, by a devoted wife to her husband just starting on a campaign! Truly that woman's faith and trust was in God, as it was the faith and trust of thousands of her country-women, for they felt that He who had called the sons and daughters of the colonies to enlist in this great cause of human liberty, against the haughty Briton and the odious feudal systems of Europe, was faithful, inspiring them with the true spirit of independence; leading their armies to victory and triumph, and often, almost miraculously, stooping Heaven to shield and protect the innocent and defenceless! Some of these were highly distinguished and greatly useful. A few of them we will specially here mention:

Mrs. Esther Simpson, the wife of Major John Simpson, the mother of four sons and two daughters, claims first the attention of the reader.

She was, in 1776, about forty-five years of age, possessed of a fine person and constitution, a warm and generous heart and intellectual head. For several years the father and four sons were actively engaged in the service of the country, and all among the most brave and useful officers and soldiers espousing its cause. They fought faithfully in the battles of Shallowford, Camden, Guilford, Kingsmountain and the Cowpens. Frequently all were campaigning at once, and absent from home in the most troublesome times with the Tories and Indians.

Major Simpson was wealthy, owning a large farm, well improved and a large family of African slaves. With this large farm and family in her charge, sufficient to engage the minds and fill the hands of ninety-nine out of a hundred of the most courageous, still Mrs. Simpson, this brave lady, found time night and day, in her own immediate neighborhood and, indeed, far around, to throw her mantle of care and kindness over her poor and suffering neighbors; ministering medicines and the most judicious nursing to the sick; the words of comfort to the dying, and food to them that needed it. She was often pleasantly called, by the country people, Doctor Simpson—so useful was she to the sick! She had been a kind and considerate mistress to her slaves, and the law of kindness had always been well tempered and mixed with a course of discipline among them, as far as necessary to maintain the proper subordination and government of so large a collection of servants, numbering near one hundred. And we record with pleasure, to the honor of that degraded race, the Africans, in the family of the Simpsons, made just returns of gratitude and faithfulness for the kindness received. She fully confided in their affection and fidelity, although she had been often informed by several of them that the Tories, more than one and even two British officers, Capt. Carlton and Ensign Storey, on one occasion had endeavored to allure them by promised rewards, as well as threats of vengeance, to join against their mistress and her family. She actually procured and placed in the hands of sixteen of the youngest of the men, guns and every other accoutrement necessary; put these under the command of her foreman, Uncle Dan, as all called him, or big Dan, as he was sometimes called, to be ready at all times to defend herself and family, and drive off, if need be, the thieving Tories from the farm and the neighborhood, in case they should attempt to steal her horses, cattle, &c.

These negroes were all genuine Whigs you may be assured. From their kind and intelligent mistress they were fully instructed in the principles of the cause and gave evidence that they emulated the spirit and patriotism of their masters. There was not one of them that would not have laid down his life in the discharge of his duty, in protecting his mistress, and indeed, any of the family. It was frequently a source of pleasant entertainment to the mother and daughters, in the absence of the father and brothers, to see Uncle Dan, of an evening, in all the pride and pomp of a military parade, in miniature, mustering his men and marching his sooty troops, to the inspirations of the piercing fife and sonorous drum, playing the universally popular national air, "Yankee Doodle." Their brave and faithful captain, meanwhile, in much mock dignity and gravity, most befitting his blushing

96   LEGENDS OF THE

honors, seeming resolved to win, by his fidelity and prowess—

"A name of fear,
That tyranny shall quake to hear,
And leave to his sons, a hope, a fame,
That they should rather die than shame."

The reader would doubtless himself have been amused to witness the staid and self-possessed look, the exercise of sound discretion, this good and simple hearted old black man kept up, down among the negro cabins and out on the farm; directing and controlling its entire cultivation, maintaining at all times complete submission to his will and judgment, subordinate to those of his mistress.

Uncle Dan had a cabin of his own, in which his kind and faithful "old ooman" as he called her, Aunt Molly (the name she bore with all the rest,) usually occupied; proud enough in all certainty of her husband, as he was for many years, foreman of the place; but now, especially since his promotion by his mistress to the high office of captain of the troops. One day after the labors of the morning and the arrival of the hour of noon, when all hands knocked off, as it is called, for dinner, Uncle Dan entered his cabin with a pleasant countenance, at once understood by Aunt Molly as signifying that he had something good to accomplish or tell her.

"Now old man," she said, "wha you guyne do, or guyne to tell me? Is'e lub to see you look good an smilin —wha is it?"

"Aye now," said he, "dese oomen's so cunning! Dey's always see sumthin' cumin'. Lookee, Molly, 'member massa's old shappaw that he hab fore he fight de Britishers and de Tories at Gilford's? O shaw, you knows him."

"Well, wha for you ax me dat, Daniel," said Molly, "Is'e noed you guyne say sumthin' 'bout massa and de wars—wha for you talk 'bout massa's big ole cock hat— wy ole man he lef him in he liber, ware he keep he book —I seed it dar. Now wha you want wid it?"

WAR OF INDEPENDENCE.   97

"Neber mine, Molly, till I ax missis, maybe she gib it to her ole Dan, dats it."

"Dar now, Daniel, you guyne be proud for sartin, you's guyne ax missis for massa's cock hat? den you's go it I nose. God nose wha you's cum to next! take care— take care, Daniel, you's guyne git a fall, dats it! Doctor Kilwell said last Sunday, when he preach, proud man go afore de fall—sumthin' dat way—he say he bible say so."

"Go way nigger, Is'e guyne talk to missis 'bout it inny how."

And having finished his dinner, neatly placed before him by Aunt Molly soon as he entered, and as they held the forgeoing chat, he went up to the great house, as they used to call it, and finding his mistress in her chamber, he very respectfully lifted his hat and bowed to her and said:—"well missis you's al'ays at work; if you's please, Is'e got to say sumthin' to you."

"What is it old man," said his mistress?

"Dats missis all de time, talk to ole nigger so good."

"Do you want to know when you'll send a load of wheat to old Walden's mill, or what do you wish to ask?"

"No, not dat, now missis—Molly sez plenty flower yet. Molly tell me sumthin' doe."

"Molly told you something," said his mistress,— "what?"

"Sumthin' marm, 'bout massa."

"What, Uncle Dan? has she heard from him—is he well?"

"No, not dat, missis, God bless 'em, I hope he well, and I believes it."

"Well, what is it, then; has Toby had another fight with Capt. Wood's Tom?"

"No, no, missis he say he fight 'em, no, Mo—Molly say doe, massa's ole cock hat in de liber, an—an——"

"Well old man what of that? His old hat has been

7

in the library ever since he got the new one from New-berne and went on the present campaign."

Aye, dats it missis, he ole hat, Is'e—Is'e ax fo' dat. Molly say de hat dar, but she say Dan to proud, an Dan go for to fall; but Is'e want it, dats flat, missis."

"Now, Uncle Dan, what in the world put that in your head?"

"Dar 'tis missis—missis, massa al'ays puts de big hat on an' he speaks to de white gemmen in de muster."

"Oh ho! that's it, Dan," said she, "you want to put on your master's cocked hat, when you muster your men! Well, well, you shall have it. Tell Molly to come and get it for you."

"Tankee, missis, tankee missis; I puts him on an I aint guyne fall neider—I isn't—yah, yah, yah; hora for dis nigger," and off he posted to his cabin.

Quite an interesting occurrence took place about the year —— when the brave General Marion, with his equally brave subalterns and soldiers, were making the proud and domineering Rawdon feel the aroused indig-nity of Americans for his cruelty at Charleston, and wherever he went with his no less cruel and reckless soldiery persecuting the wives and families of the Whigs with the most unheard of and inhuman violence. Major John Adair was, with his two sons, John and William Adair, at the distance of thirty-five miles, under the com-mand of Marion and General Sumpter, when a British Major, with a corps of about seventy men, called upon Mrs. Adair, who met the Major in her parlor. As soon as she entered, in a haughty and very insolent manner, he said to her:

"Madam, I have called this morning to see your d—d rebel husband and sons, and must see them! Where are they?"

She promptly answered that they were all from home, with General Marion, at Ninety-six, thirty-five or forty miles off.

"Well, Madam," he said, "it is my intention to see them before I leave, and I shall, therefore, call and take breakfast with you in the morning. If you do not have them here, then, to introduce them to me, I will burn your house and take away your negroes." Then, with a great air of haughtiness and impudence, he made his bow, marched his corps to a spring, contiguous to the farm, and encamped. Fortunately, late that evening, Major Adair, having been informed of the descent made by the said British officer with his corps in the direction of his home, obtained permission, and with a troop of sixty men, active cavaliers, well armed and mounted, set out and at about sunrise reached within sight of his home, and discovering the British encampment at his spring, in a moment resolved to attack them. He found almost every man sound asleep, dreaming, perhaps, of the rant and rollick they were to enjoy in the morning.

He conducted his valiant corps within a very few yards before any alarm was given, and with the exception of four, killed by his men in the first fire upon them, made the whole, Major, Captain, and all, prisoners of war. The redoubtable Major Kidd, the promised guest of the lady of his conqueror, Mrs. Adair, was now a prisoner and under a strong guard. At about eight o'clock, the following morning, Mrs. Adair, having been made acquainted by one of her brave sons, John Adair, with the events of the night, of the rapid march and rencontre, went immediately with him to the camp. When she came into the British Major's presence, she most gracefully accosted him, and said, "Sir, according to your appointment I have prepared breakfast for you; I shall expect you to partake of it; and then, if it be necessary, shall have the pleasure of introducing to your acquaintance my husband and sons." Trembling and pale, with contrition and fear, the humbled officer endeavored to excuse himself from taking breakfast that morning, as he was really "a little sick." The most courteous lady in-

100   LEGENDS OF THE

sisted he ought, as the breakfast had been prepared for
him, specially! He still urged his excuse in the most
humiliating tones, but she insisted in somewhat peremptory
terms, hinting by the way that among the waiting viands
she had been careful to have some coffee, (browned rye)
made of the genuine production of "our own beloved
America;" and so she marched the Major to her own
table, at which he presently seemed to forget his morning
nausea at the stomach.

Alas! that any American, male or female, of the days
of the revolution, should be an infidel! Ah, see God in
all this! But, as to the redoubtable British Major, it
may be justly said,

> "Shame and confusion, all is on the rout!
> Fear frames disorder, and disorder wounds,"

Alike resolute were many other of the matrons of that
day. Indeed, there were many of the most fair and respectable maidens, whose words of encouragement and
smiles of approbation to the young Whigs of the other
sex, contributed to no inconsiderable extent to awaken
their spirit and enlist their unfleshed swords in many
deeds of daring and valor. Among the former was found
the Amazon, Mrs. Polly Rust, the mother of Ben Rust;
commonly called by the Tories, Major Poll, who, often
with a rifle on her shoulder and dirk and pistols at her
girdle, patrolled the neighborhood, and was to the Tories
often a more formidable enemy than one or two dare encounter. She was a plain, stout woman, perfectly fearless, and from her sound discretion, unquestioned resolution and prowess, might well be denominated, as she often
was, the commander-in-chief of the entire community of
heroines. Such, also, were the wives of Lawrence Smith,
Simeon Tillis, Robert Caswell, and many others, who,
while there was a call for their husbands and sons to enter into the army of the country, fearlessly banded together to defend themselves and their neighbors, with a

firmness and invincibility that was truly heroic and almost incredible to any but such as are familiar with the history of the dauntless achievements of the heroines found in the earlier settlements of the West and the wars with the savage tribes. It was often the practice of the Tories, when British officers stealthily crept into the country as spies, or when small companies of British soldiers and Tories ravaged the country, to point out to their Captains, Majors, Colonels, the most captivating of the young daughters of the Whigs, in the neighborhood, and if by more gentle means they could not be subjected to their base lusts, forcibly to steal them from the protection of their mothers and friends, their fathers being away to fight the enemy, bear them to a distance, and subject them to the feculent embraces of these heartless leaders, the more certainly to secure the promised rewards of profits and official station in case British rule was maintained.

These victims to the diabolical machinations of the royalists were more numerous than would by many be supposed, to the utter shame and lasting dishonor of the king's partizans. Yet, however, in every occurrence of the kind, a more determined purpose was awakened in the ranks of the Whigs to battle for liberty and to revenge upon the heads of these detested miscreants the unspeakable insults and injuries practiced upon them.

Many of the slaves of the Whigs were seduced from their allegiance to their masters, sometimes armed and induced to fight against them; but at all events, carried off to distant parts, or forced on board British vessels and suffered to starve to death for want of food and clothing, so that nine out of ten, became a total loss. Some, however, and we may truly say the greater number could not be induced by the Tories to betray their masters, notwithstanding all their promises of reward or favor; and many of them, in the absence of their owners, most faithfully and heroically fought for, and effectually defended

their families and their property against the predatory
assaults of small companies of either British or Tories.
Indeed, in several instances that might be identified and
established, these grateful creatures, prompted by the
purest affection for the families to which they belonged,
not only periled their lives, but often suffered death in
the conflicts with the Tories and Indians, meriting the
highest praise for their fidelity and disinterested interposition.

A most interesting anecdote might here be recorded of
two African slaves who lived in the family of Lawrence
Smith, who emigrated to North Carolina in 1769 from
Louisa county, Virginia, and settled in the vicinity of
the Shallow Ford of the Yadkin. In this place he lived
till about the year 1786, when he removed to Kentucky
and resided until his death, about 1812. The first of
these two slave, Cæsar at the commencement of the revolution was about thirty years of age, tall in stature, and
spare in person, yet of a very clear and sound judgment,
for a Virginia slave; the second, aged about twenty-five
years, was remarkably strong and active, of quick perception and very great cunning. These, as the master early
entered the colonial service against the British and Tories, and often for months absent at a considerable distance from home, most faithfully conducted the entire
business of the farm, and on various occasions, when attempts were made by Tories and small groups of British
soldiers to commit depredations upon the stock—and who
twice attempted to break into the house and rob (as they
often did in other cases) and commit great violence on
their mistress and two daughters, then just grown to
womanhood, effectually beat them back. On a third occasion, testing to the severest extent the undaunted courage and unfailing fidelity of Cæsar and John, was a fearful conflict with five Tories and a Cherokee. Big Bill
and Joshua Harpe, Peter Hudspeth, Bill or William Ernest, Joseph Bettis, the Tories and Tipposa, the Indian.

The two first, Bill and Joshua Harpe, sons of the Scotch brothers mentioned in the earliest chapters of this work, had been, within two or three days preceding the event which we now describe, several times seen by John and Cæsar, rather suspiciously sauntering around the farm of their master. Suspicions of the honesty of their purpose were immediately entertained by the servants and in a consultation they had upon the subject, Cæsar remembering and speaking of his having seen big Bill Harpe on some former occasion, and having learned his name and the bad character he bore where he was known, they determined to double their vigilance in guarding the premises; keep their guns and butcher-knives in proper order, so as to be able to seize them at any moment, and sleep at night only by turns, one or the other of them being constantly on the watch. They knew that it was pretty generally known thrughout the country that their master Lawrence Smith and his sons, were then in South Carolina, and under the command of General Marion, as in a fight at —————— they had received great applause for feats of great bravery and dexterity in the battle against the British and Tories. For said Cæsar, "dis mus be so, or why would Capt. Adair come all de way from tother side Charlotte and tell missis and de young ladies, 'bout it; an den, Capt. John Wood, who fight dare heself, come an brag to missis and de young gals so 'bout it? I tell you, Jack, ebery body know massa, now, and whar's at dis time."

"Dar now Cæsar," said John, "Is'e jist tink dat bery ting mysef. Dis mornin' Is'e in de wood cutin' lode,— you'se gone to mill—Is'e look up an dat littlest one cum creepin' right up to me, had's gun. John got's gun dar, too, settin' up gin de tree, and hab dis 'ere same long knife massa stick de big bare on de Boo Ridge tother year. He cum putty close, I looks at him putty hard, he cums a little closer, an say halloo—Is'e say halloo, too— he say you'se lib 'ere? Is'e say lib wid massa,—Is'e git-

104　　　　LEGENDS OF THE

in' mad by dis time. He's den say, you massa not here —I den say dat none you bisniss. He den look all 'round, see nobody, an you wants to lib wid you's massa? Is'e den look 'round, mysef,—see nobody. Is'e say you's ax me, I wants to lib wid massa? you's got better home for me? He's say O yes, down in de Cumbeland county, wid Ginil McDonald and on de putty ship. Is'e say, I die fuss. He den talk no mo',—look 'round long time, den go way,—like he's cum. Is'e tell you, Cæsar, he's bad man, an dangerous!"

"I tink so too, Jack, an dats flat."

"No' mine dis nigger, ketch sum dem d—d black Britishers, sum days, bad."

That night these two simple but faithful Africans remained in the kitchen all night, keeping the door open so as to better hear any noise from without, scarcely either of them closing his eyes for a moment. Early in the morning, supposed to be about sunrise, one of the Miss Smiths, a beautiful black eyed girl about sixteen years of age, with a young colored woman, went into a lot a little back of the yard, and skirting a thick woods to milk, where they had been engaged but a very few minutes before the five Tories and Indian, above mentioned, leaped over the fence next to the timber, each of the whites armed with a gun and long-knife, and the Indian with a large club and tomahawk! Hudspeth came up to them first and seized the darky round the waist, who engaged him instantly in a most desperate struggle, screaming and shouting for help, to be heard a half mile off; at the same moment Josh Harpe laid hold of Elizabeth Smith and attempted to bear her in his strong arms toward the thicket from whence these vile wretches rushed. Her piteous screams and shrieks pierced the air in despairing tones. At this terrific moment the two darkies leaped into the lot, armed with guns and a long-knife girted on or to their waists, and instantly engaged the bandits in a most desperate fight! Cæsar came up with

WAR OF INDEPENDENCE. 105

Josh Harpe and gave him a deep stab in the left shoulder from which he immediately fell, loosing his grasp upon the young lady, while John rushed up to Hudspeth, still struggling with the strong and active colored girl, who seemed his full match at the game of a wrestle or fisticuff, and gave him a fatal thrust in the neck, with his long knife, cutting one of the carotid arteries, and he, perhaps, never breathed after.

Just then, however, most unfortunately, the despicable Indian drove his deadly tomahawk into the lower part of the side of the head of poor John, from which he instantly sank to the ground, and though taken to the house, and placed under the most assiduous nursing of his very kind and skillful mistress, he died in ten days. As Cæsar struck down Joshua Harpe, he was seized by the arm with the right hand of big Bill Harpe, while with his left, he grasped and held the fainting young lady. Bill Earnest also struck him a violent blow on the head with the barrel of his heavy rifle, which rather glancing, it failed to more than stagger him to one side. At this important and most momentous crisis, Capt. J. Wood, whom we have heretofore described, who was at the time of the attack passing, hearing the screams of the young women, leaped from his horse, ran to the spot, and shot the Indian through the heart just as he had stricken poor John with the tomahawk; then wheeling upon Bettis, big Bill Harpe, and Bill Earnest, who were holding Cæsar and endeavoring to stab him, instantly let him go and fled like terrified wolves to the adjoining wood and entirely escaped. John was immediately taken up by Cæsar, and Lucy, the young colored woman, and borne in their arms to his mistress' chamber, leaving Josh Harpe still alive but believed by Capt. Wood to be dying. Capt Wood conducted the affrighted and almost fainting Miss Smith to the house of her mother, and the fond sympathizing embraces of her affectionate sister. No farther attention was paid that evening to Joshua Harpe. But during the dark of the night that followed, big Bill Harpe, his cousin, and Earnest, stealthily came and bore him away. He was afterwards recovered and permitted to live for years a no better man; living with his yet more vile and terrible cousin, big Bill, growing worse and worse—indulging more and more firmly in the fatal doctrines of the decrees of God, and fully believing, as they said, that he had from all eternity determined and decreed them to be thieves, robbers and cut-throats, because they felt an insatiable thirst within them, to perpetrate such deeds; and therefore, as they were without the power to do other-wite, they must needs follow their destiny, strive as they may to change—do what they could to effect an escape from that supposed purpose! And may we not conclude that this opinion of God and man's condition, that the notions put forth in the world of the irrevocable decrees, the doctrine of fate, are indeed the master stratagems of the great enemy of God and man to allure man from all just sense of personal accountability for individual action which deadens every sentiment and sensibility of the soul that prompt to virtuous life? Substituting and adopting in their stead, as rules of life, the inbred corruptions of a fallen heart and depraved nature; teaching satan's delusive incantation, sung by one of Britain's poets.

> "There's a divinity that shapes our ends,
> Rough hew them as we will."

Nay, in the name of reason and the judgment of all men of common sense, does not the bare existence of the fact that God permits men, even in this enlightened day, the nineteenth century, to live, propogate and act out such dishonoring doctrines, prove that he who willeth not the death of a sinner, but rather that he turn from his evil ways and live, has appointed a day in which He will judge the world, not by any law of fate or immutable decree applied to any man, personally, but a law based upon man's volition, consistent with His conception of the purest reason—a law of righteousness?

CHAPTER X.

"Such and so finely bolted did'st thou seem,
And thus thy fall hath left a kind of blot,
To mark the full fraught man, and best indued
With some suspicion.   I will weep for thee ;
For this revolt of thine, methinks, is like
Another fall of man."—*Shakspeare.*

"But such is the infection of the time,
That, for the health and physic of our right,
We cannot deal but with the very hand
Of stern injustice and confused wrong."
King John, Act V., Scene 2.

"This fellow pecks up wit, as pigeons peas ;
And utters it again when Jove doth please :
He is wit's peddlar ; and retails his wares
At wakes and wassels, meetings, markets, fairs :
And we that sell by gross, the Lord doth know,
Have not the grace to grace it with such show.
This gallant pins the wenches on his sleeve ;
Had he been Adam, he had tempted Eve :
He can carve, too, and lisp ; Why, this is he
That kiss'd away his hand in courtesy ;
This is the ape of form, monsieur the nice,
That, when he plays at table, chides the dice,
In honorable terms ; nay, he can sing
A mean most meanly ; and in ushering,
Mend him who can : the ladies call him sweet :
The stairs, as he treads on them, kiss his feet ;
This is the flower that smiles on every one,
To show his teeth as white as whale's bone :
And consciences, that will not die in debt,
Pay him the due of honey-tongued Boyet."
Love's Labor Lost,—Act V., Scene 2.

It will be remembered by the reader, that in the early
part of these Legends, the female school of Rev. James

108   LEGENDS OF THE

Frazier, a Presbyterian Minister, at Hillsboro', was mentioned, and at which Maria, the daughter of Capt. Davidson, was a boarder and pupil. He was there and everywhere spoken of as a man of very accomplished and profound learning, eloquence, and oratory. Indeed, so perfectly captivating and fascinating were his manner and
style in the pulpit, that often he was followed in his appointments to preach, a great distance, by many hundred: Some twenty miles, and some forty and fifty—to
enjoy his transcendant ministrations. His name and
fame became very great throughout most of the colonies ;
but especially in Pennsylvania, Virginia, and the two
Carolinas. While making Newberne, in North Carolina,
his home, and in charge of a prosperous congregation of
Presbyterians in that city, it was his habit sometimes, to
visit and preach at Philadelphia with eminent success, as
it was said,—sometimes in Richmond, Virginia, and
many places for a considerable distance round those
cities, with very great acceptability and apparent power.

On one of his appointments in the year 1775—distant
from Richmond about twenty miles, in Caroline county,
near the Pomonkee river, at the old Reedy Church, he was
met by a very large congregation, and among the rest,
the universally known, truly pious and hospitable Mel-
chesideck Brame, who was a ruling Elder in that church,
together with the greater portion of the white members
of his large family. By this venerable and hospitable
old gentleman, after the services closed, the reverend
stranger was cordially invited to accompany him home,
and accepted the invitation. He partook of Mr. Brame's
hospitality, attended with all the assiduity and polite cordial welcome of a Virginia gentleman, for which that State
was even at that period, famed afar, and remained till
nine A. M. the second day, when he had to attend an
appointment at Hanover Town, for that day, at noon,
made as he came on from Richmond. Mr. Brame, several of his daughters, and his two nieces, Misses Happy

and Elizabeth Thompson, his wards, resident in his family, accompanied him.

On their way to church, at Hanover Town, a distance of five miles, the Rev. Mr. Frazier was observed to be most assiduous in his attentions to the pretty black-eyed Miss Happy Thompson; and when, at the bridge, on which they crossed the Pomonkee, from the Caroline side, her steed took fright and appeared to be on the point of plunging down from the abutment, over a precipice of twenty feet, or more, into the foaming stream below, the reverend gallant most opportunely and fortunately, who was riding by her side, leaped from his horse in great exposure of his own life, caught her's by the bridle, stayed his mad career, and saved the life of the rider. He at once received the thanks of her uncle, sister, and cousins,—nay, the most unqualified compliments of all, for this inimitable feat of activity and gallantry.

Meanwhile the young lady herself, deeply impressed with a sense of the dreadful danger from which she had been saved, and of gratitude to him by whom it had been accomplished, burst into a flood of tears, and for a time, lifting her eyes and hands toward Heaven, in silent ejaculations and thanks—presently turned to the reverend gentleman, and in the sweetest accents of voice, said:

"Oh! Mr. Frazier, tell me how can I ever repay the debt of gratitude I owe you?" He looked at the beautiful girl for a moment, with the greatest intensity of expression in his countenance, and said to her in rather an insinuating and under tone:—

"I cannot now, but may at some more proper time." And mounting his palfrey, the company immediately proceeded to cross the river, and to Hanover Town.

When they arrived, there was a verly large concourse gathered at the meeting house, within and around the door, more than sufficient to fill the house, come from all the adjacent country, and even many ladies and gentlemen from Richmond. In a few minutes the minister was very cordially greeted by the great and good Mr. Samuel Davis, then in charge of the Presbyterian congregation at that place, whose exemplary character, for piety and distinguished learning, was then and especially since, highly appreciated and proclaimed throughout all the country, but more particularly throughout the Southern and middle colonies, where he had preached most, and his labor of love was best known. To this venerable gentleman Mr. Frazier said, in the blandest words :

"I was not aware of the pleasure of meeting you here, on this occasion, and the honor of your being one of my audience, or I might have directed my preparation to a text and sermon something better suited to your taste and experience. But I have not time now to change, and must proceed with the one I had contemplated." To these remarks the excellent pastor, only answered :

"Doubtless it will be all well enough, as I trust, sir, it will be a preaching of Christ and him crucified."

Mr. Frazier then arose in the pulpit. The hymn was sung by the congregation, and the other usual initiatory services being passed, he selected and read for his text from the 2nd chapter of Ruth, and 13th verse, in these words :

"Then she said, let me find favor in thy sight, my Lord ; for that thou hast comforted me, and for that thou hast spoken friendly unto thine handmaid."

The minister remarked :

" These are the words spoken by Ruth, the Moabitess, daughter-in-law of Naomi, to Boaz the Bethlehemite, when she accompanied her mother-in-law in her return from the land of Moab to Bethlehem, in Judah, in pursuit of bread, (there being a great famine in Moab,) and after the loss of Elimeleck, her husband, and her two sons, Mahlon and Chilion. All who have read the Bible will have remarked in what beautiful terms of tenderness and filial regard Ruth addressed Naomi in answer to her

WAR OF INDEPENDENCE. 111

entreaties, not to follow her in her forlorn travel to the land of her people, in Judea; but to go again to Moab, and to the worship of her own Gods, in that land. And Ruth said, ' entreat me not to leave thee, or to return from following after thee: for whither thou goest, I will go; and where thou lodgest, I will lodge: thy people shall be my people, and thy God my God. Where thou diest, will I die, and there will I be buried: the Lord do so to me, and more also, if aught but death part thee and me.' "

" When they arrived at Bethlehem, in Judea, it being in time of harvest, Ruth, going forth to glean after the reapers, was providentially led among those in the fields of Boaz, was by him seen engaged in gleaning after his men, and he said unto her ' hearest thou not, my daughter? Go not to glean in another field, neither go from hence; but abide here fast by my maidens. Let thine eyes be on the field that they do reap,' &c. Then she said, ' Let me find favor in thy sight, my Lord,' &c., as in the text."

The preacher then proceeded to deduce from the words of the text, an analogy between the impoverished condition of Ruth—fleeing with her mother-in-law, Naomi, from the famishing land and people of Moab, to the land of Judea, for bread; the deep state of dependence into which she had been brought by sin for subsistence; the softened condition of her heart and mind, under these circumstances, toward her fond mother-in-law; the touching supplication to the wealthy Boaz, for his favor and aid in her trying circumstances; and the condition of a convicted sinner, saved, it was true, by the election of God, from before the foundation of the world, now convicted of sins, also foreordained, but ultimately designed to bring him to the knowledge of God and salvation through Jesus Christ.

That in such a state of mind, the sinner, thus brought to supplicate God, was prepared, not only justly to appreciate his bounty and loving kindness, but to ask—though it was long before vouched for according to God's election and eternal purpose, just as the favor and loving kindness of Boaz had been bestowed and declared before the damsel, Ruth, made her supplication (expressed in the text)—for his favor and benevolence. He dilated largely and eloquently upon the mercy of God exhibited in creation, redemption, and providence; and especially in his foreordination and election. Spoke of the wonderful adaptation of things, in nature and creation, to the comfort, happiness and safety of man. Then of the loving kindness, displayed toward his elect from all eternity, in the gift of the Lord Jesus and his atoning sacrifice, whereby, and through whom alone, they received the bread of eternal life. That, when in the condition of sinners—exposed to death eternal, through the eternal election in Christ, of which they were made partakers—they were saved, and are therefore laid under the most illimitable obligations to adore, obey, and honor Him, from whom such salvation comes.

He then closed with a few striking illustrations, as he said, by way of enforcing the arguments advanced. These he "*amplified* and *simplified*,"—one particularly. With great apparent solemnity and pathos, he urged upon his hearers, as emblematical of the duty toward God from one of his *chosen elect*. He said, " It was like that gratitude, which, all would say was a just return from a beautiful young lady to her protector, who had, when the danger of instant death, or some other terrific injury by land or sea was imminent, at the hazard of his own life, timely interposed and saved her."

Here the divine closed his unique sermon. After prayer, by the venerable Davies, the congregation was dismissed with the blessing.

The Rev. Mr. Frazier, having to reach his appointment at Richmond that evening—took his leave of Elder Brame and the young ladies of his family, and set out for

WAR OF INDEPENDENCE. 113

that place; kindly, however, saying to the old getleman, that " he believed he should accept of his invitation to preach again at Reedy Church, on next Sabbath week, after which he would spend some several days beneath his hospitable roof." Mr. Brame, only a little crustily, responded:

" Ah, yes. Then I will have the appointment given out in time, and shall expect you."

Journeying homeward the young ladies interchanged many remarks relative to the sermon they had just listened to. Some said it was a good deal odd in its doctrine and general topics of discussion—in its conclusion, rather difficult to comprehend. Miss Mary Brame said, for her part she could not see any sense or application in the most of the preachers' illustrations, as he called them, at the conclusion. Especially, that in which he instanced the case of the beautiful young lady in peril of life. " Indeed, I could not understand it. He seemed to look at that time, Cousin Happy, (Miss Happy Thompson) right at you, as if he wished to say something to you particularly."

" I don't see why he should wish to speak to me, Cousin Mary," said Miss Happy. " He saved me, I really believe, this morning, and for it I am truly thankful to Heaven, and truly grateful to Mr. Frazier; but I reckon he had no allusion to me, or that circumstance, in his sermon."

"It may be so," said Mary, "but at the time, from his look and all, I thought it very queer."

" Well," said Gregory Baynham, who was along with the company and heard the conversation between the two girls " now the thing is not hard for me to understand I assure you. That Scotchman is not only a great preacher, but a very cunning one, depend upon it. Aint he a bachelor, Miss Happy?"

" Indeed, Mr. Baynham, I do not know, I suppose he is tho', he is certainly a fine healthy looking young man,

8

114   LEGENDS OF THE

and might be an object to be caught by any young Virginia lady."

"Ah! ha, ha," said Baynham, "do you think so Miss Happy? well, then you will be sure to have a chance for that or else I am much deceived."

"O fie—fie, Mr. Baynham, the farthest from it."

"If I hadn't reasons," said he, "I wouldn't say it, Miss."

"What reasons, Mr. Baynham?"

"Why, nothing very particular; but enough for me—that's certain. He asked me a heap about you, yesterday, I know, as we walked in your uncle's garden; wanted to know, mighty particular, what was your age and fortune, and all about you. I should'nt have thought much of that, if he had'nt, to-day, soon as you got to the church, taken me one side, and asked me the same over again, pretty much; and then, how many brothers and sisters you had. Then, when I saw he could'nt keep his eyes off of you all the time he was preaching, think's I, there's something in it. I don't know much about love affairs, being a bachelor myself; but—"

"But," said Miss Mary, "Mr Baynham, you're a pretty cunning one."

During this chat on the way, the worthy old elder rode along, quite alone in his position and humor, saying nothing to any one until addressed by his niece, Miss Elizabeth Thompson, and asked, "what he thought of the sermon?"

"Why, Betsy," he said, "don't you know I do not often express my opinion of the preaching of my brethren? I confess I was not as much pleased to-day as I was at Reedy Church. To-day I could not keep up with his remarks. Perhaps, however, the fault was in me, not the preacher. He said a good deal about God's eternal purpose and the doctrine of election from all eternity, but although I believe it was all scriptural, and right, I am like my venerable brother, Parson Waddle, who told

me, one day, he did'nt see much use for it in the pulpit."

A minute or more intervened and the old gentleman
said:

"Hi, ho; this is a strange world after all, niece, I
find."

By this, the company reached Mr. Brame's and all
proceeded to his dwelling. In a few minutes, his kind
old lady and domestics united in spreading out before
them a warm and sumptuous dinner, prepared and kept
warm until their return from church.

Little more was said among them of the sermon or
any of the incidents of the day, or more than a simple
narrative of the occurrence at Pomonkee bridge, and the
fortunate rescue of Miss Happy Thompson, &c., to her
affectionate aunt, Mrs. Mary Chiles Brame, by whom, in
all tenderness and motherly care, she had been nursed in
infancy and reared to womanhood; except a pleasant
and facetious remark or two by Mr. Gregory Baynham,
who wittily suggested:

"It was only one of the tricks of that little crafty ur-
chin, Cupid, to get into Miss Happy's pony, to flounce
and flounder as he did, and give the parson a fine opportunity to display his Scotch gallantry and Edinburgh
manners, and properly prepare the way for a matrimonial
catastrophe of some sort."

"Ah, now, Mr. Baynham," said Happy, "it would
be difficult to find your match for such things anywhere.
I really believe if I was going to die you would contrive, someway, to laugh at it."

"Well," he said, "we'll see; and if something does'nt
come of this bridge affair to make me cry, I shall get off
pretty well. These starting ponies, sometimes, bring
about wonders."

CHAPTER XI.

Thoughts on the designs of Providence in opening up the way from the old world to the new—The almost miraculous preservation and prosperity given to the earlier emigrants from Europe &c.—Some touches of the history of the revolution in the middle colonies, particularly in North Carolina—The conflicts with the Tories—Their abduction of three young and beautiful Whig ladies—The pursuit and execution of a number by Capt. John Wood and others.

> " Slaves fight for what were better cast away—
> The chain that binds them, and a tyrant's sway;
> But they that fight for freedom, undertake
> The noblest cause mankind can have at stake;
> Religion, virtue, truth, what'er we call
> A blessing—freedom is the pledge of all."

> " Fair freedom has a thousand charms to show,
> That slaves, how'er contented, never know—
> The mind attains, beneath her happy reign,
> The growth that nature means she should attain,
> The varied fields of science ever knew,
> Opening, and wider opening on her view."—*Cowper.*

As yet, these fugitive pages have given but few and brief details of the severe battles fought by the patriots of the colonies, against the enemies of the country, nor is it our intention or design so to do. These are in the general, well and satisfactorily given by the histories and biographies already published, now quite numerous and reliable, all exhibiting the heroism, skill, moral courage, and fixedness of men, resolved for themselves and their posterity to be free.

New details of these may never be wholly uninteresting in view of the great prize, liberty, for which they were fought on the part of our fathers; but especially when the intelligent reader sees, as we respectfully think he ought, the hand of God's overruling providence manifestly displayed in their behalf, and regards such divine interposition, as we verily believe he should, as but the completion of that stupendous reformation, or revolution, begun and most miraculously accomplished, in the re-publication and establishment of the true principles of christian liberty, obligation and happiness, through the feeble instrumentality of Martin Luther; and finally, in the inspirations bestowed by Him upon George Washington and his compatriots of the American revolution.

Publishing to the old world, and the new, nay, to all mankind, man's natural rights in society, the revolution of 1776 finished the superstructure of religious liberty, and while the principles of the protestant spirit remodeled the church, those of the American era, society and government. Daughters of the same divine parent, the religion of the Bible, they have found a new family of men among the nations of the earth.

Here, in America, from the feebleness of infancy, exposed and sometimes almost destroyed in the midst of and in defiance of disasters, the most threatening and calamities the most alarming, the little colonies at Jamestown and Plymouth, grew and spread out under Heaven's protection, like green bay trees; ever the shade and asylum of the politically and religiously oppressed of earth, till, changing the figure, to manhood grown, taught by the reformation that when civil and political liberty was invaded, independence was no less a duty than a right, they cut the gordian knot of colonial obedience to the British throne, defied like men its power, and God gave them the victory! So that in holy triumph the inhabitants of the colonies, one and all, might justly have sung, as indeed many thousands did sing,

Sound, sound the loud clarion, o'er Atlantic's broad sea,
Jehovah has triumphed, for America is free!
Sing—for the pride of the tyrant's now broken,
　His cohorts, his horsemen, his navy so brave!
How vain all his boasting! the Lord hath but spoken,
　And cohorts, and horsemen, are sunk in the grave!

118   LEGENDS OF THE

But the reader will perceive that in the preceding remarks of this chapter, we have,—in an effort to give a somewhat enlarged view of the principles of the war of independence, and the manifest providence engaged in the cause of human freedom, by which, united with the free choice of the people to engage in, and hand to hand, and shoulder to shoulder, struggle for liberty, it was ultimately accomplished—we have rather anticipated that happy event, and raised the triumphant song sooner, in a chronological point of view, than it was properly and actually sung.

The incidents of the war of which we have spoken, may be appropriately considered as occurring, some of them, at its commencement, and others long before its termination. Yet we have some to present to our readers, several, we believe, fraught with thrilling interest and highly illustrative of its dangers and horrors, the natural products of the times.

One of the earliest and most effective measures adopted by the first colonial Congress of the Whigs in North Carolina, was the establishment of committees of safety in each county, and appointing for that purpose from ten to twenty of the most courageous and active resident Whigs, whose appointed duties were of the most plenary character, partly civil, and partly judicial. They were expected, in the first place, to go as far as practicable among the Tories or royalists, explain to them personally the general principles of Whig resistance to the parent government, and in the event of the king and ministry disregarding their innumerable supplications and petitions, to fight to the last extremity till their liberties were made secure and fully acknowledged,—to use all their influence by persuasion and argument, to convince them of the propriety of these principles, in view of their rights guaranteed by the British constitution, and the charters of the colonies, and of the absolute necessity of Union among our citizens in any event, to a speedy and

WAR OF INDEPENDENCE. 119

successful issue of the terrific dangers and trials then impending over the common country.

And again, in the event of these efforts being unsuccessful, and failing to get them to sign a declaration to the effect, declaring an acquiesence in those principles, pledging to the utmost reasonable extent, aid in the cause of the country against all British aggression and usurpation, to imprison them or otherwise put it out of their power to give aid and comfort to its enemies.

To this end they were charged to keep and maintain a sleepless watchfulness upon all within the limits of their respective counties, and thus secure the safety of the citizens and the greatest success to the cause of the revolution. In general, these remarkably extensive powers were exercised by these committees with much moderation and a becoming observance of prudence and humane discretion. Being very generally selected from among the wisest and most impartial of the citizens, with few, if any, perquisites attached to their duties or official acts, they with surprising energy acted the parts assigned them, looking to the preservation of the safety and quiet of society and the prosperity of the cause of freedom as their ample reward. On some occasions, however, under the influence of great and sudden provocation from the Tories by thefts, robberies, murders, and other crimes, if possible, more despicable and henious in their character, perpetrated upon undefended innocence, these committees adopted the most stringent measures; and in many instances, inflicted in the most unprecedented modes the severest punishments. Indeed, these seemed indispensable, especially when the armies of the British invaded and overrun the colony, under the command of Sir Henry Clinton, Lord Cornwallis, Tarlton and others, and when the Tories were much more daring and reckless in a continual harrassment of the neighborhoods by murder and rapine.

Not a few of the most beautiful and highly prized of

the young ladies of the most respectable families, as we have already mentioned, and for the diabolical purposes suggested, were abducted and clandestinely borne to a great distance from their friends, to despicable lodges and secret repositories, and murdered or made miserable and loathsome for all future life!

O, never, never shall we cease to remember with the most heartfelt sympathy the fate of the lovely Mary Walden, the cherished and only child of the venerable Walden, mentioned heretofore as among the patriots at the Mecklenburg Convention; nor that of the beautiful little Harriet Eskridge, torn with savage brutality from the very embrace and arms of her widowed mother, to whom she had flown for protection; nor the unspeakable sufferings, heart-rending agony of poor Charlotte Fitzhue, who, not an hour before, united in matrimony to Mr. John Lawrence Wright at the old Duplin Presbyterian meeting-house, returning to her father's in company with her husband, together with their bridal attendants, was with her party, attacked by four despicable royalists, two Scotch and two Irishmen. Her companion being shot from his horse, leaping from her saddle, she ran instantly to him, but at the moment of his last dying embrace, was rudely ravished from those arms, already enfeebled and powerless with the agonies of death, and borne to a great distance from friends, home, and all sympathy!

These sweet girls all lived to tell the horrid sufferings when found and restored to their despairing relatives and friends. But each, in inconsolable grief, soon, like stricken flowers in the morning of life, drooped, withered and sank into the repose of their lonely graves.

These terrible miscreants, when captured, as some half dozen of them shortly after their horrible crimes were, though unfortunately not all, swiftly suffered suspension by the neck, like other dogs, as every one will expect and approve, under the famed "second section" of Major General Jack Lynch, Judge. The first section of which

WAR OF INDEPENDENCE.   121

learned code very briefly and laconically treating of catching or shooting before hanging; and the second, discussing the doctrine sufficiently in *extenso*, hang and then try them by a jury composed of the rope or grape-vine, the tree and the hangman—"judgment for the commonwealth."

But let us turn for the present from these sickening pictures of fallen human nature to scenes more pervaded by the spirit of grace. Indeed, we are inclined to the opinion, gentle reader, expressed by a rough but strong minded old local preacher who, addressing his congregation, said with great apparent earnestness: "I tell you what it is my brothers and sisters, thar's a great deal of human natur in man!—and human natur is a grand rascal!" Emphatically so, say we, aside from the grace of God.

Well, it will be remembered, the Whigs of North Carolina, in the year 1775, elected and organized at Hillsboro' a colonial congress. That body had always been in the habit of opening its session with prayer by some minister of the gospel. This, it is true, the venerable old Whig, Dr. Caldwell, had usually done for them. But on the occasion to which we now allude, he was sick, unable to attend, and considerable delay was the consequence. Late in the evening, when all were beginning to fear they should have to break up, or proceed without the performance of that introductory, Colonel Francis Nash, one of the members, walked into the hall and introduced the Rev. George Mecklejohn, a newly and thoroughly wrought and fashioned successor of Peter, or some other of the Apostles, in high church parlance, and then "he opened the congress by *reading prayers*." He expressed great objection to serve them, for a while, but ultimately submitted to the performance of the service.

The gist of this story is, that Mecklejohn, a high church man in his religion, that is, one believing in all the superstitions of the divine right of kings and magistrates, a high Tory in his politics, was, when found by Colonel Nash, in Hillsboro', just returning from a convention of Tories, called together by the right hand machinator of the royal Governor, Jo. Martin, sent there to adopt some measures to thwart and obstruct the proceedings of the colonial congress then about to organize in that town.

In the meeting of the Tories, he had with all apparent fervor supplicated the divine approbation and succor on all their undertakings, and yet, while acting with and for the Whigs, he prayed with equal apparent earnestness and openly for the blessings of Heaven upon their cause, and for the success of all their undertakings to free the country. Reader, think you God ever appointed and called such a minister? Could he have been the successor of an Apostle?

That Mr. Mecklejohn, under the influence of his European education, his particular opinions in favor of the supremacy of the church of England, should differ with his Whig neighbors, was not surprising; but that he should pretend to favor the one while he was advocating the other was abominable. He was, however, not the only one, by hundreds, that sought by a deceitful, two-faced course, to shelter himself from responsibility in regard to either side. There were even those that foisted themselves into high places!—contrived to get themselves appointed to high and responsible offices in the Whig government!—yet all the time the aiders and abettors of their enemies. Such was the character of Farquard Campbell, a Scotchman by birth and education, a Covenanter by profession, yet who managed to be made a member repeatedly of the colonial congress, till he was detected and fully convicted of treachery, and justly punished. Others of the Tories, becoming alarmed at the probability of the success of the Whig cause, or at the stringency of the treatment they were likely to receive at their hands, under the semblance, at least, of repentance for and retraction of their Tory professions,

WAR OF INDEPENDENCE.   123

hastened, as it seemed, to give the pledge to go in future with their Whig neighbors for liberty and the rights of freemen.

The greater portion of the Whig leaders, members of the committees and other offices, as we have already declared, were disposed to adopt and practice the most conciliatory course toward the Tories, or royalists, so as to bring them into a union with them and destroy the hopes of the officers of the crown for aid by reason of an intestine division.

In many instances success attended their efforts. The case of Mr. John Coulson, of Anson county, a man of considerable fortune and influence, and who had been guilty of many offences, finding himself compelled to take an open position on the one side or the other, sent to the colonial congress at Hillsboro', the following confession. We here copy it, as it exhibits, in substance, confessions made and pledges given by many others, viz:

"I, John Coulson, do, from the fullest conviction, solemnly declare, that I have been pursuing measures destructive of the liberties in general, and highly injurious to the peace of the colony; and truly conscious of the heniousness of my guilt, do now publicly confess the same, and do solemnly and sincerely promise, that I will for the future, support and defend, to the utmost of my power, the constitutional rights and liberties of America; and in order to make atonement for my past guilt, that I will make use of every effort in my power to reclaim those persons whom I have seduced from their duty, and also to induce all other persons over whom I have influence, to aid, support, and defend the just rights of America. In witness whereof, I have hereunto set my hand, this 22nd day of August, 1775."

During the latter part of the year 1775, a numerous association of Scotch Highlanders, direct from the mother country, settled on the shores of Cape Fear river. Their principle men, or leaders, having suffered very much on

124   LEGENDS OF THE

account of their attachment to the Pretender, to the crown of Great Britain, and close adherence to his cause while in Scotland, having there lived in continual awe of the reigning sovereign, George III., had now fled or migrated to North Carolina in search of the peace which the extent and solitude of her forests seemed to ensure.

These Highlanders, however, greatly encouraged and reinforced Governor Jo. Martin, the last, as we have before stated, of the Governors under the British authority in this colony, who, having fled from his residence to, and on board of the British ship on the Cape, from whence he issued several proclamations and held his Court, managed with great craftiness by operating on their fears; threatening them, here, to prosecute and punish them for their treasonable conduct in the old country, and offering them a release from these dangers upon the condition of their embracing and unflinchingly adhering to the cause of the king.

To a man they entered into his measures and identified themselves with the Regulators—whom he had in the counties of Orange, Anson, Guilford—and others in the use of like cunning and threats, and who, with the Highlanders now under their leaders, commenced preparing for the fight; so that the banks of Cape Fear, and the beautiful valleys of its tributary streams, Deep and Haw rivers, flowing through the counties of Moore, Orange, Chatham, Guilford and Randolph, comprising the very heart of the colony, were overrun with this species of population.

They became every day more and more imperious, impertinent, and threatening; encouraged continually by the false promises of Jo. Martin, who, from time to time, on board of the ship at the mouth of the river, communicated to them pretended intelligence he had received from Europe, to the effect that speedily a large army of forty thousand troops, a considerable navy, and other mighty helps, would soon come to their aid and overrun the entire continent, and reward them more fully for their services. It is not, therefore, to be wondered that the great body of these Tories, coming to the country with all their European prejudices against, and ignorance of a republican government, not to speak of the vile corruptions of European habits, ignorance and crimes, should fall the ready dupes of these intrigues; nor, that having habitations in the bosom of society and in the midst of the Whigs, they became the most dangerous and terrific enemies.

They almost at once formed leagues for plunder and rapine, and sought by every means conceivable to harrass, vex, and even to destroy the Whigs that seemed to stand in the least degree in their way. The four Harpes, John, William, and their sons big Bill and Joshua, being among the most active; having been longer in the country than the Scotch and Irish generally, better acquainted with the localities of the land, as well as the most worthy and wealthy among the Whigs, they exercised a decided influence in directing and abetting their nefarious plans and schemes of depredation upon them. There were those among the Whigs, not a few, who, notwithstanding, felt the general disposition to pursue milder and more conciliatory action toward the Tories; yet, the greater number of them acted with great promptitude if not cruelty and violence toward them; often making them feel the most awful retaliations for their crimes.

There was, however, to their honor, no acts of assaults and injury perpetrated by them upon the defenceless females of any of the Tory families, or upon any Tory who was not known to be in league with Tories in the perpetration of crimes. At this we really rejoice, for the honor of the cause and the country.

Of this latter class of Whigs we give the names of Colonel Ezekiel Folsom, Captain J. Wood, Ben. Rust, Patrick Dillingham, Sylvester Stone, Tiberius Head, Seaburn Jones, and others, living dispersed throughout the several counties above mentioned, and in other parts of the province; nevertheless, well known to each other, and accustomed to act in great concert. The two first, Folsom and Wood, were more active and less scrupulous than any of the others, especially the former, in the means employed to bring the Tories into their power as well as in the punishments inflicted upon them when taken. Indeed, so cruel and unheard of were the punishments of Folsom, that it was made the subject of serious expostulation and complaint against him on the part of many of the more humane and generous Whigs. Nay, it was sometimes believed, that the Colonel, in some instances of his most harsh and cruel proceedings, sought by false pretences and unfounded charges, only to gratify his personal quarrels and private piques against some of his countrymen, though generally regarded as friends to the Whig cause. It was not so with the brave Wood. His distinction in this respect, was his untiring vigilance and unswerving perseverance in following, whithersoever he might flee to any place or distance, every Tory known to have been engaged in aiding and assisting the British in committing any thefts, robberies, murders, or rapine of any kind, perpetrated in his part of the country.

It was principally owing to his great enterprise and perseverance that the three vile wretches that were guilty of abducting and ruining forever the beautiful little Harriet Eskridge, of whose melancholy fate mention is made in a former portion of this chapter, were brought to a just retribution for their crimes, and she restored to her affrighted and almost murdered mother.

These Tories bore the names of Jacob Simonds, Jedediah Burk, and Sam. Jenkins. The two first, tolerably nigh neighbors of Mrs. Eskridge, and the third from an adjoining county. They had borne the unhappy Harriet to a hunting lodge, distant from her home thirty-five miles, situated in an extensive forest approaching the head-waters of Haw river, fifteen or sixteen miles from

WAR OF INDEPENDENCE. 127

the nearest inhabitants and wholly deserted and unoccupied, except once, or perhaps more frequently, a year, companies of hunters would shelter there of nights for two or three weeks at a time.

The pursuit of these horrible men, their final discovery and execution by the brave Capt. Wood and his two friends, Ben. Rust and Peter Radford, at the door of their despicable den, was for many years a favorite story of the burly Ben. Rust, always narrated by him in most facetious and graphic style, and in his own peculiar jocose vein and manner. Making a description of this tragic end of the three miscreants, and with great zest detailing their doleful looks, cries and supplications for mercy, as well as their horrid distortions of person and action; dangling in the air, when swinging by the neck in the agony of death, the subjects of the most sportive wit and hilarity. He would always begin by a sort of warning to the young ladies, in general, in much apparent gravity, saying:

"Young gals what's purty like, had ought to be mighty careful how they show 'emselves to youngsters these days, specially if they ain't goin' to marry 'em right off, for the rascals, the Tories, ar'nt very partickalar how they get 'em, and is mighty apt to any way. Now them's my rail sentiments. Poor gal! now if Harriet Eskridge had'nt looked so pesky-like, at that rascal Jake Simonds, which Capt. Wood and I, and that other man, swung up at the hunter's den, jest when she seed he wanted to get tolable nigh and to court her a bit at widda Elliott's quiltin, the week before, and jest let him fondle a little, and make blieve a while, heed'r gone about his business arter a while, and maybe shed'er never bin hurt any, or bin a bit the worse on't. Now them's my sentiments.

"Well, I hain't told you yet the best on't. Well, poor gal, she was took off mighty bad one night. The fellows went to her mamma's that Saturday night, all on good horses; but one was stole from Bill Tate over in Tryon, a month before. Well, when they got to her mamma's they seed the poor gal, and a proper purty one she was, walking about in the truck patch, and they all jumps over the fence and she seed 'em and gets mighty skeard like, and runs and hollows plum to her mamma in the house, hollowing ' O! mother, mother!'—well, Jake, he follers on, too, and he and that 'tother villain, Jed. Burk, pulls her right out on her mamma's arms and off they puts, fast, I tell you. Three or four days arter that, Capt. John Wood, a brave man as ever breathed the breath of life, comes and sees me, and says:

" Ben Rust, that poor widda Eskridge 's lost her darter ; Jed Burk and Simonds, and another fellow stole her last Saturday night, little before dark, right from her mamma's arms and went right off with her. Monday I hears on't and rode and rode, and hunted and hunted, all through the county, and the most I larnt was from old man Price and his two boys. Says they, ' that night we was out 'possoming and seed three fellars ridin' mighty hard, and one had a poor gal in's lap afore him ; the poor thing is begging and begging, on they went, passing close by us, and along the path that goes right towards the pilot mountain.'

" ' Now,' says Capt. Wood to me he says, ' Ben ' says he, ' you're a purty good woodsman, will fight I know, and you're tried, I've come to get you to go with me and Radford to try and find them Tories, and poor little Harriet, and if we ketch 'em,' says he, ' we'll have some fun ' says he.

" ' Well, now,' says I, ' thems my sentiments percisely, Capt. John Wood. I'll go ' says I, ' and if we ketch 'em I reckin we'll make 'em pesky Tories dance for it and save the little gal too.'

" And so we started and took Pete Radford along, and we fust struck out to the Yadkin like, and come to the big woods as they call 'em ; rode mighty hard that day, but not in a strait rout, sorter crooked like, this way and

WAR OF INDEPENDENCE. 129

then that way, till most night, and then we heard nothing of 'em. We all stopped, and Wood says, says he, ' Boys, let's rest awhile and talk a bit; and we'll eat a little as I am gitin' purty hungry. I've got plenty of good jirk venison here in my bags and some purty good cakes my old ooman gin me this mornin.' So we all set down close to a branch, and eat and drank awhile. At last says Capt. Wood, says he, ' Boys we're on the wrong hunt. Them fellers did'nt come out this tract nor towards the Arrarat, that is the pilot mountain, at all, at all, but they took out towards the head of Haw river and t'other side the big woods, and that's the way they went. And now says he, I have just thought of it; I fully believe I can guess where they went and are at this very time. There's, way out toward the head of Haw, a hunter's camp or cabin, where I seed Sam Jenkins once, last year, with a passle of fellers on a huntin' expedition.'

" Says I, ' Captin, how far,' says I, ' is it off?' He looks all around, thinks awhile and looks 'round agin, and then says he, ' Boys its about twenty-five miles, and in the best huntin' ground this side the Blue Ridge.'

" Says I, ' well, Captin, I'm good for goin' right to that place ; but we must look out for some place to roost all night, as the sun is purty low now, not more'n hou high, and we can't travel these woods, no rode, nor path, nor nothin' to steer by in the dark. Well, and how'll that be ?'

" Says he, he says, ' Ben, you're right ; but,' says he, ' we'll take the course and go it long as we have light, and if we come to any water we'll stop, hobble our nags, to get a little grass while we sleep, and in the mornin' take the track again bright and early.'

" And so we all started, and went right fast, and when dark was comin', thinks I there's no water, nor no branch, nor spring here, and so we went on. Presently says Capt. Wood, says he, ' Boys here's a right purty spring

9

running down from that hill, and then we stopped, hobbled the nags, eat our beef tongue and venison jerk, built a fire and went to sleep right quick. But before we went to sleep boys,' says he, ' I'll tell you how we'll do in the mornin'. We'll try and git to that huntin' den by ten o'clock. When we git 'in a half mile or so, I'll creep to the place and watch a bit, and then I'll creep nearer and so I'll see who's thar, and if they ain't all thar we'll wait and watch till if any's out huntin' or so he comes in, for I want to ketch 'em all three, and we'll save the gal. And,' says he, ' we'll have to work mighty particular.'

" Well, and so we did, you may depend. For, soon as daylight come through the trees we hitched up and started, and kept on purty brisk, till the sun begin to get on my back like.

" Byme by, Capt. Wood looks back, he says, ' now boys I know where I am.' I once killed a big buck right long this holler, and that den is about one mile over yonder, and so he went ahead. Presently he says, ' now boys stop here.' Hold my horse. I am goin' to creep up now; don't you see that cabin there? and don't you see there's a little smoke comin' out of the chimney? but, says he, I must see if my rifle's all right, and my powder all right, and pick my flint; and, you boys, must do the same.' Says I, ' very well, captain.'

"And, so he goes creepin', and creepin', and then stops, and peeps over the little hills like. Then, here he comes, runnin' strait back, jumpin' like a skared wolf; and, says he, ' boys they're all there, the poor gal and all! Now, we must have some fun. Well, says I, if Ben. Rust does'nt make them devlish Tories dance, this day, then Polly Rust is not his mamma.'

" ' Capt. Wood, how'll we proceed to business,' says I.

" ' Peter Radford,' says I, ' how do you feel? did you ever see a Tory dance?'

" ' No,' says he, ' I don't know as I did; but I've seen

WAR OF INDEPENDENCE.   131

'em run, and I'm thinkin' if we ain't cautious, and get to
the door before they see us, they'll run, too, and we'll
loose 'em at last, one or more of 'em.'

" ' Well, Pete, we must take care not to give 'em a chance
for that,' says the brave captain. 'We must, in the first
place, creep very near to the back part of the cabin.
Peter, you must stop right still, when I say 'Harriet.'
Ben, will then follow right after me up to the door, and,
if I am shot down, he must rush right in and hallo for
you, and you'll come, of course, and shoot, or do any
thing you can to catch the villains, and save the gal.
Now, come on, boys.'

"And so Peter and I tracked right after the captain.
He crept round to the side, like, of the old cabin. He
stopped a little, looked around at Pete and me, and then
said, ' Harriet,' and made two or three jumps in, right at
the door. I followed close behind him. The Tories all
kitched up their guns, and run to the door, too, and says,
what do you want ?'

" Capt. Wood says, ' I want you and must have you
quick.'

" Jed. Burk, attempted to jump by us through the
door; but the captain punched him on the side of his
head with the muzzle of his heavy rifle, and he fell back
into the cabin. Then Sam Jenkins tried it, but had no
better luck. Simonds fired his gun—just missed the
Captain's head, and shot through my left hand thumb.
He then tried to break out of the door; but with my
right fist, I tapped him on the side of his neck, and he
fell to one side. By this, Capt. Wood, was down on
Burk and Jenkins, and with one foot on Burk's breast,
and 'tother on the throat of Jenkins, hollering loud for
Pete to run and bring a rope from his saddle-bags.
Quick Pete was there with it. I had'nt more than
doubled a lick or two on Simonds, before he began to
cry loud and long for quarters. I give him a stamp or
two more on his cussed black Dutch head, and told him

132   LEGENDS OF THE

if he did'nt be still, I'de kill him right away.   He laid
right still, ha! ha! ha!   But I believe he couldn't do
any better; for I had let him have my heavy boot heels
on his neck and breast purty smart.   ' Now,' says I, ' you
black Dutch devil, where's the poor gal you stole and
killed ? '

"Says he, ' O! I kilt no gal, Mr. Rust—there's Harriet, now lyin' in the corner.'

"Sure enough, there she was just opening her eyes
from sleep-like; and tied by the hands crossed behind
her to a big log in the corner of the room, most dead!
I jist kitched Jake Simonds by his long hair on his black
Dutch head, with my left hand, and dragged him right
up to where she lay tied, and with my right lifted her
up.   She could hardly stand.   I soon cut her loose, and
the poor gal kitched me round the neck, and said, ' Is
this you, Ben Rust ? ' and began to kiss me, ha! ha!
haw! haw!   Says I, ' not now, Harriet—not now.'

" By this time, Capt. Wood and Peter, had t'other two
rascals tied fast together.

"Says I, ' Pete, bring my halter from my horse's neck
to tie this Dutchman ! '

" He soon brought it, and mighty quick I had him tied
snug enough.   Harriet had by this time run to Captain
Wood, fell down on her knees to pray, like, and thank
God that he had at last sent us to deliver her.   I thought
all the time it was I and Capt. Wood, and Pete had done
it.

" Well, now, friends, the best part is got to come yet.
Says Capt. Wood, says he, ' Boys what shall we do next ?'
Now, I say, says he, ' hang these fellers right away.'
But, says he, ' we hav'nt rope enough, nor is what we
have strong enough.'

" ' Law,' says I, ' Captain, that's easy told ; for I seede
plenty of purty grape vines as I cumed along down by
the last branch we crossed, and thought then, they'd do
very well to hang a dog with.   Well, I can soon get some

of them, if we can do no better.' The villains looked mighty bad and sheepish.

"I said to Burk, ' You white-eye Irish devil, what did you steal this poor gal for, and sarve her so?'

" ' Faith, an' your honor, Misthur Rust, you'll plaze ax Jeak Simonds for the likes o' that. He tould us the gal scorned him, and wad ha' neithen' till say to the likes o' him, and he'de die or have her all to himsel'; an' so Jenkins and mesel' coomed along.'

" ' Yes,' says I, 1 says ' Capt. Wood and I'll soon make you all dance for cumin' along. You'll be mighty apt to go along purty quick, as well as eum. And now, Captain, says I, I'm just ready to go and get the grape vines if you say so? And off I and Pete puts. Soon we brings four nice long ones.'

" ' These three will do,' said Pete; if one don't brake, and so he pulled down another proper one right away; we trimmed 'em, and I had 'em at the door, lively—and I says, ' Now for it, Captain.'

" He says, says he, ' we'll take Jake fust.'

" ' Very well,' says I.

"So Jake begins to cry and holler, ' myne Cot, hab marcy—Jake bees no mo' Tory, no ryaller mo'; Jake stealsh no mo' galsh; me beeze cood vig all de time.'

" ' Ah! ha!' says I, ' we know you'll steal no more gals, and this purty nice grape vine will make you a cood vig, as you call it.'

" By this time, I puts the grape vine in a slick running noose, as folks call 'em, and pulled him right out of the door and under the scaffold pole, put there for the hunters to hang their bucks upon of nights, to keep 'em from the dogs—high enough, too, to swing Jake and the rest of 'em on. Pete runs upon the cabin and out on the pole like a cat, and says he, ' now throw up 'tother end.' Up it went, quick he ties it. 'And now," says I, ' here goes.'

" ' Shtop a leetle,' says Jake.

" ' Stop,' says I, what for?

134   LEGENDS OF THE

" ' Jake steals no mo' galshs—no mo' 'orses—no mo' nuttin' ! '

" ' Yes,' says I, ' them's my rail sentiments, and so here goes ! '

" Swings back and forth, jist like the pendelum of another old Dutch clock, he did.'

" ' And now,' says I, I says, ' Captain, fetch on 'tother ; I don't care if you fetch all on 'em, for I jist thought they'd all look purty dancin' together up there,' and they did purty quick, I tell you.

" ' Ha ! ha ! ' says Pete, ' now you all go it right.'

" All of us then got off very quick, left 'em swingin' and crossin', and crossin' and swingin', and that night took poor little Harriet to widda Eskridge. I seede her mama come and meet her ; and I don't want any more to see a gal took back to her mama, I tell you.' "

" If thou tell'st this heavy story right,
    Upon my soul the hearers will shed tears."

" I'll say of it, it tutors nature : artificial strife
    Lives in these touches, livelier than life."

"Mad world, mad kings, mad composition."

"If it be aught toward the general good,
    Let honor in one eye, and death i' the other,
And I will look both indifferently ;
    For let the gods so speed, as I love
The name of honor, more than I fear death."—

Shakspeare.

CHAPTER XII.

The attack upon and murder of Capt. Jno. Wood by twelve Tories, sent forth by Col. Ferguson of the British army to destroy him—His burial by his son.

" He was a man ;
The which, no sooner had his prowess confirmed
In the unshrinking station where he fought,
But like a man he died."

Macbeth, Act V., Scene 7.

We have had occasion already several times to introduce in our remarks Capt. John Wood, and sufficient, perhaps, has been said to acquaint the reader with the general bent of his character and disposition. Of his patriotism none could doubt. Few men ever rendered more efficient partizan services to his country and more effectual checks to the mischievous Tories that so abundantly lived in his quarter of the colony. The consequence was, that he was the object of their greatest terror and most deadly hatred.

In a former page we spoke of his surprising vigilance and untiring perseverance in pursuing them and hunting them down, to bring them to punishment for offences against the peace and safety of the Whig families in any of the counties contiguous to his home. Of this, indubitable evidence is given in the manly feat narrated in the last preceding pages. Not a few others of like import could be furnished, but at present, at least, we will not enlarge farther than to remark, that a very remarkable amount of ubiquity seemed to characterize his daring intrepidity of action and usefulness during the three years he lived after the commencement of the war. For it was a matter of wonder to all who knew him—and

136   LEGENDS OF THE

they were many in all parts of North and South Carolina as well as in much of Virginia and Georgia—how
rapidly he would visit most of the neighborhoods of some
eight or ten counties in the two Carolinas and never
seem to be out of his own. Was there a theft, a murder,
or any other act of rapine perpetrated by small parties of
Tories, British or Indians, instantly he was appealed to,
his aid sought to pursue them, and his assistance by personal effort or the most effectual counsel and advice freely
given. Frequently, also, he would be found in the armies of the Whigs, conversing with the officers in the
most familiar terms. They all knew and highly appreciated his character, for the most indomitable courage and
military capacity ; often proffered commissions to him to
command in their divisions, if he would accept ; but
which he invariably declined, saying he was sure he
could do more good in his predatory mode of conducting
the war, than in any position he could take and confine
himself to particular portions of the army, or its operations. He on several occasions, fought bravely in battles
under Sumpter, Green, and Marion, and was regarded as
invulnerable to balls or bayonets.

Often his friends admonished him of the great risks he
incurred in his rapid movements, traversing through the
country at all hours of the day, and sometimes night, in
the most perilous pursuits of and encounters with the Tories. He always responded by the trite and almost silly
answer, he " would'nt die before his time came."

Alas, noble Whig! unfortunately for thee, thy country,
and especially thy most amiable family ! it came too
speedily ; and in most merciless and cruel form ! He
had but the night before, returned from one of his rapid tours through the country and a visit to the army.
At about two o'clock in the evening, sitting in his chamber with his excellent lady, his two daughters, Rosa and
Susan, and his youngest son, Henry, about fourteen years
old, his servant-woman sprang into the room and

said, "there is a great number of men coming to the house, all with guns, and some running." The Captain had barely time to leap toward his rifle, sitting in the corner of the chamber, before two of them entered the door and rushed upon him in great fury. Not having time to raise it and shoot, so swiftly did they approach, he could use it no other way than with great force upon the head of one of them, striking him a most deadly blow, smiting him to the floor, and crushing in the upper part of his skull. Instantly the room was filled with them, and four or five leaped at and upon him, like so many tigers; one of them stabbing him in the side with a large bear or butcher knife; they at last overcome and bore him from the house into the yard, where they at first proposed to shoot or hang him. Most terrible indeed was this scene to his family. Mrs. Wood and Rosa immediately fainted, and the latter seemed never to revive. Susan, less nervous and sensitive than her sister, only ran from place to place in the house screaming and weeping, as if deranged. Most of the servants, white and black, were at a distance, on the farm, as also Frank, the eldest son, of whom we have heretofore spoken, now eighteen years of age. Having heard, however, the loud talking and screaming at the house, he, with several of the hirelings, ran in great haste and reached the yard enclosure, just as four of the gang with his father in their arms, were bearing him out-side, and proceeding to a thick grove of timber, hard by. The white men all in a moment entered the dwelling and closed the doors. But the brave boy, Frank, at first followed the desperate villains till three of them that were walking by the side of the men carrying off his father, lifted their guns and swore if he attempted to follow they would instantly shoot him. He was wholly unarmed, and recognizing most of the men as Tories he knew to be of the most despicable and desperate charcter, he halted, concluding it would be futile for him to attempt, thus alone, to rescue his father, he turned and ran in another direction, yet determined to see what they should do to his beloved father. So into the woods he also entered, circled around in the direction they were taking, and when they stopped at the distance of about four hundred yards from the house, he crept as near to them as practicable, without being discovered, and hid himself in a thick cluster of small pines, and some fallen timber; still near enough to witness the heart-rending scene, and sometimes to hear distinctly many of the words spoken and conversation held with him, before they murdered him. He saw these brutal murderers strip and bind his parent to a large tree and with hickory rods quickly gathered from the thicket at hand, whip him till his lacerated back in a hundred streams poured forth the tides of life. He spoke not a word to deprecate their fiendish wrath in the least. But when with the most bitter blasphemies and curses he was told by one of them, they would thus make his torments atone for the lives of the many royalists he had hung and shot," with a look of insuperable scorn, and a voice of terrific fearlessness, he answered:

"But it has taken twelve of you Tory thieves, murderers, and dogs to accomplish it! Now hear me, and mark what I say. Nick Simonds, there is one, thank God, who, though not here, and does not witness his father's tortures, will, though now a boy, visit these cruelties a hundred fold on you and your despicable clans ere he will consent to sleep in his grave in peace." Then lifting up his eyes toward Heaven, and crying with a loud voice, "My God, my family, my country!" his head fell upon his breast, and he spoke no more. Nick Simonds, as he ceased to utter this dread threat and prophecy, seized his rifle, presented it at the bosom of the dead or dying man, in the act of firing, when Bill Earnest, one of the gang, said to him, pushing up the muzzle of the gun:

"Nick Zimanst, vat for youst shoot te tead manst—he tead—he speakst no mo' agins?"

Instantly these horrid savages cut loose the cords by which his hands were bound around the tree, and finding him totally dead, threw his body unceremoniously into a heap of brush, formed by the top of a large fallen tree; prepared to depart and soon disappeared from the sight of the agonized son. Going off they passed nearer still to where Frank lay concealed. Mike Stalcup said to Nick Simonds walking by his side:

"Well, we've done a good day's work arter all, in killin' that d—d rebel. I thought he would kill two or three on us any how, if we got into a scuffle wid 'em; but did'nt he hit that Irish bugger, Jim Follis, a tarrable lick now?—I gosh, he jist mashed in his whole head, and made the brains fly proper."

"Ah, he did!" said Nick, "but vee's cum in too fast for 'um, and I reckin we strung 'um 'bout right den. Do ye dink, Col. Vargerson, (Ferguson) vat gib de vifty ginnis for dis vork, vill gib us te ode vun hunthred and vifty for dis vork—vell I gish dwenty for dis time. Diebel, vat for dat vig hang Jake, and gist caize him dake de gal to de hunter's cabin? Ah, ha, he gits stick mit mine knife for dat, and very much vipping, too py tam."

"O! I reckon Col. Ferguson 'ill pay it all right," said Stalcup. "He said he would; if he don't, Col. Tarlton or Gen. Clinton will, I know—somebody's got to cum it."

Thus conversing, they passed beyond the hearing and from the sight of young Wood.

When these two heartless scoundrels were thus talking, moving slowly past him, still hid in the pine thicket, the other nine being considerably in the advance, and out of sight, he could scarcely restrain himself, armed as they were, and, notwithstanding he had nothing but a small pocket knife, from rushing out upon them and striving at once to revenge his father's cruel death upon their miscreant heads. But his father's dying words and prophecy were still ringing in his ears, and thrilling his aching heart. He felt convinced it was of himself he spoke and relied on him to avenge his death. He therefore resolved to avoid the hazard and consider how he should accomplish it. Soon after they had all disappeared he rose from the place, and ran to the spot where he saw them cast his poor father's gory corse. In all the agony of a distracted and terribly tortured mind, and wounded heart, he drew it forth from the brush heap, and having again and again embraced it, yet warm and bathed in blood, still trickling from a thousand wounds, he gently laid it down and ran to the house to seek assistance to remove it. All had fled, or been forced away! Mother, sisters and servants, all had disappeared! The imagination, however, highly wrought, could not justly depict, in words sufficiently eloquent, the horror that then possessed his soul! Had those dreadful men whose guilty hands were freshly steeped in the life's blood of his murdered father, passed by and borne them all off to share his fate, or even one more horrible and terrible? Or had an equally desperate clan borne off his beloved mother and beautiful sisters, to subject them to the loathsome fate of dozens in the country, of whom he had heard? Horrible thoughts! unspeakable agonies for a time destroyed all power of action, and enchained him in dread consternation. But the reader will presently learn, that all this, upon the heart and mind of this young man, whose earliest dreams as well as thoughts of life, had been filled, and it seemed feasted with tales and visions of human suffering and of blood, was but as the chafing of the chained or caged lion, the better to prepare him to be ushered into the bloody amphitheatre, and the more certainly and furiously to tear and destroy the doomed victims of barbarous Rome. Astounded and paralyzed for a short time, he prostrated himself upon the green sod of his father's yard, rolled from side to side in unutterable grief, shedding, however, not a tear, although enveloped

WAR OF INDEPENDENCE. 141

and steeped in tortures almost infernal! Suddenly, however, he sprang up, rushed to his mother's chamber door, pushed it open, leaped in, saw the body of the Tory killed by his father in the attack first made, and by its side his father's and the dead Tory's rifles. He passed hastily from room to room of the dwelling, returned to the chamber, and stood for a moment in the midst of silence profound. Then recollecting for the first time he had left his parent's corpse upon the ground, exposed to be abused by hogs and other depredating animals, he determined instantly upon burying it as well as he could, unable to place it more securely. He sought on the premises for tools to excavate the grave. In the garden he found a mattock and spade, and with them hastened where he had left all that remained on earth of his heroic sire.

By this time night had begun to spread its dark mantle over earth and sky; but the moon, which had risen at or a little before sunset, had driven her peaceful chariot upon an unclouded heaven for more than two hours above the horizon, sheding forth her softest and clearest light, before the deep, long grave was completed. Then this heroic young Wood turned to his father's lifeless corpse, which lay near at hand, and falling upon its cold breast, still bare as the base scourgers had left it, and in the gushing tides of filial affection he laid his throbbing head upon that cold bosom, called upon God, holy angels, and the departed spirit of his father, to witness the vow he then made—in the dying words and prophecy of that parent—never to rest satisfied till he had wreaked a just and full vengeance upon the eleven that stabbed and scourged him to death, or as many more of the Tories!

Reader, could you have listened to the entire detail of that most tragic narrative flowing from the lips of that very son—could you have seen those fury-flashing eyes, distorted countenance and clenched teeth, as did the writer see that son, then grown old and decrepid, and whose head was then whitened by the frosts of many winters, entering, as he told the story, into all the thrilling feelings and sentiments that, at the first, filled his soul with anguish and vengeance—acting and gesticulating as at first those feelings and sentiments naturally prompted and dictated,—aye, if you never before had conceived and fully comprehended the extent and climax of fallen and corrupted human passion and rage, you would then have had it fully and most vividly exhibited before you.

But then had he verified his father's prophecy? and had he fulfilled his own dreadful vow? This we will in a future chapter disclose.

Child of the brave, hear the echo of glory,
    That breaks from the hills of our country now free;
And the voice of our fathers, immortal in story,
    Which speaks in the lessons of heroes to thee.

The sound of the battle I heard on the mountain,
    The foe-men I saw—Oh, our fathers were there!
I saw their red blood as it gushed like a fountain;
    But what is the echo of glory?—and where?

'Tis the sound of the war-song we learn'd from our mothers,
    The war-song of heroes who bled to be free;
'Tis the echo we heard on the hills with our brothers,
    That speaks as the voice of the thunder to thee.

O, soft are the breezes that play 'round their tombs!
And sweet with the violet's wafted perfumes,
        With lillies and jessamines rare;
The traveler, outworn with life's pilgrimage dreary,
Lays down his rúde staff, like one that is weary,
        And sweetly reposes, forever there.

WAR OF INDEPENDENCE.   143

CHAPTER XIII.

Parson Frazier again—His return to the neighborhood of Elder
    Brame—His courtship and marriage with the rich, young, and
    accomplished Virginia lady, Miss Happy Thompson, and their
    settlement upon a portion of her fine estate at Hillsboro', North
    Carolina, together with other interesting touches of Virginia gal-
    lantry and courtship in the Old Dominion.

" They say, all lovers swear more performance than they are able,
and yet reserve an ability that they never perform; vowing more than
the perfection of ten, and discharging less than the tenth part of
one. They that have the voice of lions and the action of hares, are
they not monsters?"—*Troilus and Cressida, Act III., Scene 2.*

ALL will remember the eloquent Rev. Mr. James Frazier and his appointment to preach again at the Reedy
Church the Sabbath week following the day of his parting with Elder Brame and family at Hanover Town. A
general notice throughout Caroline and Hanover counties
had been given of the meeting, and on the day when he
came to fulfill it he found a large assemblage of the people of all classes and sexes. Elder Brame, Miss Happy
Thompson, his ward, and his two daughters, Amy and
Sarah, met the reverend gentleman. Miss Mary Brame
and Miss Elizabeth Thompson declined accompanying
them, agreeing and remarking, " they had no need of a
lecture on love affairs or obligations at that time, and
they would rather not have one from the Rev. Doctor
Frazier at any time."

" Oh, ho, sister," said Miss Happy Thompson, "I
suppose you and Cousin Mary are reserving yourselves to
be the more attentive auditors of the lectures on those
subjects to be addressed to sister Elizabeth in the love-
sick, sighing, and weeping pathos of Capt. Martin Haw-

kins, and Cousin Mary, when the highly cultivated and sentimental Mr. James Smith, is the orator."

" Well. Cousin Happy," said Mary very playfully and a little sarcastically, " I trust in either case the text will not be the fits and starts of a poney bewitched, and a famishing Ruth."

" Come, come," said Elder Brame, scarcely refraining from a loud laugh himself, " your sportiveness is little suited to the reverence due the Sabbath day. But it's just like you, my little girl; you cannot forego your wit whoever or whatever may be the subject of it."

" Ah! never mind, Uncle," said Happy; " I love to witness the playful wit of my Cousin Mary, even if I am myself the victim of it."

The sermon of Mr. Frazier being over, and obtaining very general approbation and applause from his audience, as was expected, he accompanied the Elder and the ladies on their return, and to dinner. It was generally said that his effort of that day was very creditable,—sustaining fully the reputation which had preceded him before his visit to the Old Dominion, from North Carolina and Pennsylvania. The learned Mr. James Smith, however, hinted in a conversation with the Elder a few days after, that he thought it was very materially, and rather too much so—as he forgot to give credit for them—made up of quotations from sermons of the Rev. Doctor Blair, of Scotland, and the famed Dr. Tillotson of England. However, he thought it was all very well and eloquently delivered.

Gregory Baynham, who was present, also said: " For my part I confess, in the matter of the sermon, I was a little disappointed. I expected it would be chiefly employed in the discussion of matrimony as an important religious duty, and as beautifully illustrative in some way of God's eternal election and foreordination. I reckon, however, those distinguished divines, Blair and Tillotson, had neither of them been captivated with a fair, young and wealthy heiress, and therefore put nothing of the sort in their sermons,—ha, ha, ha, ho! Well, I should like to hear what Miss Happy thinks on the subject, anyway."

By the by, it was pretty well understood among the most observant and 'cute of the family that Mr. Baynham himself had been thinking for the last three years of the pretty Miss Happy Thompson, and had rather desired to administer upon her fine estate of fifteen or twenty negroes, twelve hundred pounds in cash, and many hundreds of acres in Virginia and North Carolina. He had even ventured so far as to ask her faithful old servant, Cyrus, what he thought of the match; and had actually, on one occasion, sighed twice, and then seemed to sit in a brown study for the space of ten minutes or more, looking most despondent. Indeed, he repeated what he either some how learned from Campbell, or Campbell from him:

> "The world was sad! the garden was a wild!
> And man, the hermit, sighed—till woman smiled!"

Farther than this, he certainly never ventured to make known to Miss Happy, in any way, his sorrows. After she was married, nevertheless, he was heard to say, "well, I could ha' got her, if I had a wanted to!" A pretty common lullaby, *that*, of all old "batcheldors."— At all events, all concluded who had the least notion of the current of Mr. Baynham's sentiments toward Miss Happy Thompson, he was not the most impartial judge of the Scotch parson's merits, in or out of the pulpit.

The parson, notwithstanding the gibes and jokes which often passed between the members and visitors of the pleasant old Virginia household of the pious old Elder, by whom and his meek and quiet old lady he was treated with marked respect and hospitality, passed his time in great apparent comfort and cheerfulness for four or five days. Sometimes he entertained himself in culling over the somewhat carefully selected, but small library of the good Elder; and sometimes in hastily snatched *tête-à-têtes* with Miss Happy Thompson; or joining in with the young ladies and their visitors in the plays introduced in the evening after supper,—blind man's buff, &c., with great hilarity and zest; faithfully complying with all the penalties inflicted in the redemption of pawns; particularly manifesting delight when sentenced to administer to Miss Happy sundry kisses by way of punishment for some delinquency or other. They took walks, jaunts on horses to the river banks, and other of the more entertaining scenes of the neighborhood. And whatever were the precise conversations between the reverend gentleman and the young lady, the result was that he felt himself authorized to address her uncle and guardian on the subject of their union; prefacing his remarks, however, by saying that before anything in the way of a consummation of that union could be effected, he should be compelled to return to North Carolina on very important business, which had in good part arisen there since he left, and might prolong his stay for five or six weeks.

Mr. Brame, after a short time spent in deliberation, spoke with great seriousness of his affection for, and duty toward his niece; enquired of the gentleman if he had been authorized by her thus to address him on the subject; spoke of her as the eldest daughter of his deceased and long lost sister, and of his brother-in-law, also no more; that Miss Thompson was heir to a beautiful estate, estimated as being worth at least fifteen thousand pounds, and in every way near and dear to himself and family. " Besides," said he, " to me and all of us, my dear sir, except as it regards your ministerial relations to our Church, and the satisfactory vouchers you hold in that respect, you are almost altogether a stranger. Now, while in reference to ordinary matters in or out of Church, those testimonials would be esteemed every way sufficient, yet upon the very serious and solemn subject on which you have addressed me, they seem to me not altogether satis-

WAR OF INDEPENDENCE. 147

factory. There is, I am fully persuaded, about to come upon this country trials and exigencies of a nature, both in respect to its civil, political and religious relations, of a peculiar character, and you must pardon me when I tell you, it would be a source of very great disquietude of mind to have, even in that way, any one connected with my family, and my niece dependant upon such an one, likely to be an enemy to the vital interests of this beautiful land; or who would countenance, or in any degree favor the course now being pursued by the king, ministers, and parliament. The Scotch," he somewhat more pleasantly continued, "in this country, very generally side with the king, and seem, with scarcely one exception, to condemn and denounce the course of the people in Boston and other places, in evading and defeating the king and his officials. Now, although I hope for better things in you, yet I do not know your sentiments nor views upon these subjects."

As the Elder ceased these very candid and rather extended remarks, in some degree of embarrassment and perturbation of mind Mr. Frazier rose and walked without saying a word, or even looking at Mr. Brame, in a somewhat hurried step, five or six times from end to end of the parlor in which they were seated. He then turned to him and said:

"You altogether surprise me, sir! Miss Thompson's estate is estimated at fifteen thousand pounds! This truly embarrasses me! I would far rather that she was much poorer in that respect, lest some should think the fortune has attracted me, instead of the lady. Now as it respects your want of a sufficient acquaintance with me, that could be easily remedied in a letter from Governor Joseph Martin, the royal Governor of the province of North Carolina, and his Secretary, Wm. Fenton, both of whom I have long and intimately known, as well as a goodly number of others who, I am assured, would unite in recommending me as a gentleman worthy of your re-

148   LEGENDS OF THE

gard any moment I would ask them.   But I presume, brother Brame, that can scarcely be necessary."

"Parson Frazier," said the Elder, "I am a plain blunt
man; sometimes I fear a little too much so.   I am, I
trust, an honest man, and therefore in this matter, where
the future well-being of my niece is so importantly involved, I think that I, as her uncle and guardian, should
be very particular.   Our acquaintance with you has been
very brief indeed; an ordinary prudence would say entirely too brief for so solemn an engagement as the one
you propose.   You refer me, however, to letters of recommendation from Governor Martin, the royal Governor of
North Carolina, and others who you say are your intimate
acquaintances, and who, you are assured, would speak
in the most favorable terms of your character, &c., and
judge this can scarcely be required?   Yet permit me to
say to you, I think differently.   My father used often to
say, ' caution is the parent of safety.'   But, Mr. Frazier,
did you not speak of the letters of recommendation of
Governor Martin and his secretary?   Now, is this the
Governor Jo. Martin of North Carolina, who sent forth
that precious and most abusive proclamation against the
people generally of that province, and particularly the
convention at Charlotte, who declared independence, as
well as the provincial Congress at Hillsboro'?   Because,
I just say, parson, if it be that man you refer to, I would
not regard his recommendation or commendation a fig in
your behalf.   His undignified language and billingsgate
denunciations in those bullying proclamations settle with
me the sort of man he is.   And so he is your intimate
friend and acquaintance, is he?"

"O yes, Mr. Brame, it is Governor or Joseph Martin
of that province, I spoke of, and his secretary,—ah, to be
sure, he *was* one of my most particular friends before we
met in America, and—and—I—I—did not know you did
not know him.   Well, well, I fell out with him, too, a
little, for his proclamations; I—I think he was a little

too strenuous in objecting to the people assembling themselves together, in any case. For, certainly, Elder Brame, they have the right to come together to petition his most gracious majesty for the redress of grievances, and such like. But I am quite of his opinion on the subject of the divine right of the king and his magistrates. Ah, sir, don't you think he was right in that?"

"No, sir," said the elder. "But, Mr. Frazier, I shall not engage in any argument with you on the subject. I do not see that that is pertinent to the object of our present conversation. I asked you sometime since if you had permission of my niece to address me on the subject of your marriage? please explain, sir."

"Oh, yes, yes, Bro. Brame, the little angel gave her full consent! ah! yes, yes "—

"Well, sir, I confess myself," said the elder, "by no means competent to the controlling of the will or actions of angels, and shall doubt very much whether in this case any angel is involved; but as I feel the happiness for life of a very amiable niece and ward is hazarded in this affair, I desire to act with becoming prudence, so far as I am concerned. I must request, therefore, that I may be excused from giving you a definite answer till I can see and converse with Miss Thompson in respect to it. And while I say to you, I will not now consent to your wishes, nor deny my consent, I will not employ any undue influences to dissuade her from what she may have determined upon. She is certainly, still, so far as the law is concerned, subject to my guardianship. But as she is also old enough to think and choose for herself in these matters, I shall by no means interpose my authority against her deliberate determination."

The parson responded, he at all events hoped that his intimacy with Governor Martin and other of his Majesty's officers in the colonies, and claiming them as his special friends, would not be made to operate against

150   LEGENDS OF THE

him—especially as their intimacy and mutual friendship
was not of a political character; "for I assure you,"
said he, "we are very much at odds on politics. I, sir,
can never be anything but an American in heart and
feeling, let what may come to pass!"

They separated. The elder only remarking he would
have a further conversation with him at three o'clock in
the evening.

Mr. Brame repaired in a few minutes to the chamber
of his lady; informed her of the purport of the conversation just had with the reverend Scotchman, and of the
difficulties with which his own mind had been perplexed
on the subject of the suitableness of the match proposed
for his young and much beloved niece. He told her he
was free to acknowledge Mr. Frazier a highly cultivated
and accomplished scholar, an ingenious debater, and
pretty sound in theory as a preacher of the gospel. But
of his personal habits and character he was certainly not
assured or satisfied. He spoke to her in great warmth
of affection for the dear girl; of her excellent qualities of
mind and disposition; her undeviating compliance with
all his requirements and commands as her guardian, and
oft-repeated acts of kindness and affection toward himself
and all the family as relations. He said she had always
been for her own merits' sake very dear to him, especially as she so much favored his long lost sister, her
mother. But he said, since under the preaching of Mr.
Wesley she became aroused to a sense of her condition as
a sinner before God, and had so earnestly sought for religion and had been converted by the grace of God, to experience His power to save, she had become doubly
dear to him. But still with all these endearing qualties,
and notwithstanding her finely educated mind, she was
young and very inexperienced, confiding in and unsus-
pecting of the teaching of others, while with the strong
allurements of her ample estate actuating mere mercena-

WAR OF INDEPENDENCE. 151

ries most powerfully by the most specious appliances and studied schemes to engage her affections and grasp her riches, she was liable to become their victim.

At these remarks of the venerable elder, his meek and very affectionate wife, who loved Happy and sister Elizabeth, her foster-children, with all the tenderness and solicitude of a fond mother, became excited to tears of real joy, in the words of praise and approbation bestowed on her favorite Happy, by her much loved husband; and after having for a short space indulged in those feelings of maternal gratification, recapitulating in her own mind her husband's words, she was awakened to the apprehension, that he himself entertained doubts of the character of the parson, and the confidence to be reposed in his future integrity of purpose and propriety of conduct.

"Dear me," she said, "Mr. Brame, can it be possible that you doubt Mr. Frazier's real character, and look upon him as a mere adventurer and matrimonial speculator? O! my, my! Can it be possible you fear he is such a character?"

"Oh!" he replied, "it may be not quite so bad as that. But I freely confess that I am not satisfied with him in these respects either. Beside, wife, you know my views in regard to the contests now growing daily more and more certain to result in a general and bloody war, between the colonies of America and the mother country; and that I have had and frequently expressed to you doubts, whether any man, irreligious or even pious, can for a moment in any degree approve and sanction the course of the king, ministry and parliament, in regard to America, and be an honest and sincere man, in anything. Such still are my doubts. Upon mentioning my want of knowledge of his character and past conduct, in our conversation this morning, and fearful of the effects likely to result in reference to all in this country, from the collisions now existing with England; also of my most unqualified approval of the former and condemnation of the latter; he protested he was a true friend to his adopted country, and could not be anything else but an American in heart and soul. But yet, when he undertook to give me references for the past propriety of his character and conduct, he could give none but the royal Governor of North Carolina, Joseph Martin, and a few other crown officers, who were his most particular friends and acquaintances. When, however, I mentioned that fact to him, he sought to avoid its force against him by saying those friends and he had fallen out on the subject of politics, and differed by great odds; and so we parted, —I promising him to converse with him again on the subject this evening at three o'clock. In truth, I cannot help remembering the old Spanish adage—'tell me the company you keep and I'll tell you the man you are.'"

"Well, my husband," said Mrs. Brame, "what have you determined to do in this matter? Our dear Happy is nearly of age—capable of choosing for herself. We know that her judgment is upon subjects within her knowledge or experience, very good, and that on all occasions and in respect to all persons, especially ourselves, her conduct is uniformly amiable and kind. But, indeed, I apprehend, if the dear child has determined upon this union, and her affections are involved, even at the present but slightly, kind treatment and gentle means may do something; but the contrary, more harm than good."

"Indeed, Mary, I think so, too," he replied. "Please however, converse with her yourself as soon as convenient, and then ask the child to come here, and I will talk to her also. What is to be said or done on the subject must be done quickly, as I suppose I must say yea or nay this evening."

Mrs. Brame immediately repaired to the room of her niece, told her the nature of the interview she had just had with her uncle, and asked if she had consented to the parson's addressing her uncle on the subject of their marriage, &c.

In great frankness Miss Happy answered that she had; and expressed many regrets that she was so unfortunate as not to meet with her uncle's approval in the matter. She then threw her arms around the neck of her kind foster-mother and burst into a flood of tears; kissing the cheek of her aunt, she began to speak of the great debt she owed to her and her uncle for all their innumerable manifestations of kindness and parental affection toward herself, her sister and her brother, reared by them from very tender years; spoke most pathetically of the pain it must forever give her to disoblige them, but stated that she had learned from Mr. Frazier the difficulties presented by her guardian, and as she deemed them, though altogether sincere, still not sufficient. She thought she should so regard them, and act accordingly.

Her gentle tempered aunt, often returning in the most affectionate manner her niece's caresses, rose, and without urging the beautiful girl in the least degree to alter her determination,—only saying it was her uncle's request she would see him in his chamber as soon as convenient, retired. In a few minutes Miss Thompson, in obedience to the summons from her uncle, entered her aunt's chamber, found him sitting alone. He rose and led her to a chair as she entered, and was for a moment or two not a little embarrassed by observing the rapid tides of feeling and sentiment coursing through her entire being, and her blushes coming and going. Presently, however, he spoke to her, and in tones the most gentle and affectionate, told her of the conversation with Mr. Frazier, what were his fears, doubts, and apprehensions, and of the pain he experienced in seeming, even in any way, to thwart her wishes. He said he should not, if she declared to him she had deliberately determined upon giving her hand to Mr. F., oppose her wishes.

Blushing very deeply, but yet with a voice of much distinctness and firmness she said: "I have learned, uncle, from Mr. F., the general purport, I suppose, of your objections, and have considered them over with all the deliberation and calmness of which I am capable ; yet with the highest regard and deference for your opinions upon this or any other subject, I must take the liberty to say, they do not seem to be substantial and overruling in their nature, and have, there ore, concluded, by your permission, to fulfill my engagement ; and I ask the kindness of your so informing Mr. F. in your interview this evening."

She then burst into tears. Her uncle gazed upon her for some minutes in silence, and with a most affectionate look, told with unmistakable force the admiration and parental regard he entertained for her. In soothing tones he declared how much he desired her happiness, and determination, as far as he was able, to do everything calculated to make it perfect."

" But, my dear niece, did the gentleman tell to you one of my difficulties ?—that I feared he, like almost all his countrymen in this country, favored and would, in the event of a revolution to take place in resisting British oppression, be found on the side of the enemies of America—did he speak of this, my child ?"

" No, sir," she said, " I never heard or thought of such a thing before, and cannot but hope it is not the case. Of course, uncle, it would not be expected that I should understand the whole matter in controversy, between the colonies and the mother country. I should say I do not. But this much I do comprehend : on the one hand is my native blessed America, and on the other a foreign land and people. I am, I feel, for my country, now and forever ; and I freely declare, if a gentleman seeks my hand, who is not my country's friend, that fact would be very far from being a recommendation, if it did not constitute an insuperable objection. But, my dear uncle, is it so ? Have you indubitable proof that Mr. F., is like the rest of his countrymen?" "O no, my child, I have not. He very roundly denies it ; and says he has quarreled with his best friends, the royalists, in North Carolina, about it. I hope also, when the trial comes it may not be so. And, my dear Happy, I shall say to the reverend gentleman at once, in this evening's conversation—although, I confess, there seems to me something wrong in this hasty engagement—I will make no further objection, and shall commit the whole matter to the providence of God, and pray for your mutual happiness in time and eternity."

Then kissing her blushing cheek, he left her to make her way back to her chamber, which she soon attempted; but having to pass the parlor door, she was seen by her sister and cousin, Mary and Sarah Brame, who, with Mr. Martin Hawkins and Gregory Baynham, had but just returned from a brief visit to the family of a relative, Mr. R. Wyatte, at the White Chimneys; and who all joined to insist that she should come in and account for herself in not being found, either her or the parson, when they were preparing for the ride, and desired so much to have them along, to enjoy the trip.

"Oh, come, Sarah Brame, said Mary, let cousin Happy alone about that, for I learn since we've got back, that Happy was engaged in the more important matter of arranging all the preliminaries of the transfer of her whole fortune, lands, negroes, pounds, shillings, and pence. Nay, what is far more, if the purchaser only had the sense requisite to appreciate it, her own precious self."

Poor Happy blushed and her face seemed to approach almost a purple color. In fact, she seemed so exhausted in strength, as to be compelled to take a chair.

"Ah, sister," said Sarah Brame, "you are too severe on our dear cousin Happy. I wonder how you discovered so much since we returned; but there's nothing like mischief can escape your inquisitive eye and ear. For my part, I cannot see why you should say all this—laughing at the dear sweet girl."

Mr. Hawkins and Miss E. Thompson, were at a little

distance from the others in the room, seeming very much
engaged in conversation. Mr. Hawkins, with his handkerchief to his eyes as if crying, and yet talking, and
Miss E. Thompson listening in great apparent interest,
with her eyes cast on the floor; neither hearing a word
of the remarks made by the Misses Brame. Mr. Baynham,
however, heard it all, and with a countenance expressive
of much more than its usual gravity and thoughtfulness.
Indeed, there was something like a dark and gloomy
shade of despair passing over it, as he listened and thought
in wonder what Miss Happy was about, and with whom,
when the young ladies set out in the morning. At last he
thought of the starting poney, at the Pomonkee bridge;
of the hero of that scene, and his own prediction that
that whole affair had been brought about by the mischievous trick and contrivance of Cupid himself; he
bawled out, "Confound all these starting ponies! it isn't
the first time I have known them to do great mischief.
O! ho, did'nt I tell you all so? did'nt I tell you so?"

"What, Mr. Baynham?" said Happy, "what did you
tell us all?"

This he answered much more in seriousness than jest
after a moments pause. "Well," he said, "I told you
all it would be well for me, if something did'nt come of
that bridge affair in the end to make me weep, rather
than laugh."

"Really," said Miss Mary Brame, pointing to Mr. Hawkins, who sat still quite close to Miss Elizabeth Thompson, with his handkerchief applied to his eyes, "I should
like to know if Capt. Hawkins has also met with a
bewitched little starting poney? He must have done,
or be about to do something very bad, as he seems crying most piteously already."

At this Mr. H. slowly withdrew his handkerchief from
his eyes and all saw them looking as red as if he had just
applied an ounce or less of cayenne pepper, or of onion
juice to them. In truth, it was said and believed gener-

aily, that he said himself after he married Miss Elizabeth. that one or both of those articles he kept by him to put in his eyes, to plead with the lady when all else failed.

At this moment the servant entered, announced dinner, and requested the ladies and gentlemen to walk into the dining-room. All arose and followed, but Mr. Hawkins, who took his hat, requesting to be excused for a few minutes, and the others proceeded to dinner.

In the evening at the hour of three precisely, the elder went to the room assigned to and occupied by the parson while at his house. He found him there and prepared to receive him. As soon as both were seated, the parson observed to the elder, "sir, I beg your pardon, but I must inform you, I have changed my views in respect to the business of which I spoke to you this morning, and, and,"——"And what, Mr. Frazier?" said the elder, looking at the person addressed, with an expression of scorn, and an eye flashing a little more of fury than the meek and quiet old gentleman was before seen for many years to display.

"Mr. Frazier, so far as I am myself, concerned, I don't know, but I ought to rejoice at the change you say you have taken in respect to a union with my niece; for I can truly say, I was not, and am not now, pleased with the idea of its taking place. But, sir, as there are feelings and rights of another, entitled to my most tender regards and protection, involved in this caprice of yours, it shall not pass without my utmost censure, and rebuke. What, sir, can justify you, a grave minister of the sanctuary of God! a preacher of the gospel of peace, in thus wounding and insulting the confidence of an unoffending and amiable young lady?"

"Oh! oh! replied Mr. F., my dear elder, are you not laboring under some misunderstanding of my remarks just made?"

"If I am, responded Mr. Brame, I shall be glad for you to explain:—Did I not understand you plainly to say you had come to the conclusion to decline the hand of my niece in marriage ?"

"Dear me, no, father Brame! no, no. I only said I had changed on that subject; and, and was going on to say, I wished no delay on account of my trip to North Carolina, and if it met with your approbation, our union should be consummated in a few days."

"Aye, that is the change, is it? Very well, very well then, I ask your pardon, parson Frazier," said the elder. "Be it so, and I confess it suits my views much better, if such are my nieces wishes; for I cannot say I like long engagements and betrothals myself; and, if this thing, or match, is to take place, let it be over at once, or in some short time. For there's an old saying, 'There's many a slip between the cup and the lip.'"

"I am, truly gratified, dear elder, that everything is likely to turn out as we wished. I understand you freely to consent to our union, and if you please, it is to-day, Friday, by the consent of Miss Thompson, we will be married here on Sunday morning, as soon as morning worship is over, and before breakfast. She told me to fix any time that would suit myself."

"Well, well, said the elder, so let it be. I will see parson Toddson to-morrow, and will get him to be here at that time."

With this arrangement between them, they parted. Mr. F. going to join the ladies and gentlemen in the parlor; the elder and his lady in her chamber. Not finding Miss Happy, he wandered forth and soon found her seated in the summer-house in the garden, and in due time and form detailed the result of the interview with her uncle, and received from her own lips a confirmation of the entire arrangement. And here we will leave the Rev. Mr. Frazier, carrying everything before him, or having everything in his own way.

According to the time appointed they were married, and he received duly from the venerable uncle and guardian, his wife's cash and negroes, and every necessary voucher to possess himself of her large estate in lands, in the neighborhood of Hillsboro', North Carolina, &c., whither he shortly after conducted his beautiful bride to that place and settled in the highly creditable and honorable employment of teaching a female boarding school, where we shall, if the courteous reader please, leave them for the present.

> " The bridal is o'er, the guests are all gone;
> The bride's only sister sits weeping alone.
> The wreath of white roses is torn from her brow,
> And the heart of the bridemaid is desolate now !"—
>
> *T. H. Bayley.*

CHAPTER XIV.

Frank Wood, after the burial of his murdered father, endeavors to find his mother and sisters—Uncle Dan and his brave African troops are introduced at his cabin—Frank returns home, and immediately afterwards enters upon his first campaign in the army of the revolution—He joins the command of General Morgan at Waxaw Bottoms—Is with the Whigs in the battle of Kings Mountain—Kills several of the Tories that assassinated his father and in that battle shoots from his horse the British commander, Colonel Ferguson, while the latter is rallying his retreating troops—Other details of Frank Woods' adventures in the service of the country, and in fulfillment of his vow of vengeance.

> " But let the earth or waters pour,
> The loudest din or wildest roar;
> Let anarchy's broad thunder roar,
> And tumult do its worst to thrill—
> There is a silence to the soul
> More awful and more startling still!"—*Eliza Cook.*

Of Francis Wood, or as we have heretofore called him Frank Wood, son of Capt. John Wood, we further narrate. After he as we stated, witnessed the savage death inflicted by the eleven Tories on his noble and venerable father—after he had solemnly vowed with his head resting upon that cold and breathless bosom, deeply lacerated and torn by their cruel hands, and dyed in its own blood, to fulfil his fathers prophecy and wreak vengeance upon these Tories for the cruelties inflicted. After having laid that manly corpse in the deep cold grave, prepared with his own hands, and raised upon it an unostentatious mound; in gloom and sorrow, passing all description, he returned again to the house, still tenanted alone by the dead Fallis, as he had left it several hours before.

WAR OF INDEPENDENCE. 161

Again he, as if still to assure himself that his mother, sisters and all were gone, visited the different rooms in the dwelling, and then visited the kitchen and several other out-houses. Not a word or exclamation escaped his lips, or any other sounds, but occasional groans that broke from his tortured breast, resembling the sullen, harsh growls of an infuriated tiger more than the natural expressions of human sorrow, but suited, nevertheless, more than sighs, or exclamations of affliction, to express the thoughts of vengeance, then absorbing and flooding his soul! The feeling and sympathizing reader will readily imagine his agonies in view of what he had just witnessed of the cruel sufferings and death of his beloved father; greatly aggravated (if aggravation were possible) by the heart rending conviction that the same merciless bandits, or others no less merciless, had borne off his meek and lovely mother, and dear sisters to murder or worse than murder, dishonor, and degrade them for life!

"Oh!" said he, when many years after, relating to the writer as twice he did these dreadful scenes, and his feelings at the time, "Sir, I could not have borne it for a minute and must have died, if throughout that terrible night with the sufferings the dread apprehensions for my mother and sisters heaped upon me, had not the last words and prophecy of my dying father threatening vengeance by the hands of his son, been still ringing in my ears, and his last defiant looks, been indeliably imprinted on my soul! Nay, even then, I should have sunk under the sense of this ponderous weight of duty to requite the cruelty shown my family upon the heads of the bloody Tories, had I not had a sort of assurance and presentiment of mind, that I should live long enough to accomplish it to the fullest extent, bringing into my crushed heart, balmy touches of hope, continually pouring upon, and stimulating my soul!"

"At length, the rush of horrible thought, seemed to abate!—Seating myself upon the door-sill of my mother's

11

chamber; lifting up my eyes, and fixing them for a time upon the moon's bright sheen, in a sort of listless revery I gazed, till my thoughts seemed calmed by her mild and genial light, and my anguished soul less poignantly afflicted. It was midnight. The moon that had risen with the parting day, was now beginning her descent toward the verge of the western horizon in calm and peaceful splendor; not a flitting cloud obtruded athwart her lovely disc! not a breeze stirred to start the fluttering leaf, or wave a blade of grass, but as if in sympathy with the dead silence of the hour, and as if in unison with the queen of night's enchantments, stilled the tempest raging in my sorrowful bosom! More composed, reason became more free and took up anew the sudden disappearance of my mother and sisters; and all-buoyant hope once more sprang up gently whispering, they had not been rudely borne away by the ruthless Tories, but being affrighted, they might have fled to some neighbor's dwelling, for shelter and protection, and be thus preserved from the horrible fate I had feared, that life I wished alone to cheer and sustain by their love perpetuated, for their protection and the purposes of revenge upon my enemies. I thought, moreover, if the Tories had been there and had carried them all off, they would have taken, also, the body of Fallis, slain by my father, still lying in the sleep of death, in that very chamber, and his rifle with my father's, still lying by his side; and also, would they have plundered the house more or less of the valuable furniture with which it abounded. But nothing, as I examined by the moon's light shining through the doors and windows, seemed to have been removed.

Rapidly as these reflections sped through my mind, I came to the conclusion that my mother, sisters, and all were most probably still safe. Gratitude towards God, their preserver, sprang up in my heart,—the slightest sentiment, or sensation of which, I had not before felt during that terrible day and night,—and I instantly fell upon my knees, to thank HIM for HIS mercy! I rose, and began to think of the course I should then pursue. The thought that I should be able easily to find and once more see my adored mother and sisters, in safely, fully softened my heart, and floods of tears gushed forth, blinding for a time my sight, although, I had not wept for years, and thought, that night, I never again could. But, where were they gone? To what generous shelter had they fled? A moments reflection satisfied me they had fled to the dwelling of Major Simpson, who, although not the nearest neighbor, was with his most excellent lady, Mrs. Esther Simpson, and entire family, the very kindest. The distance was three miles. Closing the doors of the house as well as I could, after I had possessed myself of my father's rifle, which I found well charged with powder and ball, and taking from the gun rack his pouch amply supplied also. I set off by the light of the moon to find them. I traveled more in a run than a walk, and at about two o'clock in the morning, reached Uncle Dan's cabin. Anticipating that all were asleep at the dwelling of the white family, yet very impatient to ascertain whether my mother and all had made good their escape to that place, I approached the good old African's door to ask admission. Before I reached the entrance, I heard voices within, and my father's name pronounced. I paused to listen. There was a conversation going on between the foreman and other negroes, reciting in part the conduct of the Tories the evening before, in seizing and carrying off my father into the woods, and lamenting in feeling terms his fate, as well as my own—saying they had learned I followed them as they passed out of sight from the house. I did not doubt then that this information had been derived through my mother, or some one who had fled with her; and that all were there safe, as was afterward found to be the fact. But again, what most particularly interested me, after I was satisfied as to my mother's safety, was a conversation which ensued in the cabin, as to the manner in which they were arranging to conduct a sort of campaign in the morning, against the marauding and murderous Tories, on the way or at my father's, if any of them were to be found.

"Now boys," said Uncle Dan, "you's see dis is berry seeist bissniss: spectin' sum on us is gwyne git kilt. Missis say, do Daniel go and take de company long and kill all dem Britishers and dem Tories if dey no go way quick; an' dis nigger gwyne 'bey missis, an' gwyne look sharp an' peticalar, caze missis sez dat way. Tom I'se de capting an' I'se gwyne fite in de fore funt o' de battles fust; an dese debil Britishers kilt dis nigger he'se gwyne for to fall or die. Den, Tom, you's for to stan right dar whar your capting stan', an' tell Jack, Pete, an' all dem tudder niggers, wha's dar wid a gun, fite!—fite! kill all dem d—d Britishers! Dar now, ole ooman, ain't dat de fust cock wha's crow for de day? Well, dis nigger gwyne for to go putty quick, dat's it.

"O, Daniel, oo—oo—oo, dat's brake dis hart! 'Member, ole man, dis nigger say,—when you's gwyne to missis for massa's cock hat—you's gwyne git proud, you's gwyne git a fall, caze Doctor Killwell say so, when he's preach. Oo—oo! lor' gawamarcy on dis po' nigger. Daniel git kilt, and dis po' nigger die too. Oo—oo—oo! lor' gawamarcy for dis po' Molly!"

"Dar now, Molly, ole Dan no git kilt. Why, ole ooman, missis no cry so an massa go to fite de Britishers at de Guilfords. You nose dat. Wha for Molly cry den? Ole Dan no fraid dem Britishers, dats flat, he's fite 'em all de time. Wha for dem Tories kilt ole massa John Wood,—take him to de wood an kilt him, an den, wha for he's take dat good boy, massa Frank? O! Molly, Dan gwyne kilt two tree dem Tory for dat! I is now. Here Pete, you's got a gun! Jack got a gun? I say all dem tudder niggers got a gun? got ambunition too? I'se say Sam, an ole man Titus you's got no gun, you's git two grubbin' hoe—two spade to go dar an' berry dat Britisher; massa Wood mash he head and he lies dar dead, now in de room. Missis say, 'Dan go for to berry dat too.' Go' by, ole ooman, I'se gwyne now—I puts massa big cock hat on now." In a few seconds, the brave old African in front of Tom, Pete, Jack, and some twelve or fourteen other young black men of the place, opened his cabin door, and seeing me at the door—for by this time the morning light being sufficient, he took a full view of me,—then jumped back into the cabin and bawled out, at the top of his voice—"O! Molly!—Molly! massa Frank no kilt! run here! run here! Massa Frank cum back to dat door." "O, gawamarcy, Daniel, wha for you's holloo so?" said Molly, "dar now, Daniel gwyne git mad."

By this time, the door was thrown wide—I was seen fully by all. Some ran one way and some ran another—all greatly affrighted—thinking it was my ghost.

Molly cried out, "lor marcy, mass Frank is done cum back! He ain't kilt neider."

The old man then clasped me in his powerful embrace greatly overjoyed. Then rushing from the cabin door, ran for his mistress's dwelling—shouting "Missis, missis, —I'se gwyne tell missis," and away he ran shouting, "Mass Frank cum back, an' ain't kilt neider! Hora for Mass Frank!" On he ran and I right after. Still he shouted till he reached within a few yards of the dwelling where he was met by his mistress, who having heard his outcry hastened and met him; my mother and sisters close behind her, in great consternation to know the cause.

"Uncle Dan," exclaimed his mistress, "what in the world is the matter?"

"Massa Frank, massa Frank, missis, cum back, an' ain't kilt neider."

By this time I had fully turned the corner of the meat-house I had to pass before I was in view of the place where Mrs. Simpson met her old black man, and I strode up instantly to the group at the door. My mother and sisters immediately embraced me. My mother returned the embrace silently; but my sisters cried out in convulsive tones, "where is father! O, where is father, brother?" O God! thou alone canst tell the agony of thought and feeling that at that moment, like fiery tempests, swept through my soul! Not only anew, but with an intensity of horror and anguish, greater than that even of the night and evening before, thundering upon my heart and mind; notwithstanding, I saw before me in life and safety my mother and beloved sisters, whom I had mourned for a time as murdered, or worse than murdered!

For some moments, I was unable to articulate a word; nor did I speak, till, looking upon the pale and haggard face of my beloved parent, the very impersonation of immeasurable despair, motionless on the spot where we met without uttering a word or sheding a tear. All the sympathies of my nature streamed from my eyes!—I wept aloud. I then took my poor mother by the hand, and led her into the dwelling; seated her and my sisters, and almost fell at their feet. My mother gazed on me for a brief space of time, and then almost in a whispering tone of voice, said:

"My son, where is your father? Did they murder him? or does he yet live?"

I said, "O! mother, my father is no more! I saw him die!"

"And how did he die, Frank?" said she.

I said, "he died like a man and a christian!"

"Did they hang or shoot him, my son?"

"No mother, neither; but they stript and scourged him to death!"

At these words my sister Rosa swooned, and fell to the floor—Susan, poor lost and ruined Susan, just ran about the room, screaming as one deranged. I lifted dear Rosa and laid her upon the sofa in the room. My mother moved not, neither spoke a word! The kind Mrs. Simpson and her two daughters, Martha and Mary, come in and applied water &c., to restore Rosa. Still my mother neither spoke nor moved—sitting like a monument of unutterable grief, gazing at vacancy! Rosa began to breathe and presently opened her eyes. My own strength returned, and I again felt energy of mind and strength of limbs. I went to my mother, and bore her in my arms to a bed in an adjoining apartment; laid her gently down, and began to think what words I should use to comfort her. O! what could I say? She looked at me for a half minute with a look of sympathy, and apparent complacency, and, before I could say a word, said :

" Frank, my son, did you see your father die? and did you hear him speak ? "

I answered these questions by relating the narrative I before have given of the dreadful scene. I repeated his last words.—his prophecy, and threat to Nick Simonds. Silent she sat for some minutes ; several times fixing her eyes upon mine, as if to fathom my thoughts and purposes. The first thing she said was, " Frank, my son, what have you resolved to do ? "

" Mother, my vow is made, my purpose is fixed to fulfill, if God spares me, the dying words of my father. I will hunt down those villains as I would the most ferocious beasts of prey, or the cannibal that had slain my best friend, and broiled and eaten the core of his heart, before my face."

She looked at me for a moment, then burst into tears— rose from her pillow and embraced me round the neck ; while in a voice the softest yet words the most emphatic, she said :

"Ah ! my son, I knew you would do it ! Truly I now see your father's blood courses in your veins. A father's heart beats in your bosom."

"I told her, then, in full detail, how I had vowed, what

I had vowed, and where my head was pillowed when my words were audibly and solemnly uttered! Again my blessed mother embraced her son; and after resting for a few minutes, worn down in body and mind, on my arm, she again reclined on the pillow from which she had risen, and fell into a calm and most refreshing repose. So I left her. She slept till breakfast was announced, and all partook except Rosa.

Previously, however, and while my mother yet reposed, my mind very naturally turned to the events of the last twenty-four hours, and chiefly was employed in the circumstances of my vow and the means and course to be employed and pursued, in fulfilling of it. Never before had my mind been exercised in reflecting much, or in a calm and reasonable discrimination of the principles of the Whigs upon which the war of independence then raging with great violence and merciless fury in many colonies, particularly in the East and South. I had, from its commencement, read with the most absorbing interest, descriptions as published from time to time in the few Whig papers which reached my father. Still, to analyze those principles, settle and determine their merits and demerits for myself, as a rule of personal action, I had hitherto failed or neglected to do. My strong minded father, I knew, understood them all, and decided that the resistance of the British authority in the colonies was just and right. I had seen him in his peculiar way lend all his energies of body and mind, to give that resistance the greatest efficiency and the most successful triumph. That judgment and course was perfectly decisive with me. Often I had thirsted in soul and spirit to be a man and permitted to enter into the army and do battle in the Whig cause. Yea, from the time I was fifteen, I began to urge him to suffer me to enlist and enter the service of the country. This as often as it was proposed was peremptorily refused; but promised I should so soon as I became eighteen, and on the morning of the day he was murdered by the Tories, having but the night before returned from the small army of Gen. Sumpter in South Carolina, then flying before the victorious Cornwallis, he said to me :

"Frank, do you know that you are eighteen years old ?"

I answered, "I do, sir. I was of that age on the Tuesday before last. I have just been thinking of it myself, and had made up my mind to ask you to equip me with everything necessary to enter the army with Gen. Morgan, now in South Carolina."

"Well, my son, I have determined to do so, and shall take you along with me to fight the British and Tories in some battle expected in a short time to take place within or near the line of the province. I have determined to set out on Monday morning—day after to-morrow—so that you'll soon have a chance to fight a little, as you have long desired."

My mother was present, but said nothing in objection. So that all considered the matter as fullly settled.

"Now, I thought, I must determine for myself as to that matter. And if I go to the army, it must be without the introduction and guidance of my venerated father altogether. But then, as my mother had said, I had the heart and feelings of my father stiring within me. I felt that the army and war were the natural elements of my nature, and most congenial with my spirit, at least, at that time. Again, I remembered with intense satisfaction, the eternal war of vengeance I had declared in my very soul against the British and Tories, particularly the latter ; and that to execute with the greatest certainty the vow made upon the cold heart of my dead father, the army furnished the greatest facilities. I determined, therefore, to set out at the time proposed by him, for that position, notwithstanding he no more lived to bestow his counsels, and guide my footsteps. Yet again I remembered the words of Nick Simmonds and Mike Stalcup, as they passed near where I lay concealed, and the reward they were to receive from Col. Ferguson for killing my father. Oh! their words, as they were remembered, rolled through my heart like drops of molten lead! Aye, I thought, in the army and in the anticipated battle, of which my father spoke, shortly to occur, I shall doubtless meet and have a chance at that villainous murderer, Col. Ferguson. Truly my soul burned for vengeance, and I felt a panting to drink his heart's blood.

These thoughts at once confirmed the resolutions already taken. In the evening I made my determination known to my mother and sisters. My mother spoke not for some time; my sisters only wept in silence. At length my mother said:

"Yes, go, my son, go; for I know your resolution and purpose will bear you out conqueror. You must equip yourself with all your father's arms and other preparations for the public service; his excellent rifle, brace of pistols, and small sword. His fine young horse you must take, as he is better broke to the military parades than yours, and will submit better to being shot from. Did you not, Frank, in narrating the melancholy circumstances attending the murder of your father say, that some of those Tories mentioned that they had been given a reward by one of the British officers for destroying him?"

"Yes, mother, two of them, as they passed near me, going from the place where they had scourged him to death, said, they were sure to get from Col. Ferguson two hundred guineas for that service, and fifty had been paid in advance."

"O, my God!" she exclaimed, "what despicable cruelty! what heartless brutality! Is this England's boasted civilization, religion, and honor! But, my son, this is the remark I was about to make: You are right to hurry

WAR OF INDEPENDENCE. 171

to the army as quick as possible, and place yourself under the command and protection of the brave Gen. Morgan. Your father told me he, together with Col. Campbell and Col. Shelby, are preparing to attack Ferguson, now posted at King's Mountain with his forces, and drive them beyond the boundaries of North Carolina at all events. He said, moreover, Ferguson had been ordered to that point by Cornwallis to encourage and embolden the Tories, induce them to take up arms and join themselves to his command. This, he said, they were in great numbers, doing every day; making his encampment at that place the general rallying point, and from thence traversing and marauding throughout the surrounding country, committing murders, thefts, and every species of cruelty. Beyond doubt, the murderers of my poor husband will not only return to the British there, for those purposes, but also to get the balance of the price of your father's blood!"

"Those are exactly my reasons for hurrying, as I shall Monday morning, upon this campaign," I said, "and I trust I shall be successful in finding them all there."

"Well, my son, go, and may God's blessing give you the most triumphant success. For this I shall pray continually. I am far from believing this undertaking of yours, for the mere purpose of revenge, would be justifiable; or believing I ought to pray for its accomplishment, if your object was revenge alone; I do not believe that God would succor you for that purpose; dreadful as have been the cruel provocations of those British and Tories to yourself and family; justifying if anything could, most unmitigated and prompt revenge. But remember, the spirit of revenge is not the spirit of the revolution; but that of patriotism and justice—God and liberty! and will be approved by Him. While then, you follow up and destroy those cowardly murderers of your heroic father, you are but serving the cause of your country in the certainty of Heaven's approbation.

172   LEGENDS OF THE

"You will not strike for private wrongs alone ;
  Such are for selfish passions and rash men,
  But are unworthy a tyranicide.
  We must forget all feelings save the *one* ;
  We must resign all passions save our purpose ;
  We must behold no object save our country,
  And only look on death as beautiful,
  So that the sacrifice ascend to Heaven
  And draw down freedom on her universe."

" But, my son, we must now prepare to return home this evening. Uncle Dan and the other men, I understand, returned awhile ago from there, after having removed and buried the dead Tory, and says he could discover nothing amiss there. He brought two horses with saddles, &c., for Rosa and myself, and we must get two from Mrs. Simpson for you and Susan. Henry can ride behind me. Susan could ride in like manner with you, but you have your father's gun with you, and you cannot carry that well with one behind you."

She then went into the chamber of Mrs. Simpson where she found my sisters ; and, having procured the horses needed, we in a little time were ready for our return. I had much suffering of mind, of which, however, I had not yet spoken to my mother, whenever I thought of my departure from home and entering the army, leaving her and my sisters, and all exposed to the depredations of the reckless Tories, who, now more likely than ever before, would attempt their injury as they would no more stand in fear of my father, and I should be far off and unable to give them any protection. My suffering, produced by the reflection, was of so painful a character, that I was almost ready to give up my trip, at least, at that time and mentioned such cause and intention to my mother.

" Fear not, my son," she said, "discharge your duty to your country, we will endeavor trusting to providence to take care of ourselves in your absence. Besides, I have been thinking of taking the course our kind neighbor

WAR OF INDEPENDENCE.   173

Mrs. Simpson has taken, and get some guns and put them in the hands of the three white hirelings and each of the three black men, to guard us from any such attacks. It is my wish that you do not refrain from going on that account."

Early on Monday morning, I set out for the army, and traveled with what speed I could to the camp of General Morgan, which was then on the Waxaw Bottoms, about twenty-three miles from Kings Mountain. I reported myself to him;—had a personal interview and settled the terms with him, upon which I was to be recognized as under his command,—being those on which my father identified himself with the public service,—to be at liberty at all times, to be absent if I could thereby render the greater and more efficient service in the pursuit of small collections of British and Tories. I had fully communicated to him the hopes I had of finding in the service of Ferguson, the hired murderers of my father, and he seemed pleased at the idea of my partizan services; especially, as my plan embraced a determination to shoot or otherwise slay Colonel Ferguson, himself, the first opportunity.

Here the writer leaves the narrative of Frank Wood, promising to return to it again in some future pages.

> "Virtue's is the only noble blood,
>   From whence we can derive true good :
> There surely is some guiding power,
>   Which rightly suffers wrong,—
> Gives vice to bloom its little hour,
>   But virtue, late and long.
> There is a fever of the spirit,
>   The brand of Cain's unresting doom,
> Which in the lone dark souls that bear it
>   Glows like the lamp in Tullius' tomb;
> Unlike that lamp, its subtle fires
>   Burns, blasts, consumes its cell, the heart,
> Till one, by one, hope, joy, desires
>   Like dreams of shadowy smoke depart."—*Anonymus.*

CHAPTER XV.

Measures taken by Cornwallis—Battle of Kings Mountain—Death of Col. Ferguson by the hand of Frank Wood—His narrative of the battle and subsequent action.

" O such a day,—
" So fought, so followed, and so fairly won,
" Came not, till now, to dignify the times.
" It is held
" That valor is the chiefest virtue, and
" Most dignifies the haver; if it be
" The man I speak of, cannot in the world
" Be singly counterpoised.

" When the English measur'd backward their own ground
In faint retire: O bravely came we off."—*Shakspeare.*

IT will be remembered among the records history gives of the events of the war of independence in the year 1780, that after the fatal battles of Camden, which resulted in the utter defeat of Gen. Gates; and at Fishing Creek, when Gen. Sumpter, was suddenly overtaken by Col. Tarlton, and terribly cut to pieces. Cornwallis, supposing that on account of these disasters the province of South Carolina was perfectly subdued to British authority, then instituted, with the purpose of making his conquests of the Whigs doubly secure and permanent, a system of extreme severity, compelling individual as well as general, submission to royal authority. For this purpose he ordered that every citizen, who had at any time, taken part with and served under the command of government officers, and was afterwards found acting and serving with Americans, to be forthwith hung; and their property confiscated, or destroyed! But these rigorous and cruel measures were not sufficient to accomplish their

WAR OF INDEPENDENCE. 175

design. The truth is, they only tended for a brief space to overawe and put down, in appearance, open resistance; while the cry of vengeance for every sacrifice so made, was preparing to become more and more general—to whet with greater earnestness of purpose the weapon of war among the people, and exasperate them to a more determined resistance to, and deeper execration of the British government.

This same detested instrument of arbitrary power and cruelty, Cornwallis fancying thus to have made complete his conquest of this province, began to look abroad for further fields of triumph and cruelty. He knew that in North Carolina, near to the South Carolina line, and dispersed far into the interior of the former, were foreigners and others, calling themselves royalists, disposed to favor the cause of the king, but whose services to that cause, had hitherto been only of a depredatory character, mainly to rob and steal from and stealthily to murder the defenceless Whigs, and their women and children! With the view, therefore, to bring them into a more permanent and useful system of organization and consolidated force, in September of that year, he ordered and detached Col. Ferguson to the frontiers of North Carolina, for the purpose of gathering them together, and inducing them regularly to enlist and take up arms in the royal cause. Many of the most profligate and abandoned repaired to his standard; and fully equipped with arms and ammunition, came under his auspices and express commands; and, we boldly proclaim, in some instances for promised rewards and bribes, they committed atrocities most merciless and dreadful, in secret abductions of innocent females, secret assassinations, conflagrations, and open robberies, provoking to the madness of fury, the Whig citizens; and making them with scarce a single exception, run together with whatever weapons of offence they could gather at home or on the way; forming themselves around the nucleus furnished by the troops and encampment of the intrepid Morgan.

On the 7th of October, 1780, under the command of that general, Cols. Shelby and Campbell, they attacked the enemy, British and Tories, commanded by Col. Ferguson, at Kings Mountain, the post he had chosen, with the greatest fury, and although, resisted with great determination and skill on the part of the enemy, killed their commander and three hundred of his subaltern officers and soldiers; took eight hundred prisoners and fifteen hundred stands of arms, together with a considerable amount of ammunition.

But who killed Ferguson? Often, indeed, it is almost universally very difficult, in any thing like a general battle to ascertain the individual, by whose successful shot, any particular enemy of the opposing combatants has been brought down. But, the recollection of the fact that there was one who went to the spot with the fixed determination to revenge his father's recent cruel death, procured by Ferguson, through the reward given to his assassins,—one who was there solemnly resolved to rush into the thickest of the fight, and seek every possible opportunity, and employ every possible means to kill him there and on that very occasion,—the presumption grows strong that that person accomplished the deed. But when, superadded to all this, is that of the positive testimony of that very one, who was never known to lie, accompanied with a detail of facts and circumstances, corroborated by the general histories of the battle, declaring in the most positive terms, that it was his rifle ball, that pierced the heart of that instigator of his father's death; the proof is almost conclusive, that the cause of the country, and of liberty is indebted to our brave young soldier, Frank Wood, for destroying that vile, corrupt, and corrupting minion of tyranny; and giving, most probably, success in this very decisive engagement, to the side of the Whigs.

WAR OF INDEPENDENCE. 177

"O, sir," he was often heard to say—when many years after this glorious victory, narrating this part of his adventurous life, with big manly tears of triumph rolling down his cheeks—"when I saw, at my faithful rifle's crack, that man, who was the prime assassin of my noble father, tumble from his charger which he rode in front of his retreating troops, pouring from his polluted lips the bitterest curses and blasphemies against the cowardly soldiers, and particularly the sculking Tories, bite the dust in the last agony of death, a weight I had often felt, too intolerable to bear, seemed to pass from my heart, and joy for the first time after I had heard my father's dying declaration at the bloody tree, sprang up into my soul. Nor was Ferguson the only one of that father's murderers, that tasted, that day, the swift vengeance of his son; visiting on their heads the punishment due to their crimes. As I had anticipated and ardently desired, they were all there,—Simonds, Stalcup, Bettis, Ernest, Grissitt, Garner, Nevin, Stodard, Patty, Jeeter, Glutson. The three first I know I shot down and believe killed, as I never heard of them more. Ernest, Grissitt, Garner, Stodard and Jeeter, I never saw till the day after the battle, and found them in the barracks among the prisoners taken. Grissitt, Garner and Stodard died at Salsbury while prisoners of war. Ernest and Jeeter survived, were exchanged and liberated. At Glutson I also took deliberate aim during the fight at the mountain, but believe he got only a slight flesh wound; he got off some way from the field soon after, and I never heard what became of him.

"When in the morning, I saw those of the murderers of my father whom I have named, taken prisoners, I was made to reflect seriously what plan I should fix to wreak upon them my recorded vengeance. Two of them were of the three that presented their guns at me, and threatened to shoot me down, when I was about to come near

12

to those bearing my father from the house out into the woods. They knew me, and seemed anxious to hide by rushing into the thickest of the crowds of prisoners, from my view. I thought of the consequences, if I there made them feel the just consequences of their crimes, and put them to instant death; but, although I then knew but little of the rules of war and the practice of civilized nations, in regard to captive enemies—a moment's reflection impressed me strongly with the conviction, that to take advantage for any cause of the condition of a prisoner, and murder him, would not only be savage, cruel, and inhuman; but to make myself the object of the scorn of all brave men, and despicably criminal.

"On that day, in a conversation with Col. Shelby, relating to him the murder of my father, that five of them were among the prisoners, together with the thoughts for a moment, I had indulged, to shoot them there in the barracks; also, what was my conclusion upon reflection; he applauded that conclusion, and said if I had been rash enough to have assailed them there I should have been immediately arrested, tried, and executed for the offence.

" It was not many days, however, before my good rifle was again brought into the exercise of a little more of sharp shooting. The brave Gen. Sumpter, notwithstanding he had been badly defeated at Fishing Creek, by Col. Tarlton, gathered a handsome number of volunteers, and continued to harrass the enemy very seriously; and thus became the object of many plans laid for his destruction. They all failed, however. During that time, with the permission of Gen. Morgan, I joined his volunteer corps. We were encamped in the early part of November, on Broad River, near Fishdam Ferry. Many Tories were also joined to the command of a Major Wemys. They attacked us there and the British and Tories were sadly disappointed and defeated. Sumpter and his brave volunteers fought them like men; killed a considerable

number, and took their commander prisoner. That same
faithful old gun with which my father so often brought
down the bounding buck, the sculking Tory and savage,
here also performed its accustomed work, and two Tories
with an English ensign, were made to feel its deadly
touches, during the fight.

"Nor did that rifle play an idle part when on the 20th
of the same month Col. Tarlton, who with his veteran
troop of horse and some Tory recruits, assailed us at
Blackstocks. We beat them back with considerable loss
of British and Tories. There I had a sort of personal interview with two Tories, Samuel Coulson, brother of Col.
Coulson, of Anson county, and big Bill Harpe. The first
I looked at very hard, and gave him questions so sharply,
by way of the fashionable courtesies of the day, he forgot
he was one of his majesty's horsemen, slid or quickly
tumbled from his charger, and never again rendered his
most gracious majesty further service of pillage, plunder
and rapine. With big Bill Harpe also I had a word.
But we did not talk very understandingly; for he was in
too great haste to run off with his redoubtable Col. (Tarlton). It would'nt do, though. My messenger, instead
of reaching his head or heart, only glanced his posteriors,
to my own and my family's everlasting grief and disgrace. For not long after that he most fearfully revenged
himself upon me and upon all of us, by stealing and carrying off my pretty sister Susan. She was never recovered.

"But I must not enter into a detail of this most melancholy tale now—by far the most hapless and trying of all
my life,—the murder of my father cannot be excepted.
Alas! for the poor girl. Some thousands of miles my
brother and myself traveled in search of her, and never
found nor heard the least trace or trait of her for fifteen
months after she was carried off; and then we only heard
that the two Harpes, big Bill and his cousin Josh, were.

180   LEGENDS OF THE

together with three Indians, seen taking off two young
girls answering the description of Susan, and Maria Davidson, daughter of Col. John Davidson, stolen about the
same time. They were seen by two men hunting at the
time, just on the east side of the great Clinch Mountain!
These hunters described the girls and the Harpes very exactly. They said they appeared to be traveling westward
with great speed; the girls mounted on horses and tied
to the saddles they rode.

"It has often been a subject of curious speculation in
my mind, why that horrible villain, Bill Harpe, should
have been permitted to escape, or had been defended by
Providence, which you please, from my true aim and
shot, and left to live for years after, the bloodiest robber
and murderer that ever lived in America; while so many
comparatively harmless and innocent Tories and British
scarcely ever failed to fall at the crack of my rifle. But
it's too deep for me. I cannot fathom it. So it is, however. Big Bill and Josh Harpe made out to live for
years, killing and slaying all that came within their
power, men, women and children, white and black. O,
I have often thought it was a thousand pities that that
rascal, big Bill, ever got away from Blackstock's, when
we fought with Tarlton. He escaped as I tell you, and I
don't know how. But the worst of it is, although this
was not the last opportunity I had at that vile Tory, and
had a fair shot at him, I could not bring him any way!
My trusty rifle, that never failed me at any other time,
seemed to have a spell, as they call it, whenever pointed
at that Scotch rascal.

"On three occasions I saw him after that, and twice we
met in battle. He was, as you know, belonging to Tarlton's command, and I with Gen. Morgan. At the battle
of the Cowpens I saw him, and I am sure he saw me.
But he managed to keep out of my way till we killed one
hundred and took prisoners to the number of five hund-

red British and Tories. But again big Bill got off with the retreat of Tarlton.

"We managed that fight well, I tell you. For although the enemy overrated us in numbers and experience, being all except about three hundred Tories, veteran British troops. Old Morgan drove them back, and had only twelve men killed and sixty wounded. It was not long after this battle at the Cowpens that Cornwallis pushed with all vengeance to overtake Gen. Morgan; determined, I suppose, totally to destroy him and his entire forces. The latter, fully aware of the superiority of the pursuing enemy, hurried us on, you may be sure, till we were all almost broke down with fatigue when we got to the fords of the Catawba where we crossed in safety. At these fords the British expected to overtake and attack us; but when they got there we had been over, baggage and all, full two hours. Night was approaching, and the redoubtable Lord Cornwallis indulging almost certain assurance he would overtake his adversary with ease in the morning, halted and encamped."

After a short pause by this remarkable man in his narrative, during which he maintained without the slightest change throughout, a serious countenance, alternated occasionally by an expression of impassioned sentiments of piety and gratitude, when his heavy lowering brow recovered; relaxing almost into a smile, and his usually fierce, small, keen blue eyes, bathed in a flood of tears, looked forth in unwonted gentleness for minutes—he then said, seeming suddenly aroused from a deep revery:

"Now I am come to a point in this here story which you'll hardly look for from me; but it's in me, and I now and long have believed the same way. Here's a clear instance in which God Almighty stretched forth his hand and saved Morgan's army. You see there's Cornwallis with his powerful army of victorious veterans on one side of the river, and Morgan with his small and ra-

182   LEGENDS OF THE

ther overworn command on the other. The former ardently expecting early in the morning to pass over and easily overwhelm the entire forces of the latter in a moment after overtaking him. But low and behold, the Heavens poured down the rain in unceasing torrents, all that night, and increased the river to such height and might, that when morning came the proud Britons dared not attempt to pass it for two days!

" This was the first time. The second was at the Yadkin. Lord Cornwallis, after crossing the Catawba, started after us again with might and main; and at the river Yadkin again encamped for the night. Here again the rains came down in floods, raised the river and compelled him to seek its passage much higher up the stream. O, I believe, my friend," he said, " that this was another instance in which Heaven acknowledged the justice of the American cause, in giving this protection to our little army.

" But still I must mention another. Gen. Green also, at another time, was hotly pursued by Cornwallis; anxious to overtake him and bring him to a battle before he got into Virginia. Gen. Green had but just crossed the Dan River, when his lordship reached it in pursuit. His van attacked our rear just as it was crossing it, and, firing across, killed our brave Col. John Davidson, who commanded our rear, and was as sound a Whig and brave an officer and soldier as ever breathed in the old North State. Too late, a third time. In great mortification and alarm at these adverse providences, he turned again southward, and established himself at Hillsboro'. Just about this time there took place rather a curious affair in behalf of our cause. Cornwallis, you know, sent Tarlton into North Carolina and among the royalists to encourage them to enlist. Gen. Green detached some militia troops and sent them under the command of Col. Lee to meet and thwart Col. Tarlton as much as possible. I was with

Lee. Well, we, marching out in the direction of the place where Tarlton was stationed, and operating, were suddenly surprised by the approach of three hundred and fifty Tories or royalists, supposing that we constituted Tarlton's forces, crying "long live the king," and shouting loud that they were his loyal subjects, in order to make themselves known and be received into the British service. But our militia, not liking the words nor the signs given, fell upon them with great fury, killed the most of them in a few minutes, and made the balance prisoners of war. I confess that even on that occasion, Frank Wood did not fail to remember his father's prophecy, nor his own solemn vow, taken upon that father's cold and lifeless bosom. For he sent them a special message or two, by way of remembrance, that both were still unrevoked. O no! no,--not yet—not yet. I saw and showed marked attention to Jeeter and Glutson, two that officiated assiduously at my beloved parent's martyrdom; and they went the way of all flesh! I don't know whether Bill or Josh Harpe were there or not. They were not among the slain, as I looked; and I don't believe they were with the prisoners, as I heard in a little time after, they both had gone to the Cherokee nation. Nor was it more than six months, before they came into the settlements with some Indians and stole the two poor girls, and were seen crossing Clinch Mountain to the wilderness, as I told you."

"Oh! when the heart has once been riven,
    The wound will firmly close no more;
Let memory's searching probe be driven
    It bleeds and quivers freshly sore."—*Eliza Cooke.*

But

"The gloomiest soul is not all gloom,
    The sadest heart is not all sadness;
And sweetly o'er the darkest gloom,
    There shines some lingering rays of gladness."—*Hemans.*

"Hope leads the child to plant the flower, the man to sow the seed ;
   Nor leaves fulfillment to her hour, but prompts again to deed ;
   And ere upon the old man's dust, the grass is seen to wave,
   We look through falling tears to trust Hope's sunshine on the grave.
   O no! it is no flattering lure,—no fancy weak, or fond.—
   When hope would bid us rest secure in better life beyond.
   Nor loss, nor shame, nor grief, nor sin, her promise may gainsay,
   The voice Divine hath spoke within, and God did ne'er betray.—

                              Sarah F. Adams.

   Then, what if memory's probe be driven
      Through the heart's core, steeped in sorrow ?
   The soul by faith paints the rain-bow of Heaven.
      And humbly trusts in hopes of to-morrow.—

                              Thos. M. Smith.

WAR OF INDEPENDENCE. 185

CHAPTER XVI.

Lord Cornwallis encamped at Hillsboro'—Marauding parties of British and Tories sent out to ravage and plunder the inhabitants—Anecdote of Maj. Hinton, in his attempt to rob Mrs. Slocum—Falls into a dry well in her cellar—A love adventure of his lordship with Maria Davidson—His utter overthrow—The Toryism and base treachery of the Rev. Mr. James Frazier toward his wife and flight to and with the British army, after embezzling his wife's fine estate—The hypocrite's picture.

"O, woman's love is not as man's—
  He turns aside awhile
  To cheer ambition's thorny road,
  With woman's sunny smile;
  But she embarks her all in love,
  Her life is on the throw—
  She wins, 'tis bliss supreme!—she fails!—
  Unutterable woe!"—*E. M. Sidney.*

LORD CORNWALLIS, it will be remembered, after two successive failures to overtake and bring the troops under Gen. Morgan to an engagement as they were retreating across the province toward Virginia, and afterwards the command of Gen. Green—and being prevented by the remarkable interpositions of Providence, above adverted to, greatly mortified and chagrined, returned to Hillsboro', and there encamped with the main body of his army.

He continued, however, to send forth in every direction, especially into the most wealthy neighborhoods and villages of the province, marauding parties of British and Tories, to plunder and sometimes, perpetrate the most wanton cruelties and rapine, upon the Whigs. These pillagers not only took forcibly whatever cattle and horses they deemed proper or of use, but were diligent in hunting out and forcibly taking from the families every article of plate, or other valuables or transportables; frequently destroying great quantities of household and kitchen furniture, too weighty and bulky to bear off, and for which they could have no use. Many hundreds of instances of the kind occurred. One or two we will mention.

Capt. John Slocum, lived at about the distance of fifteen miles from Hillsboro'. While he was upon a tour in the American service in the army of Gen. Green, commanding a company of volunteers, one of these marauding companies of British, from their camp at that town, commanded by one Capt. Hinton, of the cavalry, with about thirty men stopped at his house, and in a most threatening and insolent manner entered and demanded of Mrs. Slocum her keys, and all the money and plate she had in her possession. She told him she had but little money, only £3 10s., she believed, and pointed him to her *escretoire* already unlocked, containing her store. As to plate she had none except a small portion hid where he might, if he could, find it. With many blasphemous and bitter curses he bid her bring it to him, instantly; threatening personal injury and abuse, if she did not produce it. She told him it was in the cellar. The brave captain, quite elated with success, and with the prospect of possessing himself so speedily of the rich booty, attempted a descent into the cellar himself, without any light, into a place entirely dark. When he entered, he called back to the lady to bring a candle. Quickly she lighted the candle; descended and pointed to the corner in which she told him the plate was deposited. Onward he hastened, anxious to grasp his prize, and in a few seconds pitched head-foremost into a dry well about twenty feet deep, dug for the purpose of draining and drying the cellar. Down he went and for some minutes was neither heard to groan or even breathe. Mrs. Slocum listened with intense interest, and was unable to judge whether he had broken his neck, or was only stunned and made insensible by the fall, for a time. She still listened, and was upon the point of making her way back into her chamber, when she heard a low feeble groan, followed by indistinct whinings, like those of a small puppy. Slowly still she ascended, and walked into the yard, where, when the redoubtable captain descended into the cellar, she had seen some of his men. She saw them all now in a meadow near the stables, chasing and endeavoring to catch several fine young horses at pasture, that were snorting and careering in defiant speed, back and forth across the field. She gave the alarm, however, and all run to the house in great appearance of fright; rushed down into the cellar, dark as it again was, bawling and shouting for their captain. By this time he had revived sufficiently, and bawled and shouted for help, as loudly as any of them. A ladder was quickly brought from the hay-mow, let down into the well, and slowly and cautiously the gallant captain ascended to *terra firma* again; calling out to be carried above as speedily as possible. Up he came, and brought to the light, exhibited, perhaps, the most perfect spectacle of slime, mud, and blood, covering and besmearing him from head to foot. His *proboscis*, coming foremost in the fall, in contact with some more solid body at the bottom of the well, poured forth a gory stream, forming its due proportion of the muck and mire with which his laces, tuckers, and frilled ruffles, were so horribly besmeared. His dallying rapier dangling and gracefully swinging at his side, bearing unmistakable evidence of his identity with his most gracious majesty's service. So discomfitted, however, was this gallant cockney, with the reception he had met with in entering the quiet abode of the toads and cockroaches at the bottom of the well, uninvited; with the rather disheveled appearance of his courtly attire, in the presence of the lady and her pretty daughters, he shouted loud and long: "To horse—to horse," and soon, with his cavalcade, disappeared; bearing off no other trophy of *beauty* or booty, than the three pound ten, and a swelled red nose.

188   LEGENDS OF THE

It is not known, however, whether the captain or any of his subordinates, after reaching head-quarters, hinted at, much less recounted, the incidents of this adventurous day; except on one occasion, Jack Tibbs, when a little severely reproved for some carelessness or unskillfulness in the execution of his captain's order to do something, a little slyly and crustily responded, " I have never yet shown so little sense, as to jump into a dry well, to tilt with a frog for silver plate."

Instances of like character of British rapacity might be here multiplied. But for the present we forbear, except as follows:

That portion of North Carolina, which is now called Forsythe county, was originally the county and possessions of the Creek Indians, the most cruel, savage, and warlike of any known tribe. In the summer of 1700, Martin Hauser, and his associates, emigrated from Pennsylvania, and penetrated into the interior of North Carolina, farther than civilization had then extended, and after various successful battles with the Indians, they took possession of the country. In order to have their little band united, and capable of resisting the attacks of the savages, they settled down together and built the town of Bethany, or as it is better known and commonly called Hausertown. This town is in Forsythe county, and in full view of the Pilot Mountain, or Mount Ararat, from the north-west, and the Samartown mountains from the north-east. The inhabitants of it were a bold and hardy race, distinguished for their love of freedom and independence; and when the revolutionary war commenced, they sided with the patriots of the country, and espoused their cause with the warmest ardor.

In the year 1776, the country around had become populated and the descendants of Martin Hauser, had greatly multiplied, insomuch, that the town then numbered some five hundred inhabitants.

" These were the times that tried men's souls." It may

WAR OF INDEPENDENCE. 189

now be said, that those that stood firm to their country, deserve the love and thanks of every man and woman who enjoys the results of the contests which took place between the Whigs or patriots, and the Tories or royalists.

When Gen. Cornwallis, commander-in-chief of the British army, marched from Chester, N. C., through the interior of the country to Little York, in Virginia, in order to dispirit and punish the Whigs, he marked the progress of his course with every sort of cruelty, blood-shed, conflagration and destruction of their persons and property.

While he was thus treating the Whigs, his conduct was very different to the Tories—their persons and property were left untouched, regarded as sacred, every protection he could afford was furnished them, and arms and ammunition (which in the then existing state of the country was difficult to be had,) was distributed in the amplest manner. When he come to the Shallow Ford, on the Yadkin, not far from where Daniel Boone was born, and about nine miles from Hausertown, instead of pursuing the direct route and following the great thouroughfare on the line of his march, he turned his course to the left and marched his whole army a circuitous road, and fifteen or twenty miles out of his way to pay an unwelcome and unsolicited visit to the little Whig village of Hausertown.

As providence would have it, when his best platoon entered the lower end of the town, it commenced raining, and continued raining very fast during his entire stay, which was more than a day and night. The army divided, the one half encamping upon the right, the other on the left of the town ; and his cannon was left in the centre under guard. Such of the men of the town, as had not joined the American army, sought the country for safety, leaving their wives and children in their houses as a sort of protection to them, and under the supposed protection of the chivalry and gallantry of the army, which they believed would not stop, but pass directly on. Their arrival was so wholly unexpected and unlooked for, that the inhabitants had no opportunity, whatever, to make preparation for the removal of their families and property.

During the stay of the army the soldiers took and destroyed every vestige of personal property in the town: all the horses, cattle, hogs, corn, hay, household and kitchen furniture, provisions, clothes, poultry, chickens, geese—all except one old gander, which afterward received the name of the " crazy army gander." He was one of a large flock and saved his life in this way:

When the army approached, this flock arose in the air and flew down the street, and, in attempting to fly to the creek, were all knocked down and killed, except him ; he escaped into a large swamp below. After the army left, this gander lived many years, but would never again associate with other geese. He spent his time solitary and alone, passing up and down the streets day and night, making sad, lamenting and mournful cries, and hence his name " crazy army gander."

While the soldiers were rumaging and hunting for something valuable to steal or destroy, they found in the cellars whiskey, brandy, and other liquors—of which the whole army officers partook and all got drunk ; and even the guard, which had been placed around the cannon became intoxicated. This circumstance has been frequently detailed by the older inhabitants with a sigh of regret, that they could not anticipate the disabled condition of the army, collect a small force, and, Marion-like. rush upon them in the darkness of night and take the whole army, Cornwallis and all.

While things were in this state, George Hauser, grandson of Martin Hauser, (who was a captain in the American army and an officer of different grades in the many expeditions of the Whigs against Tories and Indians unconnected with any Continental or State armament) came reconnoitering about the town. He was a large athletic man, seated on a fine horse, provided with a pair of

WAR OF INDEPENDENCE.   191

horseman's pistols on his saddle before him and his sword by his side. Concern for the safety of his wife and child caused him to go with all the speed of his horse, impulsively to his own house, where, before he was scarcely down from his saddle, he was surrounded by soldiers, taken a prisoner, and his hands bound behind him, and kept all that night by a strict guard, unprotected from a constantly drenching rain. The General kept his head-quarters at Peter Hauser's house, (the cousin of George) and the situation of George by some means becoming known to Peter's wife, in the morning when the General was about going to his breakfast, she took occasion to meet him, and implored his release on bended knees in the most earnest and impassioned appeals. The General granted the request of the lady, thus made, and ordered his release, with the privilege of passing where he pleased.

After the army left, nothing that was useful or that could be carried off remained. The household furniture, ploughs, wagons, &c., were cut up, piled in the streets and burned, and nothing but the incessant rain saved the whole town from total destruction.

The army of Cornwallis marched thence through Old Town, Salem, &c., to Guildford Court House. The people of Old Town and Salem, being Tories generally, experienced very different treatment from the British Army. Couriers were sent in advance to notify them of its approach. The citizens were fully protected in their persons and property, and they were fully compensated for whatever the soldiers received.

During the continuance of the British general's stay with his army at Hillsboro', and immediately upon his arrival at the place, he renewed his acquaintance with the Rev. Mr. James Frazier, who as we have said he had seen and known in Europe,—was introduced to Mrs. Frazier and the Misses Mary C. Brame and her sister Amy Brame, daughters of the venerable Melchesidec Brame, of Caroline, Virginia, and Miss Maria Davidson, daughter of Col. John Davidson, killed at Dan River by the British. These ladies were then on a visit to Mrs. Frazier; the two Miss Brames having fled to Hillsboro', to escape the vile and villainous rapine then being perpetrated in the southern counties of Virginia, by the traitor Benedict Arnold, Col. Tarlton, Gen. Phillips, and the British troops,—under their command, daughters of the "first families" were often during this period, made the especial objects of their most brutal practices and horrible assaults.

To these ladies his lordship manifested many polite courtesies and seemed particularly desirous to treat with marked attention the young and accomplished daughter of Col. Davidson, who was but about one month before in Gen. Nat. Green's command, killed when retreating before Cornwallis. Miss Davidson and her widowed mother deeply mourned, dressed in the sable habiliments of heart-felt sorrow, and their loss. Maria could scarcely ever look at the General without weeping. Still however, his lordship from motives of sympathy, it may be, knowing her great loss and consequent sorrow, or from motives less creditable and disinterested, sought by every means respectful and on every occasion practicable, to manifest his attention; which, though productive of much embarrassment of mind to the sensitive young lady, was nevertheless, under the sentiment of modesty, and the dictates of a good mind received with constrained politeness; until on one occasion, while she continued her visit at Hillsboro', and was walking in company with Mrs. Frazier and the two young Virginia ladies, upon a fishing excursion, accompanied by his lordship, and several of his young subaltern officers, Col. Burton, Maj. Tarlton and one or two others,—she and the General being at a little distance from the others, in the rear. In very direct terms he declared his passion for her, and attempted to

WAR OF INDEPENDENCE.   193

place his arm around her beautiful person, and press with
his her ruby lips.

Instantly the indignity was repelled with the greatest
promptitude, with a look of insuperable scorn at which
his king might well have trembled; fixing her eyes steadfastly on his, yet shrinking a pace or two from his touch,
she said, "My lord, I am, it is true, the orphan daughter
of Col. John Davidson, slain through your instrumentality, in the army of Gen. Green; yet acting under the
behest I suppose of your duty, to your master, the king,
and the sanctions of honorable war; but know you not
that to those sanctions, and the force you here command,
there are limits, you dare not and cannot transcend or
overleap, only in the use of brute force such as we learn
your traitor Benedict Arnold, and bloody Col. Tarlton,
are now practicing among the defenceless maidens of
Virginia? To that alternative you are now however,
come, and defied by Col. Davidson's orphan daughter and
with the like unconquerable spirit that stired him to the
resistance of British oppression!"

His lordship blenching from the majesty of her defiant
gaze, and glancing his eyes up and down her handsome
and fully developed person, as if to determine its power
and capability before a farther encounter; and as if to
ascertain whether it truly corresponded with the dignity
and heroism of her mind, spoke not for a moment; then
said, with a slight effort at facetiousness, while his whole
countenance indicated anything else but pleasurable sensations.

"Well, indeed it seems to me Miss, these western
shores produce nothing but heroes and heroines: and
well may his majesty's ministry and Parliament begin to
doubt the conquest of such a country of rebels."

Then, in rapid steps he passed on, leaving the invincible heroine to meditate undisturbed upon the triumph
she had achieved, and make her way as she might in follow-

13

194   LEGENDS OF THE

ing her friends. These Cornwallis quickly overtook with a
degree of embarrassment, covered by a sort of forced pleas-
antry of manner, he responded to the enquiries of Mrs.
Frazier for Miss Davidson, by saying, he left her in a deep
study and meditation, in which she did not wish to be
disturbed, and having just thought of an important call
for his presence at his cantonment bid them a pleasant
evening, and passed hastily on in the direction of his
quarters.

Soon Miss D. overtook her friends. They rallied her
upon the sudden loss of her *gallant*, expressed sympathy
&c. She blushed very much, and, from the appearance
of her eyes, seemed to have been weeping a little. Yet
she passed off the playfulness of the company with all
proper reserve, betraying in neither word or act, the
scene that had occurred between her and the lord commandant of his majesty's forces in Hillsboro'. The incident however, whatever impression it made on the discreet Mrs. Frazier and the others, did not escape the
keen penetration and inquisitive mind of Miss Mary
Brame. After their return to the parson's, she sought
the earliest opportunity to mention it to her cousin, and
express some apprehensions that in some way the pretty
Carolina lady, had given such a prompt repulse to the
besieging general, that he would not be likely shortly to
renew his attack, nor again come within gunshot of that
fortress. " We shall, therefore," she said, " be deprived
in future of his grace's visits."

" Ah now, cousin Mary," said Mrs. Frazier, " that is
just like you! Experience, war, nor anything else has
made you forget your old habits of irony and sarcasm.
Taking your irony as you I know mean it, I am led to
apprehend something serious occurred. Did his lordship
offer any indignity to poor Maria? I shall regret it very
much if he did. She is a truly an excellent child, of the
noblest and most generous nature. She has lived with

us more than three years and was always as dear to me as my sister; but now since she has lost her noble father, and is an orphan, she is doubly endeared to us."

"O, indeed, I do not know, madam, what occured between them," said Miss Brame," but from the looks of both, and the evident embarrassment of his lordship, when he came up to us and left us, I thought it was all quite odd enough."

"Well," said Mrs. Frazier, "I will call Maria and ask her about it."

She called Maria, who immediately entered, anticipating the object, and blushing at the thought that it would be her duty to speak with the fullest candor to her beloved friend.

"Well, my dear girl," said Mrs. Frazier, "cousin Mary thinks something very serious has taken place between you and his lordship, and he will not be likely to visit us again shortly, on account of what happened."

Maria, then, with all the artlessness of a child, narrated every particular, as we have given them; adding only that she had previously made up her mind to treat his lordship with all reasonable politeness at a distance. "But," she continued, "when he put his hands upon me and sought to bestow his caresses, I felt the insult, and spurned his approaches, as I have said."

"Right—right—served him right, dear Maria," said Mary Brame, "and I heartily approve and honor the spirit with which you sent the presumptuous lordling adrift! Ah! now, cousin Happy, I am able to answer the question you asked me the other day. Why was it, you asked, that all the Virginia ladies fled like an affrighted flock of young wild turkies whenever any of the British, such as Arnold or Tarlton entered the State; while those of North Carolina flew not at all? The whole thing is now explained to me in the good sense and spirit, fortitude and womanly firmness, with which this dear girl has met and foiled this lordly Englishman."

196   LEGENDS OF THE

"Indeed, it may be so, cousin," said Mrs. Frazier,
"and I shall myself prize the dear child after this more
than ever. I am sure my husband will also, when I shall
tell him of it."

> "Who with heart and eyes
> Could walk where liberty had been, nor see
> The shining footprints of her deity?
> Nor feel those God-like breathings in the air,
> Which mutely told her spirit had been there?"—*Moore.*

Early on the following morning, which, however, was
the first opportunity the lady had after the events of the
fishing excursion, and the insult of his lordship offered to
Miss Davidson, the reverend gentleman her husband,
having remained nearly all night at the marquee of the
commander of the British forces, as for some weeks before he had been in the habit of doing, Mrs. Frazier recounted to him the conduct of Cornwallis, and the prompt
yet lady-like manner in which Maria had met and re-
pulsed his overtures and attempted familiarities. She
declared her increased admiration and affection for the
sweet girl; her determination, so long as she remained
at her house, and under her protection, to afford her, to
the fullest extent, that protection; and declared her deepest regret that his lordship should have so far forgotten
and so returned the courtesies and very respectful attentions with which she herself and Mr. Frazier had invariably treated him as a visitor and guest, and this notwithstanding they saw in him nothing but the enemy of their
country, employed and sworn in his majesty's service, to
crush and destroy the liberties of the people: they believing that that state of things ought not to restrict his
claims to the hospitalities of their domestic circle. But
this she could not in future do, as he had ventured to set
so light an estimate upon them.

"Indeed, and upon my faith, Mrs. Frazier," said his
reverence, "you are quite severe upon his lordship this
morning; and permit me to say to you, quite too much

WAR OF INDEPENDENCE. 197

so. Why, madam, do you not know, that a great fondess for the ladies, and the performance of feats of conquest and gallantry among them are part and parcel of a brave British officer's excellencies and highest boasts? Really, Happy, you would not do among the ladies of quality and fashion in London and Edinborough; for the most fastidious and prudish among them would not make half so much ado about it, if his lordship had pressed his amour to a far more delightful and exstatic extent with the pretty little country girl!"

To these very strange expressions Mrs. Frazier made no response for several minutes. But fixing her eyes upon her husband with an expression of amazement and anguish of soul, she stood puzzled to determine what to say, or how, properly, to resent and show her scorn and contempt for the minister of the gospel who thus flippantly, if not mendaciously, could utter them. At length she said:

"O, my God! can it be possible that such sentiments as these are entertained and declared by my own husband?" and burst into a flood of tears. Then catching her little boy, about two years old, in her arms, the pledge of their union, who had clambered to his mother's knees, was about to retire from her chamber, when in a somewhat boisterous and peevish tone of voice and gesticulation, he said:

"It is unnecessary, madam, thus to fret and fume against Lord Cornwallis, his gracious majesty's commander-in-chief in both the Carolinas and Virginia, as all you can say or do will neither punish or even reprove the improprieties of which you charge him; which it is most likely he attempted upon the country lass! Indeed, if she really entertains the dislike she expresses for the noble lord, she and you, and all of us, ought to be thankful to him that he has not before now sent a sergeant and his guard to conduct the young woman to his quarters, to cheer and console him for the *numerous loves* and *de-*

198   LEGENDS OF THE

lights he left in coming to America! But you and she may have no further trouble on the subject, as his lordship informed me last night, he should in a few days march his army from Hillsboro', and perhaps to Virginia, where joining with the brave Arnold, Tarlton and Phillips, he will make an easy conquest of the rebels there also."

Suddenly she turned upon him, and with a look that told of a bursting heart, her eyes no longer dimmed with tears, but blazing with indignation, said:

"Sir, this language, and these sentiments were not anticipated from you! They certainly stamp with dissimulation and falsehood declarations, years ago made to me and to others; and to such I now forever respond, they can never find the least approval in my mind or heart! Your noble lord, as *you call him,* may indeed march his powerful army to my beloved native province; may indeed triumph there for a season, as he has done in North and South Carolina; but mark what I say, *the day is not far distant when those rebels, as you dare to call them, may make him rue in bitterness and anguish that he ever left his numerous loves and delights, to battle against the liberty of America!* Aye, and if it may please his friend, the Rev. Parson Frazier, to do so, he can communicate to his noble lord what his wife, Mrs. Happy Frazier predicts, and most trustfully prays and believes, will be fulfilled." With these remarks she left her chamber with her infant in her arms, and saw him no more till the morning of the second day afterwards.

On the morning of that second day, she had risen early from her couch, leaving him in bed, to set about her household affairs, supposing him to be asleep, as most probably he was; willing that he should indulge a morning's nap as it was past midnight before he had returned from Cornwallis's camp, where he had spent most of his days and nights since his lordship had made Hillsboro' his head-quarters. But in passing from her bed to the bureau on which she had placed her own apparel the evening before, she came in contact with the chair on which he had hung his when preparing for bed during the night, which with his coat and all fell to the floor, and from his pocket two letters and another paper dropped upon the floor before her. These she picked up and saw that the letters were directed to her husband—"Rev. Mr. James Frazier," in a female hand. She hastily opened them, being unsealed, and read the address in each, "my dear husband," subscribed, "from your affectionate wife, Janette Frazier." Filled with feelings of alarm and indescribable embarrassment, she hastily attempted to refold the letters, when from the noise made by the rattling of the paper or some other cause, Mr. Frazier awoke, sprang out on the floor, near her, and with the most bitter threats and blasphemous imprecations, accused her of basely rifling his pockets for dishonest purposes; and snatching the letters from her already paralyzed hands, he pushed her quite across the chamber, declaring he would murder her if ever she was alike guilty again.

She fell and fainted. They never more spoke to each other. She never more saw him. The loud and boisterous talking of the reverend gentleman, followed by the heavy fall upon the floor, alarmed the servants in the room below, and the maid-servant running up into her mistress' apartment, finding her still breathless on the floor, gave the alarm, and it was more than an hour after ere, with the most assiduous attentions of the three young ladies, and the aid of a variety of appliances of a stimulating and restorative character, she was revived. Still, however, when from time to time apparently restored, sinking again and again, during the day, into insensibility.

In a short time after Cornwallis left Hillsboro', and this remarkable pretender to the Redeemer fled from the country, after having sold all the slaves, and very valua-

200   LEGENDS OF THE

ble mills and lands received of his Virginia wife, pocketed the whole, leaving the deluded lady with her innocent little boy dependent upon her lands in Virginia and a few servants for a support during the residue of her hapless life.

From this melancholy and vivid picture of human depravity, the heart grows sick, looks out for relief, and the sentient mind finds none but in the solemn yet reasonable conclusion, there must come a general judgment, a day of final general retribution.   Aye, to the hypocrite a

> "Great day of revelation!   In the grave
>   He shall leave his mask, and stand
>   In native ugliness!   He was a man
>   Who stole his livery from the court of Heaven
>   To serve the devil in; in virtue's guise
>   Devoured the widow's house and orphan's bread;
>   In holy phrase transacted villainies,
>   That common sinners durst not meddle with!
>   At sacred feasts he sat among the saints,
>   And with his guilty hands touched holiest things!
>   And none of sin, lamented more, or sighed
>   More deeply, or with graver countenance,
>   Or longer prayer, wept o'er the dying man,
>   Whose infant children, at the moment, he
>   Had planned—to rob."—*Pollock.*

WAR OF INDEPENDENCE. 201

CHAPTER XVIII.

Frank Wood again at home—Learns the dreadful intelligence of the abduction of his sister Susan and Maria Davidson by the Tories and Indians—Visits with his mother the monument she had erected over the grave of his father—Visits with his sister Rosa the family of the Simpsons, and something is told strongly signifying a love match between two young lovers.

> While man possesses heart and eyes,
> Woman's empire never dies.

In a few days after the event related by Frank Wood of the capture of the Tories, seeking to unite in the British service under Col. Tarlton, he became satisfied that the whole of the vile men, who had combined and cruelly murdered his father, were all dead, except Ernest; and that with that exception, he had fulfilled his father's prediction and his own solemn vow, when it might be almost in truth said for the first time he permitted himself to think of his home, and mother, and sisters, and the forlorn and unprotected condition in which he had left them. He felt that he had rendered some good and efficient service to his beloved country, since he had joined the forces under the command of Gen. Morgan; that her condition and prospects of being finally successful in the achievement of the liberty for which her heroic patriots so ardently struggled and panted, was improved and brightening; and he concluded to obtain from his colonel a brief furlough and spend a few weeks at his home, and in the society of those loved ones.

Candor, however, compels us to say it was not only to see his beloved mother, to ascertain the condition of her mind and domestic affairs, nor to enjoy the pleasant society of his interesting and much loved sister, that most powerfully operated to induce his return to his native neighborhood and the home of his family. That neighborhood was also the native neighborhood of Mary Simpson, with whom he had in the morning of life been made acquainted; had been a pupil with her in more than one country school; had spent in company with her, her sister, and his own, many delightful days in childish gambols over the farm of their fathers, or in the beautiful groves contiguous; and had half in earnest and half in jest, interchanged a thousand pledges of boyish love, reciprocated in the various plays in which they joined, and the redeeming of pawns and forfeitures, fashionable in those more primitive days and times. For her, from a small boy, he had always felt a more than common attachment. But he had no distinct idea that his prepossession in her favor, amounted to the thing he had heard called love, until she was far away from him, nor until he had accomplished the chief object of his sudden and early entrance into the army, and the service of the country; and found time to meditate upon home, and analyze and determine upon the true character of the feelings and sentiments prompting his return. He knew he loved as he ought, his mother and sisters, and yet he found he could not separate the joy he should experience in being in the domestic circle at home, from the keener anticipations of delight, in beholding the pretty black-eyed daughter of Maj. John Simpson. He concluded, therefore, and we think very rationally, that he loved Mary Simpson, very intensely,—unless the palpitation in his bosom, which he sometimes felt when she was the subject of his meditations and thoughts, might be some pestilential disease or affection of a strange and unusual character, caught in the army, of which it was often productive. At such times, he derived comfort, from the thought that if he reached home in safety, he could consult the mother of

WAR OF INDEPENDENCE. 205

Mary, on the case, as she had been for years, looked upon as the veritable horn of the altar of all medical safety,
throughout the country.

Home he went therefore; found his meek and quiet
mother and pretty sister Rosa, in reasonable health, but
deeply afflicted in consequence of the sudden disappearance of his youngest sister Susan. It was then more
than two weeks since she set out on a visit to Martha
and Mary Simpson, accompanied by a small black boy,
who about sunset of the same day, came home and stated
that while on their return, two white men with guns and
long knives, and three yellow men with little axes in their
hands, suddenly ran into the road, surrounded the young
girl, seized her bridle, while one of the white men
sprang behind on her horse and holding her in the grasp
of his right arm, with his left, took hold of the bridle and
quickly rode off out of sight, through the thick woods.
At first she seemed to die and to be ready to fall from
the horse, but was held up by the strong man behind her
—presently she began to scream for help and he (the
black boy) heard her screaming in that way, long after
they passed from his sight!

With many tears Frank's mother told him the sad tale,
and said she had not since heard a word of her; whether
murdered, or what had become of her!

"In what direction from where they took her did the
boy say they went when they got out of sight?" asked
Frank.

"I cannot say," his mother replied, "I did not ask the
boy Jesse. I will send for him and you can enquire."

The boy was called in and many inquiries were made
of him by Frank; but he could give no very distinct idea
either in regard to the course they took or the discription
of the two white men. He only said, in describing the
men: "De two white man look mighty big, black, and
imperdent; and de injins berry mad; Miss Susan mighty
skeard."

204   LEGENDS OF THE

After a few moments reflection and two or three turns
back and forth of his mother's room, Frank turned and
said to his sorrowful mother, "Oh, mother! I fear my
poor sister is forever lost—lost—forever lost! I will as
soon as I have rested a little, set out to learn her fate if I
can find the course she was taken, and the place."

A long pause ensued in the remarks of the mother and
son, the silence that prevailed being alone broken by
the repeated sobs and deep drawn sighs of Rosa, seated
at a distance from her mother; the perfect impersonation
of patient suffering and heartfelt sorrow. Frank still in
hurried steps walked the floor of his mother's chamber,
meditating upon the fate of his ruined sister, anxiously
seeking to determine upon the best course to be persued
to find and rescue her. He remembered that his furlough
had but five weeks to run at the first, and at the expiration of which, he was bound to report himself to his
commanding officer. His heart also reminded him that
among the most controling motives prompting this return
to his home and obtain their respite from the public service, was that he might behold once more the most idol-
ized object of his heart's affections. These very perplex-
ing thoughts and conflicting duties almost unmanned him.
While, however, thus tortured in mind, he saw the meek
eyes of his mother, intently fixed upon him, expressive of
a desire to say something to him, yet hesitating to express
herself, he approached and stood near her ; yet for a time
she remained silent. Then at last said :

"Frank, have you remembered your father's threat to
his murderers, and your own solemn vow ?"

"Truly mother," he replied, "I have not only remembered them, but more than fulfilled them."

He then seated himself by her and related in substance all that he had done, from the time he had joined
the army under the command of Gen. Morgan ; the battles in which he had fought ; and the Tories and British
he knew he had slain in those battles ; as they have al-

WAR OF INDEPENDENCE.   205

ready been laid before the reader in the preceding pages.
When he ceased, she looked into his face,—her tears fast
streaming from her eyes and in silence rose, embraced
and kissed him. Again resuming her seat, after a pause
for a minute or more, in soft and emphatic terms, said:
" It is all right my son,—it is all right! Come now with
me, I wish you to take a short walk with me, till I show
you what has engaged much of my attention since you
have been absent."

So saying, she placed her bonnet on her head, and taking the arm of Frank, walked forth toward the grove to
which his dreadful enemies had borne his father, and to
the fatal tree, where with remorseless hands the cruel
scourgers bound, lacerated and tore the manly body of
his heroic sire, and to the lonely grave, wrought by
his filial hands. In silence unbroken, she led him where
an unostentatious tomb, reared by conjugal affection told
the passing stranger, there slept the remains of one of
America's earliest patriot heroes; the loved companion
of her youthful joys and most cherished memories! Already the greenest turf artistically carved and placed,
grew upon the humble mound; fitly emblemizing the
perennial memory of his public life and private virtues!
At the foot she meekly kneeled and wept for a few minutes. Then turned her gentle eyes, filled as they were
wont to be, with all a mother's love; still swimming, yet
smiling in tears, with a voice in the sweetest and most
distinct tones said, " Frank, my son, this is your mother's
monument, to the cherished worth of your heroic father,
and these tears his funeral eulogium, spoken at his grave
by one who knew and prized him most, his widowed relic,
your afflicted mother."

Hitherto Frank had not spoken, but unable longer to
forbear, he kneeled, embraced, and kissed his mother,
and with tears streaming down his manly cheeks, exclaimed,

206   LEGENDS OF THE

" O, mother! may God grant to me, just such a monument at my grave, and just such a funeral eulogy!"

Slowly they rose and in silence, as they came, retraced their steps to the dwelling; his mother saying, " Did you not say, my son, it was your intention, soon as you had rested from your long fatigues, to set out in search of your lost sister?"

"So I said, and such is my purpose, mother," he answered.

Nothing further was said, till in her chamber seated, she said, " Frank, have you taken a final discharge from the army or are you required again to return; and at what time?"

" My furlough, mother, is but short; I am required to report myself at Gen. Green's quarters, on the first day of August next. I know that the cause of the country never more needed all her forces. Cornwallis I learn is already on his march to enter Virginia, and uniting there his powerful army with the commands of Arnold, Tarlton, and Phillips, already there, committing wherever they go, the most unheard of plunder and rapine; and will, unless providentially and promptly checked, by our brave Washington and Green, utterly overrun and ruin that beautiful province."

After a few minute's pause, during which she seemed in profound thought, his mother said, " It may surprise you, Frank, to hear from me, the advice I now shall give you. I know full well the fraternal love in which you have ever regarded your lost and ruined sister; and I should far less regard you as feeling and cherishing the generous spirit and bravery of your father, if I thought you would not risk life, fortune, or anything else, to save the poor girl. Nor will you doubt for a moment her mother's love, or the agony to which she would not submit if thereby she could secure her from her dreadful and inevitable fate. But alas, alas! her doom is ere now

WAR OF INDEPENDENCE. 207

irremediably fixed. She has now been more than three weeks at the mercy of the brutal savages who stole and bore her to the wilderness. It is impossible to misunderstand their despicable purpose, or to anticipate, if she yet lives, it is in less than unspeakable ruin ; and if you could now find her and restore her to the embraces of her relatives, crushed in heart and mind, to another state of circumstances and existence instead of that she now endures, she must still loathe herself, and will lingeringly pine away and die. In view, therefore, of the improbability of your finding her with the most instant and diligent pursuit and search, the little real good, if any, to be accomplished, if crowned with success, the imminent danger impending over our country, and the essential service you may be able, if you return to the army, yet to render it in this trying crisis, your mother advises your return according to your furlough ; and may God give you a lion's heart and giant's arm, still to strike and exterminate its cruel enemies."

" Then indeed, my blessed mother, will I return in due time, trusting in God, and your prayers still to be able to serve my country, and if I fall it will be but to share my heroic father's lot; only like him, I shall not leave behind me such a widow and four dependent children. But mother," he continued to say, " so deeply interesting and engrossing have been the subjects upon which all our thoughts and conversation have turned, I have had no opportunity to ask you or my beloved sister about our kind neighbors, and particularly of the noble soldier, Maj. Simpson, his wife and daughters—are they all well ? Is the major and his brave boys still in the service ? and does the faithful old Dan continue to command and muster his men ? to guard the neighborhood ? Oh ! if he and his brave boys had been at hand when my poor lost sister was attacked and stolen by those desperate Tories and Indians, they, I verily believe, would have rescued

208   LEGENDS OF THE

her or perished in the effort.   But alas! there was none there to save her."

"They are all well," replied his mother, "or were so when we last heard from them.   The major and his sons are still in the army with Gen. Marion, near Savannah, and uncle Dan still draws on his master's cocked hat, and parades his men.   Yes, truly, Frank, I believe too, if the good old black man had been with his company at hand, he would have saved my poor Susan or lost his life.   For Mary Simpson told us when visiting us last week, how the good old man wept when he heard she had been carried off; and said, 'if Gor-a-mighty pleased dis old Dan been dar, he shoot two tree dem Britishers, and two tree dem red Ingins,—but he cum, and dis nigger no dar.'"

"Mother, when was Mary—I—I mean Miss Mary Simpson, here?" said Frank.   "Did she seem well? and did—did she"—

"O, yes, brother," innterrupted Rosa, who, sitting near her mother, heard his hurried enquiries about the Simpsons, and particularly about Mary,—"yes, yes, she makes very particular enquiries about you whenever she sees any of us.   And when we told her we had learned, that at the battle of King's Mountain you had certainly shot Col. Ferguson and several of his hired Tories, that he got to murder father, she laughed, clapped her hands, and cried all at once, and almost shouted with joy.   O!" she exclaimed, "I prayed for it, hoped for it, and fully expected it, of that courageous young man.   Aye, he is so much like his brave father!'"

"And did she say this, Rosa?"

"Indeed she did, brother, and much more, but I can't remember the half.   O! how the dear girls and Mrs. Simpson wept, when they heard of the fate of our poor dear sister.   But alas! all our sympathy and pity cannot avail.   Did you hear, brother, that about the same time she was taken off, Maria Davidson, daughter of Col.

WAR OF INDEPENDENCE. 209

John Davidson, who stayed with us the night before the Mecklenburgh convention, and who was killed by the British in the skirmish at the crossing of the Dan River, was stolen off also, and has never since been heard of?"

"No, sister. Did they say by whom she was taken, and whether there were any Indians with the party?" inquired Frank.

"We did not learn about any Indians," she answered. "Do the Tories," she asked, "always have Indians along with them when they go upon such an expedition?"

"Sometimes they do," replied Frank. You know one Indian was with the Harpes when they went with the other Tories, to carry off Elizabeth Smith, Mr. Lawrence Smith's daughter; and you remember our father shot the Indian, Tiposa, through the heart, just as he had cleaved the head of the poor black John?" "O yes, said Rosa, I remember it very well; and after father came up and shot the Indian the other Tories got off."

"O! mother," said Frank, "if on several occasions during my late campaign when I met with, and more than once shot at that horrible Tory, big Bill Harpe they call him, I had only been half as successful as I usually am, I should have swept from earth that dreadful bloody thief, and we would not, in my confident opinion, be this day mourning as we are, our poor lost Susan. I have thought it all over and fully believe that she has been stolen by the two Harpes; and that when they lately returned from the Cherokee nation to which, I heard in the army, they had fled six or eight months ago, they brought with them the Indians Jesse saw. It has always been a thing I could not account for, that I should so repeatedly miss my most deliberate aims at him. But he has been spared some way still to run his vile course. Providence has still permitted him to live. God have mercy upon us all! We are all subject to his power and many things occur which human wisdom cannot comprehend. Well, yet, mother, we have not talked quite as much about the

14

210   LEGENDS OF THE

Simpsons as I wished, though I can hardly think what more to say of them."

"Shall I tell you, brother?" said Rosa.

"I don't care," said the brother. "What is it, sister?"

"Why would you not like to have mother say that she would be pleased to have the pretty little Mary for a daughter-in-law, if Harry or somebody else would marry her?"

"O! sister, you sport with us."

"Frank, we know you have long loved Mary as a sister," said Mrs. Wood, "and it may be that that love has ripened into a still more tender character. If that is the case, hesitate not to confide the secret to your mother and sister. Truly, I esteem that sweet girl as highly and almost as affectionately as my own daughters? and of course, if you were not so young, that you should make her my daughter-in-law."

"Well—well, mother, we will not say more about it now," replied the brother. "Sister, would you not like to ride over with me to Maj. Simpson's to-morrow?"

"Yes—yes, indeed, I would, brother, and will promise to do all I can with the wily little jade in your behalf, and take you at once, for better—for worse."

"Ah, Rosa! what an elastic and playful heart and mind you have. It were well it is so. For no one could live long with such a sensitive mind and under the severe trials you of late have had to bear without it. But we'll go in the morning, remember."

> "Unsullied and pure is the future's broad scroll;
> And as leaf after leaf from its folds shall unroll,
> The warp and the woof, they are woven by me,
> But the shadows and coloring rest, mortal, with thee.
> 'Tis thine to cast over their brightness and bloom,
> The sunlight of morning—or hues of the tomb."—*Mary Gardner.*

In the morning of the next day the brother and sister, according to the arrangement of the previous evening, visited the pleasant family of Maj. Simpson. Having to

WAR OF INDEPENDENCE. 211

pass near uncle Dan's cabin, they had little more than arrived in full view from the door, before they were discovered by the kind, simple-hearted aunt Molly, who came running to meet them, crying out as she ran:

"Dar now, Daniel, Mars Frank cumed agin. Mars Frank cumed agin! Dat you, Mars Frank? I knows it is, an' Miss Rosa too."

Soon uncle Dan followed, having taken time only to find and adorn himself in his old cocked hat, and to buckle on his broad sword. Here he came, walking along; his sword swinging sometimes on one side, and sometimes on the other—and then again crossing between his brawny legs, almost tripping him up in his hurried strides, shouting as he came:

"Gora mighty bress you, massa Frank; you is comed agin, and I knows it. Molly seed massa Frank fust, an' runned fust, but dis ole nigger is cumed now an' got he cock hat on to see him too; hora for dis nigger! Hora for massa Frank! He done cum from de King Mountain, an' he aint kilt neider—yah, yah, yah!"

"I am glad to see you, too, my worthy old friends," said Frank. "Are all the family well, uncle Dan? Have you heard from your brave old master lately? Where was he, and was he well?"

"He well, Gor bress him, down at Sawannas, ready for to kill de Britishers dar, too. Ride on, mars Frank, Mise Rosa. Dis ole Dan gwyne wid you, hole de hosses when you's gwyne talk to Missis, an' de young ladies. Halloo, Molly, you's gwyne too? O, dese 'omans is al'ays gwyne too, mighty fast."

"In a few moments they reached the yard gate and alighted; but before they reached the door of her dwelling, the good Mrs. Simpson, with Martha, met and greeted them with great cordiality. Mary also ran to the door, then started back and disappeared. They were seated in the parlor but a few minutes before the questions after the health of the Wood family generally, and

212   LEGENDS OF THE

Frank in particular; when he had arrived at home, and
how long would it be before he purposed to return to the
army, were quickly asked and answered, but accompanied all the time with a look and appearance of impa-
tience in Frank. He arose from his seat, hastily walked
the floor a few times, and then with a brisk step made
his way to the matron's chamber in search of some one.

"Ah, ha! mother," said Martha, "don't you see I
told you how it was? that if ever Frank lived to get back
and get here, you would know who of us all was the
greatest attraction. I'll venture he has found sister before this time, and I dare say he kissed her! I wish I
had been there to see them meet."

"Aye, yes," Rosa remarked, "I reckon, Martha, you
guess quite correctly."

"No wonder, Rosa," said Mrs. Simpson, " she knows
the walk of these young Whig soldiers very well, and has
had no little experience, if Lieut. Lee can steal a few
days from the army to come and see us. He has only
done so, however, in the last four months, twice!"

"O, mother," said Martha, " now I do say that is too
bad; and—and—O, here they come. I knew Frank
would bring her from her hiding place."

They entered the parlor side by side and seated themselves near Rosa, who was sitting on a sofa. Frank's
heretofore sad and melancholy countenance seemed evidently changed to a more cheerful aspect than it had
shown from the time of his father's murder. And the
pretty Mary's was much more than usual (though such
was its wonted livery), beautifully dressed in the sweetest
smiles.

"Ah, brother," said Rosa, "I verily believe your ride
has already made you quite well. Yesterday you looked
weary and quite wayworn. To-day, and particularly
since we arrived here, your usual blush and cheerful
smiles appear. Last evening when you were telling mother how bad you felt, and feared you would have to ap-

WAR OF INDEPENDENCE.   213

ply to some physician and take medicine, as you might have brought with you the camp-fever or some other bad complaint, I feared from your looks it might be so; but now I know you are altogether well. The looks and rejoicings of uncle Dan and aunt Molly or Mrs. Simpson, or somebody else, has doctored you up already. Come, tell us who has wrought this miracle?"

"It was'nt I," said Martha, "and I don't think it was mother, though she is everywhere called a first rate doctor. And yet I don't think it was the broad grin of joy expressed by the good old African, uncle Dan, nor the fat, hearty and jolly appearance of aunt Molly. My little sis, this wonder must have been effected by you. I should like to know such an efficacious remedy myself."

"Well, upon my word, Miss Martha," said her mother, you play off your wit and irony quite prettily this morning, on all of us; but particularly your sister and Mr. Wood. It might not be the best thing for the cause of the country, now that it so much needs officers and men, if a certain young lieutenant of the army, who could be mentioned, who often gets himself set down on the sick list, obtains leave of absence every month or two to rusticate for his health in Mecklenburgh county, for weeks at a time, especially at Maj. Simpson's fine country residence, was to find out you were so wonderfully advanced in the healing art as you and Rosa seem to think your sister has become. He might abandon the cause of liberty altogether, and be inspired by the sanitary remedies of his physician."

"There, now, sister Martha—take that," said Mary, "mother best knows how to administer to your case—all will agree after this."

"O! mother, you always take Mary's part. If I did not love you both so much, so that I can sometimes scarcely tell which the most, I should be jealous of her; but indeed, I love her so ardently, (casting her glance on Frank) I could almost love any one she fancied, though

214   LEGENDS OF THE

he were a huge, rough young soldier; and though he had but just slain dozens of the enemies of his country."

" Come, come, now, you must not exaggerate Miss Martha," said Frank, "I have only slain fourteen, instead of dozens. Yet I don't see that that should be a ground of objection, as it is only twelve or thirteen more than Lieut. Lee has buried; especially as I promised, in a few weeks more, to endeavor to duplicate that small number."

" Bravo," said Mrs. Simpson, "God give you speed while you maintain the right."

" Well, now, let us all retire to the dinner table; some of us, at least, feel more like eating than fighting, and are likely to enjoy it with far greater zest."

" While partaking of the abundant repast prepared by the direction of the mistress of the house, the glee and repartee of the two young ladies, Martha and Rosa, still continued, till Frank, when a short interval occurred, in a grave and thoughtful tone of voice, enquired of the matron, if there was any prospect of Maj. Simpson's returning home in any short time. Being answered in the negative, or, that she was unable to form any opinion. His countenance assumed a still graver aspect, and Rosa detected, or said she did, a deep sigh to follow.

" O! brother," exclaimed his sister, " that is certainly no great cause of difficulty, I should suppose, as you better could reach him at his quarters in time for your purpose; and we would all unite in your petition. Would'nt you, Martha? and you, Mary?"

" Certainly," said Martha, " if my sister will head the list of endorsers."

The pretty little Mary blushed very thoroughly, fled from the table, and, in her haste to disappear, turned over her chair, producing such a thundering and rattling on the uncarpeted floor—for carpets were little known and less used in those revolutionary times—that all but Frank sprang up also, and upset one or two more! But the young soldier, who had so repeatedly heard the musket and rifle's crack, and the cannon's roar, was little disturbed in his equanimity,—seeming, in fact, to begin afresh his banquet, and only observed to his sister, that she was as famous for raising a rumpus as Gen. Morgan, wherever he went; quick in generalship and finding an alternative in every emergency.

Thus the evening passed very pleasantly, and its enjoyment heightened much by the parade extraordinary of uncle Dan, mustering and marching his company in his mistress's yard, as he said to Molly, "for mars Frank to voo de troop, an' tell massa Morgan how dey does, an' he go dar to de army agin."

"Aye, now, Daniel, dar tis agin! you's gwyne show massa's ole cock hat to mars Frank an' de ladies. You'se no gwyne to massa Morgan—no howse."

"Well, den, you'se gwyne I's gwyne too, an' dats flat," said Molly.

"Ah, dar tis!" the old man exclaimed, "dese omens al'ays cumin an' gywne too."

Presently the old man appeared, marching his men into the yard in gallant style, beating time with quite a military step to the tap and flam of the drum and the keen squeak of the fife playing a martial air.

Delighted with their visit, Frank and his sister returned at evening to their mother's, and there we will leave them for the present until the young soldier's furlough required his setting forth to join again the army. We shall not, however, refuse our patient readers the natural and delightful privilege of conjecturing, that the young gentleman often thought it beneficial to his health to visit at Simpson farm; yea, every day, to have the benefit of the medicine to which the merry young ladies, Martha and Rosa, so wittily and facetiously alluded.

> "Warriors and statesmen have their meed of praise,
> And what they do or suffer, men record;
> But the long sacrifice of woman's days
> Passes without a thought—without a word."—*Mrs. Norton.*

216   LEGENDS OF THE

CHAPTER XIX.

Frank Wood sets out from his home in North Carolina to join his regiment under Gen. Green according to his furlough—He is transferred and attached to the division of the army then under Gen. Lafayette in Virginia—In course of time, with that division, he was marched to the vicinity of Yorktown, and when joined to the other force of Gen Washington, marched to entrap and besiege Cornwallis at Yorktown—When Cornwallis capitulated and provisions were made and completed by Gen. Washington, safely and securely, to dispose of the many thousands captured at Yorktown and dispose of the large amount of munitions of war there given up in the capitulation, obtained leave from Marquis Lafayette to return to his home and his friends in North Carolina—On his way Frank Wood has many thoughts of his country, seeks to look into her future, and prays for her prosperity—Finds and consummates his previous engagement in marriage with Mary Simpson.

EARLY in the morning of the day following that on which the reader has seen the brave and most indomitaable Frank Wood take leave of his betrothed bride, Mary Simpson, he rose and partook of a morning repast; and having made a hasty visit once more to the little monument erected by his mother over the sleeping dust of his honored father, and having returned to the house, his horse made ready, he took leave of his beloved mother and sister and set forth to join his regiment in the army under the command of Gen. Green at ———, whither he learned at Guilford it had marched and was temporarily stationed. On his way he passed the dwelling of Mrs. Clarissa Davidson, the doubly bereaved widow and relict of Col. John Davidson, killed by the British at the crossing of Gen. Green's army at Dan River, when pursued by Cornwallis's forces to that point. With her he had before formed no acquaintance. Her patriotic hus-

WAR OF INDEPENDENCE. 217

band, however, he had for years well known, and was with him when he was killed at the crossing of the Dan. For him and his memory he entertained the highest gratitude and esteem, and thought it his duty to call and enquire after her health and condition. He found her the picture of inconsolable grief, and worn down with a true mother's horror for the fate of her poor daughter, Maria, ruthlessly stolen and borne off by unknown savage villains, and of whose sad destiny or unimaginable sorrows she was still wholly left to conjecture. All she had as yet heard she had been informed by the little son of her neighbor, that he saw her swiftly borne along an obscure path-way which passed through a dense forest, held in his lap by a dark looking and fierce man on horse-back; she screaming and calling for help. Besides that she had heard nothing.

Frank then told her of the sad circumstances of the disappearance of his sister Susan, about the same time, and of what he had learned through the medium of the hunters at the foot of the great Clinch mountain, who saw two girls tied on their horses, accompanied by two white men and several Indians, briskly urging their course across that mountain toward the vast wilderness of the West; and that from what they said of the appearance of the men and of the two girls, he was induced to believe the two Harpes, big Bill, and Josh, were the men that had stolen his sister and Maria. Mrs. Davidson agreed with him in the opinion, inasmuch as she had heard, she said, that the two had about that time been seen in the neighborhood of their father's, John and William Harpe, and had been missed from the country for many months before, shortly after the battle at King's Mountain. She had heard much already of their murderous practices and devotion to the cause of the king, which was fully confirmed by the statements of Frank Wood. He then bid the sorrowful mother farewell and proceeded on his way to the army.

218   LEGENDS OF THE

That night he came to Hillsboro', and at the inn where he stopped for entertainment, he met with Walter Brame, the son of the old elder, Melchesidec Brame, who, sent by his father, had just arrived from Virginia; having heard of the treachery and villainy of Parson Frazier, his flight with the British army under Cornwallis—to accompany the luckless wife, Mrs. Happy Frazier, with his sisters, Mary and Amy, back to their home in Virginia. From young Brame he learned the villainy of the parson, and being invited by him, the young soldier went to the residence of Mrs. Frazier and heard from the ladies a narrative of the conduct of that despicable hypocrite. They all were to set out on the ensuing morning for Virginia, and it was agreed that the young soldier would accompany them till he was compelled to take the route necessary to reach the army of Gen. Green at ———. On the way the two young men agreed, each to employ every opportunity and means which might occur, in or out of the American service, or American army, to catch and punish the renegade Scotchman in some appropriate way, for his cruel conduct to the unhappy woman whom he had decoyed from her peaceful home, robbed of her ample estate, and left with her infant son to be the victims of suffering and want, and of the disparagement consequent upon his disgraceful conduct.

It so happened that it was not long after these young patriots separated, Frank Wood to join his regiment, and Walter Brame to escort his sisters and Mrs. Frazier to Caroline county, Virginia, ere they met again and knew each other in the army of Gen. Washington near the position of Cornwallis and the defences he erected at Yorktown against the combined assaults of the Americans and French. Each in his respective division fought bravely. Young Wood among the continental troops of North Carolina attached to the command of the marquis Lafayette, the regiment commanded by the brave Col.

WAR OF INDEPENDENCE. 219

Nash, while Brame in the militia was attached to the same division, several times they each in storming the enemy's redoubts, or laboring faithfully in the erection of batteries, exposed to the raking fires of his cannon from his heavy batteries as the Americans advanced upon the British lines. Meanwhile, each in compliance with their mutual promises on the travel from North Carolina to Virginia, kept up a constant enquiry and most diligent look out, to ascertain whether his reverence, Parson Frazier, was among the besieged. They learned from several captured prisoners that he was, and was attached to the quarters of his lordship, the British commander-in-chief.

"I should like very well," said Frank in a conversasation with Brame about his reverence, "to add his name to the list of my *elect ones* from the Tories of North Carolina, and perform his funeral obsequies even in his lordship's presence; making the music of my sweet singing old rifle, in short metre, chaunt the solemn dirge. We must, however, Brame, abide our time, and until our beloved Washington shall capture or kill these gathered foemen of our America, and an opportunity occurs, (which I feel we shall have shortly,) to reckon with that dreadful hypocrite for a portion, at least, of his base frauds and crimes. One of the prisoners who gave me the information of his presence in Cornwallis's army, confirmed the fact that he left his wife in Scotland when he came to this country, and that she had followed, and was now in Nova Scotia. O! rely upon it, sir, he is a very fit subject for the most earnest animadversions of my laconic rifle."

Days and weeks came, passed, and crowned with continued success the efforts of the besiegers. Victory perched at last on the banner of Washington and Liberty. Cornwallis capitulated, and surrendered himself and his entire surviving forces, prisoners of war; together with his ample supply of munitions. But what became of the

220   LEGENDS OF THE

Scotch parson? We regret to have to say that through the timely negotiation of his favorite commander, Cornwallis, and the dignified clemency of the American commander-in-chief, as my lord's quarters were becoming too hot and dangerous for the natural non-combative temperament of the parson, he was permitted to quit the British camp, pass through the patriot lines undisturbed, and speedily made his way to Nova Scotia. There he was last heard of. We here transcribe the brief correspondence of the two commanders, by which this important privilege for Mr. Frazier secured him for the present, immunity from the just punishment for his base crimes. Frank Wood never saw him. We now give the correspondence between the two generals on the occasion. Early in the morning of the day preceding the capitulation of Lord Cornwallis, one of his aids was seen approaching the American chief's quarters bearing a white flag, and the following brief note from his lordship to Gen. Washington :

" *Gen. George Washington, Commandant, &c,*

"SIR: Confiding in your generous clemency and known desire to ameliorate, as far as consistent with your duties and the public good, the unnecessary cruelties and asperities of war, I have the honor, respectfully, to address your excellency in behalf of the Rev. Mr. James Frazier, late of Edinburgh, Scotland, now within the British lines at this place ; and ask your permit for him to pass unmolested to Williamsburg, preparatory to an embarkation to Nova Scotia, the home of his family. He is not now in arms and has not at any time been, against the colonies ; I therefore in confidence in his behalf solicit that your excellency give him the permission requested. (Signed)   CORNWALLIS,
                    Commander-in-chief of British troops
                        at Yorktown, province of Virginia.
    " Oct. 18, 1781."

WAR OF INDEPENDENCE. 221

"YORKTOWN, Va., Oct. 18, 1851.

"To the note of Cornwallis, commander of the British forces at this place, and of this date, the American commander-in-chief has the honor to reply to the request of his lordship, that it is his wish and purpose, as far as he deems consistent with his duty, to remove and pass by, as he has heretofore endeavored to do, all the cruelties and asperities of war in this contest. Americans war not against women and preachers, but enemies, and therefore hereby grants to the Rev. Mr. James Frazier the permit and passport enclosed herein. Respectfully, &c.,

GEO. WASHINGTON."

For the above correspondence the writer of these legends is indebted to an original letter of Gen. Washington, addressed to elder Melchesidec Brame, from Mount Vernon, dated the 19th of May, 1782, found with Mr. Brame's private papers at his death, preserved by the author's honored father, Maj. James Smith, executor of Mr. Brame, and now before us.

Gen. Washington's communication to the author's grand-sire, elder Brame, seems in answer to one previously addressed to the general by him, enquiring concerning Frazier and all the information he possessed of the man. Its genuineness has never been questioned. At all events, the base Scotch imposter hastily disappeared from Yorktown and was never again heard of in the United States.

Thus essentially closed the belligerent operations of the king against the patriots of America, and their independence, *all glorious*, was permanently secured.

Frank Wood continued after the siege at Yorktown, the capitulation of Lord Cornwallis, and the universal bursts of joy and thanksgiving of the whole people, from Maine to Georgia, had subsided to some extent, and effectual provisions and dispositions made by Gen. Washington, to secure the great body of officers and soldiers taken

222   LEGENDS OF THE

prisoners at that place; and the removal of them, together
with the great amount of arms and munitions of war to
points of greater security. He appealed to Gen. Lafayette, personally, to whose division he had been attached
before the siege, for permission to return to his home in
North Carolina, for the comfort and protection of his
widowed mother and orphan sister; representing briefly
the circumstances of his father's death, the unprotected
condition of his family, and the abduction of his youngest
sister Susan, by a banditti of Tories and Indians; that she
if not already murdered, was held captive in a condition
in the vast wilderness, worse than death. He also informed the General, in a few words, the true and distinct
understanding between himself and Gen. Morgan, when
first he entered the army. His request was readily granted by the good old marquis; yet, he promising, if again
his beloved country imminently demanded his personal
services, to repair instantly to his proper position, and
efficiently, as heretofore, to battle in the cause. The
next morning, at an early hour, he bid farewell to his
companions in arms, to Walter Brame and a few others
of his brave associates, and set forth inspired by the most
joyous hopes of home and country, anticipating in a few
days, by good speed in the travel, to see and embrace
once more his venerable mother and much beloved sister.
As he journied, he was the subject of many thrilling
thoughts, very bright and buoyant hopes, and sweet anticipations for himself, his family and his beloved country.
Of that loved country he mused and with thought intense,
solicitude profound, striving to see foreshadowings of her
future grandeur and glory. He thirsted to catch in his
mind's eye, straining through the vista of rolling years,
glimpses of her future destiny among the nations. But
confidently believing the war was essentially ended or
would, shortly be, her independence secured, she must,
under God, work out her own glory, or shame; and anx-

WAR OF INDEPENDENCE.

ious thoughts rushed athwart his mind. He might not, however, be regarded as properly instructed and fully versed in things of scriptural faith, and what justly belongs to a christian man's trust and dependence on the Almighty's overruling providence, to give form and substance to his hopes and prayers for her future history; yet from the lessons received from the lips and examples of his pious and well instructed mother, though so young himself, superadded to his experience, amidst the trying vicissitudes of his very adventurous life, he prayed for that country in pious poetic strains, not unlike that of his countryman, Pierpont, inspired by the same subject, in strains devout:—

> "God of peace!—whose spirit fills
>   All the echoes of our hills,
>   All the murmurs of our rills,
>   Now the storm is o'er;—
>   O, let freemen be our sons;
>   And let future Washingtons
>   Rise to lead those valiant ones,
>   'Till there's war no more."

Or as Gregory says:

> "Not hirelings trained to the fight,
>   With symbol and clarion glittering bright;
>   Nor prancing of chargers, nor martial display,
>   Nor war-trump be heard, mid their silent array;
>   O'er the proud heads of freemen our star-banners wave,
>   Men firm as their mountains and still as the grave."

Thus while urging his faithful steed onward to his home, it is reasonable, and such was in truth the case, that thoughts not only of his country and her future history and destiny, also of his beloved mother, sisters and brother, but yet, above all, of her " whose witching smile had caught his youthful fancy," thrilling his soul and commingling with most engrossing force and delight, the moments that made up the sum of his journey. In four days he reached that cherished home,

224   LEGENDS OF THE

> Where early life he sported,
> And Mary first had courted.

His meeting with his mother and sister was of course
very agreeable, as he found them in health, hopefully reposing and trusting in the guardian care of him who has
revealed himself, the orphan's father and widow's friend.
He was meekly greeted by them both, only Rosa's joy
was less tempered than the calm and chastened embrace
of maternal affection that silently and impressively beamed
from a mother's eye and ever spoke to his heart. It was
night, and in an interchange of narratives of the passing
events since his departure to join his regiment, was the
evening's entertainment until the war-worn soldier and
wearied traveler sought his bed, but not before he had
learned from them the health, &c., of the Simpsons, and
had informed them of his intention to visit that family on
the coming day, requesting the company of his sister.

That day came and ere it was noon, he had the pleasure to find Maj. John Simpson and his two sons, like
himself, just returned from the tented field and at home.
By these, as also the balance of the family, generally, his
visit was most cordially received. There was one there,
however, that did not half so soon as his impulses of affection desired, but she replete with modesty, while disciplining her blushing beauties and stilling the tides of
maiden feeling, was the last of all to welcome his return.
Still when they met,

> "The crimson glow of modesty o'er spread
> Her cheek, and gave new lustre to her charms."

It was not many days ere Frank addressed Maj. Simpson and his wife to consent to their union. They gave
consent, and the father in the fullness of a father's confiding hopes and solicitudes for their mutual blessing, may
be imagined by the reader thus to have addressed the
successful suitor:

WAR OF INDEPENDENCE.

" On you, blest youth, a father's hand confers
  The maid thy earliest, fondest wishes knew ;
  Each soft enchantment of the soul is hers;
  Thine be the joys to firm attachment due."

They were shortly after married, and among the happy participants at the marriage feast; none were more happy than the good old colored foreman, Uncle Dan, and his garrulous old ooman, Aunt Molly.

15

226   LEGENDS OF THE

CHAPTER XX.

Thoughts on the effects of times, surrounding localities, circumstances, physical and metaphysical, climate, topography of country, education, manner of life and action to make the man a giant or a pigmy, a philosopher or an ape, a hero or a poltroon—Capt. Jack Ashby—His feats of activity and bravery—Trip to Kentucky—Escape from the Indians at the falls of the Ohio.

> " O, there is moral might in this—
> My mind to me a kingdom is.
> Sound it in the ears of age,
> Stamp it on the printed page,
> Gladden sympathising youth
> With the soft music of this truth,
> This echoed note of heavenly bliss,—
> My mind to me a kingdom is."— *Tupper.*

> "'Tis education forms the common mind ;
> Just as the twig is bent the tree's inclined."—*Pope.*

THERE is no fact better sustained and established in the history and records of human action and character than that cities crowded full, and even countries dense in population, neither germinate nor rear the minds of our race, which shine forth as lights of genius, enterprise and usefulness—to eliminate science, advance art, elevate thought, and swell the tide of social kindness and prosperity—like the broad horoscope of the wilderness, the vast contiguities of sun and shade, hill and dale, mountain, cliff, and by the side of the roaring cataract.

Nor is this difficult to account for, or its causes to develop. Mind is always—matter sometimes, imitative. Man is everywhere, and always, an imitative being ; universally affected in sense and sentiment by the creations and objects which surround him. This principle in physics as well as metaphysics, we think, is demonstrated more or less in the experience and observation of every reflective individual, by the analogies of nature, and the proofs of Holy Writ. It is not, however, designed to depart from the original purpose of this book, so as to enter into disquisitions applicable to the one or the other—physics or metaphysics; and therefore we shall not extend these fugitive suggestions farther into those almost illimitable fields of reason and speculation, but leave them for the more enlightened, curious, and imaginative, to pursue or portray; only remarking, however, that in cities and more densely populated countries, in proportion to their greater aggregation and association of the everlasting debris of fallen and corrupted human nature, is the increase of vicious examples. By its lurkings from the detection of reason, and the light of heaven, the untamed and untutored mind the more naturally and quickly glides into the universal whirl of fashion, and sinks into the *Scylla* of imitation; or drives with most destructive force, upon the *Charybdis* of vicious example. But O, lead it out into the broad expanses of creation; teach it to look, though it be but as " through a glass darkly," at God and the grandeurs and harmonies of His creation; teach it its comparative littleness and insignificence, and yet its comparative dignity and value to the teaming myriads of objects around; teach it to seek and ask for wisdom at wisdom's fount, and the mighty purposes of its heart, life, and immortality, it will rise, enlarge, and ripen to apprehend, adore and imitate as far as finite may, the *infinite*, in mercy goodness and love. Yea, in its diversified exercises, though such a mind in its native darkness may, for a season of gloom and despondency, by false philosophy betrayed, look upon creation and providence as only leading " to bewilder and dazzling to blind, still like the poet's hermit, it also will rise from nature to nature's God"—discern His justice, truth, and mercy, engaged to illuminate and beautify even the loneliness and

228   LEGENDS OF THE

darkness of the grave. So striking is the figure, so
beautiful are the thoughts, embodied in the stanzas of
Beattie—unrivaled in the judgment of this writer, by anything in the language—that we suspend for a moment the
narrative, to follow these reflections, and give these lines
in full to our respected readers.

"At the close of the day, when the hamlet is still,
 And mortals the sweets of forgetfulness prove,
 When nought but the torrent is heard on the hill,
 And nought but the nightingale's song in the grove:
 'Twas thus, by the cave of the mountain afar,
 While his harp rang in symphonies, a hermit began:
 No more with himself or with nature at war,
 He thought as a sage, though he felt as a man.

'Ah! why, all abandon'd to darkness and woe,
 Why, lone Philomela, that languishing fall?
 For spring shall return, and a lover bestow,
 And sorrow no longer thy bosom inthral:
 But, if pity inspire thee, renew the sad lay;
 Mourn, sweetest complainer, man calls thee to mourn;
 O soothe him, whose pleasures like thine pass away:
 Full quickly they pass—but they never return.

'Now gliding remote, on the verge of the sky,
 The moon, half extinguish'd, her crescent displays:
 But lately I mark'd, when majestic on high
 She shone, and the planets were lost in her blaze.
 Roll on, thou fair orb, and with gladness pursue
 The path that conducts thee to splendor again.
 But man's faded glory what change shall renew?
 Ah fool! to exult in a glory so vain!

''Tis night, and the landscape is lovely no more;
 I mourn, but, ye woodlands, I mourn not for you;
 For morn is approaching, your charms to restore,
 Perfumed with fresh fragrance, and glittering with dew:
 Nor yet for the ravage of winter I mourn;
 Kind nature the embryo blossom will save.
 But when shall spring visit the mouldering urn!
 O when shall day dawn on the night of the grave!

WAR OF INDEPENDENCE.   229

"'Twas thus, by the glare of false science betray'd,
That leads to bewilder; and dazzles, to blind:
My thoughts wont to roam, from shade onward to shade,
Destruction before me, and sorrow behind.
O pity, great Father of Light,' then I cried,
'Thy creature, who fain would not wander from thee;
Lo, humbled in dust, I relinquish my pride:
From doubt and from darkness thou only canst free.

—' And darkness and doubt are now flying away
No longer I roam in conjecture forlorn.
So breaks on the traveler, faint, and astray,
The bright and the balmy effulgence of morn.
See Truth, Love, and Mercy, in triumph descending,
And nature all glowing in Eden's first bloom!
On the cold cheek of Death, smiles and roses are blending,
And Beauty immortal awakes from the tomb.'"

Man is no more the creature of accident than the victim of fate. Neither is he always, however, subordinate to his power of volition and choice of action, in his obedience or disobedience to the laws of his nature, and his accountability to his final judge. We mean, therefore, to affirm, that the time, the place, the stupendous theatre upon which, in the providence of the Almighty governor, the men of the revolution were born and raised and acted, were calculated above all others, to fit prepare and qualify them for that trying occasion.

What think you, reader, would have been the result, if Washington and his compatriots in the field, and in the counsels of the colonies, in that terrific struggle and trial of manly courage and moral firmness, had been the germs and growth of the sickly hot-beds of the vice and effeminacy of densely populated cities, or countries? If our men of war and in the cabinet, had been London cocknies, Paris beaus, or the gay Lotharios of my lady's dressing-room? or the fawning flatterers of power luxury and ease? How would the haughty Briton have triumphed and the last state of our fathers have been made seven times worse than the first? Let it be forever remembered, then, that our

230   LEGENDS OF THE

Washingtons, Henrys, Adams, Ashes, Putnams, Sumpters, Greens, Schuylers, Randolphs, Madisons, Grahams, Woods, Alexanders, Marions, Morgans, Waynes, Ashbys, and Davidsons, were sons of the wilderness; of toil and hardship; had drank from the pure and uncontaminated fountains of the free and heaven-towering mountains of the Alleghanies, and their adorning forests. Sleeping oft upon the bare bosom of earth, in the midst of the howlings of wolves, and the yellings of hostile savages!—canopied alone by the heavens, or the rolling streaming clouds,—inured from the earliest life, to employments in sports and business, most effectual for the development of the whole mental and physical man,—and their minds and spirits induced with fortitude the most enduring, and courage the most unflinching. Such were the men, and hundreds others, that officered our armies; and such were the men generally, by them commanded, and led to battle and victory.

But having said thus much upon the general character and qualifications of the officers and soldiers that periled their "lives, their fortunes, and their sacred honor, for the country's freedom; of whose deeds, as officers individually, and as soldiers generally, history and biography has already sufficiently spoken; especially as regards those whose acts in the estimation of the writer, were upon a broader scale, and effected wider interests. We will now proceed with narratives of the lives and adventures of a few individuals, hitherto not noticed or known in history or biography; nevertheless, setting forth human character, and the feats of indomitable courage, equally illustrative of the primary purposes of all historic record, which we understand to be, to teach patriotism and virtue, by the force of ever living examples.

We therefore, introduce to the reader, Capt. John, or (as he was sometimes called) Jack Ashby, born in Virginia, and reared in the immediate vicinity of the Blue Ridge, Fauquier county. From his early youth he was accustomed to the labor and business of a farmer—at intervals to the sports of the huntsman, and sometimes to the pursuits of the aborigines, that then inhabited to some extent the vallies east of that mountain, but mostly and uninterruptedly, in what is now and was then generally called the valley of Virginia. To the dense and unbroken forests of which he was early accustomed to go once or twice a year, to hunt and kill bear, and deer, and sometimes elk. His expeditions were usually crowned with great success. He was not only delighted with such sports of the forests, but also those of the field and was for many years of his earlier life, after he became married, much famed for rearing and training many of the most successful racers and breeders in the colony, at that early day. Few men of his time, although his size was small, heighth not more than five feet eight inches and a half, usual weight about one hundred and thirty pounds— could stand before him in the fashionable games of pugilism. Indeed, when he was in his seventieth year, and weighed precisely one hundred and twenty pounds, the writer was told by a gentleman of unquestionable credibility, he fairly whiped (one immediately after the other) two bullying young men; and, pitching at the third, also young, stout and active, made him run, before he put on his coat! So extraordinary were his feats at boxing and bruising, that it was a common saying, "he could whip his weight in wild cats." The gentleman above referred to, had made a match race for a mile, and the best two in three having (his horse being the oldest) to carry one hundred and twenty pounds against the catch, got the old captain, then, as we have already said, weighing exactly that amount, in his seventieth year, to ride for him, and won the match.

Still, such were the tastes and opinions of the times, and notwithstanding the advanced age and unstable habits, (as every body would now regard them,) of Capt. Ashby, he was looked upon as a gentleman; everywhere respected and taken by the hand among the most punctilious F. F. V's. So much was he a man of truth and honesty, of indomitable will, and unchanging purpose, that none doubted his promises, and most certain fulfillment, whether they were of rewards for merit or punishments for crime or offence. In the war with the French and Indians and in the army of Gen. Braddock, at the time of his celebrated defeat, near the junction of the Mononghahela and Alleghany Rivers, he commanded a company of the Virginia militia, composed principally—nay, almost exclusively of the real mountain-boys, as they were called; raised in that part of the colony bordering upon, and just east of the Blue Ridge. Men of the most brawny arms and athletic powers, as the men of that portion of the old dominion are to this day; and it is a fact well known, often spoken of and commented upon by his cotemporaries, that during that entire campaign, in the management, control, and disciplining of his rough, daring, and insubordinate militia company, not an instance occurred in which the employment of a court martial was had upon the case of any of his men, to inflict punishment according to the rigid rules of British military discipline, for any of the numerous offences, great or small, committed by them.

"O no," he would say to his fellow officers, and sometimes to those who were his superiors in command, and when admonishing him of the unmilitary mode in which he punished offenders. "O no, gentlemen, your martial law does not suit me, nor any of my men; we are not used to it, *by zooks*"—a common oath with him. "For if, in the first instance, the offence is only a slight one, such as a neglect of duty, disobedience of orders, or getting drunk, or stealing a little,—the proceedure by your regular court martial is too much trouble, too slow in its mode of operating, for my purpose. The punishment would be either whipping, which is too degrading for one of my free Virginia boys, or it would be imprison-

WAR OF INDEPENDENCE.   233

ment, for which I could not spare one of them from business. And if the charge was of offences of a higher grade, and subject to severer punishments, such as shooting or hanging or expulsion from the army, it would then be a total loss of the poor devil from the service, and I have none to spare, myself; and so I choose, by zooks, to give him what he needs right away, and then let him go about his business. The fact is, as I have in substance already stated, if one of my men commit only some ordinary act or neglect of duty, or disobedience, I first order him to stand before me and take one knock down; and that's all I give him unless he jerks off his coat, or jacket, then only two or three, if he fights pretty bravely. But, if he makes no fight, he is given one thorough knock down, and a kick or two in his posteriors, which ' wounds honor, you know, more than deep wounds before,' yet still he goes to his duties. But, Colonel, if it is for sleeping on guard, mutiny, or any such capitol offence punished by shooting or hanging, that's what my boys are not used to, by zooks, and I just give 'em such a beating and bruising, as they will never forget, or want again, and so I let them go still,—by the powers."

In that campaign it will be remembered by the reader as history narrates, that this same Capt. John Ashby, furnished to the public service, several wagons and teams for the transportation of baggage, camp equipage, &c., and that the brave Daniel Morgan, of distinguished revolutionary fame and usefulness, was one of the drivers of those teams, belonging to Ashby; and who for mutiny, knocking down and kicking a British wagon master, under whose command he was placed, was court martialed and sentenced to receive one thousand lashes from the hands of the drum major of the regiment to be administered, five hundred at one time, and five hundred in four weeks if he survived; that he, in due form received the first instalment and survived! Capt. Ashby being, on the day when the second was to be inflic-

234   LEGENDS OF THE

ted, officer of the day, remitted and pardoned him from receiving the other five hundred. Morgan lived therefore, and when the revolution came, distinguished himself more than almost any other, as a predatory and partisan commander. Whenever intelligence reached the brave old Captain, of the efficient service and distinguished bravery and skill shown by Morgan in the cause of liberty, he was sure to say:

"Now that's, by zooks,—that's just what I expected, and told them cursed fool British officers, on Braddock's expedition. Morgan has lived to do good service to his country. But had they shot or hung him, or even gin him them tother five hundred lashes, for thumping and kicking Totten, the British wagon master, he'd abin no furder use to any body, by zooks."

It will moreover be remembered by the reader of the French war with the colonies, that as soon as the dreadful defeat of Gen. Braddock, had become known, an express was sent to Lord Fairfax, then resident near Winchester, informing him of the battle and defeat of the army, and the fall of the commander, Gen. Braddock. This intelligence was forwarded from Fairfax to Lord Dunmore, then governor of Virginia, in a very few hours. Ashby was the express sent from the army to Fairfax, and, in an almost increditable short time, accomplished the trip across the mighty Alleghany Mountains through the untracked and unbroken forests and wilderness of that then gloomy and savage country.

At seven o'clock in the evening he delivered his message to Fairfax, eat a prudent supper and slept till four o'clock next morning, when at the earnest solicitation of my lord,—although he had already borne the wonderful fatigues of the express to that point fasting, and enduring an entire loss of sleep, he undertook and conveyed the tidings also to Williamsburg, and to the governor and actually delivered it in the short period of thirteen hours; a distance of two hundred and ten miles. Cer-

WAR OF INDEPENDENCE.   235

tainly, a most wonderful feat, and which very few then, or at any time, could have performed.

Few in his day or now, possess like nerve and bone and indomitable courage. In the trip from Winchester, he impressed thirteen horses, most of which were never of any use afterwards.

There is a pass across the Blue Ridge, in Fauquier county, Virginia, (the earliest and almost the only one for many years, in traveling from the eastern part of that state to what is now called the valley), called Ashby's Gap; from the fact that it crossed that mountain near his residence, then in the neighborhood of Battle Town. But more particularly, perhaps, from the wild and most adventurous freak of Capt. Jack, in driving his wagon and four horses laden with two hogsheads of tobacco, down the steep and very precipitous side of that mountain without in any way locking the wheels,—saying, "Curse the horse that can't outrun a wagon!" So he cracked his whip, away he went, helter skelter, and long before he had half reached the foot of that stupendous declivity, the tobacco pitched upon the horses, knocked him from his saddle full thirty feet to the one side of the road, rolled over and crushed two of his horses, broke the hind leg of the third, and ceased not to roll, bound and pitch till fully upon the plain at its base; while fragments of his wagon strewed the road for several hundred yards. The old fellow received no serious injury, but in the loss of his property, and was often heard, when describing the feat to his friends, to say, " By zooks, I have rode many races in my time, and beat many a one, but never in so short a time was there as much foul riding."

In those days, before the chain-lock for the wheels was invented, the usual lock employed was, to bind one or more considerable trees, with limbs and all, to the hind wheels of the wagon, and so slide down in safety. This was altogether too slow, common and vulgar a mode of business for our intrepid old soldier. He was universally

236   LEGENDS OF THE

pronounced thenceforth, however, a much better driver
of the British, Tories, and Indians, than of a wagon.

At what time, or in what year, Ashby first came to
Kentucky, is not certainly known to the writer. Enough,
however, is known to fix the period at a few years after
the coming of Daniel Boone; for it is believed to have
been in the summer or fall of 1780, and a few months after the act of the Virginia Legislature, in May of that
year, establishing the town of Louisville. He came to
that place in company with Benjamin Porter, and Charles
Wells, with whom at some point high up upon the Ohio
River, he met, having known them also in the French
war, and induced to accompany him to locate some military bounty warrants of 1763, several of which he actually
did locate in the bottom between Beargrass and the Ohio
and along up the bank of the river. Afterwards he and
his companions passed over the Falls and landed at the
point about where Tarrascon's mills are built.

There he designed to make another location of several
thousand acres more, but in a few minutes after landing
their pirogue at that point, they were fired on by six or
eight Indians and neither being struck, they hurried back
into their vessel, rowed out into the river toward the opposite shore, but had not more than reached the middle of
the stream, before they discovered a number on that bank
also. The Indians continued to fire upon them, but missed them continually, except that Ben. Porter had his hat
knocked off into the stream by a ball passing entirely
through the crown. Down the current with as much
speed as possible, they glided, keeping as near the middle as practicable; while all along for miles, and 'till near
dark, the Indians continued the shots at them, without doing any damage, being scattered upon either shore,
or keeping pace with their canoe or pirogue as it passed.
Two days and nights they thus went, fearing to land—
constantly seeing Indians on one or the other of the shores,
generally on both at once. Fortunately, however, they

were provided with a small supply of provisions, consisting of dried venison, one beef's tongue, and a little hard bread.

At an island, as the Captain supposed, two hundred and fifty miles below the Falls, they landed. This island being thinly covered with trees, they were enabled to detect any savages if present, or if attempts were made to get to them from the shore, to defend themselves, or get off again into the river, before they arrived. There they kindled a fire, laid down and slept by turns until next morning. One of them always on the watch. Then with like precautionary measures they continued their journey down the Ohio.

During their stay upon the island, they were fortunately enabled to take a fine young doe, that they discovered swimming from the Kentucky shore, and so added, in the way of meat, largely and sumptuously to their scanty stock of provisions. Some consultation here took place as to what scheme they should adopt, to extricate themselves from the dilemma into which they had fallen. They doubted the possibility of returning by way of the river, as it had from some cause risen considerably, and the force of the current materially enhanced the danger of the savage shots from the shore, as their speed would necessarily be much less. To attempt to find their way through the mighty wilderness, so great a distance to any of the stations of which they had any knowledge, filled as they might well suppose, and did judge from their continued appearance on the river, as they descended, with the wily savage foes, and without a certain supply of food, seemed madness. They did not then settle upon the course they would pursue. After however, the taking of the fine fat young doe, the old Captain observed to his companions:

" By zooks, friends, this is doing pretty well, and I have no doubt game is very plenty all the way along the river. Now I'll tell you what I have been thinking, since we have had this piece of good luck, I have thought, let the worst come to the worst, these red devils can only compel us to keep the river, and travel down it 'till it brings us to the stopping place, or somewhere else, and I have, by zooks, a sort of natural curiosity, any way, to see where these mighty waters go. So I think we'll just drive on down this current, and look into that business: and when we get out of meat, I am sure we can get plenty of game, whenever we stop a while to look for it, and we'll get, arter a while, among the Spaniards at New Orleans, and there get aboard of some ship, or trading sloop and go round to Charlestown, or some place farther toward home, some of these days. That we'll try, if you are willing?"

Both of his companions were brave men,—accustomed to hardship in hunting, and both he knew to be somewhat accustomed to Indian warfare. Porter at once agreed with Ashby, and said he thought they had better keep to the pirogue and sail downward. But Wells, for a time, with considerable warmth resisted the proposition. He said, he did not like the idea of getting among the bloody Spaniards—would rather risk it among the Shawnee Indians, rowing slowly up the current,"—and threatened leaving the boat and trying to return by land alone, rather than risk the diseases on the river, and the Spanish people. He finally submitted, however, and, as we have said, they kept on down the river.

Nothing of particular note occurred with them, until they reached the mouth of the Ohio, and on the point formed by its junction with the Mississippi, they landed. Hauling their pirogue out of the water and into a thick cluster of cane, they passed some distance from the river, built a fire and formed as well as they could, a shelter by cutting and spreading over a sort of frame-work, made with small poles, a quantity of small but tall cane or reeds. Here they also found some game, deer and wild turkeys, and remained and rested two days. Here again these

WAR OF INDEPENDENCE.   239

wanderers, though far distant from their homes and the haunts of all civilized society, were instrumental in rescuing and saving a very pretty and amiable young French girl, the daughter of an alcalde or magistrate of Kaskia, from being carried off into the wilderness inhabited only by the Chickasaw Indians, and subjected to all the horrors of a forced residence among savages, and a fate more terrific than death itself—companionship and submission to the brutal desires and will of one of them, the most degraded and debased.

On the morning of the second day after their arrival at this point, Capt. Ashby, with his rifle and hunting apparatus, walked along the bank of the Mississippi, toward the meeting of the waters, and had advanced in that direction but a short distance before he heard or thought he heard human voices. He paused and listened. Again he advanced, heard the same voices, but although now he was satisfied it was human voices that he heard, he was unable to comprehend the language spoken. Stooping very low and almost crawling, he was enabled to see the source from whence the words came, and discovered three Indians and one white man on shore engaged in the talk, appearing from the earnestness of their speech and gesticulation as in a dispute or quarrel, while a pretty young lady sat in one of the two bark canoes, still in the water fastened by bark cables to the shore. She was weeping and exhibited, as she sometimes lifted her face upward, a countenance of despair and unbounded alarm. He was not long in coming to the conclusion that she was a prisoner, as he saw that she was bound by cords to the side of the canoe, and that she had been stolen from some white inhabitants somewhere, and thereupon he began to evolve in his mind the plan in which safety and practicability, for himself and friends, must be considered, if they attempted to rescue her.

He hastened with cautious steps as he had come, after he had discovered the voices, back to the cane hut, found both of his companions, but Porter asleep. Quickly he was aroused. Ashby then told what he had discovered and heard, and, with his common asseveration, "by zooks," developed his determination to rescue the young girl, if at the risk of his own life. Instantly his friends seized their rifles and other accoutrements for battle; quickly, and with hasty cautious steps, all were seen moving toward the point where the captain had seen the party.

" We live in deeds, not years; in thoughts, not breaths;
 In feelings, not figures on a dial.
 We should commit time in heart throbs. He most lives
 Who thinks most; feels the noblest; acts the best."—

P. I. Bailey.

" Still may we battle for good and for beauty;
 Still has philanthropy much to essay;
 Glory rewards the fullfilment of duty;
 Rest will pavilion the end of our way."—<i>Salis.</i>

WAR OF INDEPENDENCE.   241

CHAPTER XXI.

Capt. Jack and his companions shoot at the Indian party—They kill the principal one, and wound another and the white man—The third Indian dives into the river and escapes—Salona Maron, the young French girl's story—She informs the Captain that the white man, Ben. James, is from Virginia—Ashby questions him and discovers his knowledge of his family—He gives an account of himself—Porter is taken sick with fever—They start down the Mississippi, taking Ben. James with them, after sinking the two dead Indians in their canoe—Porter dies and is sunk in the remaining Indian canoe, opposite Chickasaw Bluffs—Ben. James is allowed to depart for his Indian home—Capt. Ashby, Wells, and Salona Maron, proceed down the Mississippi—They arrive at New Orleans safely—Are treated well by Miss Maron's aunt and family—Capt. Jack and Wells, arrive at San Augustine, where Wells is taken sick and dies—Capt. Jack finally gets home after an absence of two years.

There's a fount about to stream;
There's a light about to beam;
There's a warmth about to glow;
There s a flower about to blow;
There's a midnight darkness changing into gray.
Men of thought and men of sense clear the way.

In a few minutes Ashby and party reached to within a short distance of the party he had discovered, and taking a position from which they could obtain a clear view and near enough to hear what was said in an ordinary voice, they discovered two of the Indians and the white man still disputing and quarreling; but as they all spoke in an Indian language, wholly unknown to either Ashby or his friends, they did not understand the subject of the dispute.

The other Indian was still nearer to them but squatted upon his haunches near to the canoe in which the white

16

242   LEGENDS OF THE

girl still sat, bound to its sides.   They also were holding a
conversation but in the French language which Wells understood and spoke fluently.   The Indian near her was
urging her to love him,—telling her of his riches,—that
he was a chief and warrior of his nation and had lately
been in Georgia with the Cherokees and Creeks, and had
killed and scalped four white men and two women, and
that if she would go with him to his nation, live with him
and be his good squaw he would make her and her father
rich.   But if she did not quit crying and go with him
freely, he would kill and scalp her too, or words to that
effect.

She wept most bitterly, seemed dreadfully terrified and
trembled much.   However, Wells understood her to say
in reply to the Indian, that she would never go with him
willingly—that she would rather die—he might kill her,
and she would much rather than be his wife; that he had
four days before, killed her beautiful little brother in the
cornfield and she hated him.   She then lifted up her
head looked toward the heavens and cried in a distinct
voice:

"O Marie mère de Dieu! priez pour moi—sauvez moi
de cette destinée horrible!   Emportez moi loiu de cette
destinée cruelle!   O, priez qua je mœur ici et que j'aille a
vous.   O je ne peu pas viure avec ce bourreau sauvage.
Oh, laissez moi mourrier!"

Just as she ended this address to the Virgin Mary,
calling to her according to the strange notion of Catholics, to save her or take her from the earth and the
cruelty of the Indian murderer, instead of calling upon
God, the Almighty Father,—Colbert the Indian chief,
for such seemed to be the name and character of him
with whom she had had the above mentioned conversation, leaped to his feet and in great apparent fury of manner, uttering and jabbering threats, darted toward her,
waving his tomahawk high over his head, and just as he
seemed to be about to strike in most destructive fury, the

WAR OF INDEPENDENCE.   243

victim before him, at a concerted sign made by Capt. Ashby, they each drew up their rifles, selected severally their mark, and fired. Colbert instantly fell pierced through the heart and never breathed again. Chickfos, another Indian, fell at the crack of Porter's rifle shot through the abdomen, and the white man, named Ben. James, fell at the fire of Wells. The third Indian being untouched, with a hideous yell leaped into the river, dived and was not seen again. Capt. A. ran to where the dead Indian, Colbert lay, seized the cable by which the canoe was fastened to the shore, drew it quickly to him, cut the cord by which she was bound, lifted her out and tried to place her on her feet, but seeming stunned, she sank to the ground and would have fallen into the water had he not caught her in his arms and bore her up the bank.

Wells finding Ben. only badly wounded, bore him up to the shade of a large beech tree, laid him down, got water in his hat from the river, washed his face and poured a little into his mouth. Presently he spoke and began to beg in English for his life.

It was not long either before the girl seemed to awake to a better sense of what was done—still, however, in great fright. Most scrutinizingly and imploringly she looked into the face of the old soldier, and seeming by that look to become satisfied he was not her enemy, she sank on her knees before him and being unable to speak the English language, or more than imitate a few words, grasped his hand, crying, father, O father! and by gestures more than words, implored his mercy and protection. He again raised her to her feet and finding she could stand and walk, he conducted her to his cane shelter. Wells came in, and, in her own language, informed her who her deliverers were, assured her of their protection and friendship. She wept and shouting aloud, claped her hands and began to return thanks to the Virgin,

244   LEGENDS OF THE

who had heard, as she said, her prayers and sent the deliverance desired.

"Oh," said Wells, "do you believe that Mary the mother of Jesus, sent us in answer to your prayer I heard you make just before we shot the Indians, to deliver you?" She answered in the affirmative.

"Well," said he, (in her own language) "we English don't believe such things as that,—we ask help in such cases of the Almighty himself; and if we get aid, we believe we must get it alone from God. Well, I don't know, nor talk much about such things; but we want you to tell us now who you are—where you are from and how you came here?"

She replied her name was Salona Maron, the oldest daughter of M. Maron—her father, who lived a merchant at Kaskaskia. He was born in France, lived in New Orleans where she, her little sister and brother were born, and he had been four or five years living in Kaskaskia, trading for furs and skins and selling goods to the Indians. That a great number of the Indians from many tribes came there. That some three weeks back these three Indians and Ben. the white man, together with a great many more came to trade, bringing much peltry and fur; that Colbert had offered, as her father told her, to give all the fur and skins if he would sell her to him, to be his wife; that her father had indignantly rejected his offer and refused to let him into his house any more. She said Colbert had six months before been at Kaskaskia, and wanted her to agree to go and live with him and be his squaw. But rejected by her father and forbid to come into his house any more, Colbert sent Ben. the white man, to court her for him, who could talk some French. He got an opportunity to talk to her, stated that Colbert was his wife's brother, a great warrior. Chickasaw chief was a mighty man and mighty rich; owned forty negroes, had a heap of money, skins and fur; would give all to her if she would go home with him and be his squaw. That she told him she would not. She would rather be killed and she wanted him to tell Colbert so. That three days after she went with her little brother to get some green corn from the field a half mile from the town; and so soon as they got into the high corn the two Indians that was killed ran up to them and with a great club knocked her brother in the head and she believed killed him, seized her and with her handkerchief, which she wore covering her bosom, tied up her mouth so that she could not speak; took her up and run with her out into the prairies for a good distance, where they had two horses, threw her up into the arms of Colbert, started in a gallop, and, in about a half a day, brought her to the river, where Ben. with two other Indians were with two canoes waiting; sent the horses off by one of those Indians, cooked some meat, eat it and in a great hurry started down the river in the canoes, tying her fast in one of them and thus brought her in two or three days to where she was rescued.

Here she paused and burst into tears, and began to plead with them to take her back to her father and mother. She said O, if they would only do that her father would make them all rich—give them his store and everything. Capt. A. who with great interest listened to what she related, having it from time to time interpreted and explained to him by Wells, said:

"By zooks, I should not know how to begin to charge for any such thing as that, my pretty little gal, even if we could take you back. Our fix is a pretty bad one too. We've got to fight our way back to Virginia some way, and can only get there I reckon by keeping the river down to New Orleans, and get round over that part of the sea on some ship or something else, and get home some way."

Understanding the captain to speak of going to New Orleans, she smiled with evident delight and new impulses of hope and joy; and with a countenance highly expressive of gratitude, looking at the generous old soldier, she said she had an uncle at New Orleans, a rich merchant, and if they would take her to him he would reward them. She told them she understood Capt. A. to talk of his home in Virginia. Heard and said that at Kaskaskia, she had learned from some Cherokees, that Ben. was born in Virginia. When about eighteen years old, going to some town with his father, they were attacked by a party of Cherokee warriors; his father killed, and he taken by them. Carrying him to their town, they were about to burn him and two others, and to have a great frolic and dance, to which many Indians from several nations were come to enjoy the sport, when a pretty Chickasaw squaw, the daughter of a chief, saw him, fell in love with him, bought him, took him to her father's town, married him, and had been his wife ever since.

"Well, well," said Ashby, "this is a strange story. If he did come from Virginia, I'll go and see from what part he was taken. I have certainly seen some one in my time that he looks like; but he's got so sun-burnt and yellow you can hardly tell if he is a white man or Indian."

And so he went to the place where he, Porter, and the wounded white man were lying on the ground, in the shade of a beach tree. Coming near to them he said:

"Well, old fellow, you are paying rather severely for being found in bad company this morning, and I want to hear how you are, where you are from, and all about you. The young gal tells me you came from Virginia—is it so?"

Ben. looked at him very steadfastly for a while, as if intending to fathom his purpose before answering, or studying how he should respond.

"Come, tell me, what is your name, and where are you from?"

"My name," he said, "is Ben. James. I came from Virginia—where did you come from?"

"From Virginia," said the Captain—"what county?"

"I believe they called the county Forkyiar. It's been fifteen years since I left there, but I remember there was a place they called Forkyiar Court-house, close by where my father lived."

"Was your father's name John James? I remember John James, who, it was said, was killed by the Indians, over the ridge, about fifteen or twenty years ago; was he your father? Was you the son he had with him going over to Abington?" Ben. rose up as well as he could, being badly wounded in the shoulder, looked again with great earnestness at the Captain, and answered:

"It was me."

"By zooks," said the old man, "I knowed your daddy and mama, and all of them, and I reckon I had seen you, too, but I had forgot you. O! I knowed your brother Jonathan, well. He went under me on Braddock's campaign, where we all got licked so. Well, where have you been all this time, and how came you out with those Indians that we killed this morning? I want you now to tell me everything about it.

"I have told you," he said, "my father and I was going to see his brother at Abington. He was shot by the Indians—Cherokee warriors. They took me and tied my hands behind my back, then packed everything upon me, and when I got so tired I could not run fast, they jabbed sharp sticks in me to make me run faster, and made me bleed all over. I thought I would die. I fainted two or three times. Then they took the packs off of me, and I went better. In three days we got to their town; they called it Nickajack. Kept me very close about three weeks, and treated me very well that time. They had two more prisoners when I got there—an old man with a grey head, and a mighty pretty Carolina gal. So one day when all the Indians from all the nations around

come, and their squaws too, they told us they were going
to burn us, and brought us up tied where all the Indians
had gathered round in a ring—the squaws was thar too—
one squaw, mighty pretty, come up to me, talked Indian.
I could'nt know what she said. I know now though.
She said, " pretty white boy, Cassata loves you,"—that
was her name. She was the old chief Chickatomo's
daughter. She then took hold of my nose and pulled it,
and then both of my ears, and did like she was going to
pull me along with her. Then she left me and went to
one of the oldest warriors, along when they took me prisoner, and they talked Indian a long time. I and the other
prisoners stood and said nothing. They looked mighty
pale and skeared. I felt so too. Cassata come back to
me again and two young Cherokee squaws with her.
This time she cut the string that bound my hands, took
hold of my hand and pulled me along with her as she
went back to the Indian ring, talking to me all the time
Chickasaw, and motioning me to follow her. At first I
did'nt understand her, and the other two squaws got behind me and shoved me along. She told me she had
bought me and wouldn't let me be burnt, and I must go
along with her and live with her in her wigwam all the
time. So she took me home with her to her father's
Chickatomo's town. She loved me, often told me so, and
had saved my life. I loved her, too, very much. I married her, lived with her. She gave me two mighty pretty
boys at first, and a pretty little squaw baby last,—no
more."

" But," said the Captain, " what was done with the
gray headed prisoner and the Carolina gal? Did they
burn them ? "

" I saw them burn the old man. Poor old man ! how
he halloed before he died ! But a large, young Creek
warrior, Wishita, they called him, bought her, too, and
took her away with him."

" But," said the old soldier, " why did you go with

WAR OF INDEPENDENCE. 249

those Indians to Kaskaskia and steal off this young French gal from her father and mother? I expect, though, you have got to be as bad as any of the cussed Indians by this time."

"Colbert, the big Indian you killed this morning," said Ben., "is Cassata's brother, Chickatomo is his father, too. He, last Spring, was up at Kaskaskia, trading skins; saw Salona Maron, and loved her mighty much. She was just got to be a woman. He loved her, he said, and wanted her to go with him to his town and be his squaw. She would not go, run off and wouldn't let him see her any more. He come back and said to me, that she was so pretty he would kill himself if she would not come and be his squaw. He studied hard about it, and shortly afterwards, with a large number of his warriors, he went high up the Arkansas. Hunted and trapped a long time—brought a heap of skins and furs home, and said to me, ' Ben., I am going again to Kaskaskia to buy Salona Maron of her father, and give him all these skins and furs to bring her to my wigwam, and if I cannot get her to go with me, I will shoot myself.'

"He wished me to go with him and try and get her consent. I went with him, talked to her for him, but she refused, and her father would not sell her, but drove him off. She said she would rather die, herself. I studied what Colbert had better do, and at last told him he would have to steal her. I told him how he must contrive it. Three days after he did steal her from the corn-patch, and I hurried to the river with the Indians, one of which he sent the horses back by, and so we came down the river to where you found us."

"But when I first found you on the river this morning," said Ashby, "you and the three Indians seemed to be quarreling and acted as if about to fight,—what was the cause of that?"

"O!" said he, "Colbert saw the other Indian that you killed at the fire of the guns to-day, who was in the

250   LEGENDS OF THE

canoe with her, trying to hug and kiss the gal last night, and when we got to the point, he said he would kill him or kill the gal.   I tried to prevent his killing the Indian, and he said the gal loved me more than him, and he would shoot me, but went to the canoe to talk to her again, and was talking to her when your guns fired."

" But, Ben, do you think that Indian who jumped into the river when you were shot, and was never seen again by any of us, was drowned? or did he just dive till he got out of sight, and then swim to the shore ?"

Fully for the space of a minute he only looked at the Captain without giving an answer, and then said: " I have told you my name, and all about my father.   You say you know him—now tell me your name and where you knew him, and then I'll tell you where the Indian, that jumped into the river, went to."

" O, my name," he answered, " is Jack Ashby.   And I knew your father in Fauquier county, Virginia, where I now live when I am at home."

Ben. looked at him from head to foot—sat silent for a minute or more—seemed puzzled in mind some way.   At last ne said, " I remember to have heard when I was a little boy that a man called Ashby, rode in a half a day two hundred miles to tell the Governor, I think it was, at the big town away down the conntry, something about Braddock—are you the Ashby ?"

" Yes, I am the man—now tell me," he said, " what you think became of that Indian ?—was he drowned, or where do you think he went ? "

" He went to his town, Chickabeauff, where he and the other Indians lived, and where I and my squaw and ba· bies live."

" How far is it, that is, how many miles is it to that town ? "

" I don't know," he said, " how many miles it is ; it will take him two days to go there and back."

" Is he coming back ? " said the Captain.

WAR OF INDEPENDENCE. 251

Ben looked him full in the face and said: "Will you take me to my home at Chickabeauff?"

"How," replied the Captain, "am I to take you there! —Is it on any river? Now, Ben. James, I think I understand you. You are fearing I will shoot you or do some other injury to you so you will be kept from getting back to your squaw and children, and are hoping that the diving Indian got across the river, and will be able to bring Indians back with him to release you and take us all prisoners, or kill us all. You need not fear this. If you think you are able with the wound you are suffering, to get home, I will put you across the river and you can go where you please. We cannot carry you in our pirogue, as there is not room for more than four of us, with the baggage, and I shall take the French girl to New Orleans with me. So when we go you will have to shift for yourself. We must go anyhow. But I want you to tell me now whether you hope the Indian will give the alarm and return with a number of Indians to rescue you and take us or kill us?"

Ben. enquired if the Indian did not yell the Indian war whoop when he leaped into the water?

"He did," replied Ashby, "a most terrible yell; and then sunk and we saw him no more."

"Well," said Ben., "that was the war-whoop, and he will come back as quick as he can."

During this long chat between the Captain and Ben. James, Porter continued to sleep on the ground, and Wells and the girl remained, conversing in the hut. Ashby stepped to Porter, awoke him, and he arose, his face wonderfully flushed with fever and an affection resembling croup or quinzy. He could scarcely speak so as to make himself understood.

Together they entered the hut and found Wells and Salona Maron engaged in preparing and spreading a plain though substantial dinner for themselves and friends. Captain A. spoke immediately to his companions of the

252   LEGENDS OF THE

conversation he had had with Ben. James,—of what he
had said would be the purpose and action of the Indian
who had jumped into the river; also the fears he himself
entertained that he would, if they did not as soon as
practicable get off from that place, return with a company of Chickasaw warriors, and kill or take them all
prisoners. He said:

"We must start down the river as soon as we eat
something. But then what shall we do with Ben. James?
In his present condition, if we put him over the river, he
could scarcely make out to get to his town, and if we
leave him here, it would be to starve, unless the Indians
he expects come and relieve him. In our pirogue there
is not room to take him with us, and besides, he will be
unwilling to go with us to New Orleans."

"Oh," said Wells, "we can make him get in one of
the canoes left by the Indians at the point; tie it to our
pirogue and carry him with us till he gets able to foot it,
any way, if he wont go all the way with us, and so then
get to his town; or else just shoot him and put him out
of his misery."

"O no!" said the old captain, "that I could not consent to. He has lived with the Indians, it is true, till he
is altogether as tricky and dangerous as one himself.
Has a wife and children among them, for whom he seems
to entertain so much affection, that he will not be willing
to leave them. He is the son of an old and very clever
father I once knew, in my county in Virginia, and has
brothers and sisters there, clever people. We must not
treat him with any cruelty. For he suffers now a good
deal from the wound he got this morning, in the shoulder,
and I reckon we must endeavor to take him with us, for
a while, at least, in the way you speak of, Wells."

"Well, Captain," said Wells, "I will go down to the
point right away and see if the pirogue and canoes are
all safe, and get back while the young girl is fixing up
the dinner, so that we can be off directly after we eat it."

WAR OF INDEPENDENCE. 253

While he was gone to the point, Captain Ashby observed the appearance of Porter to be that of a very sick man, under the influence of a most distressing fever, and complaining in much apparent agony of a pain in the head. He explained to him his intention of starting from that place in a short time, and the cause. Porter, however, suffered so much that he could scarcely comprehend what was said, and only replied he could not live, and especially, exposed to the intense heat of the sun in the pirogue. Wells soon returned, and said the pirogue and the Indian canoes were all at the point; but that the wounded Indian whom they had left on the shore, believed to be dying, had risen and contrived to drag Colbert, shot through the heart by Captain Ashby, into one of the canoes, and was there himself, evidently dying, lying by his side.

"Poor wretches," said the captain, "such is not an uncommon virtue with the Indians generally in regard to their dead or dying. They always make a like effort, as I learn, to get off or hide them, so intense is their dislike of leaving them to be scalped by their enemies. Well, we must now hasten our dinner and get away from this place, as we are constantly in danger of an attack from some party or other of them coming to this point, upon one or other of these rivers."

Accordingly they hastily partook of the dinner, of which they scrupulously gave to Ben. James a reasonable share of the best and most delicate portions, and all hastened with their share of baggage and the residue of the dinner prepared yet unconsumed, together with their small store of venison, turkies, &c. yet remaining.

Porter was still very ill, having been unable to partake of any portion of the food prepared, and being now barely able to walk, while Ben. James, whose complaint of great pain from his wound, cheerfully agreed, when the plan of Captain Ashby was explained to him, to accom-

254 LEGENDS OF THE

pany them to the Chickasaw Bluffs. Indeed, he said he would like to go to Virginia with Captain Ashby if he was well of the wound he had got, and if he could only see his squaw awhile before he went. That since the talk he had had with him about his brothers and sisters there, he felt more desire to see them again than he had felt for many years.

When they reached the point they found the two Indians on one of the canoes, as Wells had represented, only that they were both entirely dead; and the old captain expressed himself mortified at being obliged to leave them unburied. He said they were human beings; and however prejudiced he might feel against them when living,—disposed to shoot or otherwise put it totally out of their power to do any farther injury—yet when dead, though savages, they were as harmless as any other dead men, and their claims upon his sympathies just as great.

Wells told him, even if they had time, they had no hoe or spade, or anything else with which to dig a grave. He thought, however, they could easily sink them to the bottom of the river, by putting some large rocks in the canoe; and while they would thereby be protected from vultures and other animals of prey, they would serve the fish awhile for food without doing anybody any harm. This they concluded to do, and in a few minutes two large rocks were procured from a convenient quarry, placed in the canoe, down it went on being pushed out a little from the shore, and no more was seen of the Chickasaw chief, Colbert, and his savage companion.

The party then instantly renewed their journey down to New Orleans—Salona Maron, Porter, and Wells in the pirogue with Captain Ashby, and Ben. James in the Indian canoe, lashed to the pirogue. Nothing of any interesting character occurred till they reached the Chickasaw bluffs on the evening of the second day; having traveled day and night, never landing; seeing, however,

WAR OF INDEPENDENCE. 255

frequently, on the shore, Indians secreting themselves behind trees, as they glided along in the middle of the stream ; and having a hostile appearance.

All the way Porter grew worse and worse. There being no medicine on board, they could administer nothing to ameliorate in the slightest degree the raging fever upon him, and with which he was threatened with immediate destruction. By the time they reached the bluffs, all believed his death in a very short time was inevitable. He was totally insane and destitute of the knowledge of anything. At that place Captain Ashby determined to land on the western bank of the river, as he supposed the eastern bank the most dangerous, being so contiguous to the habitations of the Chickasaw and Choctaw Indians. Here they built a temporary covering as at the mouth of the Ohio. Every attention was shown to poor Porter. Salona, true to all the sympathy and tenderness of her sex, unceasingly stood or seated herself by his side. Often dipped from the river, water, and bathed his head, hands and feet, burning with fever; while to the most distressing and alarming extent he raged and screamed with delirium. He often talked of his home, his family and friends ; would seem to converse with his wife and children, fancying they were present, and addressing them sometimes with all the affection and expression of countenance the tenderness of paternal affection could indicate in words or gestures which, although she did not understand the language employed, repeatedly excited her to tears ; and when he spoke of his home, his wife, and his children, even the veteran Ashby shed many tears. But the sympathy, care, and tears of his friends could not avail; and on the morning of the second day after their arrival at the bluffs, he breathed his last.

Now a like difficulty occurred to Captain Ashby and Wells, to that in respect to the burial of the two Indians at the mouth of the Ohio. Common humanity moved their solicitude to give something like a decent burial to

256   LEGENDS OF THE

the bodies of the Indians; but now poor Porter, their
friend, the companion of their enterprise, sharer of their
peculiar dangers and distresses, had also died. His mortal remains alike invoked a decent interment. It was,
however, being unable to avail themselves of any instruments by which to excavate a grave, determined to place
his body in the remaining Indian canoe and sink it to the
bottom of the turbid Mississippi, and so in a few minutes
it was in much solemnity interred, and not without
tears gushing from the pretty blue eyes of Salona and
from those of his hardy companions. Even Ben. James,
who received his most painful wound (so far as he knew)
at the hands of the deceased, seemed to weep a little and
exhibit a countenance of much seriousness.

Immediately after this scene, the two travelers, Ashby
and Wells, began to think and prepare for the further
pursuit of their journey. The first thing to be done was
to dispose of Ben. James. When they first came to the
Chickasaw bluffs, the captain deemed it most prudent not
to let him go till they were ready to leave themselves,
lest he, before their friend Porter had died or grown better so as to enable them to proceed, should inform the Indians of their presence at that point and induce an attack; but
now they were prepared to set off, how should they dispose of him? They then told him he might, if he choose,
be set over on the Chickasaw bank, go, if he was able, to
his town, or go with them to New Orleans. Ben. choose
the former, and after thanking them for the care they had
bestowed upon him, and requesting the Captain to inform his relatives in Virginia of his being yet alive, and
his place of residence, bade them and the young lady
farewell, and being taken to the bluff he started for his
home.

In a short time our friends were rapidly rowing their
little bark down the rapid current of the great father of
waters. In ten days' sail they reached Natchez, where
they landed for a few hours to enable them to lay in a

WAR OF INDEPENDENCE.   257

supply of comforts and provisions for the balance of the trip to New Orleans.

In three days they reached its levee without having any occurrence of an interesting character on the way, traveling day and night, as the nights were calm and clear, and the moon shone with more than her ordinary brilliancy. Having found the family of M. Maron, the uncle of Salona Maron, that is, his widow and two children, he having died the year previous at Cuba, they received her and her two friends with cordiality and treated them during their stay with marked hospitality and politeness.

At New Orleans our friends remained for five weeks, being unable sooner to procure a passage through the Gulf upon any vessel to the Southern or South-western part of the Atlantic on the Continent of North America. There they bid farewell to their pretty little Salona, who, from some intelligence received from Kaskaskia, hoped shortly to be sent for by her father and to reach her home again in a few-months. She seemed greatly affected at their departure, wept much, and having by this time attained a slight knowledge of the English language, employed it all in expressing her grateful obligations to the old captain for his kind and very parental care for her safety and comfort, as well as in her native language, the gratitude due to the kindness of Wells.

They were in three weeks landed at St. Augustine, where they were necessarily detained for weeks seeking a vessel by which to reach Charleston, or Savannah, or some other point more contiguous to their home in Virginia. At St. Augustine Captain Ashby was so unfortunate as to have to bury, also, his last companion in this most tedious and adventurous trip to the wilderness of the West. They had not been at St. Augustine but little more than a week ere Wells was attacked with a most virulent and strange fever, and in a few days brought to his grave. To one of less sturdy nerve this was, indeed, calculated to overwhelm, embarrass and afflict the mind; but al-

17

258   LEGENDS OF THE

though the old soldier felt as intensely as was by any
means reasonable, still he was not wholly discouraged,
and in two weeks embarked in a small trading sloop, and
after considerable and frequent delays at different points,
landed at Norfolk, Virginia, from whence in about a
month from the time of his embarkation at St. Augustine,
he reached his home in Fauquier county. He found his
wife, who had never heard from him from the time of his
departure—having been gone more than two years, and
she fully believing he had perished.

Many other incidents and adventures of this brave old
soldier might yet be recorded, but we forbear at this time.

CHAPTER XXII.

Thos. McClanahan, another native Virginian—Incidents of his boyhood—His skill and perseverance as a huntsman—Chases a buck on foot six miles—Runs him into a farmer's cellar, where he is found next morning, killed and taken home in triumph—Tom, at the age of eighteen leaves his home, and joins the continental army—Travels one hundred miles on foot to whip a man who insulted his father, and having done so, immediately returns—Is engaged in the battles of Brandywine, Morristown, Monmouth, and Trenton—Returns home after the surrender of Cornwallis—Renews his acquaintance with Miss Ann Green—Courts her—Asks the consent of her brother, Col. Robert Green—Is refused.

"Youth's dreams are but flutterings
Of those strong wings whereon the soul shall soar
In after-time to win a starry throne.
The future works out great men's destinies ;
The present is enough for common souls."--*Lowell.*

THOMAS McCLANAHAN, the oldest son of the Rev. William McClanahan of the Baptist Church, was born about the year 1754-'5, in Westmoreland county, Virginia, and was about eighteen years old, when the battles at Lexington and Bunker's Hill were fought. His earliest indications of mind and character in future life, were those of a great devotion to all the amusements common to boys ; particularly those requiring the greatest activity, adventure and hazard, and, an unabating thirst for fun, sport, and amusement. He was particularly fond of the chase, and with his pack of hounds in pursuit of the fox or deer, when only ten or twelve years old, he would follow on foot, from early day until night,—contriving, to the astonishment of all acquainted with the fact, to "come in at the death," to use the fox hunter's phrase, as early as

260   LEGENDS OF THE

any of the gentleman who were mounted upon their fleet-est and best trained hunters.

On one occasion, hearing his hounds upon a full cry, as he and several believed who joined in the sport, after a fox—he on foot and they well mounted,—they pursued for several hours before it was discovered they were in full chase of a deer. All the others immediately declined further following the cry, believing it was useless. But little Tom, still followed on, hissed on and encouraged his dogs,—now greatly wearied and dispirited. Still the most faithful and enduring of them, kept up the pursuit and on they went, and the bounding buck being at a little past sun set, sadly wearied and severely pressed by the pack, for safety and shelter leaped into a gentleman's cellar. Into the cellar the dogs went also; and, when their little master got up, they were yelling and terribly worrying the buck. Calling them all off, with the consent of the farmer, he closed the cellar-door, and left old antler to rest himself as well as he could in his newly chosen quarters, until morning.

That night at about eight o'clock, he reached home on foot, a distance of five or six miles from where he caged the buck, astonishing his father and mother with a detail of his wonderous feat. His father was wholly incredulous to his narrative; and being himself a man of scrupulous truthfulness, hating a falsehood most cordially in any one, but especially this as he thought in his promising boy. It is very probable, but for the timely interference of the mother and her exhortations to his father, to await the discoveries he might make in the morning of the truth or falsehood of his statement, he would forthwith have shown that he was not disposed to "spare the rod and spoil the child," but practice upon the monition of Solomon and the doctrines it was designed to teach in parental discipline. However, the mother's teaching—pursuant to the wise maxim of Davy Crockett, being of a wiser practical applicability; " be sure you are right and then

WAR OF INDEPENDENCE. 261

go ahead,"—prevailed, and the tired boy was let go to his bed that night with an unstriped night-shirt, to await the development of the morning.

At early daylight the parson set out with Tom, to seek the truth of the matter. At the house of Capt. Gibson, peeping into his cellar, they discovered his buckship by his shining eyes wide awake, and awaiting his visitors, to the great gratification of the parental heart, and the proud triumph of the brave boy. Quickly the game was throttled and prepared, *secundem artem*, to be transported to the home of the mother and all the family, to give to all, not excluding the courageous pack, joy and gladness, which the latter most unmistakably evidenced in the loudest yells and howls of applause.

At school our young hero was not considered nor posted as a dunce or even a dull boy, but as dedicating all his capabilities and time, to sport of some sort or other, and in pranks and sportive tricks, upon his school fellows, which they all were at perfect liberty at all times to return good humoredly without the least hazard of giving offence to him. But if one or a half-dozen of them, at a time, took offence at any of his sportive pranks or tricks, and angrily resented, or attempted retaliation in anger, woe be unto them all. No school discipline or law, or scarcely parental command and authority, could stay his vigilant hand from administering the most prompt and severe punishment. An awful thrashing was the inevitable consequence, unless speedy concession or honorable reparation was made. Then, instantly, the fullest forgiveness and restoration to favor would as certainly follow.

His scholastic attainments were but small; although his sensible and judicious father, would have delighted much in extending his opportunities for learning, to the placing him in the best schools of that early day. But for study and learning he never showed the least fancy or relish. A game of play, or amusements of rough roll and tumble; a foot race, a match at fisticuffs, or fox or deer chase, ever had the greatest charms for him; and would not be foregone for the acquirements of any knowledge from books. His parents having the ability to indulge him with time and leisure, to gratify his passion for any or all of those amusement, they constituted almost his entire employments. It was the surprise of all who were made acquainted with his wonderful feats in following his hounds, in a deer or fox chase, for whole days. When asked the way in which he bore and accomplished it, or how he had trained himself to be able to bear it, he mainly accounted for it by referring to his early habits of practising long races, refusing to drink water or anything else, to quench the thirst that naturally occurred. He relieved thirst most readily and effectually by plucking, as he ran, (almost everywhere to be found in forest or field,) the leaves of the *cornei cervinum*, or white plantain, as it is commonly called—chewing them and swallowing the juice, expressed as he ran.

At the age of seventeen he went to his parents to permit him to join in the service of the country. He had often before, even at the age of sixteen, urged his parents to consent; but they invariably refused him. Having now passed his seventeenth year, he insisted, as his beloved country needed his services, and as he possessed the health and constitutional vigor and activity to render the most effective aid in the glorious cause of liberty, they ought to consent. "At all events," he said to his father, "it is my intention to go with or without your consent, and I must employ the best means I can to procure the necessary equipage expenses to the army."

To this candid declaration of his purpose, neither of his parents replied, and left him to his own reflections. Still he was resolved to go. The more he thought of it, the more increased was his anxiety to be a soldier in his country's cause.

In a few days, therefore, having borrowed a small sum

of his neighbor, Capt. Thomas Gibson, together with his saddle and bridle, he was one morning missed from home, together with his father's fine rifle and fine young blood mare. Little doubt, however, was entertained by father or mother, that he was off in fulfilment of his determination to go to the army, somewhere. They were not mistaken. Having learned that his uncle, Col. Thomas Marshall, with his regiment, was posted at or near Williamsburg—thither he went with all practicable speed, and having made himself known to the colonel, and received the appointment of corporal, in one of his companies, became at once, somewhat noted; but more for his tricks and pranks and love of fun, than for any indications of military prowess and discretion.

In Col. Marshall's regiment, in two battles, he had fought bravely, before his family at home knew where he was. Nay, the first reliable intelligence they had of him, was brought them by a neighbor, who happened at Fredericksburg, about thirty-five miles from the home of the father, and who told young McClanahan's parents, on returning home, that he had witnessed a most bloody pitched battle between Tom and Peter McCormack; that Tom. having heard that Peter had abused, cursed, and attempted to strike his father while conducting a meeting of worshipers at the Baptist church of his neighborhood, and having sent McCormack a challenge to meet him on that particular day at Fredericksburg; they met and fought it out, Tom, giving him a most awful beating, although he had within three days before. under a brief furlough from his colonel, traveled on foot one hundred miles to reach the appointed spot at the time specified.

He very soon set out for a return to his post at Williamsburg, only addressing a brief note to his father, informing him and his mother of the meeting, the cause, and the victory, without note or comment; apologizing for his haste in returning, on the ground of the little time he had in his furlough yet to run.

264   LEGENDS OF THE

A vast number of like instances could be mentioned as occuring in the life of this truly brave young man, wherein his feats of pugilism—now almost by every respectable citizen regarded as disreputable, but then looked upon, according to tbe prevailing fashions and customs of the country in every circle of society, as altogether praiseworthy, making the greatest and most successful bully the most respectable man—were very extraordinary. But we shall not, here at least, pursue his history further in detailing them.

In the continental service, Thomas McClanahan was esteemed one of the best of soldiers; always in battle found at his post, and in the hottest of the fight. In general, in or out of the army, his personal encounters—and they were remarkably numerous—found some palliation in the fact that they were very seldom personal to himself or on his own account, but on account of some other, whose injury he resented, or whose cause he espoused.

About twelve months before the treaty of peace between the colonies and the parent government, and the acknowledgment of their independence, but subsequent to the capture of Lord Cornwallis at Yorktown, where McClanahan was present and took part in that most crowning feat of the revolution—this young soldier left the army and returned to his home at his father's, in Culpepper county, Virginia. From a small boy he had been acquainted with Miss Nancy Green, the orphan sister of Col. Robert Green, of revolutionary notoriety, a gallant officer, generally regarded as wealthy, nevertheless proud and haughty in temperament, and who had reared his sister as his own child from very tender years. With Miss Green the young soldier, early after his return to the neighborhood, renewed his acquaintance,—having from his boyhood felt the greatest attachment for her, even when they were at school. While he was in the army, often, very often, she was the subject of his most cherished meditations and the object of his purest affection. The bold soldier was not long in soliciting her hand in matrimony, though he was yet in his minority, and she only seventeen. To their union her brother was bitterly opposed. To the refusal of this brother and guardian, our hero coolly responded, that it was at least his duty and altogether respectful for him to ask his consent; but if Miss Nancy was the woman he judged her to be, they would be married shortly, the colonel's objection to the contrary notwithstanding.

CHAPTER XXIII.

Young McClanahan informs his mother of his determination and requests her assistance—She breaks the subject to her husband, and they agree to provide their son with funds to consummate his object—Miss Nancy and her lover fix upon the course they intend to adopt.

"When daylight was yet sleeping under the billow,
    And stars in the heavens still lingering shone,
Young Kitty, all blushing, rose up from her pillow,
    The last time she e'er was to press it alone;

For the youth whom she treasured her heart and her soul in
    Had promised to link the last tie before noon;
And when once the young heart of the maiden is stolen,
    The maiden herself will steal after it soon!

As she look'd in the glass, which a woman ne'er misses,
    Nor ever wants time for a sly glance or two,
A butterfly, fresh from the night-flower's kisses,
    Flew over the mirror, and shaded her view.

Enraged with the insect for hiding her graces,
    She brushed him—he flew, alas! never to rise.
"Ah! such," said the girl, "is the pride of our faces,
    For which the soul's innocence too often dies."—*Moore.*

In the evening of the day on which he had received the haughty repulse of her brother, Thomas McClanahan, sought and obtained an interview with the blushing young maiden; revealed to her the reception he had received; and told her the defiant answer he had made to him. In all the calmness he could command, protesting his undying attachment for her, he asked her if she would make good his prediction of her course, and elope with him across the Potomac and marry him as soon as he could make all necessary arrangements? She blushed and wiped from her rosy cheeks a few pearly drops; then, with a timid glance at her lover's manly visage, fully expressive of the fervency of his affection for her; owned he had for many years occupied and possessed her highest regards, and said to him: "I will fulfill your prediction to my brother. Choose your own time and I will not disappoint your expectations."

On his return home that evening, he related to his mother his engagement to Miss Green; the refusal to their union on the part of her brother, dwelling with some emphasis upon the abrupt and disparaging manner in which he had given it—pretty directly basing his objections upon the ground that his sister was of a family, so much superior to him or any of his connections in rank, if not fortune. His mother with dignified calmness listened to his relation; and, seeming to meditate awhile on all that he said in relation to what touched families replied:

"I am surprised my son, at what you are stating. I had not dreamed that young as you are, with all your passionate fondness for sport and fun you had ever bestowed a thought upon matrimony, or the ladies; but did Bob. Green, dare to intimate that the Greens claimed the respectability of the Marshalls and Markhams, from whom your mother is directly descended? Well to me that gives no little surprise! But his impudence and presumption is only verifying what I said to your father but a few days since—that this revolution would not only produce a wonderful change in the political affairs of the country, but give to the poorest and most plebian families of the colony the right to claim equality and equal respectability with the first families of the land; even though such families as my own, were descended from the dukes duches, and barons of England!" And, warming still more and more as she spoke, she said, "Now, Thomas, my son, I assure you, I am almost ready to say I am altogether opposed to your connecting yourself in any such way with any such newly fledged pretenders to respectability as the Greens are; and if your father, Parson McClanahan, would join me, I would forbid it altogether if I did not admire the dear girl so much myself. But my son, what will you do—will you give it up? I am satisfied that the vulgar pride of Green, will make him persevere in his opposition, and then what will you do?"

"Still have my own way, mother," he responded. "There is only one difficulty in the way, and that is a few hundred dollars are wanted."

"What for?" asked his mother.

"Miss Green, mother, has already said she would be mine, and go with me to Kentucky, or anywhere I wished, when we were married; but that can only be accomplished by a trip across the Potomac and out of this province; as her brother who is her guardian will not consent to our license here, and more than I now have will be necessary for our equipage and expenses."

"Never fear about that, Thomas, your father will, I am sure, attend to that. If, however, he will not, your mother, since Bob. Green, has chosen to put his objections upon the grounds of family respectability, will see that it shall not be wanting,—a few hundred pounds will suffice and show to that accidental Col. Green, that in her veins runs the blood of the Marshalls and Markhams, the descendants of England's proudest dukes, lords, and barons!"

Now Tom was fully satisfied he had touched the right chord of his mother's usually unimpassioned mind, and confidently believed what she had told him on the subject of his getting the money requisite, from one or both of his parents. Of his father's generous impulses he was rather doubtful, unless he could obtain the aid of his mother, who like every prudent wife always held and upon an emergency could exercise an overweening influence upon her husband, and, in such matters, a power quite irresistable. "And now," he said to himself, "Col. Green, will find I made no vain boast, when I told him I should carry my point in spite of him. But what is better than all I shall prove to my Nancy, that she is giving her hand and plighting her fidelity in marriage to no mere beardless boy, as her brother impudently hinted this morning."

That night, according to his anticipations, his mother had a regular sitting with the sober and dignified old parson her husband. She with no small degree of earnest feeling, detailed to him their son's engagement; his appeal to the brother and guardian for his consent to the union; and with much of scorn and emphasis becoming the proprieties of a true Virginia matron, told him of " the impudent insinuation of Col. Bob. Green, that Thomas' family and family connections, were not so respectable as the Greens, impudently calling our manly soldier, a beardless boy! "

"A beardless boy, did he say?" replied the parson, and, after a slight interval he repeated " a beardless boy? Ha-ha-haw-haw! Now Molly, I'll just say to you, for I would not like for Tommy to know that I said so, or thought it, if Col. Green thinks him a beardless boy and stands much in his way hereafter, large and haughty as his colonelship, Bobby Green is, he'll find himself, one of these days, terribly thrashed by the *beardless boy*. I I should regret it, even if he provokes it, yet you may be sure of what I tell you. But did you not say that Green cast reflections upon the respectability of Tommy's family and his father and mother? and rather grounded his refusing his consent on that reason? Well, that takes me altogether by surprise! For I have always thought few of the first families of Virginia—no, not even the Fairfaxes, the Dunmores, Amblers, Keiths, or Randolphs, could hold their heads above the Marshalls or Markhams, your kin here, and in Europe. As for mine, they are, except a very few, all in Europe also, they having hitherto had so little sense, it is true, as to refuse to come to this beautiful free country—yet I suppose loving and ready to fight, according to the old Scotch Church covenant, for the king and his babies. Yet I have always heard they were honest. But, what does Tommy intend to do now?"

"Why," said the lady, "what would you expect, Mr. McClanahan, he would do? Did you ever know him turned from what he had deliberately determined to accomplish? I love him for it; only he does not deliberate as he ought before he acts. But I'll tell you what he said to the colonel's impudent refusal. He just calmly told him he was determined to marry his sister in spite of all he had said or could do, and so left him. He told me such was still his purpose, but that he had not money to bear his expenses to Dumfrieze, and then across into Maryland with his pretty bride. Now, husband, this is what I want particularly to talk to you about. You may be sure he will contrive to take away the girl, someway, even though he has to hazard his own or Bob. Green's life, and I can't bear the idea of his going off to get married dependent upon Green or anybody. For you may be sure he loves the pretty girl too much to be turned now. And besides, she is a good child, as I know. The very best of all the Greens."

"Well now, wife," replied the worthy parson, "I am not a proud man, I believe, but I feel pretty much like you about this matter, and as Col. Green is pleased to put on these airs, I will give the boy one hundred pounds, anyway, and if I had my tobacco sold I would make it one hundred and fifty pounds; but I reckon that'll do for the present with what he has of his own, and you can tell him so. Yet don't hint to him what I said about his whipping Green. He might suppose I wished him to do it."

"And," said the old lady, "I'll give the boy—what I please."

All this she hastened to communicate to her son, and had the pleasure to witness the joy it imparted to him.

He thanked and kissed his mother again and again, and exclaimed, " O, my Nancy! I have long since resolved to make you all my own if I lived to get back from the army ; and now I'll do it, stand who will in the way."

The next day he visited his kind old friends and neighbors, the Gibsons, enlisted the generous husband and wife in his behalf, and they dispatched a servant girl to the colonel's with a secret message to Miss Green, to visit them to tea that evening. Promptly she complied with the request, and to her equal, at least, if not surpassing gratification to that of her young and ardent lover, she found him there. It was not long ere the young lovers embraced an opportunity, in a walk to, and along the banks of the Rappahanock—which beautifully coursed its busy tide near to, and almost around, the fertile farm of their friends—to enter into a mutual detail of the events which had occured since last they met, and sweetly commune on the prospects before them. Young McClanahan said :

" Come, tell me, dear Nancy, what the colonel, your brother, has said to you in respect to our marriage ; and whether he seems to be as much opposed as ever ? "

" I have not had any conversation with him since, but once, and that was not long."

" But, dear girl," said he, " do you see you have not answered my question ? Did your brother say anything to you about my asking his consent to our union and my answer to his objections ? Please let me know what he said so I may be the better able to shape my course in the future."

" O ! " she said, " I really can't remember all he said about it. I confess, Thomas, I feel under obligations from the relation, even now existing between us, and from the reason you have just assigned, for your wishes to know what my brother says, and how he feels in reference to our engagement. To speak in great candor to you, though it be to expose my own brother's follies, but I am not assured of your prudence in bearing it. If you will promise to be counseled by me in respect to him, and will at all times restrain and control your resentment and too great an impulsiveness of feeling and action, I will tell you all I recollect of what he said about us."

"Well, Miss Green, I promise upon the honor of a gentleman all you require."

"I know, Mr. McClanahan, your natural sensitiveness and the usual promptitude with which you are likely to resent injury or insult; I will, nevertheless, confide in your word, and I must tell you, my impetuous brother seems to entertain the bitterest hatred towards you, and the most irreconcilable objection to our marriage. Here let me stop, and please do not require me to say more. My brother has always been tender, affectionate and kind to me, from my earliest childhood; and never, that I remember, before last night, looked at me or ever spoke in tones of disapprobation or reproof; but O! my God "——

Here her voice ceased, and she wept silently for several minutes. Wiping away her tears, however, presently in a calmer spirit she said: "I have told you, sir, sufficient to show his continued opposition, and all, in substance, that you asked to know; except one thing, which, perhaps, you ought to be informed of."

"And what, dear Nanny, is that?"

"He said if I did not then promise totally to discard you, he would in a short time take me where you should never find me."

"And did you promise him?" he quickly asked.

"O! Thomas, can you suspect I did? Is not the freedom with which I have spoken of our engagement, the speed with which I hastened to attend our dear Mrs. Gibson's invitation to tea this evening, assurance enough that I did not, and could not so promise? No,—no! I made no such promise."

As she said this he drew the gentle maid closer to him,

gently pressed her panting bosom to his own and kissed, more than once, her blushing cheeks and ruby lips.

"But, dear Nancy, did he say where he would take you, and when?"

"Nothing," she replied. "He left me soon after he made the threat, and when he found I would give no such promise, but spoke with firmness of my determination to fulfill my engagement with you, O! how dreadfully and bitterly he stormed and raved, and talked of vengeance. But, my dear friend, you must remember your promise! Remember it is his sister, who feels for him a sister's love and a thousand obligations for favors she has received at his hands, notwithstanding his errors, who pleads for him."

"Dear, affectionate, and grateful heart!" said he, "I love and prize you the more for this exhibition of your generous nature; and shall hope to profit by your discreet example. For your brother's safety and entire escape from all my vengeance, for his unjust insults and personal abuse, an angel pleads, and makes the wolf a lamb, at whose feet the lion, at your bidding, will meekly crouch.

"Yet, dear girl, we have not said a word on the subject of our marriage—or when and where you will be made wholly mine? Your brother and guardian will, I am now convinced, never yield consent. Nay, will, instead thereof, studiously labor to make it impossible, as you have already declared, and, doubtless, he has ere this, resolved to place you secretly beyond my reach, and will speedily attempt to execute his plans. I fear not, though he can ultimately succeed, or ever hide you from my love. But as even in the assurance of certain ultimate victory and success, the discreet general will still choose between the various means, to avoid the incidents of postponement and expense, I think we had better marry at once, and put an end to all his schemes to thwart our wishes."

"I have already," she replied, "promised to be sub-

18

ordinate to your wishes in that regard. I have no choice as to when or where. But, Thomas, you have not yet said anything as to the mind of your own respected parents, who, so far as I know, still, as your natural guardians, hold a legal and reasonable control over you, while under age. Are they willing to receive me, the defenceless and almost penniless orphan, as their daughter-in-law?"

"Aye, dearest girl, most willingly. Indeed, only fancy how my mother's sweet words in your praise, when I first mentioned our engagement to her, thrilled my soul with delight! She spake of her knowledge and respect for your long lost mother ere your birth and up to her death—that she had always known and loved her little orphaned Nancy for her mother's and her own sake; and when I told her of your brother's objections and the grounds he suggested for his opposition, the true mother's heart, with the strongest impulses beat, and she told me, at once, not to fear—a mother's and a father's liberal hands should be stretched forth to supply me in all necessary aids. To-day she told me she had spoken to my father in regard to it, and my wants, and delivered my father's message that he would enable me to go ahead."

"Dear and most generous friends! May Heaven's smiles ever rest upon them," she exclaimed; "and did your kind mother, the friend of my long sainted parent, say that she knew and loved her for her virtues? O! these words shed bright sun-shine into my sometimes darkened and lonely soul, and drop the sweetest and richest aroma, as it were, into a heart that has often almost desponded! All is well, then, dear friend. Your mother's kindness to me has long been known and greatly prized and appreciated; but yet, I trembled lest I might be regarded as an intruder into her family."

"Oh! in that light I am sure she could never regard you, dear Nancy. But let us, dear girl, determine upon

WAR OF INDEPENDENCE.

our future course; you are willing that I shall direct the time and place, you say, of our marriage? It remains, therefore, for us to determine the means by which we may escape your brother's interference. We must elope to some one or other of the adjoining States; in this we cannot obtain license. To elope to Maryland—about forty miles distant, we must now settle how we shall effect it. My opinion is, to avoid difficulty with the colonel, your brother, we must not let many days pass ere we go. For my part, I can be ready by next Sunday, which is now four days off. Can you consent to that time, and will you suggest where on that day—morning, noon, or night—you will meet me? For I should not be able to come to your brother's for you, as I might have to encounter his insults and personal interference, and do not wish to come into collision with him, as I hope to keep my pledge to you in regard to him. I could not trust myself in that case. I even fear you will be so closely watched that you will not be in future permitted to visit your kind friend, Mrs. Gibson, unguarded. When, then, will we meet, prepared to set out? Of course, you will be accompanied by some lady friend in the trip. I shall get young Jonathan James to accompany us."

"O! Mr. McClanahan, these are things of which I have scarcely thought before, and am much at a loss now to answer your questions. But I will endeavor to do so. I will meet you at the back of my brother's barn, which is, you know, near to the grove of pines that skirts the western side of his farm; and do not doubt I can bring along with me the beautiful Miss Polly Wright. We will meet, if you please, at the hour of seven in the evening."

"Very well, Nancy, at the appointed hour I will be there; and I like your selection of Miss Wright as quite fortunate, as she is the flame of my friend James. I believe he has been courting her ever since he got home from the army."

"O, it fits finely every way, for she will be the more ready to accompany us," said Nancy, "when she learns her lover is to be one of the party."

Thus conversing, the lovers entered the parlor of the family from whose house they had half an hour before walked.

WAR OF INDEPENDENCE. 277

CHAPTER XXIV.

The lovers consummate their marriage—A description of the bride's person—Col. Green's chagrin and disappointment—His wife's sensible advice, and the colonel's final reconcilement to what he could not help.

"There are gold—bright scenes in worlds above,
    And blazing gems in worlds below;
Our world has love and only love,
    For living warmth and jewel glow:
God's love is sunlight to the good,
    And woman's pure as diamond sheen,
And friendship's mystic brotherhood
    In twilight beauty lies between."—*R. M. Milnes.*

"Love, passionate young love, how sweet it is
    To have the bosom made a paradise
By thee, life lighted with thy rainbow smile!"—*Landon.*

"Then doubt me not—the season
    Is o'er when Folly made me rove,
And now the vestal, Reason
    Shall watch the fire awak'd by Love,"—*Moore.*

Shortly after the young lovers entered the parlor of Gibson's dwelling, as stated at the close of the last chapter, they were invited to meet the inmates of the house at tea, and soon thereafter, the young soldier took leave of Miss Green, hastily whispering in her ear, "Remember the place and hour; and if life is spared me, I shall be there to meet you;—till then farewell!"—and bowing to Mr. and Mrs. G., hurried home.

He then addressed a brief note to his friend, Jonathan James, informing him of the contemplated trip across the Potomac into Maryland, and requesting a visit from him early on the next day to consult, arrange and prepare for the trip. This note he sealed and placed in the hands of his father's faithful old body servant, Toby, directing him to deliver it to his friend, and none other; and at the hazard of his life suffer no one to take it or get possession of it, till he found Mr. James. "Aye, neber mine, Mas Tommy,—ole Tob neber lib dis long in ole Vaginy an' know nuttin. Nobody neber gits dis 'spatch noway, mine I tells you. Mas Tommy, aint dis de berry way Ginel. Washinton. sent dat 'spach by dat Maj. Creg, I hear masser read 'bout in de big newspaper, an de Britisher make he gib he up, and gib he up to Ginel Conwalle, stiddy Massa Fayette? I die fuss an de Britisher neber done gits dis 'spach fom dis ole nigger."

"Ah! now, Tob, this is your way," replied his young master: "you are always talking about the army or something happened there; and will have your talk out, no matter how great the hurry you ought to be in. Don't you see you are losing too much time, and you've yet got to go five miles to Mr. James', and back to night."

"Neber mine, Mas Tom, dis ole nigger gwyne do it, an no mistake." And so he started.

In a few minutes his mother sent for him to come to her room and placed in his hands one hundred and fifty pounds—one hundred sent him by his father, and fifty contributed by herself. "Here, my son," said she, " we hope this will do for the present; more shall come, when needed."

With grateful acknowledgements he received the bills and a few doubloons, making the sum, put them in his old greasy buckskin army purse; stuck his hands a kimbo, and said, " Now let Bobby Green come along."

" Well," said his mother, " you'd better say young man, 'now Tommy Mac., go along;' for from what I was told to-day, by one of our lady neighbors, you will have pretty hard work, to get hold of the sweet-heart in a few days."

"Ah, what did she say, mother ?" She replied she had

WAR OF INDEPENDENCE.   279

heard Bob and his wife talking of Nancy's foolishness,
and heard him say he was going to some city in a few
days; and she was sure he is going to take the dear girl
with him. "Are you going to run away with her Thomas, and when and how will you fix it?"

He then told his mother of the interview that evening,
and of the plan they had adopted: that he had just written to Jonathan James, by Toby, to go with them; and
Miss Green, expected Miss Wright, to be her brides-
maid."

"Yes—yes," she replied. "that is the reason why Capt.
Gibson's old Harry stopped here a few minutes, enquiring
of your father the way to Maj. Wright's over in Fauquier.
Did you leave her at Capt. Gibson's when you left there?"

"Yes, mother."

"Ah! yes that's the way of it. He said he had to
carry a letter there. But he wouldn't say who from or
who to."

We pass over many amusing incidents that occurred
in connection with the hurried preparations of the lovers
and their attendants, in the trip to Maryland. Engaging
the patience of our respected readers no farther for the
present, in regard to the marriage of Thomas McClanahan, of whom we shall, hereafter, in detailing some of the
events of the earlier settlements of the West, have much
more to say, only to remark that the young and beautiful
Miss Green, with her equally interesting bride-maid,
Miss Wright, met the two young soldiers, McClanahan
and James, at the time and place agreed upon, by the
lovers, upon the banks of the Rappahanock, and without
delay or difficulty, most pleasantly the gallants journied
with their respective intended wives, to Dumfries. There
at Rose Hill, the beautiful residence of Rev. Dr. Thomas
Bonnell Thornton, they engaged the services of that venerable gentleman. He accompanied them across the broad
Potomac, to the fisherman's hut on the Maryland bank,
and there were the sacred rites of matrimony solemnized

between the runaways, according to the ordinance of God, and the forms of the old English Church, of which the reverend gentleman was an unfashionable, though intelligent and truly pious minister.

We would present to the reader a more particular introduction to Miss Nancy Green, just made the bride of our young patriot, Thomas McClanahan, as we have seen, and of her no less beautiful bride-maid, Miss Mary Wright. They were within a few months of the same age; the bride, a little the oldest, and both a little over eighteen years. To the former, the connisseur in beauty of form and symmetry of features, would probably accord the palm; to the latter would be ascribed the greatest approbation and attraction in sprightliness of temperament, quickness of perception and justness of judgment. The young bride in person exhibited a mould remarkably attractive. A skin white as alabaster; a neck and bosom —in short an entire bust, full and expansive; portraying nature's fashioning, in her most artistic handy-work; and indicating a fine adaptation for health and endurance of pain and suffering; soft deep blue eyes, adorned the expression of her face, shaded with jet black eye-lashes, and a full flowing suit of hair, dark as ebony, hanging in clustering ringlets down a beautiful neck. Her heighth was a little above usual, and altogether she was possessed of a fine person. The distinctive qualities of her mind was that of continued quietude and sunshine. Never greatly buoyant with hope, nor depressed with sorrow or despair ; sensible ever to passion's touch, quickly shown in vermillion blushes unaccompanied by any other ebullition of passion; and when sorrows and suffering came, as oft they did in after life, she exhibited a fortitude equalled only by that of the suffering Viola, "smiling at grief." Of her pretty brunette bride-maid, little more here need be said, as the reader may be fully assured she was in person and mind everything her enraptured lover, Capt. Jonathan James, could think or wish in a bride.

WAR OF INDEPENDENCE. 281

Of the effects produced upon Col. Green, and his very amiable and kind lady, who had most tenderly reared and educated her sister-in law, Miss Green, from a very tender age—affectionally supplying the place of a mother, we need not particularly remark, on account of her elopement. We only say that with the colonel, who was not a little inexorable in his prejudices, however hastily and indiscreetly formed, seemed greatly discomforted when he discovered in the morning his pretty bird had flown.

"Why Amelia," he said to his wife, "you have nourished and reared that disobedient sister of mine, to a poor purpose!—to marry that wild adventurer and be dragged in a year or two I suppose to the wilderness, or God knows where—among the Indians in Kentucky or any place he pleases. O, I wish I had him here now, he'd never again run on foot another race with the hounds after another deer or fox or anything else—a mere beardless boy!"

"Husband! husband!" said his lady, "hear me but just a minute. Your sister, it is true, is yet quite young, and I cannot say that she has been prudent in the choice of a husband, but I am sure it is by this time too late to remedy it. Nor will I pretend to say Thomas McClanahan is not worthy of her and will not make her a good and worthy husband. I am sure he is a very brave and heroic young man. His superior officers say he is a brave soldier, and you know he is able to take his own part with any body, though he is a beardless boy, as you call him."

"Well—well, wife I am, perhaps, a little too hasty, but I don't like to be overcome in this way by that young man. Why, if you could only have seen how he looked me in the face, when I told him he should not have her, and he replied he would in spite of me, you'd have hated yourself to see me so outdone."

"Ah! husband, it is now, rely upon it, too late to make the thing any better, and as your pride of character is only a little touched, in the affair, I think its best now to let it pass, and receive them when they come back, as friendly as we can and make the best of it. The least said, the soonest mended."

"I don't know yet what I shall do," responded the colonel, "I love my sister, and it was my duty to protect her. What I shall purpose hereafter, may depend on circumstances; but I hate to be thus headed by a mere boy."

"O, how much more doth beauty beauteous seem
 By that sweet ornament which truth doth give!
 The rose looks fair, we it esteem,
 For that sweet odor which doth in it live."—*Shakspeare.*

"Nor steel, nor fire itself hath power
 Like woman in her conquering hour,
 Be thou but fair,--mankind adore thee!
 Smile,--and a world is weak before thee!--*Moore.*

WAR OF INDEPENDENCE. 283

CHAPTER XXV.

McClanahan removes to New River—Is famed for his pugilistic encounters and victories—A conspiracy to whip him—Seven men
undertake to do so, but after five of them being by him nearly
killed. the other two run and leave him victor—He, with his family, emigrates to Kentucky—Reach and reside at Boone's Station
—McClanahan's intimacy with Daniel Boone—Has several severe
combats with Indians—Delights in the occupation—Boone makes
him commander of a company of rangers, and sends him to the
settlements on the Ohio to watch the Indians—His success.

" Give me a look, give me a face,
    That makes simplicity a grace;
    Robes lo sely flowing, hair as free;
    Such sweet neglect more taketh me
    Than all the adulteries of art:
    These strike mine eyes, but those my heart."—
                                            Ben. Jonson.

In the foregoing notices of the early life of Thomas
McClanahan, we are aware that the incidents are not remarkably calculated to distinguish him from the thousands
of the young and chivalric sons of the colonies. in the days
of the revolution; but as constituting an initiatory and
appropriate introduction to the entire narrative of his
whole life. They also serve to confirm us in the opinion
heretofore ventured in this work, and still adhered to,
that the time and the circumstances by which the heroes
of that glorious struggle were finally successful in achiev-
ing our liberty, and were, necessarily, in the nature of
things and the providence of the Ruler of the universe,
certain of final victory. We, therefore, are induced to
believe that the future of this somewhat daring and adventurous young man will increase the interest of the
reader, and therefore we will now give a narrative of his

284   LEGENDS OF THE

pioneer character and proceed to exhibit his after life, both before and after his emigration to the West.

In a few months after his marriage and return to his home with his pretty young bride, his father made him a deed of conveyance to a valuable tract of land which he owned on New River, not very distant from Abington, at that day very sparsely populated ; to which, in the course of a few months later, he moved and settled, with his family. There was at that time no portion of the State of Virginia east of the Alleghany mountains as little inhabited or less known. It was, not many years previous to his removal, that the hunting herds of Cherokees, Creeks, and other Indians then inhabiting the entire valley of the Mississippi, South and West, had ceased to penetrate into that region, and as might have been expected, he found living in his vicinity those not far in advance of them in civilization.

They had brought with them all the wild and vicious practices, habits, fashions, and homely customs, which were found in that early day everywhere prevailing, more or less, in all the better portions of the country from which they had recently emigrated, leaving behind them nearly everything calculated to adorn, enlighten and ameliorate the asperities of social life. The men were almost universally swearers, gamblers and bullies ; some renegades from justice and the just animadversions of the laws of civil society.

Game was very plenty. Deer, bear, wild turkies, and other desirable game, were very abundant ; inviting and alluring to the hunters. It will, therefore, not surprise any who have read of his early habits and delights, that hunting at once chiefly engaged the fancy and engrossed the time of young McClanahan. Neither will anybody be surprised when they are informed that he was soon found engaged in the most desperate trials of his pugilistic skill and tact, and set down as the most dangerous and successful bully in all the land.

It will be recollected by those who are acquainted with

those days, that even in the most civilized circles, frequent meetings for the trial of strength and prowess in boxing and fighting matches were among the choice of their entertainments at gatherings for musters, log-rollings, corn-shuckings, shooting matches, &c. The fashion was to consider and treat him as the greatest and most distinguished man in all the land, who had conquered the greatest number of his fellows in the games of "hardest fend-off" and fisticuff. The reader will not, therefore, be surprised to learn that young McClanahan was, after his settlement on New River, plunged into these fashionable employments, the results of some of which were, that while he invariably boasted, as truly he could, of the most unquestionable victories in every trial, though not without a few black eyes and red noses, together with a few weighty verdicts for damages and bills of costs for his sports in bruising; yet so notorious did his name and fame become for such feats, that prided bullies of counties and neighborhoods fifty and sixty miles distant from his residence, came to his house, sought an interview, and made a trial of his skill in turning out bruises and perfectly satisfying their desires for such distinctions. None ever came for a second trial! So remarkably expert were his exploits in this line, and so frequent had been the occasions in which he had taught that description of combatants for the bully's fame, that it began to be rumored and fully believed that he was, in fact, a sort of super-human being. Some said he was certainly a direct descendant from Lucifer upon the principle of the modern doctrine of a small fragment of the Baptist church, called the "Two seed Baptists." Others who had heard the tales that spread throughout the land of the celebrated Peter Francisco, of revolutionary wonders—swore he was the sun of that giant, they were certain; and others said if one could not be found in all the country to conquer him, yet they were sure if a number would join in, they could accomplish it.

Accordingly it was so determined on. He had to be whipped some way. Seven men (a prophetic number) were therefore selected out of a Captain's company, who were understood to embrace the next muster or some other general gathering of the country, to accomplish it. No such meeting came till the muster. In the mean time, some one who had heard of the conspiracy, informed McClanahan of it. He determined to prepare, as well as he could, for the trial. Visiting a blacksmith's shop, he had a couple of steel plates made to fit exactly his shoe, or boot heels, so that when with screws these plates were fixed on his heels, an edge jutted over the hind part of the heel taps, the eighth of an inch, which was as keenly sharpened as the edge of a knife. With these weapons, over and above those furnished him by nature alone, he went to the muster, suffered himself to be decoyed by the seven bullies into a room, and the door to be locked upon him. Quickly the contest began. But even while the resolution of the seven was being told him, he sprang at one of them, seized him by the neck, ears, or some other part, threw himself upon his back, dragging him upon himself, and with the entire strength of his uncommonly muscular arms hugging him tightly, began with his heels the work of raking him from his shoulders to his posteriors in a most butcherous style. Meanwhile the other associates stood by, seeing that their comrade was uppermost, and as they supposed, all the time making fight, shouting hurra, John or Jim or George, (as the case might be) "give it to him, whip him!"—until it suited McClanahan to let him loose and spring and grab another of them and use him in the same way; leaving the first stretched on the floor dead or dying as it seemed, bleeding and helpless, at least; and so he passed on to the third, fourth, and fifth, using them up, each in turn, till the sixth and seventh, taking the hint that their time for a like fate was at hand, hastily unlocked the door, and ingloriously fled, carrying the entire balance of fight, in

WAR OF INDEPENDENCE.   287

the select seven heroes, out of harm's way, and leaving McClanahan victor of the gory field, booted and spured to ride over another seven *select militia*.

After this extraordinary demonstration, great and distinguished honors met him and were shown him at every public gathering. At all log-rollings, house-raisings, corn-shuckings, foot-races, quiltings and weddings, by all the country, male and female. O, poor human nature! The consequence was, with our young hero, in the exhuberance of his love of fun and sociability, joined with the flattertng attentions shown him by his neighbors, luring to many evils and costly escapes, beset him, till his liberal patrimony melted away like the drifted snow before the direct rays of the mid-day sun, leaving himself and interesting family subject to the narrowest means of comfort.

About the year 1782, joining in with a company of some twenty or thirty men with five or six families of women and a number of small children coming to Kentucky, all on pack-horses; (for to cross the mountains and pass the wilderness then with wagons or other carriages, was altogether impracticable,) he, with his family, set forth for Kentucky. Few incidents in the way occured worthy of note till the company reached what is called Powell's Valley, where their camp was attacked in the earliest dawn of the day, and one man and one woman killed, and one man and a little boy severely wounded. The men instantly sprang to their guns, loaded and prepared for battle, rushed forth into the woods from whence they understood the report of the Indian guns came, and discovering some Indians at a distance, some behind trees and others retreating in a run, fired and killed one Indian and wounded two others. The number of Indians was supposed to be about fifty warriors, and a few squaws. They were also supposed to be Cherokees.

In a few days more the cavalcade moved on to Boone's Station and Harrods. McClanahan and a dozen or two went to Boone's. They had not been there but a few days before the Indians attacked and besieged Boone's Station, which lasted ten days. Ordinary men coming into the country and in so short a time after being subjected to so severe a trial as that station suffered on that occasion, would have felt great alarm. But to our young soldier there was presented, though a new scene, one which above all others seemed to be suited to his adventurous nature, and the theatre on which his native genius was best enabled to show its superiority of prowess and energy.

Soon after his arrival at the station and he was known to Daniel Boone, who is known by all familiar with his history that among his other peculiar traits of character, he was distinguished for his power in looking in the face of the most entire strangers and immediately forming the most reliable opinions of them. Being thus gifted, Boone saw at once the moral courage, integrity of purpose and probable usefulness, every way, of our hero, in resisting the incursions of the savages. It may not, therefore, surprise any who have become acquainted with his history, in the pfeceeding pages, that young McClanahan was immediately taken into favor and enjoyed the greatest confidecne of that extraordinary leader in the conflicts with the savages in the first settlement of the valley of the Mississippi. The writer well remembers to have heard him often say, when narrating many of the feats of enterprise and bravery of that extraordinary man in fighting, pursuing and destroying the wily savages, that he, above all others, was the greatest natural man he had ever known, and the most perfect woods-man; with the most ready and useful knowledge of the savage character ever seen.

Sometimes in the hunting expeditions, when provisions became scarce in the station and want of food was likely to become extreme; when the greatest danger and terror existed; and when it was well known that the sur-

WAR OF INDEPENDENCE. 289

rounding forests were filled with savages of the most ferocious character, McClanahan, at the break of day,
would leave the fort alone and travel for miles in hunt of
game, and almost always returned laden with supplies,
composed of the most choice portions of deer, sometimes
the tongues only of deer and buffalo, and sometimes three
or four fine turkies.

On one of those occasions, his readiness in a fight as
well as fleetness of foot, were put to the severest test.
The weather was warm, and he had glided through the
forest till he had gone the distance of two or three miles
from the station. An opportunity presented of a shot at
a beautiful young doe. He shot it, hung it upon a sapling,
removed the intestines to lessen the burthen of taking it
on his back. This was just on the declivity of a small
sink, at the bottom of which he espied a small stream of
water issuing forth. Being considerably heated and
thirsty by reason of his walk and the heat of the day, he
descended to the bottom, set his gun against a tree at
hand, and kneeling, drank from a small pool. He slaked
his thirst. But as he rose from his knees and straightened
to an erect position, a large Indian warrior, making the
significant *booh* of the Indian, pitched at him as if to
seize and take him prisoner. As he plunged, McClanahan most dexterously met him with a stroke of the tomahawk he scabbarded on his left side, striking him on the
right side of his savage head, felled him to the ground;
with his left hand he snatched his rifle from the tree and
with all his wonted speed fled up the small rise of the
sink, ran towards the fort about two hundred yards, took
a tree and looked back for a minute to see the result.
Assured in his mind the Indian he had knocked down
was not distant from others, perhaps many, and if he
paused but for a moment to put an end to him, they
would come upon him and probably kill him, he fled
as stated. But when he looked from behind the tree, he
found his conjecture true; for he saw two Indians run-

19

ning in pursuit with their rifles a little elevated and ready to shoot. He stood still, covered by the tree, till they came within seventy or eighty yards, took sight, and one of them, at the crack of his gun, fell. The other stopped a moment to look at his kicking companion; but fearing when the Indian yelled and started again toward him, he would be down upon him before he could possibly reload, our hero set forth again with his accustomed speed, loading as he ran. After running the fourth of a mile, finding he had greatly the advantage in speed over the savage, he took another tree, and when the Indian got within a hundred yards from him, let slip at him; but whether he hit or not he never knew. To the station then he made his way without farther adventure.

Next morning he and four others of the men in the fort, steathily crept to the ground, found his deer still hanging, but found no Indian, dead or alive,—saw much blood, and where it seemed some one had been dragged. They bore his game to the station.

Frequently he was out on expeditions as one of a company of spies sent forth to range along the banks of the Ohio river, principally on the south, and often on the northern side of that stream; very frequently encountering considerable numbers of the Indians seeking to make incursions into the feeble settlements of Kentucky for purposes of murder and rapine. On several of these spy expeditions, McClanahan was in command of the company; ever intrepid and daring. Having under his authority at one time forty young and hardy soldiers, and when on the Ohio river, he learned that a number of the Mississinawa, and perhaps a few Pottawatami Indians had, within a few weeks, attacked two boats coming down with emigrants, near the mouth of the little Miami, killed six or seven—two men, two women, three children, and took off, as prisoners, two young ladies of very respectable families—Lucy Smith and Harriet Lane. They were tracked from the river, some distance towards the

WAR OF INDEPENDENCE. 291

north and in the direction of the Mississinawa towns. He determined to hazard the great danger and "take the responsibility" if his men would agree to go with him, endeavor to find their way to the nearest of the villages, and, if possible, rescue the unfortunate girls.

He called a sort of counsel of war,—told the men what he wished to do and had determined with their consent to do. Taking the vote, all went for it, except one and the captain dismissed him from the company, proffering, however, to put him across the river, for they were camped on the northern side, if he chose to return to the station from which he came; saying, he did not, as they were certain to have some pretty hard fighting, want any one to go into that business, unless he was willing to go his death. His name was Turner, and when he was told by two of the men they were ready to put him across the Ohio.

"Well, now," says he, bursting into a loud camp-laugh, "boys you see my name is Turner, and I turn toward that hunt for them gals as heartily as any on you,—so go as soon as you please—I'm up to the hub for it."

They raised a great laugh and shout in the camp, and all set about a preparation for the trip; some in jerking up a good store of venison and preparing deer tongues, and the like. They were then encamped, as we have said, on the northern bank of the river, near the mouth of the Big Miama; having recently received a good supply of ammunition from Fort Washington, just a little before established, now Cincinnati, while some engaged in moulding an additional stock of bullets, &c.

The distance to the Mississinawa villages none of them knew, nor the exact direction, and there was neither road nor trace to direct their course or travel; but the next day they set out on the expedition. Capt. McClanahan had derived some idea of the locality of the Mississinawa Indians by conversations with several of the men that were out on Gen. George Rogers Clark's expedition to

292   LEGENDS OF THE

Kaskaskia and Vincennes. He was himself a fine woods-
man, but one of his men, Bland Ballard, was believed to
be unexcelled in all the West. Added to his experience
as a great hunter, was that of the most towering love
of adventure, and above all the most irresistable moral
courage, beautifully commingled with the kindest and most
generous sympathies for his fellow-men. Of the bravery
and almost superhuman powers of endurance of this man,
we have much to narrate and will do so in an appropriate
part of this book. In one of his recent tramps along on
the Ohio, he had accidently met with a young man in a
thick forest, entirely bewildered, lost and nearly famished
for want of food ; having eat nothing but the bark of the
spice-wood bushes, broken off as he wandered, and the
tender buds of the hickory branches found in his way. He
was one of the men on board of one of the boats attacked as
above mentioned, and the only one known to have escaped,
except Harriet Lane his sister. They were with their father and mother and a few of the children, (who were all killed by the Indians,) emigrating from Maryland to settle
at Harrod's Station.

After sharing with young Lane, a portion of his jerked
venison and dried buffalo tongue, and waiting by his side
till with these refreshments, rest and sleep, his wearied
and emaciated companion was revived and refreshed,
young Lane communicated these further particulars of
the capture of the boats. They were a little before sundown gliding quietly down the stream within fifty or sixty
yards of the northern shore and passing an abrupt bend
in the river, below which and within a few steps on the
north side, a creek mouthed in which were hid two Indian
canoes, from which and from a number of Indians on the
bank, the boats were suddenly fired upon. The two men
working the oars, on his father's boat, were instantly
killed ; also his mother and father. He himself jumped
into the river and swam to the same shore above the point
unobserved by the Indians ; landed and crept into the

WAR OF INDEPENDENCE. 293

hollow of a very large sycamore, close to the water's edge, and hid himself. He saw a part, at least, from the hollow in which he was hidden, of the killing of those remaining on the boats and saw them take and tie the two girls. Those from the canoes took possession of the boats, managed to land them below the mouth of the creek, where all of the savages got on board and pushing them again out into the river, in the midst of the most horrid yells and screams, sailed out of his sight. In the hollow of the friendly sycamore he continued during the night after the dreadful catastrophe. At light in the morning he crept forth, and along down the river a few miles, undetermined whither to direct his steps for safety; wholly unarmed, but having some indistinct and undefined hope of discovering the destiny of his sister and Miss Smith, as well as the fate of the boats. Near evening he came to a place where he discovered a fresh bank of ashes and beneath a little fire still lingering. This place evidently was recently deserted by many persons, as the grass and leaves seemed recently trodden down for a large space around the fire. Still looking more closely, he discovered a small wooden tray, split at one end, used by his mother on the boat in kneading dough. This he remembered; whilst near by, he also discovered a small portion of a middling of bacon which seemed cut from the balance with a knife and thrown in the edge of the water. He also saw or thought he saw one corner of a boat sunk out in the river yet near enough to the shore and surface of the water to be seen. He further discovered that the track made through the beaten grass led off from the fire in a plainly marked course directly northward, and in following it for a half mile or more he found the garter of his sister which he readily recognized, and doubted not she had dropped it as she was dragged or driven along by her captors, into the wilderness. This he picked up and had still preserved in all his ramblings. He then returned to the river, but being unable to cross to the Kentucky

294   LEGENDS OF THE

shore, and utterly ignorant of the entire country, starving and distracted, he rambled off from it, became bewildered and lost, when he was found by Mr. Ballard.

After that generous young pioneer of the West had fed and nursed young Lane for two days, supposing he could now make his way to the station called Drennon's, and directing him with particularity how to steer to cross at the grassy flats his course to Drennon's Fort, and dividing with him his store of provisions, they parted. Ballard steered in a course to bring him to the Ohio, near the mouth of the Big Miami, before agreed upon by the spy company as the place for their next encampment and general rendezvous for a time, and until it should be agreed to be changed. There in the evening of the day he found the entire company, related to Capt. McClanahan, the foregoing adventure and narrative of young Lane proposed to him the effort to overtake if possible the savage captors of the two young ladies and rescue them at all hazards; and had the heart-felt gratification to find a ready and willing acquiescence in that affair. On the second day the company started on the expedition, in pursuit of the Indians, and to find the Mississinawa villages.

> "Know that pride,
> How'er disguised in its own majesty,
>   Is littleness.
> True dignity abides with him alone,
> Who, in the silent hour of inward thought,
> Can still respect and reverence himself
> In lowliness of heart."
>
>   "Strongest minds
> Are often those the noisy world
> Hears least."— *Wordsworth.*

CHAPTER XXVI.

The party overtakes the Indians—After destroying forty of them, they release Miss Lucy Smith and Harriet Lane, and conduct them in triumph to Fort Washington, now Cincinnati—Lucy Smith is married to one of the Rangers—The first wedding ever celebrated at Cincinnati.

"Heaven alone is just! Men in adulation record,
  The infla ed warrior's or statesman's reward;
  Whilst woman's sweeter virtues, and patient sacrifice of days,
  On earth pass, without a thought, without a word of praise!
    O! I would not live always here."—*Lelia.*

NOTHING very strikingly interesting occurred with Capt. McClanahan and his brave company of rangers or spies for five days after they, as we have seen, marched from the banks of the Ohio, to find and deliver the two unfortunate girls, captured and borne off by the Mississinawa Indians. Almost all of the company were young, active, and very athletic; not one of them was more than twenty-eight years old, and none was under the age of twenty-two. Great cheerfulness was depicted in every countenance and their almost boyish hilarity and sportiveness were so great as to preclude nearly entirely the maintainence of necessary discipline, and the caution indispensable to safety and success, in the country of their wily savage enemies. Having learned from a man who had been captured at Drennon's Station a year before, by a roving gang of Shawanee Indians, carried by them through the Mississinawa villages, and who had ultimately escaped when well nigh the head waters of the Wabash river, that these villages were situated chiefly between the sources of the Big Miami and those of the Wabash, they were little at a loss in directing their course through the trackless wilds which they had to pass.

296   LEGENDS OF THE

The weather was clear, calm, and pleasantly warm; the nights unclouded and serene. The north star therefore, as to the mariner upon the bosom of the trackless deep, meekly and truly pointed out their course. Onward in vigilance and cheerfulness they wended their way, till the evening of the fifth day, when, arming at the bank of a small stream, they were about to build a fire and encamp for the night, when they heard the sharp crack of a rifle, and, in somewhat suppressed tones, the Indian yell was heard down the stream, appearing to be within the distance of a quarter of a mile.

At once convinced there were savages at hand, a counsel of war took place, and Ballard and Basey were ordered in the most stealthy manner to examine in the direction they heard the explosion, for Indians, &c. In a few minutes they reported the discovery of an Indian fire, surrounded by at least fifty, and also two white girls, who were apparently tied by a hand each, together, and bound to a tree. Quickly a slight retreat was resolved upon, and executed in the most silent and secret manner, to the distance of four or five hundred yards, and to a very advantageous position, covered by a bend of the creek and high cliff. Here they kindled a small fire, sent out a sufficient guard, and determined to wait till it was entirely dark as an unclouded night was likely to be; and then act in the way best favoring success in reclaiming and releasing the captive maidens.

The moment for action speedily came. All were ready, and all anxious for the fight. In a few minutes they had a full view of the savages, and also of the unhappy captives, seated on the ground, side by side, and discovered them to be in the range of the shots from the spies, from the position in which they stood. Quickly, at a whisper to his men by the captain, they changed their position and at a given signal, all fired—ten or twelve savages instantly fell! Those not killed or wounded seized their guns in great confusion and disorder, and commenced shooting at random; as they could not see the whites who stood in the woods, until their fire was put out. The spies loaded and fired the second round—shot somewhat in the dark also, killing some more, however, and wounding others; then, according to the plan of attack, all rushed forward with their tomahawks drawn in their right hands, their rifles in their left, and contending with the Indians for a minute or so, drove them or killed all that remained to fight.

The two girls seemed at first frightened into an almost demented condition. As soon, however, as a torch was lighted and they were enabled to see and find themselves surrounded by white men, imagination alone can measure the grateful transports of joy, that filled their tried and trembling hearts. This was exhibited now in almost distracted exclamations and supplications to the men in the most pathetic terms, for mercy and protection, and anon in triumphant shouts of joy, when assured by the captain, that they were their friends, that it v for their rescue they had come, and they should be restored to their friends.

The ground was for a distance around where the fire was kindled surprisingly covered with dead or dying Indians, but with much pain and regret they discovered also among the slain, a small French lady that had also been brought off by the Indians from Heckerwelder, the Moravian town, situated near the Muskingum river. The body of the young woman, the rangers, if they had had anything with which to excavate a grave, would have buried. But nothing of the kind had they or could they procure.

O! how deplorable a thing is war, blood-shed, and carnage, even with poor heartless and infuriated savages! Still they are human beings—their bodies human bodies! their spirits or souls, though untutored and undeveloped by science or civilization, are human spirits or souls, for which the red currents of atoning-blood as freely flowed as for those of the civilized man. And not the least of the corrupting and brutalizing of war's effects upon the hearts and minds of even civilized men, are its tendencies to excite, cultivate and cherish the degrading and iniquitous thirst for human blood; to shut up all the generous sympathies of our nature, and demonize our noblest attributes of mercy and charity. Modern European laws of warfare have greatly ameliorated, it is true, the terrific coincidents of international conflicts, by respecting the rights of private property, and extending humanity and kindness to the sick, wounded and captured. Nor less do such demonstrations of human sympathy and christian feeling obtain and control the conduct of the government officers and soldiers of civilized America. Nay, indeed, it may be truly said, they are more cherished, and maintain a more universal respect and wide-spread control here than in any other portion of the civilized world. But it must be confessed that these ameliorations of war's asperities and cruelties, are due to civilization alone. War naturally teaches no such mixture of mercy with its wonted and congenial cruelties. In man's primitive and unchristianized state, since his corruption by the fall, he knows no object in his wars, but the extermination of his enemies, by death or captivity. Such characterized the wars of the Jews, in their palmiest days of national existence! Such those of the Greeks and Romans, at the zenith of their highest boasts of semi-civilization and science. Unfortunately, however, for American honor and character, our people, in these respects, in all their wars, have had in every case, with savages to endure their accustomed practices and cruel examples in war, such as the slaughter of prisoners and the indiscriminate murder of women and children! While in all other of our wars —twice with Britain, once with France, and lastly with Mexico, the most savage and ferocious tribes of Indians in every instance have been armed not only with guns, but tomahawks and scalping knives!—and brought into the conflicts; encouraged, inspired and improved, so far as British, French, and Spanish artistic inventions, the boasts of their civilization, could be made to bear, in new modes of savage cruelty and ferocity.

And although in reference to the savages that those European nations, while at war with us, employed and encouraged in their savage cruelties toward us, yet towards Britons, French, and Spanish, we acted in strict conformity to the usages and rules of civilized nations at war. It is the regret of every right-minded and philanthropic citizen that in regard to the barbarisms, we have been tempted, in the spirit of the "*lex talionis*," or law of retaliation, to follow in some instances their examples and practices of savage cruelty and malignity; and visit upon them the rage of a war of extermination, and not merely of conquest! We would to God, that for the honor of our beloved United States, its civilized and christianized reputation, among the nations of earth, such items as those of the far-famed Nickajack victory; and distinction of the Georgia assumption of territory, governmental possession and authority, over the lands the homes and graves of the fathers and mothers, brothers, and sisters, of the Cherokee Indians; and of the conduct of McClanahan and his intrepid fellow rangers, in the fight we have just described; as well as a thousand other occurrences in disregard to and in outrage of the most common sympathies of our nature, did not stand forth to bedim and blacken the fair and beautiful pages of our country's history.

We have said that, at the two fires of Capt. McClanahan and his men upon the Mississinawa Indians, when they rushed upon them, tomahawk in hand, and killed and wounded them all, or nearly so, strewing the ground with the dead and dying—but we mean not to say, by word or thought, in the foregoing reflections, there was any wrong. For if in mortal combat and war unto death with our enemies, there can be justification (and we certainly do not doubt it), this is a case in which nothing could be more just, nothing more deserving of the highest approbation than such a rescue of the captured girls.

But to explain our meaning, and to fix the application of this case with others referred to, with the view we have been taking of wars of all kinds, but especially with barbarians or savage tribes or nations—it will be recollected that beside the dead and dying found by our rangers, strewing the ground, there were twelve or fifteen only wounded or disabled; and who, if it had been possible to have taken care of them and treated them according to the dictates of humanity, as civilization teaches, might have lived, gone home to their wives and little pappooses and furnished them with food. But these also our pioneer Kentuckians, coolly put to death, and left them and all the others to feed the wolf, the panther, and the vulture of the wilderness !

History, however, scarcely furnishes an instance of a war between a nation civilized and one barbarian, in which the former did not, to a greater or less extent, adopt the warfare of the barbarian. Our wars with England and France, toward whom we observed with unwavering strictness, the humanity of civilized warfare, must not constitute the ground of blame to us alone. Sometimes, in reference to the savages whom those nations prompted and employed and brought to the conflicts, they did nothing to restrain their barbarous excesses and cruelties. The blame is at their doors respectively. The cruelty was all their own.

But to return to the completion of the incidents of Capt. McClanahan's excursion to rescue the captive girls. Often did the writer witness in the latest days of the old soldier, with what pleasure he would recur to this incident in the history of his public service, as giving him more pleasure to remember and recount than any other portion of his active life. Often when relating it, and speaking of the wild transports of joy and delight manifested by the girls when they found themselves delivered, and surrounded by, and under the protection of their white American brethren, the big tears would roll from his eyes and chase each other down his aged and time-furrowed cheeks. Ah! 'tis sweet, when we have passed far down the hill of life, to be able to look back on life and know that for others, as well as ourselves, we have not lived in vain—that we have sometimes, at least, relieved the distressed, bound up the broken heart, chased away sorrow from the afflicted, and imparted joy to a suffering soul.

All united in treating the poor girls, in their return to Fort Washington (now the splendid city of Cincinnati), with the most respectful regard and politeness. At night, there being but very few blankets among them, the best pallet practicable was made for them in the best place; and when they would accept of two or three of the soldiers' coats or hunting shirts thrown over them, the donors were cordially delighted. Thus in seven days they reached the fort and placed the orphan strangers under the care of Gov. St. Clair and his most accomplished lady, living in the garrison, and went forth to renew with their accustomed vigilance their duty as rangers along the banks of the Ohio. In this trip they were absent fourteen days, and had slain forty-two Indian warriors, and in return, but one of the party receiving a slight wound in his leg.

At parting with the two young captives, all were quite affected. While the girls wept and expressed in very touching terms their gratitude to each of the company for their deliverance, not a few tears were seen to steal down the manly and hardy cheeks of the brave pioneer soldiers. The pretty Lucy Smith, whose gentle manners, beautiful black eyes, bright auburn hair, and skin fair as health's rosy tints could paint, even though exposed as she had been during her captivity and return, was truly captivating. She at first seemed very deeply melted in

302   LEGENDS OF THE

tears, and almost inconsolable. But when the noble young ranger, Charles Wilson, looking upon her with silent but fixed attention and admiration, approached her, took her hand, softly pressing it, and said to her in whispering tones, she should not long be left at the Fort wholly among strangers, for in two weeks, by her leave, he would see her again at Fort Washington, the despair of her pretty face changed to its usual cheerfulness and smiles. Then they parted. He in his heart saying:

> "From this hour the pledge is given,
> From this hour my soul is thine:
> Come what will, from earth or Heaven,
> Weal or woe, thy fate be mine."—*Moore.*

While with equal power she felt, and seemed to say:

> "Farewell, and blessings on thy way,
> Where'er thou goest, beloved stranger;
> Better to sit and watch the ray,
> And think thee safe when far away,
> Than have thee near me, and in danger."
>
>   —*Lalla Rookh.*

The reader will be pleased to learn that in fulfilment of his promise, young Wilson, in less than three weeks, did return to Fort Washington; sued for and obtained her hand in marriage, and with the consent of Gov. St. Clair and lady, they were in a few days the first pair united in marriage at Fort Washington.

We may also gratify the reasonable solicitude of the reader to follow further the results of this matrimonial exploit in the wilderness, and remark, that the generous young soldier having obtained his discharge from his captain, he withdrew from the spy service, returned with his pretty bride to visit her relatives, to the eastern shore of Maryland, and there and afterwards when they returned to the West, laudably gave to their country a lively flock of young Americans.

WAR OF INDEPENDENCE.   303

CHAPTER XXVII.

McClanahan's account of Harmar's defeat—His own miraculous
escape from death—Makes his way back to camp, much to the
surprise of his comrades, who had given him up for lost..

"But strew his ashes to the wind
    Whose sword or voice has saved mankind—
And is he dead, whose glorious mind
        Lifts their's on high?
To live in hearts we leave behind,
        Is not to die.

Is't death to fall for freedom's right?
He's dead alone, that lacks her light!
And murder sullies in Heaven's sight,
        The sword he draws :—
What can alone ennoble fight?
        A noble cause?"—*Moore.*

IN pursuing further the incidents of Capt. Thomas
McClanahan's life, we have but few to narrate fraught
with much interest, either in regard to his public or private service, until the expedition to the Miama towns or
villages, in the Fall of 1790, under the command of Gen.
Harmar, and when that officer, by the order of Gov. St.
Clair, as the immediate medium of Congress and the
President, was sent to quell, if possible, the incursions of
the confederate tribes of Indians, within and bordering
upon the boundaries of the northwestern territory. He
was upon that campaign, holding the lieutenancy of a
militia or volunteer company from Kentucky. He was
at the fight with the Indians at the junction of St. Joseph
and St. Mary's rivers when the defeat, commonly called
Harmar's defeat, took place. As this venerable old gentleman, when near seventy years of age, several times de-

304   LEGENDS OF THE

tailed these facts to the writer, he made at the time a written statement of the same, which he asks permission to transcribe in the old captain's own language :

"I was, on the day of Harmar's defeat, more properly called Hardin's defeat, one of the Kentucky militia, and in that unfortunate battle with the Maumees. There was a small creek that mouthed in the river St. Joseph just above the junction of that river with the St. Mary. The army occupied the best position, as it was supposed by the field officers, to fire successfully on the Indians, who were by them at that time, believed to be principally embodied about three hundred yards back from said creek, but covered from our view by some large timber and a considerable amount of tall sedge grass. The army was then directed to cross the creek, which they did. The company of militia of which I was lieutenant and Millen captain, marched and crossed in front, the federal or regular soldiers commanded by Maj. Wyllys in the center, while one or two companies of the militia were to bring up the rear. Our company had barely reached the opposite shore of the creek before the Indians, rising from a bank formed by a sort of lagoon, a very short distance in front (a position they had taken unobserved), began to fire with all vengeance and effect upon us, and particularly upon the regulars, now in the act of crossing. In a very few minutes, as well as I could judge, they killed and badly wounded the whole of them, insomuch that on looking back, the creek seemed perfectly dammed up with the dead or dying, and red with their blood.

"We all rushed forward, notwithstanding the Indians were thick before us, nay, indeed, almost surrounding us, taking to trees. Near me, and in full view, my captain was shot down; a ball striking him near the center of his forehead and a little above his eyes. Finding myself now again with Indians all around me, I sought a better position, ran a few yards farther out in the woods, and had to leap a large fallen poplar across my way. Placing my left hand on its top, with my rifle in my right, I leaped it. At the time I sprang, I have reasons to think many shot at me; as the bark of the poplar was knocked up into my eyes and all around me, yet I was untouched. Two pair of extra moccasins tied to my belt around my waist must have been, at that time, shot through with more than one bullet, as I found afterwards three distinct holes in them. They could not have been made at any other time without striking my body.

"Again I took my position behind a tree, from whence I loaded and fired twice. But again finding myself surrounded by the enemy, who had for a time ceased firing, and in every direction seemed closing in upon us, with their tomahawks waving high over their heads, I started on a run in the direction I saw the fewest of them. In doing so I met a tall old Indian, quite gray, decorated like a chief, with a young warrior on each side, all with uplifted tomahawks waving over their heads. These I had to pass; and rushing up to the old chief, jabbed the muzzle of my rifle against his naked abdomen and fired, seeing the powder burn all over it; I clubbed the gun, instantly knocked down the young ones by his side, right and left, and jumped over them. At that instant a small Irishman, of our company, ran past me, saying:

"Och! lutennon, and what shall we do now?"

"I said, 'run like the devil.'

"On he scudded, with might and main, but I never saw him more. I ran, myself, about a half a mile, as well as I can now judge, up the creek, loading and firing once before I reached the place where I leaped down the bank, and imperfectly concealed myself under its low clay bank, which had been, when the water was high and the current strong, carved out in the clay, leaving, as it was, at this time, at a low ebb, a small cluster of water willows growing on a small sand bank directly between me, as I lay in the curve, and the main current there flowing. There, as incredible as it may seem, I

20

306   LEGENDS OF THE

was at the mercy of an overruling Providence, almost miraculously kept undiscovered by the keen lynx eyes of a dozen, at least, of the savages, who, in full view, came and dipped water, and some of them waded past me up the stream.

"I am not superstitious. For many years, both before and since that time, notwithstanding what I had from my earliest boyhood read in the Bible and been taught by my pious parents, I believed in no spiritual existences, neither in Heaven or hell. But it is due to mercy and truth for me to say, in this narrative, of that alarming condition in which I then laid, stretched along the bank, that I was induced to choose that place, and seek safety there from the hosts of savages, by having plainly presented to my natural or mental vision, a hand, the appearance of which I can never forget; pointing directly to that spot for safety.

"As the Indians waded into, and past me, in the stream, resting at full length on my right elbow, nevertheless with my gun cocked and ready—determined to fire if I discovered one looking at me, and put his eye out. But great was my surprise and absolute bewilderment, as I heard over my head, by the jaring of the ground, Indians walking up and down the bank, and giving water to their wounded, as it seemed, from their horrible groans and screams. For when the step would appear to be a little beyond and above my head, supposing that from thence it would be perfectly easy to see it, and imagining sometimes I felt the deadly ball twisting into my crown; yet strange as it may seem, I tell with truth the stranger circumstance, that while in that state of alarm, such was my fatigue of body and mind, I fell asleep, and did not awake till it was quite dark.

"With the utmost caution, however, I rose, first resting on my knees, then stood up, listening to every whispering breeze and rustling leaf; then slowly and cautiously directing my steps to the ground on which the

WAR OF INDEPENDENCE.   307

battle commenced, feeling, that from thence, I could best
direct my course back to the camp, at which we had left
Gen. Harmar and the largest portion of his troops, two
hours before day. The moon was about an hour high,
and by its light I stealthily crept, entered the field of
death, went to the spot where I had seen my captain fall,
turned his body over and put my finger into the hole in
his forehead where the ball with which he was killed, entered. I knew, even by that light, many of the slain of
my company; although their features were very greatly
distorted in the agonies of death. All were scalped, and
rifled of their arms and accoutrements, as well as much
of their apparel.

" While thus passing about in this awful and solemn
scene, to the relief of my troubled thoughts, upon the subject of finding my way back to the camp, I heard the
booming roar of the cannon, fired at camp, to direct the
return of any straggling soldiers, through the dense forests,
through which they must pass. Thus it was fired at the
end of each hour through the night. I was aware, that
to catch such and put them to death, would be the effort
of the Indians, and therefore resolved not to travel on the
route along which the army had in the morning come,
but at the distance of some hundreds of yards, occasionally turning to it to be assured I was steering the proper
course. Once so returning to the track or road made in
the morning, I came in sight of Indian fires, and just before me saw lying on the ground the figures of two men,
who appeared to be asleep. I knew, therefore, if they were
Indians, as I thought them to be, and I attacked them and
failed to kill them, a noise from shooting by me or them, or
a yell by them, would at once bring hundreds of the savages about me, and death would be inevitable. I, nevertheless, thought it was so fine an opportunity to give two of
the infuriated destroyers of my friends on that hapless
day, their eternal quietus, I would try it anyway. In
preparing for my frontier campaigns against the Indians,

308   LEGENDS OF THE

having been accustomed to the use of the bayonet and the musket, I at a neighboring blacksmith's shop procured a butcher's knife wrought, handle and blade, of steel—the handle made to fit exactly my large-bored rifle, so as to do very well on an occasion of need as a bayonet, and when pushed down pretty well, answered very well as such. So with my gun in my left hand, my tomahawk in my right, one of the Indians I could pin to the ground, and cleave the head of the other at the same instant with my axe in my right hand. Thus armed, I crept to within a step of them, paused again to reflect upon the danger to which I should be exposed by a failure, concluded it was too hazardous, and began slowly and cautiously to retreat, walking backwards till I reached near thirty yards, and then turned and ran at no slow pace out into the woods and resumed my travel for Harmar's camp, which I reached at about eleven o'clock at night,—spoke to the sentinel, who knew my voice, and admitted me within the lines.

"Among my numerous friends in the camp much apprehension, I found, had been entertained by them of my being among the slain. One had agreed he would take this, and another that article to my wife at home, of my small store of camp equipage and clothing. I had the pleasure, however, easily to convince them all, I was not killed, and to permit me to take charge of my property without let or hindrance."

> "Night closed around the conqueror's way,
>   And lightnings showed the distant hill,
> Where those who lost that dreadful day,
>   Stood few and faint, but fearless still.
>
> "The soldier's hope, the patriot's zeal,
>   Forever dimm'd, forever crossed?
> Oh! who shall say what heroes feel,
>   When all but life and honor's lost?"—*Moore.*

WAR OF INDEPENDENCE. 309

CHAPTER XXVIII.

Lord Rawdon's inhuman execution of Col. Isaac Hayne—Death of Hayne's wife and child—Some thoughts on these sad occurrences.

> "Authority!
> Show me authority in honor's garb,
> And I will down upon the humblest knee
> That ever homage bent to sovereign sway ;—
> But, shall I reverence pride, and hate, and rapine?
> No! when oppression stains the robe of state,
> And power's a whip of scorpions in the hands
> Of heartless knaves, to lash the overburthened back
> Of honest industry,—the loyal blood
> Will turn to bitterest gall, and the o'ercharged heart,
> Explode in execration,"—*Shakspeare.*

In pursuing the sketches of those extraordinary men, Captains John Ashby and Thomas McClanahan, who, for years in Virginia, took part in the war of American independence, and coming to the West, shared largely in the perils, dangers and toils of the bloody conflicts with the savage allies of Britain, in the wilderness, as fitly characteristic and discriptive of the courageous and hardy sons of the colonies,—whom God, in his providence, had transplanted from the shores of the Old World ; released from the chains of European political and ecclesiastical tyranny, and reared under circumstances by which they were inured to the endurance of trials and hardships, calculated above all other training, to make them the unconquerable advocates of civil and religious liberty ; and most effectually to resist British oppression in the new hemisphere—our respected readers may have supposed we had relinquished our tales of the war of independence, as it was sustained in the older portions of the colonies, and taken our transit across the Apalla-

310   LEGENDS OF THE

chian heighths of America, to view in accordance with
our pledge in the title of this work, the earlier settlements
of the West. But, with their generous indulgence, we
wish yet to interest them with the narrative of the
achievements of our fathers at Eutaw Springs, King's
Mountain, Guilford, Yorktown, &c., &c.; where their
efforts were crowned with the most glorious triumphs,
yet untold and unpublished in any of the histories,—or,
if spoken of or mentioned at all, in very meagre terms,
pertaining to that heaven-blessed epoch of all our country's greatness and glory.

We therefore proceed to speak of that good and heroic
victim to British malignity, and martyr to the cause of
American liberty, Col. Isaac Hayne. Taken prisoner of
war, at the siege of Charlestown, South Carolina, when
invested and conquered by Gen. Clinton, he took the oath
of allegiance to the British government upon the *express
condition*, and *distinct agreement*, that while he would
not engage in the war against the parent state, so also he
was not to be in any case, compelled or required by
the British authorities to take up arms and fight against
his own beloved country. He accordingly was permitted
and actually retired to the position and enjoyment of his
home and family—the society of his most accomplished
and beautiful wife and two innocent babes, as a private
citizen. Thus he remained, until in violation of the condition of his oath of allegiance, and the solemn promises
of the commanding officers, he was summoned by authority of Lord Rawdon, left by Cornwallis in command in
South Carolina, to join the British standard. He refused,
and was in consequence, charged with treason, brought
before Col. Balfour and a court martial, and sentenced to
be hanged on the 4th of August, 1781.

In vain did he urge his just defence before that court.
In vain did the innocence of his wife and helpless infants,
plead for his release from crime and punishment.

Strangely, however, several historians in America in

writing of this extraordinary event and unjust treatment on the part of the British officers at Charlestown, take occasion to pass a flattering and most unjustifiable compliment upon Rawdon, to the effect that in his deep sympathy for that unfortunate young patriot, he, Rawdon, greatly desired to arrest the violence and cruelty of his sentence, but was overruled by the other officers, and signed as commander the order for his execution. What! Rawdon, a sympathizer for Hayne? The man that had given countenance to and himself repeatedly ordered the unceremonious execution of dozens of the citizens of South Carolina, in every cruel and inhuman form, almost for no other offence than that of having once in some instance or some war, in which his king was engaged, borne arms and fought in his behalf, and afterwards fought under the banner of the Whigs for liberty! And who had in a thousand instances connived at, to say the least, if not himself the immediate actor in it, the forfeiture and confiscation of the property belonging to innocent men, women and children, under some pretence of treason to the king in the revolution of the American colonies, then going on openly and avowedly! Such a man moved by sympathy in behalf of Col. Isaac Hayne! The signer of his merciless death warrant, have feelings of sympathy! As well might it be published by historians that the mousing cat has sympathy for the victimized mouse within its claws, the wolf for the lamb, the tiger for the innocent fawn, or the dreaded and despicable hyena for the corpse scratched from its grave.

Col. Hayne, by the order of Rawdon, was ignominiously hung in the presence of his lovely little boy! —who after witnessing his father's last expiring struggle, upon that same bloody scaffold, instantly expired himself! Aye, and the heart-stricken wife and mother, having lingered but a brief space behind, a monument of British injustice and brutality, then died also.

312   WAR OF INDEPENDENCE.

What was his crime and with what was he even charged, before the court martial by which he was tried? Taking up arms in the war when a paroled prisoner, and refusing to obey Rawdon's summons to fight in the British cause, in the war in which he was a prisoner on parol! Having taken the oath of allegiance to the king when it was distinctly agreed and understood in taking such oath, that he was not to be required so to do. The former charge he denied, and it was left without the shadow of proof to sustain it. The latter he confessed as true.

He had, he said, refused to obey Rawdon's order to fight in the British cause against his country—against his countrymen; and "this was the very head and front of his offending," before his arraignment. But there were several secret causes operating to seal his fate. One of these was a vile determination about that time prompting the British officers to make a victim of some distinguished young American, right or wrong, justly or unjustly, to wreak their vengeance upon him for the just punishment of Maj. Andrew, as a spy in the army of Gen. Washington. And another was, old Balfour owed Col. Hayne a deadly hate for having told him to his face, when brought before him, to answer to the charge and responding to his haughty address, how much he detested and defied him, for his vile treatment of the inhabitants of Charlestown, while their temporary governor, and his thieving extortions made upon them, to enrich his private coffers. His destiny became thereby irrevocably sealed; yes, to the haughty words addressed to him by Balfour, when a prisoner about to be arraigned and tried for his life, before him, Col. Hayne. knowing his crimes and extortions under cover of authority, as above mentioned, and despising him and his power, when the former said to him, in the most insulting manner: "How dare you, sir, have the insolence when his majesty commanded, and through

313   LEGENDS OF THE

Lord Rawdon, required you to enter his service, to put down the d—d rebels, how dare you disobey." Hayne replied to him in the spirit of a freeman:—

"Authority!
Show me authority in honor's garb,
And I will down upon the humblest knee
That ever homage bent to sovereign sway:
But shall I reverence pride, and hate, and rapine?
No! when oppression stains the robe of state,
And power's a whip of scorpions in the hands
Of heartless knaves to lash the o'erburthened back
Of honest industry,—the loyal blood
Will turn to bitterest gall, and the o'ercharged heart,
Explode in execration."

This fixed his doom. This truthful discription of Col. Balfour, and of his disgraceful administration, had the effect only to infuriate Balfour's ignoble heart, incapable as it was of any sentiment of magnanimity or compassion; and Hayne was hung in the presence of his family, and his hosts of weeping friends—and his little boy virtually murdered. One only of the once happy family survived —Robert Y. Hayne!—all murdered by British cruelty!

I have said this barbarian course of warfare characterized the acts of the British in this war, especially in the earlier portion of it. I repeat the assertion. When the revolution began, it is evident to any one who will read its history, mark the conduct and observe the language employed toward the colonists by the British, here and at home, that they regarded themselves, as waring against uncivilized savages; a mere banditti, an undisciplined, semi-civilized, irrational body of insurgents, or presumptuous rebels, and mercilessly adopted their course of conduct, that is, to mortal conflict, as between savages. Hence they justified the employment of the most ferocious and brutal savages, armed and sent forth to tomahawk our men, women and children; enlisted and incited the Tories, little less brutal and ferocious than the red men of the wilderness, to carry murder and rapine to

WAR OF INDEPENDENCE. 314

the families and hearth-stones of every patriot; and lastly, though not least, in point of heartless brutality and iniquity, armed the slaves and sent them forth to butcher and destroy without discrimination of age or sex, their masters and mistresses, and the families to which they belonged.

But, we admit, toward the latter portions of that ardent struggle—after it was found the people and armies of the colonies, had the power and as a principle of self-defence, under the circumstances the moral courage, to retaliate upon them, for their frequent practices of savage and brutal conduct in the war, some improvement was manifested, perhaps, in matter and manner of their hostile tactics. Here, again, it might seem proper our chapter should close, and other topics of a legendary character be introduced; but having taken a view to some considerable extent, of the plan and principles upon which the government of England, and the officers sent here to subdue the Americans, commenced and conducted the war, we cannot forego the privilege of turning with pride to a contemplation and contrast of the men, who in the continental congress of 1776, organized, gave form, body and spirit to the great continental confederation and league of the colonies; and who brought forth and proclaimed to a wondering world, the birth of a new national existence, based upon the broad palladium of moral, rational and religious liberty! "The rights of man!"— Freedom from all unscriptural, political and ecclesiastical bondage. Yet upon these the proud Briton affected to look with contempt, and treat as mere adventurers the people whom they there represented; the army by them organized, and by them in dignified conclave regulated and controled, to maintain the mortal conflict, according to the laws of civilized nations, and the dictates of christian philanthropy.

Of Thomas Jefferson and John Adams, in an earlier portion of these Legends, we have already sufficiently spoken in terms of praise. Nor was it among ordinary or less than superior minds, those two enjoyed a sublime preëminence. With them sat a patriot sage, the practical philosopher of nature and science, than whom it is not the boast of any nation to claim as her son a better writer or more profound thinker,—Benjamin Franklin. There sat also a Patrick Henry, a Richard Henry Lee, a Samuel Adams, and a host of others, whose manly diction, cogent eloquence and thrilling oratory, would have well compared if not surpassed, England's boasted Chathams, Burks, Sheridans, or Grattans. Were such men mere adventurers? No—no. They were greatest among great men —mightiest among the mighty; standing loftiest in a body or assembly of men, more than half of whom would, with honor and usefulness, have presided over the deliberative counsels of any nation.

Hear the language they breathed, the sober thoughts they indulged, and the conclusions to which they came, after the adoption of the declaration of independence, in reviewing the ground they had taken and the costs of its maintainance. "I am not transported with enthusiasm," said one. "I am well aware of the trial, the treasure, and the blood it will cost, to maintain this declaration; to support and defend these States Yet through all the gloom, I can see a ray of light and glory. I can see that the end is worth more than all the means."

It was not the rash adventure of reckless and uneasy spirits; having everything to gain and nothing to lose in the enterprise. For their country's sake, for civil and religious liberty's sake, they risked their all "their lives their fortunes and their sacred honor." Nay, who does not know that Adams, Jefferson, Henry, Lee, and Franklin, and others, distinguished in the nations, counsels and the army, could, by bowing the suppliant knee; by flattering and fawning, have won the loftiest stations in the British empire? Could have reveled in the royal bounty? Could have shared the imperial counsels, and could have

WAR OF INDEPENDENCE. 316

stood in the shadow of that throne they shook to its base?
But with a full comprehension of the whole subject and of
the seeming desperation of their choice, they chose principle, liberty and their country's glory! And the dread
voice of authority; the array of an empire's power; the
pleadings of friendship; the yearning of their hearts toward the land of their father's graves; that land the great
and earliest champions of civil constitutional liberty still
made venerable; no not even the hideous visions of the
British gibbet deterred them.

They were anything but adventurers; anything but
restless malcontents. Loving peace, order, law and a
manly obedience to constitutional authority; yet chiefly,
loving freedom and their country, they took up the ark of
her liberties, with pure hands and firm hearts, and bore it
through in triumph! For their confidence was in God.

"Oh, confidence divine! the good and just,
    Who still on heaven repose their pious trust,
    New laws for attiring seasons can create,
    And thwart the stars malign, and conquer fate."—*Tasso.*

" Life is not lost, from which is brought
    Endless renown."—*Spencer.*

" When liberty is gone,
    Life grows insipid, and has lost its relish."—
                                                    Addison.

CHAPTER XXIX.

There are, who with purpose dare pursue
Ways wicked and false, rather than true:
All evils they practice, and take most delight
In the ways of the vicious, in conscience's spite!
Who early in youth listen to sin's vain delusions,
Yield faith, and practice Satanic persuasions.
And, though bad to worse, and good to better, tend,
Downward they plunge, nor upward ere ascend.
Thus in Satan's snare early captive led,
To crime and iniquity in early life are wed:
In natural progression, are sure to graduate
In villainies most horrid! then charge it all to fate.
—*The Author.*

It will, by all who have given the preceeding legends a perusal, be remembered that frequent mention is made of the notorious cousins, Bill and Josh Harpe, the sons of John and William Harpe, Scotch covenanters and brothers, who, like their sons and all Scotchmen of that day in this country, were Tories, or as they called themselves, Royalists, devoted to the maintainence of the king's authority.

The fathers, however, prudently kept clear of the vile practices into which most of the friends of the old king entered—such as murder, robbing, and rapine; but their vile sons, the continuance of whose dreadful lives we now propose to delineate, ran greedily into every imaginable excess of those crimes. Having been sedulously inducted by their fathers into the peculiar doctrines and tenets of the Calvinistic school, the doctrine of eternal election and reprobation in their broadest and most unqualified sense, fully believed every character, good or bad, was inevitably and immutably fixed in God's foreor-

WAR OF INDEPENDENCE. 313

dination and decrees from all eternity; and feeling within themselves a love of iniquity in all its forms, took *that* as evidence conclusive, that they were not of the elect to life and glory; and therefore determined, as they on more than one occasion declared publicly, that they were decreed to be damned, and would therefore indulge to the full, all their love of crime, and so fill up the measure of their destiny.

Nor are we prepared to say that, from the premises assumed, their reasoning and conclusions were not strictly logical. Always asserting for ourselves, and all scriptural record, and all rational deduction, that the entire doctrine is neither in consonance with man's accountability to his Maker for his moral actions, obedience or disobedience, nor with the idea of his being the subject of rewards or punishments. Nevertheless, such was declared, as we have said, to have been the opinions and faith of the two younger Harpes, and such, we believe, in a vast variety of cases, were the sentiments of many, so taught, most dangerous in its consequences, and most dishonoring, of all others, to God. Of this, in truth, the utter recklessness of life and acts of these most brutal and terrible men, seem to go very far to establish.

It will be remembered, also, by our readers, that for a time approaching the close of the revolution, so formidable had the Whigs become to the Tories; so fiercely did they follow them, that these, with many like them, fled, some to the settlements and stations formed in the West, and others to the neighboring savage tribes, from Georgia and the Carolinas. Big Bill Harpe and Joshua Harpe, having, at the King's Mountain and other of the battles they fought under the British standard side by side with a number of Creek and Cherokee warriors, and a few of their chiefs with whom they became intimate, went to the Cherokee nation. For about nine months they remained with them at their town, near the head waters of the Tennessee, called Nickajack. Much of that time they

319   LEGENDS OF THE

went upon marauding expeditions with their savage allies, to the settlements in Tennessee and Kentucky. Big Bill was with them at the battle of Blue Lick and at the attack by the Creeks and Cherokees, on the station where Nashville is now situated, and at Bledsoe's Lick, seven miles from the beautiful site of Gallatin.

At about the expiration of nine or ten months, the two Harpes, with four Cherokees, stealthily returned into North Carolina, made their way to the vicinity of Hillsboro', and contrived to capture, as we have already related, Maria Davidson, while Cornwallis was at Hillsboro' encamped with his army. They bore her off to the hunter's cabin, of which we have also spoken, where she was detained for more than a week, and until Big Bill Harpe, in company with one Moses Doss and two Cherokees, Antoka and Ochetta, went to the neighborhood of Mrs. Wood and seized Susan Wood, daughter of Capt. John Wood, on her return from a visit to Maj. Simpson's, as we have also in another legend described.

The two unfortunate girls were not personally acquainted, but had often heard of the family to which each belonged. Maria, during the time, had been kept bound by cords, and subjected by Josh. Harpe to the most brutal and hateful outrages. The relentless villain, after pretending to entertain a long and deep seated love for her, although he had never before avowed it—and after having employed all his powers of persuasion to obtain a voluntary consent to his wishes, but which she resisted, notwithstanding she knew she was without hope of escape from his inexorable power. She loathed and detested him as a villain, and told him so, in the bitterest hate and scorn; hoping, thereby, to provoke his vengeance, and to obtain death at his hands. But it had the effect only to provoke his violence in gratifying his diabolical passions. Poor Maria! more dead than alive when the other villains came in bringing the hapless Susan Wood, felt a slight and momentary gleam of hope spring up in

WAR OF INDEPENDENCE. 320

her heart, from the natural feelings of the sorrowful, on the principal "misery loves company." For it was not long before she saw poor Susan, in open day, subjected to the same brutal force, by big Bill Harpe, as she had been by the other, more than once. They remained at the hunter's cabin, however, but a few hours, after they were joined by Bill and his accomplices bringing Susan; and each of the unhappy girls being tied by a strong rope to the saddles on which they rode, on horses, led by the two Harpes, the whole party set out toward the Blue Ridge, crossing it in a northernly direction, entered the vast *terra incognita* beyond it, being often loosed and taken from their saddles, even in day-time, to endure the lustful dalliance of their bestial tormentors. Thus they traveled rather slowly, crossed the Alleghanies, and without anything occuring of strange or very novel character to retard their progress through the mighty waste to the nearest settlements of the Cherokee Indians, except that of a terrible combat between big Harpe and Moses Doss, whom Harpe slew in the end, leaving his body where it fell in the wilderness, horribly mangled and disfigured.

The cause of the quarrel was not very distinctly made known. It was, however, believed that Harpe was under the influence of a freak of jealousy; having, as he thought, seen or discovered a disposition on the part of Doss, to plead for and secure a less cruel treatment toward the unfortunate girls, and a disposition to comfort and console them in their awful condition.

Seldom the poor unfortunates were given an opportunity of conversing with each other. Indeed, they were forbidden to converse, and threatened by their despicable tyrants with some terrible punishment, if they did.

The gang found it necessary on several days during their journey to hunt and prepare provisions. At such times, the girls, with the exception of one or two left to guard them, were quite alone; and as the guard would often sleep almost the whole time of the absence of the

WAR OF INDEPENDENCE.   321

nity of conversing with each other. Indeed, they were
forbidden to converse, and threatened by their despicable
tyrants with some terrible punishment, if they did.

The gang found it necessary on several days during
their journey to hunt and prepare provisions. At such
times, the girls, with the exception of one or two left to
guard them, were quite alone; and as the guard would
often sleep almost the whole time of the absence of the
Harpes, they found an opportunity to talk to each other
and interchange sentiments of condolence and sympathy
for their mutual sufferings. Thus their bursting hearts
seemed relieved. Without these communings, as they
both declared, after they were rescued from the control of
the Harpes and brought into the town of Russellville,
Kentucky, whose inhabitants, with some exceptions,
treated them with great kindness, they must have died
on that dreadful journey. They learned from the conversations of the Harpes that they were going to dwell with
the Indians. They said, so terrible was the reality of
their condition, they strove to put the thoughts of that
reality as far from them as possible; nay, even sought to
forget they ever had a beloved home, beloved parents,
and had enjoyed the bliss of freedom and society. They
felt they had drank to the very dregs the bitterest cup of
suffering life, and hoped for change, as no change in the
wide circle of vicissitude in human suffering, could be but
for the better.

Alas! poor young women; they little thought or knew
the deeper stings of sorrow yet to be endured by them.
There were chords of affection and feeling yet to be rudely
broken, of which they were yet unacquainted, and which
did not, in fact, then exist, but the rending tortures of
which they were doomed to feel.

Maria Davidson was of a more sensitive and delicate
mould, mentally as well as physically, than Susan Wood,
and consequently less qualified to endure suffering in
either. Miss Wood possessed a more robust person and

21

322   LEGENDS OF THE

a less sensitive mind, accompanied by a sort of elasticity
of temper, by which she was enabled to parry or blunt
the poignancy and agony of pain.

In twenty days they reached Nickajack. This was an
Indian town situated high up near the Tennessee river;
inhabited by about three hundred Cherokee Indians, in-
cluding warriors, squaws, and children. When they arrived, the Harpes seemed well known to the Indians, and
from what the girls saw, had been looked for by them.
Considerable joy seemed expressed by all, but particularly by the women and children. They all crowded
around them, appearing very curious, and took much
pleasure in examining their dress and every exterior appearance. They were conducted to several wigwams,
and were brought to one in which they saw only an old
Indian and his squaw—both very gray. Here Susan was
told by big Bill Harpe, she must live. Maria was taken
to the lodge of a tall warrior whose squaw had not long
before been killed by a panther, who had left three pappooses, the oldest about six years, and the youngest about
two years of age. There, Joshua told her, they were to
live.

Greatly alarmed and disgusted with the appearance of
the Indians around them, and dreadfully sick and wearied with the long continued mental and bodily suffering
through which they had passed, each in her respective
lodge sunk on the ground and sat reflecting on the dreadful condition in which they were placed, with the worst
imaginable forebodings of their future fate. For some
days the treatment from the Harpes they had been subjected to in the earlier portion of their imprisonment and
journey, had not been repeated, and they took some
slight consolation, indulging the hope the wretches had
relented and would not in future so assail them. O!
vain the thought, vain the hope. They were not long
thus meditating before their respective brutal tormentors
came, aroused them from their vain delusions and demon-

strated more violence than ever. Each having spread upon the floor some buffalo, bear, and deer skins, in addition to those used on the travel, required each his victim peremptorily, to lie; preparing to take their positions by their sides. Alas, poor, lost and ruined girls! Better far you had not been born, or had been strangled in the birth, than live the hapless victims of such a despicable doom.

But we will no longer dwell on the unimaginable sufferings of the poor girls, for more than two years in that miserable little Indian village. Twice they became mothers, and as often each witnessed during that time their tender offspring cruelly and most brutally murdered by their brutal fathers after they had lived long enough most affectionately to engage and fix a mother's love.

It is true, the two Harpes were often away with the Indians in depredating expeditions against the white settlements in Tennessee and Kentucky, sometimes to hunt, often for the space of two or three months; yet on such occasions they remained subject to the most constant vigilance and watchfulness of the Indian warriors left behind, and the Indian women. They were, however, generally treated by these savages with far less cruelty than by the Harpes; and experienced some relief from their absence.

At the expiration of between two and three years, the exact time not remembered, on the night previous to the attack by some Tennesseeans and Kentuckians under the command of Capt. A. Jackson, late President of the United States, upon Nickajack, when he sacked the town and put every Indian, man, woman, and child, to death, the Harpes learning in some way that the troops were coming and would be there the next day, hurried off secretly, with four Indians, two of those that were with them when they stole Susan and Maria from North Carolina, and two others. They went some eight or ten miles from Nickajack that night, and hid in a cane-break.

Next day one of the Indians went to the place stealth-

324   LEGENDS OF THE

ily, returned at night and told the Harpes the entire village had been burnt and all the Indians destroyed ; they
then set out, traveled two days and a half to the western
end of a great mountain, believed to be the Cumberland
mountain, where, finding an abundance of game of every
kind, they encamped, and remained about nine months,
during which time Susan Woods gave birth to another
infant boy. While encamped at that place, big Bill
Harpe, with two of the Indians, went to Powell's valley
to get horses ; were gone three weeks, and returned with
four, which they had stolen. But their further operations we will unfold in another chapter.

WAR OF INDEPENDENCE. 325

CHAPTER XXX.

Rev. William Lambeth's adventure with Big Harpe—The Harpes leave their camp at the Cumberland Mountain, and start for the Ohio—Meet with, murder and rob two Marylanders—Maria Davidson's account of that horrible crime—They waylay, murder and rob a young Virginian—They are chased and secured in Danville jail—They escape and make their way to Springfield—The two ruined girls their victims, being free, discuss the propriety of seeking the sympathy and protection of the settlers—They decline doing so—The Harpes return to the women and start for the neighborhood of Snelling's Station—Again they steal horses and journey towards what is now Columbia, Adair Co., Ky., where they are believed to have murdered Col. Trabue's little son—Continue their journey and operations of murder and robbery into Tennessee, are chased back to the Mammoth Cave, but not captured—Big Harpe murders his own child.

Mean though I am, yet not wholly
So; since sovereign mercy for me abounds, and
Undertakes my cause.

In me by nature, since the fall,
No merit does abide ;
Captive in evils thrall,
All virtue I deride !

Yet by the merits of a Savior's blood.
Freely on Calvary shed;
Repentant, I may follow good;
His merits raise the dead !—*The Author.*

RETURNING from Powell's valley, it is worthy of record that Big Harpe actually displayed a feeling evidencing, to a small extent at least, that his vile and most depraved heart, was not utterly incapable, at some times and under some circumstances, of the exercise of something like mercy and a forbearance to shed human blood. It is probably the only instance in all his life, after the com-

326   LEGENDS OF THE

mencement of his murderous career, in which he had
any one, old or young, in his power and showed less than
a fiendish barbarity.

The Rev. William Lambeth, a young Methodist minister, aged about twenty-three years, sent by Rev. William
McKendree, then presiding elder of all the West,—afterwards Bishop McKendree, of that church,—was traveling from Baltimore Conference, across the mountains, to
form a circuit and preach to the settlers, in what is now
called Middle Tennessee, and the Green River portion of
Kentucky. He had to pass through that part of Tennessee, lying between Knoxville and Nashville, which
was for many years called the wilderness; there being
no civilized inhabitants occupying it. In his journey
through this wilderness, one night he had kindled a
small fire near the foot of a broad spreading beech, to
cook a little supper as well as to keep off wolves and
panthers during his sleep; and hobbling his horse to
graze on the contiguous cane and grass,—spreading his
blanket-pallet, and committing himself to the care and
keeping of Almighty God, he laid down, making his
saddle-bags his pillow and the moon-lit heavens his only
covering. He was asleep but a short time when he was
awaked by the neighing of his gentle horse. Continuing
awake, wondering at the cause of the neighing, and concluding the horse must have heard or smelt some other
horse. In a few minutes he saw creeping toward him a
large man who, as he rose, seized him with an iron grasp
and strong arm, and by the dim light of the moon he
discovered him to be a white man, though terribly black
and ragged, in his attire, and ferocious in his countenance.

With a blasphemous oath he swore if the least resistance was made by Lambeth, he would instantly murder
him. Lambeth being a very small man, only measuring
five feet five inches in heighth and weighing only one
hundred and nine pounds, stood perfectly still; but in a

mild and slightly agitated tone, asked what he wanted ?
In a broad sort of Scotch dialect the man replied:

"I want all your money and must have your horse,—
you must give them up right now, or I will kill you."

Lambeth took from his pocket his purse of about thirty
dollars, gold and silver, and told him there was his horse
and he could take him. He took the purse and found
Lambeth's small bible in his bosom, where he had placed
it when he laid down to sleep. That, he quickly seized,
rapidly turned over the leaves from beginning to end, apparently looking for bank bills. There were none there.
But he discovered on the marginal or front page, written
in plain letters, *William Lambeth*, and also the name
George Washington. To the latter he pointed and asked
if that was the name of the American general. Being
answered in the affirmative, he said, "That is a brave
and good man, but a mighty rebel against the king."

He then asked, if Lambeth had ever seen Gen. Washington, and where; and being answered that he had in
Richmond, Virginia, he enquired what the latter was
doing away out in the wilderness by himself. Lambeth
told him he had come to preach the Gospel. He asked
if he preached from that bible, and being answered affir-
matively, he enquired if he had ever been in the country
where he was going to preach. "No" was the response.

"You can never get there without your horse," he
said, and then pausing, as if in a deep study, loosing his
grasp at the same time,—"Nor," he after a minute said.
"can you do without your money,"

L. told him he could try. A few moments then again
intervened and he said, "You must keep both," throwing
down the purse, and saying, "My name is William
Harpe," quickly disappeared. Harpe never spoke of this
meeting to any one, except to Susan Wood, who said in
Russellville, to the writer, that when he reached the camp,
"He told me he had seen the little preacher in the
wilderness."

328   LEGENDS OF THE

Lambeth himself frequently spoke of all the circumstances, as above detailed, many years afterwards; twice in the writer's presence, in narrative, and once in a sermon from the pulpit, in arguing the special protecting Providence of God, over his servants,—instancing also God's closing the mouths of the lions in saving Daniel, in their den; and in quenching the fires of the dreadful furnace into which the tyrant cast Shadrack, Mesheck and Abednego.

From the camp at Cumberland Mountain, in a day or two after the return of Big Harpe, with the Indians who had gone with him, bringing the horses stolen from Powell's valley, they all set out to go to the Ohio through Kentucky, entering near the Crab Orchard.

The Harpes having once or twice passed through that part of Kentucky, on expeditions against the inhabitants there, and Boone's Station, knew the localities pretty well, and knowing, as good woodsmen, when they were coming pretty near the white settlements, the Indians dare not go among them, they separated and the Indians steered directly for Muldrow's Station, to secret themselves in the neighborhood, till the Harpes came, having gone from the Crab Orchard to Logan's Station, from thence to Harrod's, thence to a settlement where Springfield is now situated, and from thence to the place at which the Indians were to meet them.

Within a few miles from the Crab Orchard, while traveling along the trace leading to Logan's Station,—two gentlemen, apparently travelers, came in company. They were both Marylanders, as was afterwards ascertained from papers in their possession. One by the name of Paca, and the other Bates. Bates was a man some thirty years of age, and Paca between twenty-five and thirty. They were both stout,—mounted on fine horses, and armed with rifles. It was agreed between them and the Harpes, that they would travel in company to Logan's. In a few hours a considerable shower of rain set in and, as Susan Woods related in Russelville, "We were detained several hours sheltering under the foliage of a thick cluster of trees." Doubts were expressed by the travelers, that there was any chance for them to reach Logan's Station that evening; and that they would have to camp another night. "Instantly," said Maria when also relating the circumstances of this part of their travel in Kentucky, "I saw from what passed between the Harpes, who, when those remarks were made by one of the Marylanders, were standing near each other,—in low whispers and significant looks between them, that some desperate purpose was occupying their minds. Big Harpe remarked to the traveler quickly and rather in a persuasive manner not to think of such a thing as going on, for they would be in danger of an attack from the Indians, as he was sure there were many Cherokee Indians then ranging in that part of Kentucky; for they had seen four of them as they came on, and he was certain they were on their track to take advantage of them at night."

"I understood this as thrown out" said Susan Wood, "to induce the travelers to keep company with them till night, knowing as he did, from having been on expeditions through that part of the country, with the Cherokees, that it would be impossible to reach the point before night, and the gentlemen expressed a wish immediately to keep together, for their mutual protection."

"I had no difficulty in forming an opinion of the scene that would that night occur," said Maria, still also relating the story. "I knew the Harpes had formed a scheme of murder and robbery. If I had dared I would have given them notice of their danger; but if I had been seen by either of them, speaking to them they would have suspected me and treated me as though I had betrayed them, and would have taken my life. I therefore could only keep silence."

Night came on, and the Station was yet at least twenty miles distant. The party came to a small branch in a

330   LEGENDS OF THE

sort of open glade, and Bates proposed that they should
there encamp and stay all night. Bill Harpe, said no;
they would go a mile farther and find water which he
thought he remembered, and more grass. So they went
on till it grew dark. Suddenly, the two Harpes, seemed
as if by accident to change position—Bill Harpe getting
behind Bates, and Josh directly following Paca,—the
two women eight or ten yards in the rear. Suddenly,
both the Harpes fired, and the two unfortunate Marylanders fell. One of them was found dead, as soon as the
light was raised, and the other, Paca, not dead, but
speechless, seeming to be trying to get to his feet. Josh
Harpe, however, soon ended the struggle, by splitting
open his head with a hatchet or tomahawk he carried in
his belt. Quickly the pockets as well as the entire baggage of the murdered men, were searched and rifled of
everything valuable. A considerable amount of money,
some gold and silver, and a large quantity of continental
paper was found.

They stripped the bodies of their clothes they had on,
and emptied their saddle-bags also of the shirts and other
apparel, which fitted the Harpes pretty well—so that each
of them appeared after that, in tolerable decent trim for
woodsmen. Big Bill, had not worn a hat for more than
two years. In a drunken carouse with the Indians at
Nickajack, his old hat brought from North Carolina, was
burnt by a drunken Indian. He "whanged," together
some pieces of deer skin, with the hair outside and wore
it for a covering to his head in very cold or snowy
weather; but not often. When he put on the pants and
coat of Bates, who was a large man, and also his hat
which fitted well, he seemed proud of his supposed improved appearance, and had the impudence, putting on a
less turbid and threatening countenance, than he had
ever shown her before, to ask Susan Wood, if she did
not think he looked like a handsome gentleman.

Josh also rigged himself out, in the clothing of Paca,—

WAR OF INDEPENDENCE. 331

and having packed up what of the goods and clothing of the Marylanders, they wished to bear off with them, they started and traveled about a mile through the woods,—stopped and camped at a small branch; leaving the almost naked bodies of the murdered men, to be food for wolves, panthers and other inhabitants of the caves and dense forests of the "dark and bloody ground."

Next morning, apprehending it might not be safe to pass Logan's or Harrod's Station with the horses, clothing and other equippage of Bates and Paca, which might be known by some one, they changed their course, steering over towards the south-west, and fell into a road or trace, leading to Green River.

The third day from the time they left the Crab Orchard, a report reached there that a wealthy young Virginian, by the name of Lankford, had been robbed and murdered, on the wilderness road, as it was then and is now called—somewhere in the Rock Castle hills. The suspicion that fell upon those despicable men, was justly founded, for they had fallen in with him near where they entered that road, traveling alone. Instantly he was shot, rifled of all his money,—his body thrown into a deep sink, and his horse escaping to the Crab Orchard, first excited the suspicion of his fate, at that place.

They were followed by a company of twelve men, who ultimately overtook them in a camp on Green River, and were all taken to Danville and imprisoned. But before their trial came on they broke jail and cleared themselves; leaving all their horses and other effects behind.

From Danville they made their way during the night of their escape, to the neighborhood of Springfield, where they camped, keeping very close till the second day, when the Harpes set out alone, as they said, to go to where the Cherokee Indians were to meet them; leaving Maria and Susan with her baby alone at the camp. In two days they returned with two horses, saddles and bridles, and two of the four Cherokees.

332   LEGENDS OF THE

While they were away the two women having a fair opportunity to fly to one or other of the white settlements and appeal to them for protection,—conversed with each other whether they ought not to do so, but fearing they would again be taken to Danville, imprisoned and roughly treated, if not condemned for the murder of Lankford, for which they were indicted with the Harpes, Maria said: "Susan, what shall we gain by doing so, even if we escape from the imprisonment and the prosecution? We are forever ruined and disgraced; and must forever be the objects of the scorn and contempt of all respectable persons, never to be received again by our relations in North Carolina, nor here or there, otherwise treated than as the debased and defiled mistresses of horrible murderers and Tories! Oh God! far rather would I die in the wilderness, yea at once, on the murderess' gallows, than endure such a torture as scorn like that would inflict." So they concluded still to abide their fate.

The same day the Harpes with the two Indians returned. All set out and in a short distance crossed Muldrow's Hill, and steering south-west, passed through the neighborhood of the present location of Greensburgh, and encamped on the bank of Green River, within that vicinity.

From this they again returned to the neighborhood of Snelling's Station, in what is now the most southerly part of Nelson County, Kentucky, where they committed several robberies and stole several horses. Again they progressed to the south-west,—entered Adair County, or what is now Adair County, and are believed to have murdered not distant from where Columbia is now located, Col. Trabue's little son of very tender years; from whom they took a small bag of meal or flour, and threw his body into a sink-hole, where his bones, some years after, were found and identified.

Again they passed on to, and entered Tennessee—and near old Fort Blunt, met with a small girl distant from

WAR OF INDEPENDENCE. 333

her home only one fourth of a mile, passing to a neighbor's house, murdered her most wantonly and left her in the woods. At the old Fort some soldiers were quartered and when, the day after, the body of the child was found, a gentleman, Capt. Bedford, from Georgia, who happened to be at the Fort, but not in command, headed, nevertheless, six mounted soldiers from that place; and getting on the trail of the murderers followed them across the Kentucky line, out into the Barrens, as they were then called, in the Green River country, and into the neighborhood of the Mammoth Cave, or at least eight or nine miles north west of Prewitt's Knob, and finally losing all trace of them, after a diligent search for more than a day and a half, abandoned the pursuit and returned home.

The fact is, as the women afterwards disclosed, they had hid in the Mammoth Cave, or some other remarkably large one, where they remained for two or three weeks.

From thence they passed down Barren River, near to the mouth of Gasper's River, and murdered a Mr. Stump, with whom they met when hunting. His body being shortly after found, the alarm was given through the sparcely settled neighborhood, and a number followed them through the country for two or three days.

Before these vile fiends, however, passed the village of Russellville, and when within three or four hundred yards of the residence of Mr. Samuel Wilson, the infant of Susan Wood, about nine months old, being very sick and crying all the morning, so that nothing could quiet it, Big Harpe snatched it from its mother's arms, slung it by the heels against a large tree by the path-side, and literally bursting its head into a dozen pieces—threw it from him as far as his great strength enabled him into the woods. This was the third of his children by poor Susan he had murdered and in like manner destroyed.

334   LEGENDS OF THE

CHAPTER XXXI.

The Harpes and Cherokees continue their blood-thirsty journey—
At the point of the Clay Lick woods they murder, strip, and mutilate the families and servants of two brothers—They are chased
by a party from Russellville and Drumgool's stations—The Harpes,
in the meantime, murder Stegall's family near the Double Licks,
rob and burn up his home—They are overtaken at the "Lonesome Oak" by the pursuing party—Big Harpe and one Indian
is killed, and the head of the former hung on a tree—Stegall attempts to murder Susan Woods—Is restrained and wholly checked
by Wm. Stewart, of Russellville—Maria Davidson and Susan
Woods are taken with the return party to Russellville—Excitement of the populace against them—They are privately conveyed
out of town to a place of safety—Maria is subsequently married.

> We range the fields and woods
> Like beasts of prey.   Murder
> And robbery mark our path ;
> Our hands are wet with human blood,
> And human life and hopes are withered
> At our touch.   Avaunt !   Hell
> Gapes and opens for our treacherous souls,
> Accursed alike of God and man —*Impromptu.*

PASSING about one half mile on the north of Russellville, this blood-thirsty party crossed big Whippoorwill
about eight miles west of Russellville, and traveling
through the very level and naked barrens of the west side
of the above named creek, entered what is called the big
Cave, where they housed themselves for the space of two
weeks, hunting in the day (for game was very abundant)
and at night carousing and debauching. On the day
before they moved from the cave, one of them discovered,
near sundown, two brothers and their families, by the
name of Titsword. Each with a wife, several children,
and a few black servants. He watched them at a dis-

WAR OF INDEPENDENCE.   335

tance until they stopped at what was for many years
called the point of the Claylick woods, saw them halt,
and prepare to encamp by the bank of the Claylick
branch. Narrating what he had seen on returning to the
cave, it was determined to make all things ready at day-
break, proceed to the place, attack the camp, rob and
murder them, and then proceed on their journey to the
Ohio, and to Stack Island. This bloody resolution, these
demons in human form but too successfully executed. At
the break of day they sallied forth, the Harpes, the two
Cherokees, and the two women. It was only about a
mile and a quarter to the fatal spot—the camp of the
Titswords and their innocent wives and children. As
soon as it was light enough to shoot, they all, except the
women, fired on the peaceful families, most of whom were
still reposing in quiet sleep, and at the first fire one of
the brothers was instantly killed, also one of the wives
and several of the innocent children! The other brother escaped unhurt, ran out from his tent, leaving his
wife shot through the heart, and one of his children mor-
tally wounded, supposing they were attacked by a large
band of Indians; got into the buffalo trace along which
they traveled the day before, and ran back eight miles,
quite in his undress, to Drumgool's station, in Logan
county, Kentucky, near the Tennessee line, precisely
where the village of Adairville is now situated. There a
company of nine men was raised, who set out immediately for the dreadful scene of cruelty and death. Some
passing by Russellville, the county seat of all Green river
at that time, where, also, ten or fifteen more set out
for the point of the Claylick woods. When they reached
the place, most horrible was the spectacle they beheld!
The ground covered for a space with the bodies of men,
women, and children, white and black! Some of them
dreadfully mangled; and some stripped to the skin.
This was especially the condition of the two sisters-in-
law. The men immediately, or most of them, set to work

336   LEGENDS OF THE

in digging a large deep grave in which to bury the dead, masters, mistresses and servants, in one common grave, whose mingled ashes must there rest till "the last loud trump shall bid the dead arise."

Meanwhile, several of the most experienced of them, went forth to find the trail of the bandits. Within a short distance they ascertained they had taken the buffalo trace along which the Titswords had traveled for some days before, and which those primitive inhabitants of this vast wilderness—the buffaloes—by hundreds, and, perhaps, sometimes by thousands, used to travel from Bledsoe's licks, in Tennessee, to the Clay lick and Double licks ; and so on to the Highland lick, near the Ohio. According to the arrangement between themselves, in the morning following, ten or twelve of the most active and efficient of the men from Russellville and Drumgool's station were to follow and endeavor to apprehend the murderers ; if Indians, destroy them, or if whites, to bring them to Russellville for punishment. Of the number of those who set out next morning to pursue the Harpes and Indians from Russellville and Drumgool's station, were William Stewart of the former, and John Mann of the latter place. The former was a man of great originality of character. More distinguished through a long life of the most hazardous adventure—possessing a nature of extraordinary malignity of purpose and action, deep design, dark and yet more certain in execution of such purposes and designs—than personal prowess or moral courage. The latter was a man of great bodily strength, indomitable courage and pacific temperament. More of them, however, we shall take occasion to speak in another place in these legends.

The Harpes, from where they perpetrated the murder of the Titswords, fled, as we have already said, along the buffalo trace on to the Claylick ; from thence to the Double licks, near which, at the distance of eight miles from the latter place, was situated the house of Stegall. They

WAR OF INDEPENDENCE.   337

found his wife and four children there, and also a negro
woman and two of her children. Stegall was from home.
They put them all to death, robbed the house of everything they desired to take off with them, and putting all
the slain in one pile in the dwelling, set fire to it and
burned it to ashes. At night the unfortunate husband
and father came home and found everything consumed.
He went that night to the house of his acquaintance,
Samuel Leeper, and told the horrible tale. Early in the
morning Stegall and his neighbor Leeper returned to
Stegall's house, saw the burning bones of the family consumed. They hunted for the tracks of the murderers,
were not long in finding them, and commenced the pursuit. On their way they passed by the residence of
McBey, another neighbor.

Still the murderers kept the buffalo trace, and traveled
rapidly. Others of Stegall's and Leeper's neighbors heard
of the occurrence and joined in the race till the number
increased to eight or ten. The pursuers traveled during
that entire day, and did not overtake them. They encamped that night near to what was called the Lonesome
Oak, well known in all that country for standing out
" solitary and alone " in the midst of a body of very level
barrens of four or five thousand acres with no tree, or
even a shrub within a mile's distance.

Again in the morning, as soon as light, they recom-
menced the pursuit and traveled about twelve miles, when
suddenly they came upon the camp of the bandits. Big
Harpe first discovered them, and instantly gave the
alarm, mounted his fine young mare, rushed to the somewhat steep bank of Pond river near at hand, forced her to
leap into the stream, swam to the opposite shore and endeavored to make his escape. Leeper followed him in
hot haste, had to cross at a place some distance lower
down the stream, but getting across, soon was upon the
plain track made by Harpe in the thick tall pea vines;
and being mounted on one of the fleetest of horses, in

22

338 LEGENDS OF THE

about a mile and a half came near enough to shoot and put a ball through Harpe's right thigh, some three or four inches above his knee, and kill his horse outright. They both fell together, Harpe's gun rolling off from him fifteen or twenty feet as he fell. Leeper came up to him while he was growling and writhing like a wounded tiger, struggling to get up and reach his gun. It was impossible. He then sunk down and commenced cursing and defying his assailant in the most ferocious and bitter terms, blasphemous oaths and denunciations. Then begged for water, as he said he was famishing with want, and seemed to sink down in a swoon. Leeper's pity or magnanimity was awakened; he ran hastily to the river, about a hundred and fifty yards distant, dipped his hat full, but ere he got back to him, Stegall had come up, and cut the murderer's throat from ear to ear, which with the next blow he entirely severed, and afterwards hung his head upon a tree at the forks of the road from Hopkinsville to Morganfield and Madisonville—a place still known and called *Harpe's Head.*

One of the Indians, who had accompanied them and was at the camp when it was reached, fled on foot and endeavored to follow big Harpe in his flight, but was unable to get more than a half a mile down the river before McBey overtook and killed him and left his body, as was also that of big Bill Harpe, to feed the wolves, wild cats, and panthers of the Pond river bottoms and dense forests.

Returning to the camp from where the Harpes and Indians had fled, and at which several of the men who had accompanied them had stopped, they found Maria Davidson and Susan Woods. Instantly Stegall recognized the calico dress of his murdered wife upon Susan Woods. His fury was greatly aroused, and he made several attempts to slay her and tear it from her person. With much difficulty he was prevented by Leeper and McBey. In vain she told him in the most humble and suppliant terms her own sad story and cruel sufferings. In vain

WAR OF INDEPENDENCE.   339

Maria Davidson confirmed her statements, and related her own intolerable sufferings. Still he persisted in his attempts to destroy her. But just at that time, the company made up at the point of the Clay lick woods and at the grave of the Titswords, to pursue their murderers, came up, and learning the incidents that had occurred, as well as the cause of Stegall's fury and threats, William Stewart, from Russellville, looking him steadfastly in the face, with an expression of countenance no man could imitate, and none misunderstand, who had the least acquaintance with him, said:

"Look here, Stegall, I reckon you once had, or now have, a mother. So had I a mother. I have occasionally, aye, several times in my life, seed men killed, but can't and won't see a woman." Still looking Stegall very significantly in the eye, he continued:

"Did you see that flash of lightning, Stegall?"

"No, sir," answered Stegall.

"Well, well," said Stewart, "a word to the wise is sufficient."

Stegall did not respond, but sinking down to a seat on the ground, began to cry quite audibly, and nothing more was said at that time about killing the unhappy woman.

In a short time after, those that had followed Josh. Harpe and the two Indians, returned, stating they had wholly failed to keep their track or overtake them. The conversation then turned upon the question as to what was to be done with the women. The deputy sheriff of Logan was along, and said it would be his duty to take them back to Russellville, as they were present when the Titswords were killed and would have to be tried. William Stewart said, " that was right, and he wasn't going to leave them in the woods no way."

So they all set forth to return to the court at Russellville. Arrived there, a prodigious excitement arose against them. The intelligence had come of many of the murders perpetrated by the Harpes as they had passed through the country, and they were placed in jail by the advice of the clerk of the court, Mr. Armsted Morehead, and several others, who pitied them very much, and believed it safest for them. Still the fury of the populace spread more and more, till threats were openly made of a determination by many to tear down the jail, which was but a log cabin, and murder or destroy them in some way. Mr. Morehead, Gen. Samuel Caldwell, and Phillip Latham, got the jailor to place them in their charge, and they sent them secretly a distance into the country, where they were taken care of till the excitement had passed. They both lived in the county of Logan many years after, where they were often seen, known and conversed with by the author of these narratives, and who received from the lips of Susan Woods herself most of the facts narrated in the foregoing pages, in reference to herself, Maria, and the Harpes, from the time they became so unhappily connected with them.

Maria married Sol. Hostetter, of Logan county, where, it is believed, she died some ten or twelve years since. It is not known to the writer what became of poor Susan.

Profoundly mysterious are thy ways, O, Lord God of all human destiny! Passing all finite comprehension.

> ' Deep in unfathomless mines,
>   Of never-failing skill,
> Thou treasurest up thy bright designs,
>   And works't thy sovereign will!''

WAR OF INDEPENDENCE. 341

CHAPTER XXXII.

Further narrative of the adventures of Josh Harpe—His escape—
His appearance at Natchez with Peter Alston—They conspire to
murder and decapitate Mayerson for the government reward—
They do so and while waiting for the reward are recognized and
seized, tried, condemned and executed.

Alas! alas! 'tis sin, man's doom decrees;
A bondage to misery and death creates!
Mercy loudly pleads to release,
But iniquity ordains man's sadest fate.—*The Author.*

WE again enter into a farther narrative of those remarkably desperate men, the Harpes; or, rather, that
of Josh Harpe, and the Indian that followed him from
Nickajack, at the time when they fled from before Capt.
Jackson, where he attacked and utterly destroyed that
place.

It will be remembered that the two Harpes, when they
were found in their camp, by Stegall, Leeper and others
on or near Pond River, fled like affrighted wolves; one of
the Indians taking the same direction, westward, with
Josh Harpe. The Indians on foot and both the Harpes
on horseback. Bill Harpe was mounted on a very valuable and fleet mare, of which he had possessed himself
after they had broken jail at Danville,—unequaled by
many in point of speed.

It so occurred that the part of Kentucky, in which
they were overtaken, and particularly that through which
they fled, was covered with the most extraordinary growth
of the pea vine, in the bottoms and indeed, throughout
the timber, while in the barrens as they were then there
called, and are still; the grass grew so thick, tall and lux-

342   LEGENDS OF THE

uriant, that it was not at all difficult to discern or follow the break in them by a man running, or especially a horse, at a considerable distance. Thus it was notwithstanding the speed of Big Harpe's fine mare, his pursuers had no dfficulty in trailing him. Those that followed Josh Harpe, however, were more puzzled, as he traveled much slower, made a less plain and distinct mark; and being less pressed by those that undertook to chase him, he had more time to pick his way and cautiously direct his flight. This was particularly the case when within a few miles from where they started, they reached the immediate neighborhood of a lick, which was perfectly bare of grass or pea vine, or even shrubbery; and there the trail was lost altogether.

Onward they pressed with celerity and reached the Ohio, near the mouth of Trade Water, where, finding a perogue fastened to the Kentucky shore, supposed to have been brought and left there by some Illinoisians, who had crossed from the neighborhood of where Shawneetown is now situated, to hunt in the vicinity of the Highland lick, as game of all kinds was there very abundant, into that they hastened, and Josh Harpe and the Indian, were seen floating down about where Ford's Ferry is situated, (on the Ohio), a little below the position of the Saline Salt Works. From that time they were not again heard of until at Natchez,—Josh Harpe was recognized, together with Peter Alston, the son of the celebrated counterfeiter, Phil. Alston, who was also from North Carolina,—who had some years before, moved to, settled, and five or six years, lived in Logan County, Kentucky, and being driven from there by the Kentuckians, fled to Stack Island, where he with the said Peter, had acted with the terrible bandits of whom we have heretofore given a description, in robbing and murdering on the Ohio, flatboatmen and passengers down that river. He, however, chiefly conducting the vile work of counterfeiting of the silver coins and the most current paper money, then in circulation in the West, having at an early period of the revolution, practiced that business in Raleigh, North Carolina, and continued in Kentucky, as long as permitted to remain there.

These two, Josh Harpe and young Alston, added to their diabolical crimes and character for murder and rapine practiced at said place. Having learned that at Natchez, then part of Louisiana, a reward of two thousand dollars was offered for the head of Mayerson, the leader and commander at Stack Island, they conceived and executed the traitorous design of murdering him, taking off his head, and, going to Natchez, demand the reward. The next day after they reached Natchez, and were waiting the payment of it, they were recognized by two young men, as two of a gang that had robbed their boat at Stack Island—murdered several of the crew, and from whom they had almost miraculously themselves made their escape.

Upon the testimony of these two young Kentuckians, they were immediately apprehended and in the most summary mode tried and convicted of murder and robbery, and immediately executed. Before his death, however, Josh Harpe made to one of those young Kentuckians and others a tolerably full disclosure of his life of iniquity, as in the preceding pages set forth, touching his bloody career in connection with his still more despicable relative, big Bill Harpe,—protesting to the very last breath, however, that he was destined by God and nature, to the crimes or acts of his whole life, and to the horrible end to which he had come. These things he stated in the callaboose, and at the place of execution, to Thomas L. Hawkins, one of the young Kentuckians we have mentioned, as witnesses against him on the trial, who was afterwards a well esteemed and useful officer in the U. S. Army, in the north-west, during the war of 1812.

Many others, however, in Kentucky and several from North Carolina, have made statements to this writer,

344   LEGENDS OF THE

personally, in corroboration and establishment of the entire narrative of the lives of those Harpes; so highly
illustrative of the capabilities of fallen human nature,
trained in false notions of God, and themselves and the
principles upon which human conduct is certain to be
finally judged, rewarded or punished, at the bar of Almighty God.

> " And must I be to judgment brought,
>   " And answer in that day,
> " For every vain and idle thought
>   " And every word I say ?
>
> " Yes every secret of my heart,
>   " Shall shortly be made known
> " And I receive my just desert,
>   " For all that I have done."

WAR OF INDEPENDENCE. 345

CHAPTER XXXIII.

Major Bland Ballard—His parentage—His father locates at Boonsboro—Removes to Tick Creek—Family locates at Tyler's Station—Maj. Bland marries—The Station becoming crowded, the Ballards remove outside the stockades—Danger from the Indians anticipated—The family of old Mr. Ballard is attacked and nearly all murdered by the Indians—Maj. Bland, hearing the attack, rushes to the door of his cabin to receive the last groan of his murdered mother—Decides to take the open ground and defend himself and wife—Is heroically assisted by his wife—After shooting seven Indians, he finds his bullet pouch exhausted—Is supplied by his wife who melts her spoons for the purpose, and exposes her life to hand the bullets to her husband—He finally triumphs.

> "Courage in arms and ever prompt to show,
>   His manly forehead to the fiercest foe:
>   Glorious in war, but for the sake of peace,
>   His spirits rising as his toils increase,
>   Guards well what arts and industry have won,
>   And freedom claims him for her first born-son."
>   —*Campbell.*

AMONG the many gallant and daring spirits that emigrated to Kentucky, at an early day, and periled their lives to rid its fertile soil and that of the vast valley of the Mississippi of the innumerable savage tribes, none was more active and efficient than Maj. Bland Ballard, who died on the 5th day of September, 1853, in Shelby County, Kentucky, at the advanced age of *ninety-four* years; possessed through life of a most daring and unconquerable spirit; knowing no fear of man, and yet alike distinguished for his generous bearing to others, and amiable conformity to and practice of all the amenities of social life and all the obligations by it imposed. Cau-

346 LEGENDS OF THE

tious, active and fearless in the pursuit of the wily savage, he was from his youth up, ranked among those upon whom the greatest reliance was placed, in the times of the greatest danger.

The father of Maj. Ballard, removed to Kentucky from Virginia, in the year 1780, with his family; settled or stopped, for about two years, at Boonsboro;—sharing during that time, in common with all then in the West, the privations, toils and hairbreadth escapes, incident to a life in the wilderness and the dangers of the destruction of himself and family, by the ruthless tomahawk and scalping knife. When it was generally believed some degree of safety had been won by frequent chastisements inflicted upon the Indians, the father of Maj. Ballard, whose name was also Bland, with the view to a permanent settlement at the falls of the Ohio, removed to a Station occupied by a few families on Tick Creek, about four mile east of where Shelbyville is now situated, then in Jefferson, now Shelby County,—Tyler's Station it was called. This Station was named after Capt. Robert Tyler, a most respectable gentleman, who early emigrated from Virginia, and first made a settlement at that place; and whose numerous relatives, generally industrious and enterprizing, now much dispersed through Kentucky, are justly numbered among her most respectable, judicious, intelligent and wealthy citizens.

Before this removal it was that the services of Major Ballard, of which we have already given some account, were rendered, in company with and under the command of Capt. Thomas McClanahan, as spies or rangers along the Ohio River, in the release of two young ladies from their captivity by the Mississinawa Indians. After his return from that most arduous and trying campaign, he became the husband of Elizabeth Williamson, a young and heroic girl, like himself, enthusiastically delighted with frontier life, inured to its vicissitudes and dangers; having witnessed more than one attack by the

Indians, upon the infant settlements and familiar with the Indian war-whoop and scenes of blood. Tyler's Station was small, and in the numerous and rapid immigrations to that place, soon became inconveniently crowded. Hence the Ballards were induced to build their cabins without the limits and line of stockades erected for the defence of the Station, and they lived there without the protection enjoyed by their neighbors. But as the Indians had for some time seemed quieted, no great apprehension was felt or fear entertained from that quarter. Nevertheless, they were not long left to enjoy the hope of security.

The Indians, always on the look-out for an opportunity successfully to assail the whites; watched the progress of things at the Station, and seeing a favorable opportunity in the defenceless condition of the Ballards and their dwellings, planned a murderous attack. At about daylight in the morning, twenty or more aroused the inhabitants of the Station, by a furious assault upon the cabin of the elder Ballard, occupied by himself and wife, and several of their unmarried children; forced the door open and before any effective resistance could be made, right away, and within the house, butchered the father, brothers and sisters! His mother for a minute or so survived them, got out of the house, but was shot down when endeavoring to reach the door of her son! The son with his wife was in bed, in his cabin, which, as we have said, situated a few yards from that of his father, was awakened at the first onset of the savages, sprang up, hurried on a few of his clothes, heard the last expiring groans of his mother, who fell near his door. He seized his trusty rifle and prepared for the desperate conflict.

Having some confidence in his skill in using his gun, and as to remain in the cabin would, he believed, the more endanger the lives of himself and his wife, he preferred the open woods for the fight, and rushing out, concealed himself as much as possible behind the trees ; keeping, however, in a position to communicate with his wife, still within his dwelling. With astonishing coolness he surveyed the ground and prepared for the deadly conflict. The wife, alive to a sense of their imminent danger, but still calm as he was brave, kept a close watch upon the movements of the Indians, and at every change of position by any of them, gave him, by word, notice of it, if he was near enough to hear, or signal, if too distant. The Indians knew Ballard, and by experience, knew the man they had to deal with. As soon, therefore, as he was discovered abroad, he concealed himself behind a tree and acted with extreme caution. It was not long before he had an opportunity to fire, and one of the most daring of them fell instantly. Reloading from time to time, husbanding his shots with the utmost prudence, he thus kept up this unequal contest till he had killed seven of his foes. More than double that number yet survived to fight. But even these bloody savages, thinking " discretion the better part of valor," left the field in Ballard's possession, and fled beyond the reach of his deadly aim. During this terrific battle, he found he had just loaded with his last bullet. He remembered there was lead in his father's cabin, but to obtain it was incalculably hazardous. He gave the signal to his wife. She understood it, and in a moment flew to a few pewter spoons they possessed, siezed the ladle and his bullet moulds, melted them upon the coals still lingering in the fire-place, quickly turned out an ample supply, and with that heroic daring, known alone among the early women of the West, like a bounding fawn darted across the space to where he stood, and placed them in his shot-pouch ! then again skipped back to her cabin without injury. Not unseen, however, by the Indians ; for they fired upon the noble woman, yet Heaven protected her, and she escaped their aim.

Another incident occurred which we think ought to be mentioned. About the moment of the fleeing of the In-

WAR OF INDEPENDENCE.   349

dians, and when Mr. Ballard could see but one that lingered behind, who seemed endeavoring to obtain a shot through a fence that ran between them, Ballard ran near to it, and both ran along side for the like purpose. The Indian fired and missed, and in a moment was the eighth victim of Ballard's unerring rifle.

For many years he lived, upon the soil and at the quiet home so bravely by his own hands won and rescued from savage invasion and control, and which he so profusely enriched with the heart's blood of the ruthless murderers of his mother, brothers and sisters. Single in heart and purpose ; peaceful, kind, and courteous towards all ; the advocate of right ; the friend and defence of the poor ; and the firm and unconquerable resister of whatever he believed to be wrong. Early in youth he sought, and faithfully battled for, a home on the loved soil of Kentucky ; and waited long there to find his grave. There, now, his honored ashes shall rest in calm repose, till " Heaven's last thunder shall shake the world below ; " till Gabriel's loud proclaim shall bid the dead arise. Then,

> " These new rising from the tomb,
>   With luster brighter far shall shine ;
>   Revive with ever-during bloom—
>   Safe from diseases and decline,"

Maj. Ballard died at his farm in Shelby county, Ky., fifth of September, 1853, and was there buried by the side of that heroic wife, long before deceased. But since the above narrative of his highly adventurous life was written, and in the — day of the present year, 1854, in accordance with an order of the Kentucky Legislature, passed at the session of 1853-4, his body, with that of his beloved Elizabeth, under the order of Gov. Powell, were taken and reinterred at the State's cemetry at Frankfort, the seat of government.

350   LEGENDS OF THE

CHAPTER XXXIV.

"William Stout"—Thoughts on the adage "Murder will out"—Why Stout came to Kentucky—His dark deeds of blood—His care of his family—Tracks and destroys the murderer of his son—Redresses the widow's wrong—Prevents Jerry Moore's trip to Missouri—Dies.

> "Will all great Neptune's Ocean wash this blood
> Clean from my hands? No: this my hand will rather
> The multitudinous seas incarnadine,
> Making the green—one red."—*Shakspeare.*

"He has done the murder. No eye has seen him, no ear has heard him. The secret is his own, and it is safe! Ah! gentlemen, that was a dreadful mistake. Such a secret can be safe nowhere. The whole creation of God has neither nook nor corner where the guilty can bestow it and say it is safe. Not to speak of that eye which pierces through all designs, and beholds everything as in the splendor of noon. Such secrets of guilt are never safe from detection, even by men. True it is, generally speaking, 'Murder will out.'"

Thus spoke that preëminently great orator and sound philosopher, Daniel Webster, in his unequalled speech against the Napps. Generally, indeed, it is so. "Murder will out." We rejoice it is so, in a great majority of the instances of murder. We rejoice and felicitate ourselves, and all who love civilization and social life, that Providence hath so ordained and doth so govern things that those who break the great law of Heaven by shedding man's blood, seldom succeed in avoiding discovery. Yet we must record, that such is the imperfection of human laws, of human perception; the irregularity and inequality of human judgment and action; the secretive powers and cautious cunning of some murderers, over

WAR OF INDEPENDENCE.   351

those of the great number alike guilty, that to the great
discomfort of society, not to speak of the dark stamp of
degradation of our race, too many perpetrate this horrible crime, sculk back into society; and often, though
again and again they perpetrate this dreadful outrage
against the laws of God, society, and humanity, are permitted to pass a long life and die in their beds the subjects of the attentions and sympathies of all our better
natures, as though they had lived honest, harmless, and
inoffensive lives. Ah! who does not see in the actual
existence of this state of things on earth, an argument ir-
resistably confirmatory of the wise and just order of the
Almighty in the appointment of a day of general judgment, " in the which He will judge every man according
as his deeds shall be! whether they be good, or whether
they be evil."

To these seemingly abstract remarks, courteous reader,
we are led, preparatory to your perusal of a brief, but
truthful exhibit of the life and character of one of the pioneers of the West, most unique in the strange comminglement they exhibit of vices of the deepest dye, and
seeming virtues of the most proper and fascinating character; with all the secret craft, cunning, malignity and
pusillanimity of the midnight assassin, and the daring,
toilsome and hazardous enterprises of men of the greatest
energy and prowess. A dastardly coward, yet relying
upon his own perfected and matured knowledge of men
and things, the machinery of the human mind, the passions, motives and purposes of the human heart in its
most corrupted or graciously purified phases, to cover and
carry out in secret and safety, his bloody deeds, he sallied
forth in a darkness almost of his own creation, and perpetrated whatever a practised and cultivated thirst for
human blood or malignant revenge dictated, from youth
to hoary age.

To many, nay, thousands, who yet live in Kentucky,
who have known the original from whose strong linea-

352   LEGENDS OF THE

ments of character the foregoing picture is truly sketched,
it is unnecessary for us to assign a name. To all others
who may chance to read these pages, the real name of
this extraordinary man cannot be material, and the fic-
tious one we shall give, instead of the real, out of a just
respect entertained for his worthy descendants and collat-
eral kin, yet living, will answer for all the purposes of
reference, while we assure them we personally knew the
man more than forty years,—with frequent opportunities
to observe and mark his physiognomy and manners,
throughout that length of time.

The birth of *William Stout*, the subject of this narrative, according to his own statement, was in the district
of Edgecombe, South Carolina, in the year 1772. There
his parents lived, and he was raised, till he reached his
eighteenth year, when he left them and never more saw
them. Of their history, before and after his birth, none
knew in this country, more than as he very seldom said
of them, his father was of a remarkably quiet and taci-
turn disposition, while he seemed proud to speak of his
mother as Amazonian in temper and spirit; stern toward
all in her manners, and inexorably revengeful toward her
enemies.

These traits of his parents were imparted by him in
brief anecdotes, in his familiar conversations with his
friends, as he chose, occasionally, to unbend his stern nature. It was always evident that his love and admiration
for his mother was preëminent. He often gave that, as a
reason for his devotion to the sex, generally, and as the
reason why he called them all sisters, and avowed himself
ready to protect them at all hazards. Very frequently,
however, when speaking of his " mammy," as he always
called her, and especially of her resolute spirit and disposition, he would conclude, in some apparent seriousness,
by saying, " she got me into a devil of a bad scrape once
by her high temper." But he never explained how.

His education was of a common grade. In nothing superior, except in a sufficient knowledge of figures and the ordinary branches of mathematics—trigonometry and geometry, to enable him to execute with reasonable correctness and promptitude, surveys of lands. His penmanship and diction were ready, in matter and manner. His heighth was a little above ordinary; person robust; features tolerably symmetrical; light auburn hair, hazel eyes, heavy eye-brows, large head, and particularly so in the rear and above the spinal column. Always eccentric in his material and style of dress—sometimes, and often so much so, he appeared attired in an entire suit made of various colored "lists," taken from the finest broadcloths, sewed together, fantastically cut and fitted to his person, while the buttons of his coat and pantaloons were quarter dollars, United States coin, with eyes attached by his own ingenuity (for he was a worker in metals), and his vest buttoned with genuine United States dimes. This dress, however, was rather for high days and holydays,—such as a fourth of July, an extraordinary assemblage of the people to worship; or the reception at his town of President Monroe, Gen. Jackson, or Mr. Clay. His conversation was always vulgar, obtrusive and profane,—generally in the order of the jocular and facetious, and desirous to cover himself in a mist of enigmas and inexplicable inuendoes. He was between nineteen and twenty years of age, according to his own statement, when he came to Kentucky, and that was about the year 1790. He died at Russellville, Kentucky, 1852.

To the writer of these legends he once said, in a sort of private way, and in his own peculiar style of talking, "Smith, did you ever know why it was I first come out to Kentucky?"

He was answered in the negative.

"Damn it, then I'll tell you. You know I loved fiddling. I larnt to play when I was a small boy. They used to get me to play at frollicks about in daddy's neighborhood, for the gals and boys to dance after. So when

I was about eighteen, I was at a frollick about a half mile from daddy's, playing away the best I could in one corner, and a whole passel of gals and boys dancing. A big black fellow, of the name of Jack Patty, come to me, and said to me, says he, 'Bill, play the tune called Captain Johnson.' I seed he was drunk, and paid no attention to him. So I played along, the tune I was at. In a little while he come again, and cursed me. Still I took no notice of him; kept on. He cursed me again, give me a rousing slap on the side of the face, and sent me half over to the floor. Bless you! I played no more that time. But jist rose up and laid Betty (that is what I called my fiddle) on a table, close by, and walked right off from the house, pretty mad, I tell you.

"I walked about and about, through the woods, then round daddy's field to the house. It was about an hour before I come home. Mammy and daddy was still sitting up. The old woman was mighty mad, and spoke to me fust. She said, says she, 'Billy Stout, Tom. Ellit come here awhile ago, and said Jack Patty had slapped your jaws, down at the frollick, and hurt you very much.''

"'Well,' says I, "mammy, he did."

"'Well,' says she, 'now, Billy Stout, if you, after that, let Jack Patty live in South Carolina, above ground, you aint the son of your daddy.' Daddy said nothing. Said I, 'mammy, now let me alone about that. I don't tell folks what I am going to do,'—and went right to bed; but didn't sleep much, for thinkin' about it. 'Well,' says I to myself, 'mammy says Jack Patty oughtn't to live above ground any more, in South Carolina. I think so too.' So I made a decree in the morning to go and look at him that night after dark. I said nothing to anybody all day. Mammy said to me after dinner, 'Well, Billy Stout, what are you going to do about Jack Patty?' Said I, 'mammy, that's my business,' and said no more to her that time.

"God bless you, Smith, I went that night and took a

WAR OF INDEPENDENCE. 355

look at Jack through a crack in his house wall, and I took a straight edge along to look at him by. Now, a straight edge is a mighty dangerous thing to look along, at anybody. So I peeped at him through a crack that night, and he dodged me or fell down, and I never saw him after that. Ha! ha! You may depend, it's dangerous to look at a fellow along a straight edge,—it is that. Well, the people all about began to say, I or somebody had looked at Jack rather hard that night; that he had set off to go to another country, or somewhere. So I thought, as they made such a big fuss about it, I had better come out and see what the folks was all doing out this way; and that is the way I come out to Kentuck you see. Ha! ha! haw!"

We have already intimated that this man's life and acts constituted an exception to the aphorism, " Murder will out," above quoted and referred to. That there are cases in which the dreadful crime of murder has been perpetrated, wherein the guilty murderer has never been brought to the condign punishment due to his crime. The universal belief has been, and now is, that this man shed the blood of many, in the midst of his neighbors, and a population the most staid, sober, and law-abiding that exists in the State, and yet went down to his grave wholly unpunished. There were hundreds convinced and ready to swear, he committed such crimes in many instances; yet no one able to testify to a solitary fact or circumstance upon which a prosecution could be predicated. The extraordinary secrecy with which the deeds of death had been conducted, in every case, baffled all possibility of conviction or proof of any fact establishing legal guilt. In many instances in which the murdered bodies have been found and identified, universal suspicion at once fixed on him as guilty; but, suspicion is not proof. There was a case where an old gentleman, who lived a few miles from the town of Russellville, was found dreadfully mangled and murdered, within a few hundred yards from the boundary of the village. Suspicion fixed at once on William Stout and a free negro butcher, who lived, also, in the county and neighborhood of the deceased. The charge was directly made against the negro, his case judicially examined, and he committed for trial at the criminal court. Before his trial, however, he committed suicide in the prison. By the side of his dead body was found a confession, to this effect:

"I did not murder Knox; but I saw it done. The deed was done by the man that everybody believes has often done such things in this neighborhood. But I can be no witness.   C. W."

This, so far as is known to us, is the nearest approach to anything like the proof of guilt on Stout; and certainly, this was not the slightest legal proof of guilt. From the first of his residence in Logan county, Kentucky, till within six or eight years of his death, murders occurred, bodies were found and identified. All who knew of these things seemed not to doubt he was guilty, but none could prove a fact sufficient to *begin* the establishment of guilt upon him. All was conjecture—all suspicion.

As prefatory to this narrative, we said above, there was a strange comminglement of the basest with the most virtuous and fascinating elements of character in this extraordinary man. We take more pleasure in pointing these last out to the reader than in depicting his horrible crimes. He was a husband and a father.

About the year 18—he united in matrimony with ——, a plain, but most estimable lady. He also became the father of five children by her—four daughters and one son. In these several relations of husband and father, it is believed he discharged most faithfully every obligation. Toward his wife, maintaining every propriety; manifesting the most appropriate affection and respect. Toward his children, giving always the strongest evidences of parental care and affection. To the education and advancement of his fair daughters, he exhibited the most proper solicitude, and although they were most of them of very tender years, when they lost their fond and prudent mother, he seemed but to double his parental diligence in their behalf, and to withhold no expenditure or any other necessary care to make them accomplished and respected. And they certainly were entitled, when they grew to womanhood, in point of personal merit and elegance of appearance, to stand well in any circle. His son was also well educated, intelligent and respectable. Settling, however, after marriage, in one of the adjacent States, peopled as yet, as frontiers often are, by reckless and lawless adventurers, he fell into a quarrel with one of that character, got into a sort of Indian fight with him, shooting from behind trees, and was shot by his antagonist through the heart. This constituted the occasion of another display on the part of Stout, his father, of his extraordinary revengeful spirit and thirst for human blood.

At the time of the murder of his son, John G. Stout, he was at his home in Russellville. His son lived and was murdered near the south-western border of Arkansas. He received the intelligence of the sad affair and without telling any one his purpose, in a few days he prepared and at the advanced age of upwards of sixty years, mounted his horse, shouldered his rifle, traveled the distance of four or five hundred miles to his son's residence, and learned all the facts from the neighbors. The murderer of his son, doubtless, having learned the character of the father, and anticipating his speedy appearance in Arkansas, had disappeared. William Stout soon ascertained the direction he had fled. He took his track, followed him with the infallibility of the most practised woodsman, as he really was, through the Red River portion of Louisiana, through the vast wilderness of the Sabine, and on the Brazos and near Brazoria, overtook and slew him. In the course of a little more than three months returned to where he had set out telling to many, and with all his dreadful vices, that of falsehood was never charged, in his own peculiar style, he had "accidentally met with Jim Bell, (the murderer of his son) and looked at him a while, away down yonder in the woods, left him and never seen him more." The man was actually found dead near Brazoria. The truth is, revenge and blood were not only his passion, but darling delights.

We turn again from the contemplation of such of his traits of character to his feats of a less sanguinary nature, and which the reader can at least smile at, as not worse than comic tragedy. We have already spoken of his devotion to woman, and pledges to be forever her protector. We relate now, therefore, some curious instances in which he showed much proof that on such occasions, he meant what he said and pledged himself to.

About twelve or thirteen miles distant from Russellville lived in the County of Logan, the widow of a man whom he knew reasonably well, before he died, but with whom or any of his family, he had not at any time, had any particular acquaintance, or association. Before his death the husband had purchased a rich and beautiful tract of land containing three hundred acres, built a comfortable dwelling, made a good beginning for a productive farmer, became sick, made his will and died,—bequeathing to his amiable wife, the mother of his three or four little children, his land and negroes and in short, everything in fee simple, only requesting that their prudent mother should raise and give to his children as she should find it convenient to bestow. But three or four hundred dollars remained unpaid and due to the vender of the land, and for the payment of which a lien was retained. The creditor, after a time, began to press for his claim. The inexperienced and faithful mother, began to fear the loss of her comfortable home. She had a neighbor who possessed the amount necessary to save it. He pretended great kindness to her and her little orphans. She borrowed

WAR OF INDEPENDENCE.   359

the sum at the rate of *sixty per cent per annum*. She redeemed the lien, paid the debt, but then she gave a mortgage to secure to her *kind neighbor*, the sum and interest, borrowed. So it stood for several years, the very kind neighbor, only every ninety days adding up the interest, making it also principal, and taking her note to be tacked on to the mortgage, and to abide a future settlement. Thus his kindness had enlarged and improved in the estimation of the worthy yet inexperienced widow, till he had her not only involved for more money than the land would sell for, upon a foreclosure of the mortgage, but also he had exacted a bill of sale for her four negroes. The thing got out and began to be much talked and complained of by her other neighbors.

Stout heard of the mortgage, read it on the record, silently waited and watched the entire progress of the money lender's doings, till on a certain day at about four o'clock, P. M., and when the usurer was passing round his luxuriant field of corn, just in the roasting ear, with his shot-gun to gather a mess of the pillaging squirrels, at a distance from his dwelling in the midst of heavy timber and a mazy thicket of tall hazle bushes, greatly interwoven with bamboo-briers, he was confronted by Stout, with his rifle cocked and presented at his breast,— the man whom most of all he feared, and least of all his acquaintance, expected to see.

His first exclamation was " My God!—Uncle Bill, what is the matter ? "

He was quickly answered, accompanied by a look of fury, unmistakably expressive of the most deadly purpose, " Throw down that gun, sir." Instantly the command was obeyed. Again, he appealed for an explanation, and in great trembling and trepidation, asked, " What harm have I ever done you ? "

" O, none that I know of, but," looking upward with a glance of his eyes, he said, " old Master has sent me for

360   LEGENDS OF THE

you. He says you are not fit to live among men, and has directed me to kill you and throw you into that sink-hole," —a deep break or cavity in the earth, very commonly occurring in that rich district of Kentucky, and which was just by where they stood.

"O! Maj. Stout, have mercy on me," and falling on his knees, lifting up his eyes and hands in the most suppliant tones, the usurer cried, "O, have mercy upon me."

"Well now," he was answered, "don't pray to me!— pray to old Master! for he says you must die. If you want I'll give you time to pray to Him, but you must be quick about it. Maybe He'll help you, I can't."

The usurer fully believed, or seemed to believe implicitly what he said to him; and then earnestly engaged in supplications to Almighty God, to spare him from so dreadful and instantaneous a death. Among the subjects embraced in his prayer was, "O! Lord have mercy on my poor wife and children."

When those words were uttered, Stout, who stood near him, looking him in all the bitterness of revenge and death sternly in the face, with his rifle still presented at his breast, said, " Aye, now that's a good prayer. Pray for your wife and children, and while you pray for them, pray also for the poor widow and orphans of J. King, whom you have ruined. Maybe old Master will then do something good for you."

"O! said the usurer, I will do anything you say I must, for Mrs. King and her poor little children; only spare my life, Major."

"I cannot spare your life, unless old Master tells me so," said Stout. Again the suppliant addressed himself to the throne of infinite mercy and grace. Prayed for the poor widow and orphans, each by name. And while in the fervor and greatest apparent earnestness of petition in their behalf, Stout said, "Ah! that is the right way to

WAR OF INDEPENDENCE. 361

pray! Did you not say a while ago you were willing to do anything I said you ought for Mrs. King and her children?"

"O!" replied the usurer, now melted into tears, streaming down his pallid cheeks, "I'll do anything for them you say."

"Well," said he, "old Master has told me, if you will do what I tell you, I may spare your life. Now you must give back her negroes for whom you have her bill of sale, and execute and record a release of the mortgage you hold upon her land."

"O! I'll do it, Major, I'll do it now,—anything you require."

"Well," said Stout, "we'll see," and taking a sheet of paper from the crown of his hat, a pen of ink from his ink-phial, which he always carried, the latter hung to his vest by a string and button, he seated himself upon a log of fallen timber and began to write. This attitude he was most accustomed to, and would have prefered to the best cushioned seat at any table in any gentleman's parlor, or at his desk. Quickly he wrote a bill of sale reconveying the negroes and a deed of release of the mortgage. He read them to the usurer slowly and distinctly, and then said, "This" (presenting the bill of sale) "you must now sign, and I will witness it and keep it for Mrs. King,—and this also you must execute but as it has to be recorded in the County Court clerk's office, you must sign it also now and go to-morrow morning to the clerk and acknowledge it for record, before him, as it is best not to have to call in two witnesses. This is a matter between us alone and I want no witnesses. And now upon two conditions, old Master tells me, I may spare your life. Now you know I will kill you, if you fail to comply, go where you will. If you do not meet me to-morrow morning, at the Clerk's office in Russellville, between nine and ten o'clock, in the day, to acknowledge the release. This is one condition. And if you raise a

362   LEGENDS OF THE

talk and fuss about it, now or hereafter, I will assuredly kill you. Nothing but death shall save you from my vengeance."

The usurer solemnly engaged to comply with all he required. He then signed his name to the papers;—Stout attested them and put them in his pocket-book, when, as it was nearly night, he started for his home, at Russell-ville, and rode thirteen miles, while the usurer went round to his house, not a little nervous and unfitted for sleep that night. He, however, duly appeared next morning at the Clerk's office, and acknowledged the release, as his act and deed, and it is not known to this day, that he ever complained in any way, or even whispered the affair to any one. But Stout did, more than once; and referred to the record, as a proof of the whole.

Now it is not surprising, if our readers shall doubt whether the threats and acts of Stout, were anything more than a hoax, practiced upon the cowardly timidity of the usurer. They may rely upon it, however, it was no joke, no hoax! C. the usurer, had known Stout, personally, for more than thirty years; had heard and known more or less of the tales circulated rifely, throughout the land of no dissimilar events in reference to the man, in a dozen or more cases. Ah! he was a man of the most perverted and vicious passions, but indomitable will. Never threatened, but always acted.

We will now very briefly give another anecdote of his life illustrative highly, as is generally believed, of his peculiar traits of character on the same side of the picture, and which is also highly calculated to show the power his strange reputation had, to alarm and deter all the bad and despicably vicious of his acquaintance, especially if women was in any way involved.

J. Moore, late of Logan County, Kentucky, was raised a farmer. For years, however, after he married an ignorant but good woman, as it was said, he lived in Russell-ville, and engaged in keeping a doggery as it was usually called. He became habitually a sot, and, of course, much perverted in natural feeling towards his wife and children. He, however, purchased a farm six miles in the country, where he lived for eight or ten years, still growing more and more excessive in drink, and more and more brutalized. Often cruelly and brutally abusing his family. He sold his farm, cashed it for four or five thousand dollars, gold and silver, and then again rented a house in the town and continued his brutal treatment of his wife and helpless children.

At length, as a sort of spite to them, he swore he would abandon them, and purchased a two horse wagon and fine pair of horses, with which to travel to Missouri; swearing he would leave them all except his oldest son, a lad, and without any provisions for their support. He made it generally known throughout the town he would start in the morning of a certain day.

The day before Moore was to start, Stout saw him standing on the street and with an appearance of great seeming simplicity, he stepped up close to Moore's side, and in a sort of loud whisper, said to him, " Why Jerry, I understand you're gwyne to Missouri, to take but one of your boys, with all your money, and leave your wife with the other five children to shift as she can, for their support.

" Yes, yes," replied he, " Uncle Bill, I am gwyne in the morning, sure."

" What! " said Stout, " and make no provision for your family, left behind."

" No! d—m 'em," replied Moore, " let 'em starve."

Stout said, looking at him with his indiscribable gaze, steadfastly in the eye, and leaning a little closer still toward him, said " Now Jerry, that's a mighty dangerous road for you to travel; for as sure as there is a God in heaven, you'll catch your death, if you travel that way." Moore started back, took a more searching look into the eye of Stout, and exclaimed, " Great God, Uncle Bill, what is that for! "

"O, God knows," said he, "but I tell you as certain as you try it you will catch your death," at the same time somewhat impressively griping his right arm above the elbow. Moore turned exceedingly pale, said not a word more, but walked directly off, never started for Missouri nor even talked of it again, but died in the vicinity some few years after.

Of many other like occurrences in the extraordinary life of this man, we could speak, but here conclude by giving, in few words, the manner in which it came to a close, without further note or comment:

About three months before, he was observed, by his neighbors, to be evidently declining in flesh and strength; seldom appearing out from what he called *his den*. He complained to none of suffering, and though, to all that called in to see him, he admitted he was suffering much and was rapidly going,—he utterly refused to take medicine, or even but a very little of nutritive food. His answer was, generally, "O, let the poor old devil die in peace. Gabriel has blowed his horn!" In the morning of the day on which he died, he with but little aid, drew on his curiously constructed, many colored, suit of clothes, heretofore described, as made of the lists taken from the bolts of fine broad-cloth, and in that attire he died, and was buried.

> "And there he sat with his sunken eyes,
>   That *old man*, thin and pale,
> While the wind in broken symphonies
>   Through the creaking blinds made wail,
> And the raven croaked on the battlements
>   In the rising Autumn gale!
>
> Ah! sad and fearful to look upon
>   Were those glassy eyes of his,
> For a soul shone out of them, had done
>   Much in its day amiss,
> And thought was a dark and bitter thing,
>   Unto that man, I wit.

"Lo! the dark clouds around him close, dim waves above him roll,
The casket perishes in death, but where's the gem, the soul?"

WAR OF INDEPENDENCE.   365

CHAPTER XXXV.

A picture of the earlier settlements in the West—State of Society—
    Who gave it tone and polish.

" So live, that when thy summons come
    To join the innumerable caravan,
    That move to that mysterious realm,
    Where each shall take his chamber in the silent
    Halls of death,"—not
" Like the quarry slave at night,
    Scourged to his dungeon ; but,
    Sustained and soothed by an unfaltering trust,
    Approach thy grave like one
    Who wraps the drapery of his couch around him,
    And lies down to pleasant dreams."

HITHERTO little has been said in respect to society, generally, and the social phases exhibited by the earlier emigrants to the West. To Kentucky they were chiefly from Virginia. But Maryland, Pennsylvania, and the Carolinas, sent forth, each, a respectable portion of their plain and industrious citizens. These last, however, seldom mixed well (except the Marylanders) with the population from Virginia, who, in a conscious possession, or supposed possession of greater polish of manners, perfection of education, though in fact the most illiterate of all, only having the superior genius to make " a little learning pass for a great deal," rather assumed, or were suspected of assuming, something like exclusiveness in the social circles, as they formed in the wilderness.

The Marylanders who came from the vicinity of the District of Columbia, or who hailed from the eastern banks of the Potomac, and could trace easily the genealogy of the F. F. V.'s., or first families of Virginia, or could claim feasibly, relationship to, or a very familiar acquaintance with those universally acknowledged dignitaries of the Old Dominion; or the North Carolinians, who though natives of that State, claimed plausibly to have come from "*near the the Virginia line,*" get along pretty well in the "*upper tendom* of Kentucky aristocracy. Then, as indeed now, the Virginians, or *Figinians*, as many in those times called themselves—now, "*gentlemen from Varginiar,*"—are, indeed, "a peculiar people; zealous of" ——good eating and drinking, fiddling and dancing, and are, in short, a great people; the most courteous, the most companionable, the most agreeable, and the most fashionable of all the nation; and in no case, to be understood, as playing second fiddle anywhere, to anybody. Of course, therefore, we must set them down, and no mistake, as taking the lead in, and giving tone to all social, political, and religious formulas.

Early was it settled as an axiom of unquestioned and unquestionable propriety by the staid and well born matrons from Virginia, in solemn council, met at divers tea tables, that all bundling of the ladies, under thirty-five and over fourteen, with their sweet-hearts, as was the habit of the fair dulcinas of Coheedum, and the Bunkumites in those days of natural proclivities, was not at all admissible until the solemnities of matrimony were duly pronounced by the parson or just-ass of the peace.

However, by reason of the general hardships all had to encounter, for want of the common conveniences, not to speak of absolute necessaries for their families, and especially their mutual dependence upon each other for the defence of the infant settlements agains the incursions of the savages, great kindness and cordiality took possession of all hearts, and spread throughout the social circles; putting aside the usual fastidiousness of the charming lady pioneers from Virginia.

O! it was transportingly delightful to witness with what amiable condescension and beautiful amenity and gracefulness of manners they received, among the new comers, even the overseers and their dowdy wives and daughters, who came in from Virginia, Maryland, and the Carolinas. So that the law of neighborly kindness universally prevailed. The male Virginians and Marylanders brought with them to the West much of the roughness, rude diversions, horse racing, wrestling, jumping, shooting, drinking, dancing, &c., usual in their native States. These diversions were often accompanied with personal combats, blows, kicking, biting, and gouging—commonly called "rough and tumble." Sometimes with what they denominated "pitched battles," in which the combatants agreed upon the time and place of meeting, stipulating the employment of fists only.

But it was not many years ere these rude sports were supplanted by the more noble ambition for mental culture and skill in the useful arts. To the rude, and often indecent song, roughly and unskillfully sung, succeeded the psalm, the hymn and swelling anthem. To the clamorous boast, the provoking banter, the biting sarcasm, the horrid oath and imprecation, succeeded urbanity of manners and conversation, enlightened by science and chastened by mental attention and respect. The direful spirit of revenge, with but few exceptions, became unknown. Civilization and elegant ease, favored by the abundant productions of the rich soil, without much labor, readily furnishing the material and subjects of commerce, changed in rapid degrees the exterior aspect of the population of the country, and gave a new current to public feeling and individual energy. Religion, also, in all her humanizing and harmonizing teachings, brought forth in her unostentatious ministry, chiefly of the Methodist church, according to her itinerant plan; always visiting the cabins of the frontiers with the same messages of "peace and good will to man," which they bore and proclaimed to the dwellers in palaces and parlors; on the other side the mountains, alike "in the city full and the wilderness waste; lifting high their voices, sounding the Gospel tocsin of warning to the wicked, and notes of grace to the believing penitent. Nay, we presume to say, had it not been for the labors of these pious, generous, self-sacrificing and most indefatigable servants of God, to a great extent, instead of our present almost Eden blooming land, we should have been, at this day, a semi-barbarian region; and our wilderness would have never blossomed as the rose, and the solitary places would have never been made glad, by reason of the coming of those Heavenly messages.

Early views of western society will pretty readily be understood and appreciated by those who, in the days of President Washington's, J. Adam's, and Jefferson's administration, were familiar with the manners, customs, and feelings of the Virginians and Marylanders. For, as we have already stated, the former, at least, gave cast and coloring to everything of a social, moral, religious and political character. Of the three former, little, it is true, was cared or felt. Of the latter, all talked much, yet few understood. All, however, were zealous politicians, Republicans or Federalists, as their respective partizan leaders, Jefferson or Adams, gave direction. Of the former—morality—little was regarded, less practiced. For religion, little was cared, less possessed. Churches were few. Christian ministers were yet fewer. Indeed, the greater majority that thought or concerned themselves about such a thing as religion and a Christian ministry, could scarcely persuade themselves there were any, except those who were of the English Church, and these came, not even as angels' visits, few and far between. None who had not sufficient evidence along with them that they had been regularly taught religion and divinity, and graduated at some ecclesiastical college in Europe or America, had a right to preach the gospel, or had the least claim to be heard. The consequence was, that religious feeling and influence occupied a remarkably contracted sphere in the public mind, and it was among the rarest things to be met with, that of an experimental and practical professor of christianity. Still, however, there were such to be found, shining here and there, as "lights in a dark place."

The time, however, to favor Zion in these western moral wastes—this wide-spread wilderness, budding to its glorious season of blossom and bloom, was fast coming, and in the providence of Almighty God, did shortly come.

24

370   LEGENDS OF THE

CHAPTER XXXVI.

Religious revival in the West—Rev's John and William M'Ghee—
    Their appointments to preach—Preaching at Red River Meeting-
    House—Its results—Preaching at Beech Meeting House—Results,
    especially on those who came to mock, but remained to pray—
    Meeting at Muddy River Church—The Meeting House too small
    to accommodate—They go out into the open air—A pulpit is erect-
    ed—First Camp Meeting—Great results.

"And they were all filled with the Holy Ghost and began to speak
with other tongues as the Spirit gave them utterance."

"And as I began to speak, the Holy Ghost fell on them, as on us
in the beginning."—*Acts* i. 4; xi. 15.

"Compared with this, how poor Religion's pride,
    In all the pomp of method and of art,
When men display to congregations wide
    Devotion's every grace except the heart;
But happy we in some cottage far apart
    May hear well pleased the language of the soul."

THE year 1799 is distinguished for the commencement
of the great revival of religion in the West, and the introduction of Camp-meetings in the United States.

This revival commenced under the united labors of two
brothers John and William M'Ghee; the former, a Methodist local preacher, and the latter, ordained a Presby
terian minister, and called to the pastorial care of a Presbyterian congrega ion in Sumner county, Tennessee.
Both had moved with their families from North Carolina,
and settled near each other in Smith county—both had
received good educations preparatory to the Presbyterian
ministry. But, when the revolutionary struggle came
on they patriotically decided for their country, and entered the army of the Whigs to battle, side by side, in liberty's cause.

WAR OF INDEPENDENCE.   371

Peace and the independence of the country being secured, they both returned to the private circle of their parents, and both professed conversion and the new birth under the ministry of a distinguished Methodist preacher in North Carolina, where they and their parents lived. After marriage, which occurred shortly after their return from the army, the elder, John, was made a minister of the Methodist Episcopal Church, and the younger, William, a minister of the Presbyterian, according to the order respectively of those Christian denominations.

It was not long after, that they, together with their families emigrated to that portion of Tennessee of which we have spoken, then almost an unbroken wilderness, and settled on farms contiguous to each other. There they industriously engaged in the business of opening, each a farm, and cultivating the soil. William, ministering as pastor of a congregation of Presbyterians in Sumner county, while John, as a local preacher of the Methodist Church, preached in a sort of itinerant style, here and there, throughout that sparsely populated portion of the state, making war upon the enemies of God and man in all the potency of the word of truth.

The two brothers were ever greatly allied to each other and often attended meetings of two day's continuance in that state. In 1799, living contiguous to that part of Kentucky commonly called Green River, poorly supplied with ministers, yet rapidly filling with immigrants, to visit which they had been often urgently solicited, in the the latter part of the summer, sent forth a series of appointments to hold together, two day meetings, at a number of places reaching toward the Ohio river, leaving it to the brethren contiguous to the respective places of appointment, as each meeting was to include a Sabbath, to make them sacramental meetings, or not, as might best suit their own wishes.

The first of their appointments was at Red River meeting-house, in Logan county, Ky., one of the congregations

372   LEGENDS OF THE

under the charge of Rev. James M'Gready, a Presbyterian clergyman. It was announced as a sacramental occasion. The two brothers, M'Ghee, came duly to their appointment, and were met by the Rev. Wm. Hoge, John Rankin, and James M'Gready. On Saturday the pulpit was filled by William M'Ghee, who delivered an interesting discourse, well adapted to a preparation of the congregation to participate in the eucharistic feast of the next day. The assembling of the people was reasonably numerous. The order of the next day's services were, a sermon in the forenoon by Rev. Mr. Hoge to be followed by a sermon from Rev. John M'Ghee, and accordingly they took their positions in the pulpit.

A large congregation for that sparsely peopled neighborhood, gathered, and filled the large old log house very well. Mr. Hoge arose, and, as he was often heard afterwards, to say addressed the assembly with a freedom and power of speech he had never felt before. Still, however, the hearers though riveted in their attention, remained silent and quiet.

As he closed his discourse, the Rev. John M'Ghee arose singing,

"Come holy spirit, heavenly dove,
    With all thy quick'ning powers,
Kindle a flame of sacred love
    In these cold hearts of ours."

He had not more than sang through the verse quoted, ere an aged lady, Mrs. Pacely, sitting quite across the congregation, to his left, and Mrs. Clark, also advanced in years, somewhat to his right, began in rather suppressed, yet distinct tones of voice to hold a sort of dialogue with each other, and to reciprocate sentiments of praise and gladness to the "Most High," for His grace and goodness in redemption. Still the preacher sang on—still the venerable ladies in louder terms praised God! The preacher, yet singing this beautiful and most supplicatory hymn, came down from the pulpit intending to take the hands of those two happy sisters, shaking hands, however, as he passed, with all those within his reach. Instantly they fell as he progressed through the crowd—some as dead men and women—some most piteously crying for mercy, and a few, here and there, lifting their voices high in the praise of the Redeemer. Among these last was the Rev. Wm. M'Ghee, who fell to the floor, and, though shouting praises, was for some time so overpowered with the divine afflatus that he was not able to rise. The other ministers, M'Gready, Hoge, and Rankin, were so surprised and astonished with this apparent confusion, in the house of the Lord, that they made their way to, and out at the door, and there continued for some minutes, whisperingly enquiring of one another, "What is to be done?" There they might have remained yet longer, had not Mr. Hoge, who returned to the door, and seeing all on the floor, praying or praising, said to his reverend brethren:

"We can do nothing. If this be of Satan, it will soon come to an end. But if of God, our efforts and fears are vain! I think it is of God, and will join in giving glory to His name."

He walked into the house, while the others presently followed. Rapidly some of those who fell to the floor mourning and crying for mercy, rose, sometimes two or more at the same moment, shouting praise for the evidences they felt in their souls of sins forgiven—for "redeeming grace, and dying love!" So there remained no more place, that day, for preaching, or the administering of the sacrament. From thirty to forty that evening professed conversion, and to have found "peace with God, through our Lord, Jesus Christ."

Their next appointment was for the Saturday and Sabbath following, at what is to this day called the Beech meeting-house, situated a little south-east of the Cumberland Ridge, ten miles west of Gallatin, Sumner county, Tennessee, and seventeen miles north-east of Nashville. Hither, even on Saturday, many hundreds of the inhabitants of the adjacent country, in earnest and anxious haste, from a considerable distance around, had come. The news of the wonderful power displayed, at the Red River meeting, on the Sabbath preceding, and "the time of refreshing from the presence of the Lord," poured out on that occasion, had spread, as if by electric communication, together with the announcement of the preaching by the brothers at the Beech, throughout much of the Green River portion of Kentucky and of all middle Tennessee. Some came to witness and catch, if happily they might, "these touches of his love," some to pray and praise, while a far greater number came to witness, analyze and expose what they were pleased to stigmatize with the stereotyped phrases and brands of infidelity in every land, and country, and in all ages, "*fanaticism, wild-fire,* and *hypocrisy.*"

We will hear the results, however, of the experiments made by many of these last, who came, as they afterwards declared, to laugh and deride.

At 11 o'clock, A. M., the two brothers, John and William M'Ghee, were at their posts, met by other ministers of the Presbyterian and Methodist orders, to learn and know for themselves what this strange matter meant. The preaching commenced. The Rev. John M'Ghee commenced the services; and the writer of these narratives well remembers to have heard from the lips of that venerable old man, when speaking of the events of that time, and of the occurrences, particularly, at Beech meeting-house, when at a Camp-meeting near the same place, in Sumner county, about thirty years after. He quoted the words from Acts xi, 15, heading this chapter. "And as I began to speak, the Holy Ghost fell on them, as on us in the beginning." And said, "hundreds fell and began to rejoice, or plead for pardoning mercy." To many, very many, it proved a most joyous season and little less than one hundred of the gathered crowds of sinners professed peace through faith in Christ.

WAR OF INDEPENDENCE.   375

And yet, the tidings of these wondrous demonstrations of power to bless and save, winged their way to regions farther and wider. And when the days came, the ensuing Saturday and Sunday, for the next meeting, of those brothers, at Muddy River, three miles east of Russellville, the gathering of the people from distant parts of the two states, some twenty, thirty, fifty and even one hundred miles, was astonishing! Some in tented wagons, some in open wagons, some in carts, some on horses and many on foot!

The meeting-house it was found, hours before preaching time, could not seat the third part of those already gathered. And still they came, by dozens, fifties, and hundreds. A temporary pulpit, therefore, was quickly erected under the foliage of a contiguous grove of thick and broad-spreading trees, seats were made of large timber felled, and laid upon the ground. Here the thousands seated themselves, and the worship commenced. Soon the presence of the all-pervading power of the Most High was felt by all. Some crying for mercy, some in ecstacies of joy and praise, strewed the ground. Many of the former were members of the churches and had been for many years such! Nay, not a few of them had been, for years, preachers of the gospel, but now, for the first time, convinced thoroughly of sin, and of their absolute need of the converting grace of God applied to their own hearts. One of those, in a conversation with the writer the universally beloved, well known and respected, Samuel Wilson, who lived on the very ground, we may say, we are now describing, and the place of this meeting, to a great age, and where now, his venerated ashes lie interred, said: "Up to the time of that meeting, from a young man, I belonged to the Presbyterian Church, and long had been a ruling Elder in the congregations to which I belonged, persuaded myself I had religion, hoped and hoped I had religion, but there I found I was deceived into that hope, that it was without foundation, and never

376　　　LEGENDS OF THE

until that blessed meeting at Muddy River did I know, *for myself*, Christ's power on earth to forgive sin. My preacher also," he said, "Rev. James M'Gready, was for a time there, among those crying for mercy, and never before, as he often told me afterwards, felt a scriptural assurance that he was born of God. This you may depend, my friend," continued this simple-hearted, but most sensible and useful Christian, "was the case with almost all of us Presbyterians there, and all through the country, at that time. We did not know what it was to have God's 'spirit bear testimony with our spirits, that we were children of God '."

Thus spoke this truly christian man; and it gives us pleasure, here to record, in honor of his name and pious life, that after fulfilling, with great dignity and universal approbation, all the relative duties of husband. father, neighbor, citizen, and a responsible public officer, he died a beloved and most exemplary member of a Presbyterian church, having lived as such more than forty-five years.

But to return to a further discription of the proceedings of the meeting at Muddy River. Above we have said the ground round the temporary pulpit erected in the grove, was litterally strewed with the slain of God's convicting power; and we, further remark, that the number of these was constantly augmented. With some apprehension of mind, some of those who lived nearest the place, saw night approaching, while the meeting grew hourly more solemn and interesting, the seekers of salvation every moment increasing,—and began to think how these mighty multitudes, from so great distance from their homes, after night, were to find shelter, and to be fed. It was believed by them, all the dwellings for ten miles round, put in requisition, would not give them shelter. What was to be done? "Eight or ten of us," said the venerable Mr. Samuel Wilson, "began to think of the same difficulties at the same time. We hurried together, as if by accident, and began to talk about it. One pro-

WAR OF INDEPENDENCE.　　377

posed one thing and another something else. I proposed that I and my neighbor, Col. Daniel M. Goodwin, should take three or four of the many wagons on the ground, hasten to our treading yards and barns, and bring all the straw we had, to spread the ground. Others to sewing together the wagon sheets, and others cutting forks and poles, on which to spread the same, together with counterpanes, coverlits and bed sheets, secured together likewise, to make tents or camps. While others should be dispatched to town and all the nearest houses to gather all the bacon, flour, and meal, and cooking utensils, necessary, in which to prepare the provisions for the multitudes. In a few hours it was a sight to see how much was gathered together in preparation for our encampment, and food for the hungry. Soon we strewed a half-acre, at least, with the straw, pushed up a large tent spreading over the pulpit and for a distance in front, and then ten or twelve smaller ones, in order, ranging round the ground where the straw and people were spread, standing and sitting. Fires were built, cooking begun, and by dark candles lighted and fixed on a hundred trees around and interspersing the ground surrounded by the tents, showing forth the *first*, and I believe still, one of the most beautiful, camp-meetings the world has ever seen."

The meeting progressed and continued for four days, night and day. Several hundreds professed conversion, many back-sliders joyfully proclaimed their restoration to the favor and blessings of their heavenly Father, and still a greater number, when the meeting closed, went forth yet mourning, and enquiring, "saw ye the Lord whom my soul desireth to love," &c.

Here then, we cease with this narrative, having feebly, we feel, but faithfully we know, traced the history of the first camp-meeting in America, and we fully believe, the first in the world, properly speaking; except those musterings of the captains and their hosts, of the children of Israel, in their exodus through the wilderness to the land of promise, and their assemblage for the worship of the God of Hosts, guided by "the pillar of cloud by day, and pillar of fire by night," are to be regarded as such. Thus briefly, also, we have given the first exhibitions and effects of the great revival of religion, which so signally marked and characterised the earlier immigrants to the eswt; effecting in a great variety of ways the various sects, and church organizations of Protestants; first in Kentucky, and Tennessee in respect to membership, faith and practice; and quickly, in the mercy of its great Author, spreading to all the populated and peopling portions of this vast continent, giving new life and energy to the great cause of evangelizing the world, and enlarging the borders of Messiah's kingdom on earth.

For the verity of the facts we have narrated, even in detail, both as it regards this great revival, and the origin of Camp-meetings, we rely upon the statements of hundreds of eye-witnesses of the events themselves, the cotemporaries and intimate acquaintances and friends of the Messrs. M'Ghee, whose lives of piety and usefulness they well knew from the beginning. All these, however as we know, are now gone down to the grave, but many of whose participation in the interesting events when and as they occurred stand well authenticated and recorded, and whose pious and useful services in the church during long lives, built up characters forbidding all doubt of the truth of their statements.

O! it was delightful to us, and to all who took an interest in religious matters, or even those who found entertainment in the earlier history of these western wilds, to listen to the grateful and joyful accounts given by many of the happy participants in this great revival of the blissful assemblings of the people at those camp, and other meetings, where, "the stately steppings of our Immanuel were so demonstrably seen! while the hearts of his joyous followers, imbued with his love, sweetly harmonized, dwelt and acted together in unity."

WAR OF INDEPENEENCE. 379

Particularly was this the case with the Methodists and Presbyterians. They admitted and believed the doctrines, as taught by the scriptures, of the direct witness of the "spirit with our spirits, that we are born of God." But for this faith and practice, many of them, we lament to say, were afterwards made the subjects of persecutions and bitter denunciations from their own brethren, who stood aloof from these meetings, and had tied their faith and practice to the Calvanistic dogmas of election and reprobation!

The Methodists always believed and taught the doctrines of the direct witness of the spirit to the believing soul. That it was by the operation of the divine spirit, the third person in the adorable trinity, through the word of His grace the sinner was convicted, justification made known and sanctification and redemption perfected. These things, however, the tenets of the Presbyterian brethren, and confession of faith, and in short, all other of the Calvinistic Protestant sects denied, and taught otherwise. Indeed how could they consistently admit them to be true? Believing, as their confession of faith, and all other of their standard writings declared, that all salvation was in virtue of, and accomplished by, the sovereign and infallible decree and gracious foreordination of God, from before the foundation of the world. To be consistent, we say, those brethren must needs be understood to differ from the Methodists on those doctrines of the immediate agency and efficacy of the Holy Ghost. Hence the denunciations, generally, of the Calvinistic orders against the disorders, as they chose to call them, of the revival of which we have been speaking, and of the meetings we have been describing, which followed under its divine influence. But many men and women, servants of God, and willing to labor, preach, and pray for the salvation of souls belonging to those orders, were among the earliest participants in that blessed out-pouring of the spirit of life and salvation, and the earliest in the field to

380   LEGENDS OF THE

do battle for the Lord at the meetings throughout the
Union, which have ensued and still ensue. And we
rejoice to say that among the most pious, useful and faithful, practical Christians we have ever known, have been
men whose creeds and confessions of faith hung solely
upon the eternal and immutable decrees of the Almighty,
yet who were daily, in the language of the apostle Jude,
"building up themselves, on their most holy faith, praying in the Holy Ghost, keeping themselves in the love of
God, looking for the mercy of our Lord Jesus Christ,
unto eternal life." Such have ever loved, with the
people called Methodists, since 1799, revivals and camp-
meetings.

For many years the honored instruments in the hands
of a gracious providence, by whom this wonderful revival
of primitive and evangelical Holiness was exhibited in
the west, and which has spread all over the republic,
wrought good in all the Christian churches, and still is
accomplishing so much for the saving of souls, the two
M'Ghees, lived in Tennessee. Each died at his post, in
the communion of saints on earth, to rise again to the
communion of saints in Heaven.

"How blest the righteous when they die!
    When holy souls retire to rest,
How mildly beams the closing eye,
    How gently heaves the expiring breast!—

So fades the summer cloud away,
    So sinks the gale when storms are o'er,
So gently shuts the eye of day,
    So dies the wave upon the shore."

CHAPTER XXXVII.

State of Western Society—Dr. Gist's story of the honey—Its disastrous results—Is confirmed by Dr. Wilmot—His additional remarks.

"But they say the bee's a roamer
    That he'll fly when sweets are gone ;
And, when once the kiss is over,
    Faithless brooks will wander on!—

Nay, if flowers will lose their looks,
    If sunny banks will wear away,
'Tis but right that bee's and brooks
    Should sip and kiss them when they may."—*Moore.*

RETURNING once again to a contemplation of the earlier settlements in the West, and to a relation of the peculiar phases exhibited in the moral, religious and social relations of its inhabitants, we remark, as before we have said in substance, that in these aspects, Virginia manners, habits and customs predominated, differing only, to any material or very observable extent, in what we may term western speed, or western fastness, as contradistinguished from the almost tread-mill progress made by their progenitors on the eastern, or Atlantic side of the Alleghanies. For, strange as it may seem, the painter of character and progress in the West, contrasting those in the older States, particularly Virginia and North Carolina, is compelled, in justice, to seem to exaggerate and deal in the marvelous.

There appears actually something in the air breathed, the invigorating and cheering draughts of the pure, limestone water they quaffed for the first time, the enlarged and enrapturing views of the vast expanse of hill and dale, forest dell and Eden-blooming prairies, of fertile

382   LEGENDS OF THE

farms, villages and hamlets springing up in a day, giving
a hundred-fold increase to the entire man, mentally,
morally and physically. The result is, therefore, that
speedily, your slow, cautious and very punctilious Virginia impractical, regenerated and rejuvenated, became a
George Rogers Clark, a Daniel Boone, a Bland Ballard, a
Tom M'Clanahan, or a Simon Kenton, aye even a Simon
Girty, a Nick of the Woods, or, "*a Horse in the cane-
break, a little touched with the snapping turtle!*" And
as to the famed hospitality of the inhabitants of the Old
Dominion, *here* they have not only been known to give
cordially to man and beast, entertainment, "aid and comfort for a night, and as much more as he pleased," to the
passing stranger, not dreaming of compensation, but also
insisting, before he leaves, he shall go home and bring
also his wife and children and share the hospitalities and
courteous cheer of their frontier cottages!

Literary attainment or much of scholastic education was
not a great deal enjoyed, or much more prized. But in
the West, the reader may rely upon it, the young gentlemen springing from the families of the genuine early Vir
ginia and Maryland immigrants quickly entitled themselves to the appellation "of fast" young gentlemen. Their
feats of learning at gin-mill grammar-schools, and geo-
graphical and arithmetical lecture schools, were truly
wonderful. Born and bred in the new world of prodi-
gies, and reared in the midst of the feats of their fathers,
killing Indians, shooting buffalo, seven-horned elk, terrific bears and ferocious panthers, narrated and garnished
with items of the most marvelous hair-breadth escapes
and miraculous successes and victories. Such constituted
the chief elements of their son's conversational exercises,
as well as fashionable accomplishments. Indeed the
great wonder is, there did not arise, and rapidly spread
all through the country as the fruitage of such an abundant planting and culture, many hundreds, nay thousands
of Munchausens, Robinson Crusoes, Arabian Nights and

WAR OF INDEPENDENCE. 383

Don Quixotes, with Sancho de Panzas. But in those days there were, if any, few book publishers in all these lands, or otherwise such a flood of comicalities as Davy Crockett, in forty lives, could never have "grinned into potatoe peelings." As it was, however, the young geniuses contented themselves generally with spinning their yarns of western adventure to the entertainment of their wonder-loving dulcineas, to the extortion of showers of "O my's!" "dear me's," and "you don't say so's," from their tidy high-capped antiquated mammas, and gruff, "I wonders," from their old fogy papas.

Specimens innumerable of these Young-America, yarn-spinning fillibusters might be given. A few we will here subjoin.

We mention first Dr. Thomas Gist, born near Lexington, and chiefly educated at Transylvania University. An expert talker, (and who of the descendants of Virginia parents are not?) a regular graduate of Pennsylvania Medical Institute, a man of wonderful sight-seeing, and a narrator of more tales of thunder and death and love and murder, than forty thousand old women could listen to or unravel, or forty thousand old fogies could begin to believe to be true. Very well.

This dashing Lothario, came, saw, and *was conquered* by the fascinating charms of Miss. Courtney Baylor, daughter of Col. Robert Baylor, late of Virginia, and his hundred negroes! All sweet and honied in hope and word, he deemed it prudent and necessary to win the fair lady by most industriously and cautiously pouring forth from his wordy battery, stories, learned by land and sea, of mortals bewitched, or by jack-o'lanterns drowned. It would'nt do. So he resolved to throw himself "upon his reserved rights and real Kentucky invention." Therefore, on his next call on his fair one, he determined upon something most delectable to her fancy and taste. So being in preparation, he very seriously and pompously delivered himself, on his next visit, in this wise:

384   LEGENDS OF THE

"Well, did you ever hear, Miss Courtney, of the wonderful occurrence that took place some years ago in Philadelphia in respect to the bees and the great amount of honey aand honey-comb got from the old church, at one time?"

Of course he was answered in the negative.

"O! I wonder you never heard of it! Why the winter I was last there attending the lectures, the session I received my diploma as M. D., the greatest bee-hive ever opened was that fall found. Forty years before, when they were putting a new roof upon the old church and when the workmen had nearly finished, there came a swarm of bees and settled on a rafter. The workmen just went on and shingled over the bees, and there they remained, working, swarming and peopling the garret for forty years, till it was literally filled to the roof with the most beautiful comb, as white as alabaster, richly filled with the most delightful honey. Sixty-five hogsheads of it were shipped to Liverpool, and there remained enough to supply every family in the city, rich and poor, high and low that winter. It was so distributed!"

"O! doctor what a ——!" said Miss Courtney Baylor.

"Alas! alas!" said her grave and truly gentlemanly Virginia father, who was near and heard the whole story, "Doctor Thomas Gist, I have now for at least the hundredth time, been compelled through politeness to sit and listen to your contemptible twaddle and remorseless falsehoods, till I have not the conscience to endure it any longer. I cannot submit to your course of falsehood, before myself and in the presence even of the ladies of my household, without sinking myself to the grade of a common falsifier. Will you please, sir, find my door as soon as you can make it convenient, and have the politeness never to enter it again? Be assured it will greatly oblige me."

The young Kentuckian looked unutterable confusion. First at his blushing fair one, who quitted the parlor

WAR OF INDEPENDENCE.   385

while the Col., her father, was yet speaking, and then he
gazed with amazement at the stern and resolute features
of the old gentleman, who also hastily rose and quitted
the room, leaving the gay Lothario dreadfully astounded,
eyes distended, mouth expanded, and every way the picture of desperation and the victim of surprise and despair.
At last, however, aroused to a sense of the necessity of
immediate action he arose from his seat, and muttering to
himself that he had never known so much honey to create
so much bitterness, seized his hat, ordered his horse and
disappeared, a used-up man.

The young and very pretty Miss Courtney B., from
thence refused any further entertainment of his proposals
in the line of courtship, and the young Kentuckian was
left free to direct his invincibilities, in future, to whatsoever like object his prurient enterprise might suggest.

This gentleman had the good fortune to boast of a lady
friend. The lady of a member of Congress, no less skilled
in arranging and adjusting all the matrimonial affairs
within any reasonable distance in the early settlements of
the West as well as of all matters of etiquette and neighborly comity of action, as her honored husband was in
national legislation. To her he made known his utter
overthrow at Col. B's, the honey story, &c. Promptly
the honorable lady showered upon him all her sympathies
in the most approved expressions of contempt for such
proud airs, exhorting him to treat the affair with silent
contempt—that the B's did not seem to her, as they
claimed to be, one of the F. F. V's, any way, entertaining, or pretending to entertain, such a disgust for
honey because it happened to be raised in Pennsylvania
and not in Virginia! And many other pretty things the
lady said, to the great comfort and consolation of the dis-
comfited Kentucky gallant. But, be it remembered, this
truly sympathising, magnanimous lady friend introduced
to his acquaintance a young, accomplished niece, just
reached the west on a visit from Virginia to her sister,

25

Mrs. Minor, at Clarksville, and to her aunt at whose house she was then spending some weeks. Indeed she was a lovely girl! And no wonder our young hero was at a loss to determine, from the first, whether the delightful words of his sympathising friend, the aunt, or the entrancing smiles and beauty of the lovely Virginia niece, Miss Nancy Barber, had brought the most consolation to his wounded heart and pride of character. At all events he concluded he must see them both shortly again or his stock of consolations would totally evaporate. Early, therefore, he again visited them, and crowned with equal success, often repeated the delicious antidote.

Meanwhile this lady friend, indeed, of our young Kentucky M. D., plied all her superior powers of inquiry and investigation, to get to the bottom of the honey story. O! she "would see if her young friend, Dr. T. Gist, was justified in the truth of the honey narrative or not. And if he was, she would let the B's know it, certain." Well, most opportunely on visiting a sick neighbor she made the acquaintance of Dr. Robert Ridgely Wilmott, attendant physician, a fine-looking, young Kentuckian, admirably (as it was said) educated at Transylvania University, travelled, as he said, over all the six continents of the earth and two or three of those of the moon. Of course there was no man had ever seen as much, or could talk so familiarly of this universe as Dr. R. R. Wilmott, born in Kentucky about the time Daniel Boone made his breakfast upon two buffaloes and a panther. His parents were Marylanders. And no lady of half the knowledge and experience of men and manners possessed by Mrs. Mary W., would be at all at a loss to determine that he was fond of talking, and wielded rather extraordinary colloquial powers.

"Well, Doctor Wilmott," said she, after a brief acquaintance, "I dare say you are a graduate of the Pennsylvania Medical University, and I should like to inquire of you what years you attended the lectures there and graduated?"

WAR OF INDEPENDENCE. 387

"Yes madam, certainly. I was a student at Philadelphia in the years 1796 and 1797."

"O!" she replied, "I verily believe that was exactly the time, or about the time, my dear friend, Dr. Thomas Gist, graduated at that medical institution."

"No madam, he received his diploma as M. D., precisely one year before I went there."

"You know him then?" said the lady.

"Know him, madam? Why as well as if I had made him, as old chums, at Transylvania and every where else."

"Well indeed, now this is fortunate," said she, "tell me if you please, Dr. Wilmott, did you ever hear any thing at Philadelphia of the many hundreds of hogsheads of honey comb, taken by the corporation of that city, at the time Dr. Gist was there, from the garret of a church and who sent one hundred hogsheads to Liverpool, besides furnishing an abundance to every family in the city for their consumption during the entire winter?"

"Yes, indeed, madam. Aye; yes, yes. But pray, my dear lady, what has prompted these enquiries?"

"Well, doctor," she said, "I will tell you," and she proceeded to narrate, in every particular, and with all due emphasis, her friend's adventure at Col. Baylor's, giving in his exact words, the doctor's story of the church, the bees, and the honey-comb, and concluding with a pretty severe phillipic pronounced against the airs of the Baylors, &c.

"Why, dear me, madam," replied Dr. Robert Ridgely Wilmott, "silly airs they were truly. For I well remember I heard not only of the shipment to Liverpool, but of a like quantity to Amsterdam, and not only the furnishing of the city, the winter your friend graduated as M. D., but I and everybody else luxuriated most gloriously upon it two years afterwards! Truly, madam, travelers that have seen a little of the world, and been subjected to a few of the occasional adventures to which the inhabi-

388 LEGENDS OF THE

tants of these mundane shores are always incident, must
be exceedingly careful, in the presence of your truth-lov-
ing, punctilious, chivalrous Virginia dignitaries, lest they
speak of something beyond the ordinary occurrences, and
exhibitions of their mill-path, or the court-house green.
Why, madam, I dare say, if I were to relate to the Baylors the hundredth part of the wonders I have seen in my
extended travels by land and sea, they would discredit
me, for a miserable fabricator of old women's fables!
And if I were to narrate to them even a single adventure
of my life,—that of my being clutched up by the Golden
American Eagle, that used to inhabit in great numbers
the tall cliffs of the Kentucky River, borne to the highest
peak of the Cumberland mountains, and there left, though
unhurt, to clamber down as best I could to the fertile vales
below, they would wholly disbelieve me! Or if I were
to tell them of the visit I once made to old Treadwell's
mutton mill, in North Carolina, where I saw one of the
very poorest old sheep, I ever saw, thrown up into the
hopper, ground over and turned out, right away, five first
rate fat quarters of mutton, two wool hats, and a leather
apron, they would want me prosecuted for lunacy! Why,
madam, Dr. Gist's honey story is perfectly *je june*, flat,
and insipid compared with either of these."

"Well, well, Doctor Wilmott, I am sure I can't tell
about that," she said, "but I am sure I can now prove to
the Baylors, by evidence they dare not dispute, they are
utterly wrong, entirely too hasty, and put on entirely too
many airs for the West, though they are Virginians.

"Oh sons of earth! attempt ye still to rise
By mountains piled on mountains, to the skies?
Heaven still with laughter, thy vain toil surveys,
And buries madmen in the heaps they raise."—*Pope.*

WAR OF INDEPENDENCE. 389

CHAPTER XXXVIII.

Religion in the West—The revival of 1799—Its effects—Dissenting of the Presbyterians and denial of God's hand in the work—Results of such denial—Cause of the organization of the Cumberland Presbyterian Church—Conclusion.

"And there was a day when the sons of God came to present themselves before the Lord, and Satan came also among them."
—*Job* i, 1.

"And again there was a day when the sons of God came to present themselves before the Lord, and Satan came also among them, to present himself before the Lord. And the Lord said unto Satan, from whence comest thou? And Satan answered the Lord, and said, from going to and fro in the earth, and from walking up and down in it."—*Job* ii, 1, 2.

In several of the preceding pages we have given some account of the revival of 1799 or 1800, which so vitally effected and powerfully controlled, generally, the religious opinions, observances, and intercourse of the earlier settlers in the great valley of the Mississippi, also of the rise and progress of camp-meetings, as consequent upon that revival; spreading on from Kentucky and Tennessee, east, south, and northeast, crossing the Alleghanies, onward to the Atlantic shores. Reference, also, is made to the general dearth of moral and religious feeling, and destitution of an evangelical ministry at the time of the occurrence; while the feebleness and simplicity of the means employed by the Almighty to bring them about, are likewise, to some extent, presented in the simple narrative of the facts, thus enabling the reader, by a comparison of these with the ordinary means employed by the Divine Ruler and Governor of the universe, as shown forth in His own inspiration—the Bible; and which, as it seems to us, judging by analogy, was a *divine influence* among the people of the west; and should, instead of being a ground of contention and bitter denunciation toward their advocates, have been gratefully acknowledged by all lovers of christianity, as productive of the happiest effects upon all that sought for, and became partakers of, its power and grace; and cheerfully and faithfully maintained and cultivated for its heavenly origin and teachings.

Thousands became awakened to their interest in the things that belong to their everlasting well being. Thousands converted to God, proved it by a long life of consistent profession and action, to be genuine. The "wicked man forsaking his way, and the unrighteous man his thoughts." "Turning to the Lord, who *had* mercy on him, and to our God who *had* abundantly pardoned him." Yet such, little as christian men may be inclined to believe it, hundreds of the *hope so* brethren denounced, both them and all the partakers and advocates of the revival, as workers of iniquity. Yea, even some of the partakers themselves, in the first instance of its exercises and benefits, came afterward to decry its divine origin, repudiating the voice, "crying in the wilderness, prepare ye the way of the Lord, make straight his paths," and joined in with infidels, and other practical opposers of God, denying that it "was a time of refreshing from the presence of the Lord;" asserting that all those that declared, in strict scriptural language, that it was a manifestation of God's power on earth, to forgive sins, that "the spirit itself bore testimony with their spirits that they were born of God," (as very many did) were all deluded fanatics, enthusiasts, bewitched by some evil influence, or led captive by Satan himself.

Of these last, however, it is hard for us to refrain from comparing them to certain of whom the Apostle Peter speaks, and compares to "the sow that was washed, turned to her wallowing in the mire"—"the dog to his vomit." These, we said, at first participated in the revival,—were for a time its advocates, and showed evident marks of, and loudly proclaimed to be themselves in the enjoyment of the converting grace of God. But they became the bitterest revilers of the brethren that adhered to the faith and practice of the privileges of the revival, and denounced them all, as we have before stated.

What, then, became of these?—we almost hear the reader inquire. This writer does not know, and cannot answer as to many of them. Some of them emigrated to other and distant regions of the country, far off in the West. Many of them, however, too many, and (we record the fact with painful and almost indescribable sensations of sorrow and regret) fell into manifold snares and temptations of Satan. Some became Fatalists, and anti-revivalists, of course. Some open and avowed Antinomians; some new New Lights; some Shakers; some Socinians; some Universalists; some Pelagians; and some "counting the blood of the covenant wherewith they were sanctified, an unholy thing," denied, at last, the divine authenticity of the Bible of God.

Now does the reader doubt and inquire—can these things be so? Is it possible that men, ministers of the Gospel, and others who thus for years lived in its faith and practice, proclaimed in language and acts of obedience unmistakable, its power to save? We say again, as we have already, in sorrow and chagrin said, that with such we were personally, and, we might say, intimately acquainted, in all their after life, and affirm solemnly, it is so. Trace, reader, the acknowledged and current histories of those times, and the years following. Look into the biographies of many of the earliest actors and participants in that remarkable revival. Inquire for the Last Days—for the "last state" of the Craigheads, the Balches, Donnells, McNamers, Bowmans, Houstons, Bartons, Stones, Rankins, Marshalls and McCombes, the Smiths, Creths, and Campbells.

392   LEGENDS OF THE

A heathen once said, "whom the gods doom to destruction, they first make mad;" and there are those, who, in the exercise of the freedom of volition choose "evil in the error of their ways," of whom God has said, "He would bring upon them strong delusions, that they might believe a lie," &c. Ought we not, humbled under a just view of our own weakness and fallibility, say with the Apostle Paul, 1st. Cor. x. 12—"Let him that thinketh he standeth, take heed lest he fall."

But, that the courteous reader be at no loss to determine our purpose in returning to, and extending our remarks in regard to the revival of 1800, as it is very commonly called, though as we have shown, it took its rise in the latter part of the summer or first of the fall of 1799, as in connection with a detail of its effects upon the moral, social and religious condition of society among the earlier settlers of the West, we state, as we have heretofore in another place stated, its progress was greatly crippled and retarded by a host of opposers. First, by the wicked of every grade in every rank, conjoined might and main with Satan and every Satanic emissary. This, however, was perfectly natural. All, as it was a work of God, a mighty means of saving sinners, would have anticipated, or expected that would be the case. But it is a lamentable fact that it was opposed, also, by the professed followers of Jesus, readers of the Bible, in the greater number of the Protestant churches, especially the Calvinistic branches of them, who decried it and its advocates as being side by side with the bitterest subjects and most fanatic supporters of the Pope of Rome, here and elsewhere. And why? Was Satan divided against himself? Was Christ and Belial in fellowship with each other? Never—no, never. What, then, was the matter? Why, then, did the Protestant Calvinistic christians oppose? A thousand explanations and reasons have been given, or attempted to be given, by some, and conjectured by others. But we must be permitted to reject them all, as altogether unsatisfactory and inadequate. Some charged the meetings consequent upon the revival, the excitement produced by those rejoicing and shouting the praises of God, together with the loud cries of sinners to Almighty God for mercy, as being nothing but "noise and confusion," "unscriptural and unchristian disorder," and they "would have none of it."

Why they said, when seekers of religion, in the forgiveness of sins, who, feeling the answer of peace to their prayers through faith in Christ, rose from their knees with tears of joy streaming down their cheeks, giving glory to God for redeeming grace and dying love, was indecent and satanic, and dealing with familiar spirits! Many of these opposers, we are induced to believe, joined in these general denunciations of the advocates and believers in the genuineness of the revival from ignorance. They were, for the most part, members of the church who never witnessed such displays of the convicting and converting power of the spirit of grace, and such seasons of "refreshing from the presence of the Lord," and who being prejudiced by the reports of the enemies of all religion, in wholesale denunciations, rife with the stereotyped charges of hypocrisy, indecency, disorder, and the like, kept themselves at a continued distance from these meetings of the sons of God. They came not within the influence of the pervading spirit of those meetings, but satisfied themselves in pronouncing the harsh judgments upon all, indiscriminately, who favored and partook of them. Hence, bitter, unchristian and unchastened revilings of brethren of the same communion, in the same church, spread throughout the land.

But it was mainly among the brethren of the Presbyterian church that bitterness, denunciation and excommunication, for belief in the genuineness of this revival, became most common. There the opposers of the revival, claiming, with great self-complacency, to be the exclusive orthodoxy of the times, and sole correct expounders of

394   LEGENDS OF THE

the word of God! having shut themselves up in their confessions of faith, and teachings that His fore-knowledge of all things was as a necessary consequence, a fore-ordination of "whatsoever cometh to pass,"—and that as the beneficiaries of the redemption of Christ, were the elect of God, decreed from before the foundation of the world and infallibly to be saved, do what they would, while all others were passed by, and left in their sins to perish do what they could; they very consistently, as we have said, repudiated and rejected the appliances and opportunities of those revival meetings, for the conviction, conversion and final salvation of sinners. As "all that mighty affair in the sovereign grace, mercy and power of God, himself, was immutably fixed, fore-ordained and decreed from before the foundation of the world."

But let us not seem even to do these conscientious, pious and sincere brethren injustice. They saw, or, very many of them at least, thought they saw, that in the revival exercises and meetings, many hundreds of the converts whom they previously knew personally to be the wickedest servants of Satan, lived changed, and for years, faithful christians, yea, from thence-forth until death. As they are justly entitled to be considered lovers of good, we respectfully express the opinion, that they should have grounded and ceased all this bitter denunciation of their brethren, the Cumberland Presbyterians (as they are now called) and the Methodists, who have always believed in these revivals as being productive of *real* conversions to the service of the living God. Should they have made these opinions, and the honest exercise of them, cause of such denunciations, nay, even of the excommunication of brethren? We think not. Yet this they did, and still do! Should the prayers of the convicted sinner to God for mercy "with strong cries and tears," at these meetings, have been called the co-workings of the devil, and such sinners' rejoicing, when made to believe their sins were forgiven and owned it before men, feeling the witness of the spirit within that they were born of God, have been made the ground of abuse and utter repudiation? Alas! alas! that mere pre-conceived opinions should accomplish such sad consequences! Yet so it is!

But our good brethren found difficulties in the way, to the maintaining such christian charity. Ah, our creeds—our confessions of faith are put in danger. "Away with it!" was then, and still is, their cry.

And what think you, reader, was the real difficulty? Why all the revival preachers and people, converts and all, believed, and taught, and professed openly, the simple scriptural doctrine of the witness of the spirit to the converted believer. They all spoke one language. They all talked of their hearts being filled with "the love of God shed abroad" by the Holy Ghost given unto us. O! all this was too bad! Aye, yes, it was anything else than a mere "hope so"—a mere, "I hope my sins are forgiven," —a mere "hope I have got religion," as taught by the Calvinistic creeds and practice. Hence they could not affiliate it, but characterised such boldness in expressions of joy and confidence in the religion of the blessed Redeemer as highly immodest and presumptuous, and worthy of a dozen other ugly names. Well, they honestly thought, or it seemed so. There was yet another thing showed itself in process of time as an accompaniment of these revival meetings, that proved beyond all controversy, as those Calvinistic opposers said of satanic origin. The bodily exercises, demoniac howlings, as they called them, the jerks and other strange phenomena settled, as they said, the matter. Some of them fully believing and declaring all these things were lying hypocrisies, would venture forth and go to the meetings. O! they would show it was all pretence, they could not be made to jerk nor howl nor bark. But in not a few instances of just such experiments these gainsaying individuals would suddenly find themselves jerking, dancing, barking, rolling, or something else unaccountable, notwithstanding

396   LEGENDS OF THE

their previous incredulity and sedulous desire and exertions to avoid it, uttering the most pitiable groans and horrible shrieks. While others would at the same time be seen to fall into excess of joy, expressed in every feature, and exhibiting faces radiant with felicity and delight. Truly these things were marvellous, yet were certainly realities.

Many conjectures and speculations were given then and now are indulged as to the cause. But we are still without having among them all any that approach, even plausibility. But suppose we admit with these Calvinistic railers, that these strange accompaniments of those revival meetings, camp-meetings, and all others, were of satanic influence or origin, are they justified in denouncing the thousands of genuine conversions that attended them as satanic also? That, it seems to us, would be unreasonable and unjust. Yet this those brethren continue to do to this day. *O! tempora—O! mores.* O! wonderful is the force of custom and prejudice for injustice and evil.

They say when the people came together in those days for the worship of God, Satan came also. Well, what of that? Was not that the case in patriarchal times—in the days of Job? Read again the quotations at the head of this chapter. And Satan still almost visibly pervades the earth. At least, his foot-prints are everywhere visible. Does he not even, sometimes, when our Calvinistic brethren assemble before the Lord, appear also?

But not to wander farther from what properly belongs to our narrative, it is right for us now to state, that those of our Presbyterian friends who believed the doctrines preached in the revival and in the utility of camp-meetings, and continued, as honest men, professing to be governed by the Bible, to preach and teach them, till by the church to which they belonged in Kentucky and Tennessee, they were robbed of all quiet, and many of them excommunicated, were compelled to form themselves into a separate church organization, and call themselves the Cumberland Presbyterian Church.

They and their successors are now going on, believing and preaching the same true and scriptural doctrines of the "*direct witness of the spirit*" to those who are born of God, and the "refreshings from the presence of the Lord"—"building themselves up in their most holy faith, praying in the Holy Ghost,"—till now the year of our Lord 1855, the church so formed by that mere handful of men, smitten from the self styled orthodox church, has multiplied and spread out through the great valley of the Mississippi, as well as through many of the older States, till it almost equals the old organization in number of communicants.

"Quench not the spirit." "Mind not high things, but condescend to men of low estate." "Be not wise in your own conceit." "He that believeth on the Son of God hath the witness in himself." "If any man have not the spirit of Christ, he is none of His." These are the doctrines which gave them, under God, their success in winning souls to Christ, and these are the doctrines that must eventually conquer the world. "Ah, what hath God wrought!"

Milton Keynes UK
Ingram Content Group UK Ltd.
UKHW030109160124
436092UK00005B/95